Seeking and Soaring:

Jewish Approaches to Spiritual Guidance and Development

Edited by Rabbi Goldie Milgram
and
Rabbi Shohama Wiener

6/22/15

בהרב לי ללי'א'כ' דלרב.

Reclaiming Judaism Press
New Rochelle, New York

Also from Reclaiming Judaism Press

Honored by the Covenant Foundation and National Jewish Book Council

Mitzvah Stories: Seeds for Inspiration and Learning
Edited by Goldie Milgram and Ellen Frankel
with Peninnah Schram, Cherie Karo Schwartz and Arthur Strimling

Sixty inspiring and provocative stories crafted by leading Jewish storytellers, rabbis and authors from across the full spectrum of Jewish life. Meant for reading and retelling across the generations. Free downloadable discussion guide.

"Exceptional, vibrant anthology." *Jewish Book World*

Mitzvah Cards: One Mitzvah Leads to Another
Created by Goldie Milgram

Each beautifully illustrated deck contains 52 meaningful contemporary Jewish spiritual practices.

New Mitzvah Stories for the Whole Family
Edited by Goldie Milgram and Ellen Frankel with Arthur Kurzweil, Batya Podos, Peninnah Schram, Mindy Shapiro, Shoshana Silberman, and Danny Siegel

A juried anthology of forty-three inspiring, inclusive fictional and true life tales by new and leading authors from across the full spectrum of Jewish life. Questions for spiritual development and discussion follow each story.

Reclaiming Bar/Bat Mitzvah as a Spiritual Rite of Passage
by Goldie Milgram

"Featured at the Jewish Futures Conference"

Provides the tools you need to create a conscious Bar/Bat Mitzvah experience infused with spirituality and meaning.

Available through most booksellers and
www.ReclaimingJudaism.org, www.Bmitzvah.org and www.Amazon.com

Seeking and Soaring: Jewish Approaches to Spiritual Guidance and Development

Reclaiming Judaism Press: http://www.reclaimingjudaism.org

Publisher's Cataloging-in-Publication data

Milgram, Goldie, 1955-

    Seeking and soaring : Jewish approaches to spiritual guidance and development / edited by Rabbi Goldie Milgram and Rabbi Shohama Wiener ; introduction by Rabbi Zalman Schachter-Shalomi.
      p. cm.
      ISBN 978-0984804870
      Includes bibliographical references and index.

1. Spiritual life --Judaism. 2. Jewish way of life. 3. Spiritual direction. I. Wiener, Shohama. II. Schachter-Shalomi, Zalman, 1924-2014. III. Title.

BM723 .M46 2014
296.7--dc23

ISBN-10: 0-9848048-7-0
ISBN-13: 978-0-9848048-7-0

Cover image: Copyright 2014 Lawrence M. Monat
Cover & Interior design: Taylor Rozek

Published by Reclaiming Judaism Press
17 Rodman Oval, New Rochelle, NY 10805
Tel: 914-500-5696 http://www.ReclaimingJudaism.org

Manufactured in the United States of America

Dedicated to our teacher and guiding light

Rabbi Zalman Schachter-Shalomi

Table of Contents

Lexicon and Glossary Brief: Hebrew Terms and Symbols

Hashpaʾah derives from the Hebrew term *shefa*, the infinite flow of Spirit, and is adopted from usage within *CHaBaD* Hasidism for Jewish spiritual direction and declined grammatically accordingly to the various roles within this field that are described on this page.

Note that the Hebrew letter *fey* takes a *dagesh*, a grammatical dot in its center that gives it a "p" sound when *shefa* is conjugated to apply to the roles in *hashpaʾah* as follows:

Mashpia [ms], *mashpiʾim* [m pl] and *mashpiʾah* [fs], *mashpiyot* [f pl], are the gendered terms for a Jewish spiritual director, mentor or guide.

Mushpa [m] *mushpaʾim* [m pl] and *mushpaʾat* [f] and *mushpaʾot* [f pl] are the grammatical forms for what some programs term the directee or, or a *hashpaʾah* client, or student.

YHVH symbolizes the Tetragrammaton from the Bible. Made of the Hebrew letters *yud*, *hey*, *vav* and *hey*, it is by Jewish tradition an unpronounceable placeholder for The Great Name once known by the high priest in Temple times.

Transliteration Notes: In Hebrew there are several letters that have a sound like clearing your throat, *khhhh – khaf* and *het*. These letters appear in this volume in transliteration as **ch**, **h**, **kh** and in a word found in the English dictionaries like Hasidism as **h**, depending upon the author and editors of a given piece. All transliteration herein is aimed at helping those unfamiliar with Hebrew to be able to pronounce words; the transliteration is not designed to help readers identify Hebrew letters of the words. There is no "ch" as in "chirp" sound in Hebrew; all "ch" combinations here-in represent the guttural khhh sound. The terms Hasidism, *hasidim*, hasidic and *hasid* all have the khhh sound at their opening, since it is not normal usage to put a **kh** at a word's opening, so they are spelled and italicized based on their dictionary usage.

Authors transliterate names referring to *rebbe*s differently, for example Nachman, Nachman, and Nahman and Berezovsky and Brazovsy.

In Modern Hebrew the final letter *taf* is always pronounced as a "t" sound. Some of our authors learned Hebrew before this convention was introduced and they use a "s" sound for this letter in some situations, for examples *atzilus* vs. *atzilut*, have the same meaning and yet are pronounced differently based on the date of birth and country of origin of our authors.

Torah, in Judaism, specifically means the Five Books of Moses. The term Torah is also often used in the phrase "Torah study" which colloquially means the study any of *TaNaKh*, Jewish biblical literature and its Jewish commentaries. The term *TaNaKh* refers to the entire canonical Hebrew Scriptures which are composed of Torah–Genesis, Exodus, Leviticus, Numbers and Deuteronomy; *Nevi'im*–Joshua, Judges, I Samuel, II Samuel, I Kings, II Kings, Isaiah, Jeremiah, Ezekiel, Hosea, Joel, Amos, Obadiah, Jonah, Micah, Nahum, Habakkuk, Zephaniah, Haggai, Zechariah and Malachi; and *Ketuvim*–Psalms, Proverbs, Job, The Song of Songs, Ruth, Lamentations, Ecclesiastes, Esther, Daniel, Ezra, Nehemiah, I and II Chronicles.

Talmud, Mishna, Gemara, Midrash, Codes, Pesikta de Rav Kahana, etc. For readers unfamiliar with post-Biblical Jewish sacred texts, *Jewish Texts: The Owner's Manual*, by Rabbi Judith Z. Abrams located at http://www.maqom.com/pdf/learner.pdf offers a simple, brief self-study curriculum and clear explanations.

Translation Note: Where terms from some of the languages and sacred texts of the Jewish people — Hebrew, Aramaic, & Yiddish — variously appear in this volume, their translations generally are provided in parentheses or footnotes, especially if the term was not previously translated in an earlier page of *Seeking and Soaring*.

Foreword

Having honored Rabbi Shohama Wiener with our 2009 handbook on Jewish spiritual direction, we are pleased to have her join Rabbi Goldie Milgram as co-editor of this volume of essays reflecting currently practices and innovations in the rapidly evolving field of Jewish spiritual guidance and development.

Hashpa'ah is the contemporary Hebrew term for what is often termed "spiritual direction." *Hashpa'ah* involves providing guidance and support for those seeking healing and spiritual development. The root of this term is *shefa*, the flow of Spirit within all that is and the condition of our spirit and relationships within this "God-Field." (Godfield is a term offered by our teacher Rabbi Zalman Schachter-Shalomi, a.k.a., Reb Zalman). The importance of this holism as foundational to *hashpa'ah* echoes in the writing of another innovator in the field, Dr. Carol Ochs:

> When we are in emotional pain, we look for immediate relief in medications, distractions, or the hard work of psychotherapy. But the pain can...be regarded as an invitation to strengthen our relationship with God, because the essential unease in our lives finally boils down to the questions of [the] whole we are and...the system as a whole.[1]

In Judaism, the contemporary field of spiritual direction initially emerges from Reb Zalman's great appreciation of the role of the rebbe as a spiritual guide. His books *Spiritual Intimacy: A Study of Counseling in Hasidism* and *The Geologist of the Soul: Talks on Rebbe-craft and Spiritual Leadership* are foundational for all who enter this

---

1   Carol Ochs, *Reaching Godward: Voices from Jewish Spiritual Guidance*, URJ Press, 2004. P. 5

field. This volume is an eclectic collection, reflecting the variety of approaches used by *mashpi'im*, Jewish spiritual guides (also known as spiritual directors) and the new field of Jewish spiritual educators. Articles cover a range of topics from vary traditional methods such as intercession, prayer, ritual and spirit guides, to more contemporary approaches such as the importance of working from the body out into consciousness, imagery for transformation and healing, and using nature as a focus for connecting to spirit.

In a recent discussion with Dr. Barbara Eve Breitman, co-editor of the first anthology published in this field, *Jewish Spiritual Direction: An Innovative Guide from Traditional and Contemporary Sources* (Jewish Lights Publishing, 2006), she noted:

> Merely 15 years ago, I referred to the contemporary practice of Jewish Spiritual Direction as an 'emerging field'. As the field has evolved and expanded, an increasing number of liberal Jewish seekers are benefiting from the unique form of sacred accompaniment and inner work possible through *hashpa'ah*. Spiritual direction has significantly impacted rabbinic education and is now offered to students in most liberal seminaries in the US as a crucial dimension of rabbinic formation.

The reclaiming of the healing power of Jewish spiritual practices is a rising phenomenon in Jewish life. In particular, restoration of *teshuvah* as a Jewish spiritual practice — the life-long process of renewing our capacity to manifest and experience life's journey in healthy and holy ways — has become so central that *hashpa'ah* is not only part of rabbinic formation, it has become an independent profession with a number of available training programs.

A major shift since the first edition in 2009 of *Seeking and Soaring* and the Addison/Breitman anthology is the increasing recognition of rising rates of depression, personal pain and vulnerability and the yearning for assistance in personal healing. This change is in significant measure due to the amplification of unresolved trauma from World War II, the destruction of the Twin Towers of the World Trade Center and other upheavals attendant to religious and political fundamentalisms. Gender and racial oppression and the struggle for inclusion also remain important factors. All together, these have led to the widespread acceptance of the term "soul" as referring to the overall locus of human experiences from joy, to love, suffering, and much more. Accordingly, among the many teachings here-in, we learn: "A small hole in the body, a large hole in the soul."

The field of *hashpa'ah* is evolving rapidly; we invite you to savor the articles so generously shared by so many leading innovators, scholars and guides in this field. Additionally, your reflections and comments are welcome on our blog at:

www.ReclaimingJudaism.org

Introduction

Guidance for the *Mashpia* (Spiritual Director)
by Zalman Schachter-Shalomi

Rabbi Dr. Zalman Schachter-Shalomi, better known as "Reb Zalman," was born in Zholkiew, Poland, in 1924. Raised largely in Vienna, his family was forced to flee the Nazi oppression in 1938, landing in New York City in 1941, settling in Brooklyn, where Lubavitch ordained him in 1947. He later received his Master of Arts degree in the Psychology of Religion in 1956 from Boston University and a Doctor of Hebrew Letters degree from Hebrew Union College in 1968. He is the father of Jewish Renewal and founded the Spiritual Eldering movement, is an active teacher of Hasidism and Jewish mysticism, and a participant in ecumenical dialogues throughout the world, including the widely influential dialogue with the Dalai Lama, documented in the book, *The Jew in the Lotus*. He is one of the world's foremost authorities on Hasidism.

I feel such a blessing in this moment that the work of *hashpa'ah*, spiritual direction, has taken on greater prominence in the Jewish life. Not many people have had the privilege of sharing regarding spiritual intimacy. It is difficult to share the inner life without first establishing a sense of respect or trust. For *hashpa'ah* this is immensely important. Both the *mashpia*, and the one who receives spiritual direction, need to share this field of trust. Only then is it possible for the barely conscious thoughts and feelings to come uncensored to the surface.

Not only in the service of his/her congregants or students, does the Jewish professional need to know about spiritual direction. In his/her own life the pressures are mounting, conflicts between the functional and ideal aspects of congregational, educational or communal leadership arise and we need someone in whose presence we can work our way through the tangles of ideals and relationships.

When I studied at the Lubavitcher Yeshiva to become a rabbi, there was no explicit person-to-person spiritual formation available at other *yeshivas* or seminaries. At our *yeshiva* and in hasidic circles the place of the *mashpia* was prominent and essential. I often would think of the *mashpia* as a prayer coach, one would show how the ideals studied could best be applied. In the hasidic hierarchy the *mashpia* was located between the rebbe and the *hasidim* (adherents). Often *hasidim* would receive directions and indications from the rebbe in which they needed to be coached in order to actualize the directions the rebbe gave them. The *mashpia*, whose task it was to teach the theory and practice of hasidic life, was in effect the Jewish life mentor. The *mashpia* also served as a role model, one to whom one could attune, like a first violin or an oboe in an orchestra. And, this way one could harmonize one's mind and emotions to the *davvener* (person praying) or among the other *mashpi'im*.

In the late 1970's I served from time-to-time as *mashpia* at RRC, the Reconstructionist Rabbinical College. Teaching the students concepts of Hasidism, "davvenology" and being with many of them on a level of spiritual intimacy, I raised the hope that spiritual direction would become part of the training of Reconstructionist rabbis, which it has under the leadership of Rabbi Dr. Jacob Staub. Rabbi Shohama Wiener offered group and individual spiritual direction during her years as President and *Mashgiach Ruchani* at the nondenominational seminary, The Academy for Jewish Religion, and the other editor of this volume, Rabbi Goldie Milgram introduced the first formal seminary course in *hashpa'ah* there in the year 2000. Programs training *mashpi'im* outside of hasidic communities continued to emerge including so far, the *hashpa'ah* training in the Aleph Ordination Programs and also Lev Shomea founded by Barbara Eve Breitman, D.Min., Rabbi Howard Avruhm Addison and Rabbi Zari Weiss. There is also the Morei Derekh Jewish Spiritual Direction Program at the Yedidya Center, co-founded by Rabbi Amy Eilberg and Linda Thal, Ed.D., and Rabbi Milgram's Jewish Spiritual Education program at Reclaiming Judaism that provides distance learning for Jewish educators in methods of spiritual education and direction for youth and families. For the people in the Aleph Ordination Programs receiving and training in spiritual direction has become a requirement, due to the urging of Rabbi Shohama Wiener, *Rosh Hashpa'ah*, Head of Spiritual Development and Direction.

Clergy as *Mashpi'im*

People, who know very well that they could go to other people helpers, go nevertheless, to a rabbi. Their expectation is that something that touched them in their life in the synagogue could help them in dealing with their issues because, often enough the content of the rabbi's sermons touched on such issues.

But are Jewish clergy ready? A smattering of psychology, social work, common sense and a willingness to help is not enough in that situation. Imperative is the rabbi's professional values clarification, the way in which she or he is able to let go of personal agendas and make him or herself fully available to the other person both as congregant and as a soul striving to be in harmony with God. Only those clergy who receive preparation for inner work, examination of conscience, and a devotional prayer life, who receive *hashpa'ah*, spiritual guidance from a trained colleague are likely to steer clear of the serious damage which spiritual intimacy presents when it deteriorates into improper forms of intimacy. Just as in psychoanalysis people talk about infatuative transference between the analyst and the client, so it is inevitable that both the rabbi and the counselee involved in spiritual intimacy would feel an attraction to each other that could create karmic pollution of the process. Equally so, clergy and Jewish educators trained as *mashpi'im* who remain in *hashpa'ah* supervision while serving, will be able to assist their students, congregants, teachers and counselees, in navigating life's journey in ever more healthy, profound and pleasing ways. They will be able to work not only at the universal level of soul, but also through a Jewish lens that allows the powerful practices and traditions of our people to be put into effective service on behalf of the individual and the social systems in which they live.

Factic versus Mythic

Let's go back a bit to the human relationship with history. Left-brainers want history; but there are facts and there are "facts." From the factual side, we don't know how many of us were in Egypt, nor how many were part of the Exodus. Maybe Ben Gurion was right and there were only 6000 people. But while that may be the reductive-factic and there may be discoveries that help with the historic part, we don't live there spiritually; we live where the archetypes are. We experience in the mythic realm where there were 600,000 men and their families and flocks and in that realm was heard: "*anokhi hashem elokekhah* — I am the Lord your God."

We can argue: How much did the people hear? Was the Hebrew letter originally with the vowel *kametz* or without? On the mythic level "what we received" was Torah giving us access to the Infinite, to that Divine Mind, so that we become committed to the purpose that the Infinite had for this group of people. As Divine Mind came down to us, It came down in the form of descending fractals. When we start looking through all the generational adaptations to Torah, we can come to realize that even in the face of all of those changes, it's the same Torah Fractals all over again, except that It is adaptable to the time, for the place and for the people, etc.

Emil Fackenheim spoke of experiencing "Sinai events." This is the sense of saying that one can break past all kinds of preconceptions about how God should be and what is our situation and then suddenly feel that "my covenant is being renewed from this contact that I have." So if I can't find somebody who has experienced in his life a Sinai event, someone who knows beyond the rational realm of thinking, I'm just going to be dealing with information and not with the real *emes* of transcendent truth. And so *hashpa'ah* trainees must learn to attain that archetypal place. This can be done through midrashic exploration, and metaphoric interpretation of our sacred stories, as well as contemplative prayer; this is often where transformative awareness happens. Anything that happens in *assiyah* (the physical world) is a result of the awareness that issues from there; at least three more dimensions are available. If we want to be able to get people to a place to connect them to *elokus* —Divinity, and if the *mashpia* hasn't yet been there, then as a professional you aren't yet able to serve. So what to do? Expand your training. As Moses, our teacher, says, "Ask those people who were there, they saw this thing, so ask them."

My sense is that most of today's teachers have lost that sense of being people who can authentically share their Sinai moments. *Hashpa'ah* training and guidance increases the possibility of attaining that sense and sharing it in our session, our sermons and our relationships. We feel it when we have "brought down Torah from that place" and people will then come over to tell us "We felt a breakthrough," beyond the mental and the verbal, a breakthrough of *atzilus*—the highest spiritual level. This is one reason they want to have *mashpi'im*—spiritual guides who are grounded in the Jewish tradition.

Let's go back to the sons of the prophets, to the people that gathered around the prophet Samuel; they wanted to know how to be *nevi'im* — prophets. When his mother brought him to serve in the Temple, he was three years old. So Samuel knew what it takes to be prepared for sacred service. What a wonderful moment arises in I Samuel 3:4-10 when Samuel hears himself called: "Shmuel…" He goes to ask his mentor, Eli, "Did you call me?" and it was not he. Finally Eli explains: "God called you." From Samuel's understanding of that "calling", his whole relationship to life and service changes.

The story of Samuel is an example where one of the children of the Biblical prophets seeks spiritual guidance. Further examples of guidance being sought are to be found in the story of Daniel and, of Rabbi Akiva and his three friends who ascended spiritually through the spiritual levels known as *Pardes*. Each example reveals the importance of having a spiritual mentor or *hashpa'ah* support group. There were also clusters of spiritually aware people who created Qumran (in Israel), and examples are to be found among the Talmudic sages and the *yordei merkavah* (a particular group of early Jewish mystics). Their spiritual questions to each other, based on the sources they have left us in sacred texts seem to have been: "How did you do that which you report having experienced?" Part of the responsibility of a capable *mashpia* is to be able to prepare and guide each generation to be able to connect to the Divine.

Hashgakha in Hasidism

In general Hasidism you'll hear very little about *mashpi'im*; that seems to be a very *ChaBaD* kind of thing. Why? Because the other *hasidim* are thinking there's a rebbe and there are the *hasidim*, and in between are the *eltereh (older) hasidim* who've been around, but they're not officially appointed to be *mashpi'im*. So one asks these elders, saying: "I want to *davven'* (pray) like he *davens*." And one might ask of such a "davvener," "What could you teach me? Will you show me now to go into the meaningful prayer experience you seem to attain?" And also, "Do you mind if I emulate you, to see if your approach helps me in prayers and spiritual development?" These are important ways "in"; for how can one do things that one doesn't yet have words for?

When that inspiring person is standing there *davvenen'* and I have a sense, not only from his body, that he is lifting up his heart at that point, how do I learn his inner experience and find my own? Through questions, emulation and follow-up guidance I can attune with some of what is possible. This is what Chayim Soloveitchik calls the mimetic aspect of Jewish life, which has been largely lost in recent decades. The *mashpia* has to be able to provide this in a kind of clean way that is full of *emes* (truth) and not polluted by ego. You can imagine how inappropriate it would be if a *mashpia* was indicating: "See how good I am," and how that could turn someone off. There are experienced people who sometimes are giving it to us in that way, and we realize, this one can't be my teacher. There's too much energetically that he wants to get for himself from showing me. Not all teachers are good for each of us. I recall an intense personal experience in that regard.

> One day while in Belgium as a youth, I was looking into the *Tanya* (a *ChaBaD* mystical text) because they hadn't invited me yet to a *Tanya* study session and I wanted very much to get into the *Tanya*. A fellow comes over to me, shuts the book and takes it away from me. *Oy*. Did I feel bad. I reached at that point for the *Mesillat Yesharim* by Luzzato and he does the same thing to me. Finally he hands me Samson Raphael Hirsch in German, known as *The Choreb*—it was such a put down, you can't imagine what a put down that was. But it also told me, are you finished yet with *The Choreb* that you want to reach the other place? It was a harsh kind of thing to do.

Today, trained *mashpi'im* learn to be kind in redirecting people who are reaching beyond their capacity. I remember about ten, fifteen years ago everybody wanted to study *Abulafia* (a major early Kabbalist). Perhaps they figured it was a short cut. This was ultimately not helpful for them, as advanced mysticism becomes chaotic and disturbing without the prior and necessary levels of grounding in the tradition. Another story is illustrative of how a *mashpia* might guide in a beneficial way for the *mushpa* (person being guided):

> My *mashpia* Rabbi Jacobson catches me one day when I'm praying. I'm contorting my face in sincerity, wanting connection so badly that it's like I'm saying: "Pretty please God," and only getting into a frustrated,

kvetchy place. He gives me a bit of an elbow in my ribs and asks: "Did you try already in a nice way and you got a 'no?' So look differently for connection, maybe an ache somewhere?" I found the ache and knew its place in my life and heart, and from there I started to smile and started to *davven* and know what? It made a difference. He had helped me. This is the kind of craft that a *mashpia* has, to be able to see if the person is stuck and needs some clues.

On the other hand, the word *mashpia* is a relationship word and the other side of the relationship is the *m'kabeyl*, the person who is receptive. Notice the word *m'kabeyl*—**kabbalah** comes from that. *M'kabeyl* is an intensive form, which is not something that is just passively receptive, but rather actively receptive, wanting to take the experience in, to participate as fully as possible. So the *m'kabeyl* also has to have a sense of "It's Torah that I need to learn." This is when real possibilities begin, knowing that I need to learn and must find my teachers and cultivate the *chutzpah* (audacity) to really inquire of them. For example:

> It was in January 1943, that I finished a glass of *shnaps* and turned to Reb Shmuel who had just been saying, "The *bochurim* (male novices) don't really do serious *davvenen*." So I say to him, "Basically, could you tell me what you do when you're in *davvenen*?' I know the words and I know the *siddur* (prayer book), but what's going on inside of you?" And he gets irritated at my *chutzpah* of asking him such a question. So he turns to Rabbi Jacobson and says, "He's in your class, you answer him." So Rabbi Jacobson comments, "Over all these years I've been working so hard on prayer and he wants me to give it to him all on one foot." So I say, "If you want us to *davven* you have to tell us the whole thing." (The outside form, the inside experience.)
>
> So Reb Avraham Pariz turns to Rabbi Jacobson and he says to him, "After all, he's right." So they all turn to Rabbi Jacobson and say "Come on. Why don't you do it?" He takes a glass of *shnaps* (whiskey), tosses it down and begins to explain, beginning with the prayer of praise "*Hodu l'Adonai*." Every time I tell this story people what to know what he told me and I can't remember his words, but I can relate the powerful knowing he gave me. I was very much the *m'kabeyl* at that time, so each time he was sharing how he was going into "*y'hi k'vod ha-shem l'olam*—may the glory of God's name be forever", he would image what it's going to be like when all join in the hope that the world will be filled with God's glory. And, for each

verse he was adding internally to that image. When he came to the *amidah* (contemplative standing prayer), he said "here's where I pray of the Divine as *ga'al yisrael* (redeemer of Israel) and feel that all the fetters are off, I'm redeemed from my struggles." Then he stops with the indication that, "the rest is not for you, that's between me and God."

That had such a significant impact upon me, because it showed me that *davvenen'* is for real, that there were some people in my community truly doing that. In 1943 people had just come to America from Europe, during the Holocaust and the ghetto uprising. This was a very hard time. We were so preoccupied with trying to find out what was happening to our families overseas, in the camps and ghettos; it was so painful and frightening. That there were *ChaBaD* teachers available to me in Brooklyn helping me to pray, this for me was a wonderful, wonderful thing. There were additional designated fast and prayer days; all kinds of things were introduced. Where people were developing this and talking about it, I needed to be with them.

Mashpia as Spiritual Guide

When you see a travel poster, it can give you a desire to go the place that is depicted. Most people haven't seen the travel poster of the higher worlds. What is it that you visit when you go to *yetzirah* (the feeling dimension)? What is it that you might experience on *Shabbos* in each of the Four Worlds? Because we live by the modeling, if we don't have a sense of what is possible, then we can't go there. Opening the imagination is so important. This is why I like those *hasidishe meisehs*, (Hasidic stories) because as Rabbi Abraham Joshua Heschel would say, "a *meiseh* is a story where the soul surprises the mind." Such a wonderful way of putting that, because it opens possibilities and shows where else one can go.

Many of the people who come for spiritual guidance haven't yet seen these possibilities. Now here is where one has to be careful not to show the possibilities too soon. You have to have to have a sense that the person is caring, and has a spiritual concern, so you can say, "let me show you there's another possibility," and "maybe we can tune into it together so you can work on that in your inner life."

It's also important not to throw it away, because if you think about how people would say in the 70's, 60's, "I was into that and I'm not into that anymore, now I'm into this?" It was as though they became a kabbalist from one workshop. This is holy ground, so determine their commitment to the guidance and learning process through guidance such as: "Work on this for a week, I'll be glad to share with you afterward. Tell me where your practice has brought you."

It is frequently helpful to encourage people to work on their longing. You might inquire: "Tell me what your spiritual longing is." Teach them how to get in touch with that; to sit quietly, eliminate phone calls and distractions and learn to move beyond reactivity. Once you feel there's longing there within them, then you can take them a little bit deeper into the treasures of our spiritual traditions. This is a very important role of the *mashpia*.

When we take a person through an issue of transformation, they are likely to have some discomfort and distress because integration of the new "knowing" takes time. So you have to take responsibility for helping them with the integration. Roberto Assagioli wrote about this in his book *Psychosynthesis: A Manual of Principles and Techniques*, pointing out that many people have spiritual experiences that upset them. After a breakthrough and until you integrate the breakthrough, you are not going to be your best self. We hardly have time for integrative processes today, so *mashpi'im* have the responsibility to slow the process to allow for it. You might say: "So tell me what you have realized up to now, before we move forward any further."

Theory - *Yishuv ha-Da'at*

Theory can be quite helpful. This begins with a Four Worlds Approach, appreciating the differences in perspective and knowing that become available through the Four Worlds dimensions: the physical, emotional, intellectual and spiritual. Instead of "shoulding" on people, "Oh, we've got such a beautiful religion; oh, you should do this and you ought to try that" we are meant to help them appreciate the IS from which spiritual development begins. We must be careful not to get lost in the business of advice and the world of action, *assiyah*.

None of this spiritual work can be done without *yishuv ha-da'at*—the mind being in some kind of a settled place. So when the person comes to see you; or when you, in your own self are looking for a little bit of *yishuv ha-da'at* (equanimity), you want to be able to be in a place where you can steer your mind without it being buffeted by all kinds of other things that you usually have to respond to. As an analogy, we go to some movies and return home tired from them, because they're moving so fast from image to image, and that's the very opposite of where we have to be with spiritual development. We have to be more in *yishuv ha-da'at*, because while information can go very quick in and out, growing wisdom takes more time. The dimension of feeling has a different schedule; it doesn't go with fast "ah ha's."

Most of the time people want to get past the feelings, because every good feeling brings with itself also some history or knowing that is asking for deeper attention and focused prayer. *Yishuv ha-da'at* reveals pain for which the *mashpia* must also be trained to help discern whether to stay with it or rather to refer out while sticking to the position of spiritual support. Most of us are not licensed as therapists; we have an obligation to know when and how to avoid entering into that domain.

Yetzirah, **Intuition, Feeling**

We don't have many words for intuition and most of us have not spent focused time considering this human capacity. We need to trust it more, although it doesn't have words. Articles in this volume about Eugene Gendlin's Focusing ™ and also methods of *hashpa'ah* that involve movement modalities as well as the imaginal methods developed by Mme. Colette Aboulker-Muscat.

The levels of human awareness that we use in *hashpa'ah* require an understanding from the domain of brain physiology. Using a Four Worlds model, in the reptilian brain we go into *assiyah*, the physical dimension—protecting our turf, making sure we have what to eat, and that we are safe. From the limbic brain (*yetzirah*) we like to be in community, and we like to do rhythmic things; we're at the level of mammals here. Then there is the cortex in which we do our thinking (*briyah*), but there's a lot of brain capacity that hasn't been invoked yet and that's the place where mental intuition is. But when we say, "it occurred to me," it really occurred from the place of *ayin* — the no-thing (*atzilut*), from the highest intuitive place. In Hebrew this is called *b'hesekh ha-da'at*, which means that you can't work at it through "I want to reach it with my will and my intention". In *b'hesekh ha-da'at*, it comes suddenly. The more one gets out of the way and becomes a *m'kubal*, a "receiver," the more pre-verbal and valuable the "knowing" becomes for many. From that place of the body's receiving we can then try out words to express and understand our experience. First we need to be clear and open to receiving it.

Reducing Resistance to God

Spiritual direction offers approaches to reducing our resistance to God. Most of us want to always talk about the nice emotions, the nice feelings, our love of God and so on. Occasionally, someone introduces the flip side, *yir'ah* — the awesome/fearsome aspects of God-experience. Then inside, or within our communities and from our *mushpa'im* we hear, "Oh, no, no, no. We don't go for that. We want love, not fearsomeness from our Godsense."

Fear not *yir'ah*, for "*reishit hokhmah yir'at HaShem* — the beginning of wisdom is awe of God." It can help to ask: "God, please, let me be totally transparent to Your will, to Your mind, I want to give over all my will—*messirat ha-ratzon*." But then, like a mouse running back to its hole in the wall might come: "But I can't trust the Master of the Universe with this thing." So try saying: "Holy One of Blessing, wait a minute! I am not ready to surrender to You." When this emerges, one understands the resistance to the desired connection. This is the place where we talk about changing our blind spot. There's a lot of shadow energy here. Even the heart does not tell it to the mouth—*liba l'fuma lo galia*. If the heart doesn't pay attention to this place, we won't be able to reduce our resistance to God.

Which is the best kiss that we get? A kiss is true when I stop offering resistance to the beloved and insisting on being me, being an other. So when I think of the *midrash* about Moses dying, the kiss he receives from God to take away his soul shows he's become so selfless that he is ready to ascend from this life into mystery. The best we can expect for most us is to reduce the resistance bit by bit.

Living Parables

Reb Shneur Zalman says everything that we say about God and our relationship to Spirit is *m'shalim* (parables); nothing is so much reality as it is a *mashal*. When we're learning Torah, on the one hand we have to be in the *mashal*; on the other hand, we have to know it is a *mashal*. In parables, we are dealing in the realm of archetypal material. By living in the realm of the archetypal traditions of Judaism, we are living the *mashal*. One enters into the role of someone in the story or lives as though there is a listening God (who knows).

Another story by way of illustration:

> I was telling a group of people about *davvenen'* and my daughter Mimi was at that time taking lessons from Lee Strassberg in New York, she says to me, "Abba (father), I know what you are telling the people. You are telling the people how to *davven* by the Stanislavsky method."

My daughter was right. We go into the *mashal*. When the *chazzan* begins, were s/he to really mean the prayer known as the "*Hi-n'ni*" (Here I am, devoid of deeds, trembling with fear, frightened..." If the *chazzan*, cantor, were there in the *mashal*, could you imagine what we would get from such a *Hinneni*? Too often what the words intend to point us to in terms of spiritual connection, and what the *chazzan* is trained and capable of doing in terms of delivering real davvening, is such a sad contradiction. The reality lies behind the words. So you have as a good *mashpia* to be in touch with that reality while you are using the words of the tradition; it is your sacred duty to show the way.

Concurrent Processes of Spiritual Support and Jewish Growth

It is a common problem that someone comes for *hashpa'ah* and they present something they talked about in therapy. You reflect with them upon the problem and have a sense that this problem is covering up something deeper or more primitive. Someone I know once put it this way: "Most spiritual work that people do is putting whipped cream on top of garbage." If the garbage hasn't been cleaned out, then the whipped cream is like going to a dentist who misses some of the rot and then puts a filling on top; it's not going to result in a good long-term outcome." A story:

> A *ChaBaD* person says to me one day, "Zalman, I know what you're doing." I said, "What?" "You want everyone to have *ahavah b'ta'nugim* (love and ecstasy) in one easy lesson." Which is saying, you want to take everyone to the top level of spirituality in one easy lesson; to guide people straight into ecstatic love for God. So I reply: "You're darn toot'n." "Why?" "Look how often religious leadership people are using God-closeness to get mileage out of you; it's like saying I want you to put on tefillin first, and to make *Shabbos* first; and, you don't get into kabbalah that easy, you have to get into the *halakhah* – the details of Jewish ways of living, first. That's the coercive 'you have to' approach of *'teshuvah tatta-a* —of the lower return', where you come in and you say you have to fix up everything on the bottom, then I'll show you something wonderful. I don't go for that.

Honor Individual Differences

To be a *mashpia*, you have to be able to honor individual differences. Most books say this is where you begin, and this is the next step, and the next step, as if everybody was on the same track and that's not realistic. So it is important to know the difference between different body types: the viscerotonic person will need to know how to celebrate more; the cerebrotonic person will need to know how to meditate to keep their mind clear; the somatotonic person, how to go do a mitzvah for other people, and to live in that.

Authenticity and Ethics Are Essential

The truth of the matter is if I wouldn't get help from God, I couldn't effectively work on the garbage. How can I get onto a healthy path without the help and love of God? I have to have some kind of sense of support and compassion in order to begin with the real work that needs to be done on the ground level. As part of the effort to lift oneself out of a situation, the *mashpia* serves as a spiritual friend to help you keep your *neshamah*—your soul together. If you have to be in the dark subterranean aspects of your life, the *mashpia* comes to say: "I'm going to give you something to nurture you, while you work your way through that."

Sometimes it becomes so clear that somebody presents an issue and you have a feeling that it's not their own real thing, probably somebody else told them that that's what they should be doing. This is called an "introject" that they are bringing. It's very important to be able to say, "Wait a minute, is this your stuff at this point?" I recall one day when my *mashpia* told me to ask the rebbe for help about things he specified. I did go and told the rebbe, as if those issues were indeed mine. The rebbe smiled and told me: "You're not at a place yet where such things become difficulties for you." It was a compassionate assessment and important, because I had introjected another's opinion of me and needed help to discern that. At that same in the *yekhidus* — the one-on-one time, the rebbe was saying to me through the physical paralysis that made it hard for him to speak: "Zalman. Every country has its own expressions, there is in America an expression: 'take... it ....easy.'" This was so wonderful. He was saying, if you want to take it, you have to do it easy.

Being a spiritual director, a *mashpia*, doesn't mean being a rebbe. It is important for you to say when something is beyond you. You may need to make a referral. Don't play all-knowing *tzaddik* (sage). Remember the garbage and the whipped cream? If you have a sense that the person before you needs another kind of ministry, such as a rebbe, psychotherapist, psychiatrist, or marriage counselor, you can say: "This is beyond my depth," or, "You need to address this and I can't help. When you finish doing it, by all means come back to me."

Setting the Stage

If you've ever been to a recording studio or on camera, you know they would have a light up there to show that you're on at that point. Similarly, it would be appropriate in the place where you're going to give spiritual direction to someone, that you initiate the session with some action. For example, lighting a candle or opening with a prayer that gives the sense that what is going to be happening is taking place in the presence of God. Engage in this work knowing that the *Shekhinah* will be there with you, witnessing.

Yekhidus and Journaling

It is appropriate after the sessions that you have with people, to pray for them and then do some journaling. The Piasetzner Rebbe of blessed memory was asked how he found time to write so much Torah. He replied that between time with one *hassid* and the other, he always took notes. It was not necessarily that he took notes about the conversation that happened, but about what occurred to him at that point. You will see how this is helpful. The journaling might be something like this: "This session didn't come off effectively, because it didn't come from best place with myself," or, you may want to say other things about surprises that happened for you in the session. Private time, this type of *yekhidus* — spiritual intimacy, is always a very special privilege that you have with people. It is professional work, so be sure to remain in supervision so long as you are still seeing people professionally, and maintain a self-reflective journal about your efforts.

Deepening Your Own Practice

One of the things that keep us on track is what we consume mentally. Be sure to read the current and traditional spiritual direction literature. Allow a sense to emerge from your reading of how God's bungee cord pulls you. Reading material from the past gives a different take on things. We are very rich today in our tradition. When I first got started, not much was readily available. I would mimeograph pieces of *M'shivat Nefesh, Hishtapchut ha-Nafesh, Likutei Eitzot* of Reb Nachman, etc. One little *hasidic sefer* was out of print completely and I needed it. I still have it at home; I wrote it out by hand, ten chapters of that book *Derech Chayyim* in order to have it for study. It's good to have several possibilities at the same time. For example, when you study something medieval like *Orchot Tzaddikim*, it is necessary to understand that those spiritual teachers were very much on the side of an old asceticism, where the *guf*, the body isn't so good and the *nefesh* (soul) is the important thing. The non-Jewish world for them wasn't considered to be so good. Read their material without buying into that view, because there's good learning in there.

For example, when you see the way that Luzatto lays out steps for spiritual development in *Mesillat Yesharim*, you've got to learn how to screen out some of the old paradigm sexism and savor the awareness he teaches for how to mobilize towards desired change. There are times when one really needs to be doing something, *be-z'rizut*; and *n'kiut, takharah*—quick, clean, and pure—and he takes you through the various stages of that. While the first stages he describes in great detail, disappointingly he doesn't offer so much when you get to the aspect he calls *ruach ha-kodesh* (Holy Spirit). But that doesn't matter; because he takes us quite a good and long way on the path.

Mussar (ethical) tracts also help us cultivate awareness and we must also be careful not to so reify that period's values as to drag them all into our times. Seek out contemporary works also, including Rabbi Rami Shapiro, who I see as our Taoist. Just as we have the two poles of Deuteronomy of Moses saying "Don't do this ever, always do that, and so on, and you don't go to the right or the left, so too, we have the other pole "for everything there is a season"; sometimes you do, sometimes you don't. Let the spiritual direction literature continually sensitize you. It's important also to read *Kuntres Klallei ha-Hinukh v'Hadrakhah*, by Yosef Yitzhak; it's translated and available as *Principles of Education and Guidance through ChaBaD*.

Read Other Traditions, Too

Outside of Jewish tradition there's also a lot of good material. There is what Buber used to call "the leprosy of habit"; it eats away at you, and then you need a refresher, a "strange attractor" in the current language to lift you from spiritual entropy. Once I had read about Ramakrishna, I began to appreciate our rebbes more. I wouldn't have had a sense of the writings of Reb Dov Ber or the Mittler Rebbe until after I got in touch with St. John of the Cross. Once you see it from the outside, then you can come back with new eyes and greater depth of appreciation and understanding.

Empowerment and Appreciation

Watch yourselves, anything that you see in a book of spiritual direction that you haven't digested within yourself, don't serve it to anybody else. Look at all the Jews returning to Judaism who are unfamiliar with what's crucial to do in practice, and what's more stringent or elective. I feel for them as they read the *Kitzur* (abbreviated) *Shulchan Arukh* (code of Jewish law), and then they go learn the *Mishna Berurah* that summarizes the laws. They take this material overly literally compared to the traditional intent. There's such a need for their teachers to guide them with compassion.

In the past the asceticism was very clearly coming from: "How do I know that I am not at the mercy of my instincts because of the control that I can exert over my body and over my instincts." And that already had its say like this: "I will not indulge my body; I will do everything for the sake of the spirit." This sort of language also appears in the Zohar where: "the strength of the body is the weakness of the soul." Today we are getting a lot closer to a different understanding, that of a goal of a healthy mind in a healthy body. The Maggid of Mezrich told his followers: "You make a small hole in the *guf* (body), you are making a large hole in the *neshamah* (soul)." This perspective brings us back to appreciation of the gift of the body, and with appreciation, sensation has permission to return in holy and healthy ways.

Inevitably, if we are starved in the limbic we are going to get passive aggressive to the world. Let me spell this one out. If I feel I never have fun, if I feel that I'm starved in this, if I don't get mother's milk from the Torah of kindness, then I am being set up to act out.

I will feel my dissatisfaction, that I'm not happy in my body, and vent it unconsciously and often hurtfully. Reb Nachman came from a period of repression of sensation, that went this way: "When I was eating when I was young, I was eating overly hot food, so that I shouldn't feel the taste." My sense now is to go in a different direction, to embrace sensations as information to be used with discernment and as a gift divine. A story belongs here:

On Hanukkah there is a teaching of the Piasetzner that is a wonderful teaching. He was saying, how can you say that God is fulfilling every mitzvah in the Torah? How can you say that God is eating? What about the mitzvah of eating matzah? How does God fulfill that? The answer he gave is that it is through us. When we eat matzah God eats matzah. Just as it says: "What is it that God has to borrow from us?" What does God not have? God is an atheist, so God doesn't have a God, except in us, to serve, through us, God can feel how that is to have "awe of Heaven, everything is in the hands of heaven outside of awe of Heaven — *yir'at shamayim – ha-kol biy'dey ha-shamyim chutz mi yir'at shamayim.*" Only through us.

So if I enjoy something in this world and I do it only for myself, I create a passivity between myself and God, and that increases the resistance. Instead, what if I say: "*Ribono shel Olam*, I want you to taste, to have this *hana-ah* (pleasure)." Doing this helps to heal the limbic, so it won't go to the passive aggressive or gluttony. So when enjoying something, let's not deny we are really enjoying it and rather create a type of prayer of gratitude by saying "This tastes good!" Today is to enjoy.

Examination of Conscience

It is important for a *mashpia* to have the practice of the bedtime prayer practice, the *kriyat shema shel ha-mitah*, where one reflects on relationships from the day and says the *shema* prayer. Review your *hashpa'ah* sessions from the day at this time and ask yourself: "How was it?" Look at it again, and pray for each person you saw. You'll want to teach this to your *mushpa-im*, as well, to help them reflect upon their relationships and time with you. There's also a story for this:

A woman comes to Mohammed, peace be upon him, and says to him: "My son is spending all his money on eating dates, would you please tell him to stop doing that." He says: "Come back in a couple of weeks." So she comes back in a couple of weeks with her son, and he says, "You should stop spending your money on buying dates." So the mother says: "That, you could have said two weeks ago!" "Well," he says, "Two weeks ago I was spending my money on dates!" So you see, if you aren't doing your own *kriyat shema al ha-mitah*, it's really important to do so.

Chasing Blind Spots

There are times when I make a mistake and I catch myself and "I say I'll never do that again", and then I do something and it's "the same bride but she has a new veil on." Yes, the same issue keeps coming up, and this has been my life issue in so many forms. It is very hard to chase the blind spot; we need to have somebody to help with that. Ask: "What is it that I don't see?" The closer you get the more you feel you have to go to the bathroom or to go and eat. So if you have a friend does not have any agenda of their own with your blind spot; that might work for you. A door opens and all of a sudden you can see the blind spot but minute later you've lost it, so you have to go again, and again, until finally you can put a foot in the door and name it, and then you can work on it some more. It's hard, hard work, but if you don't attempt to do some blind spot chasing, it's going to interfere with your capacity to be of healthy service.

Kurt Lewin talked about "life space," meaning that when we do it only in our head there's no life space assigned to it; but, when you understand it is a matter of: "*v'asu li mikdash v'shokhanti v'tokham*—make me a sanctuary and I will dwell within you," you can become the observer of the blind spot as well as receive the support you need to intervene with your patterns. This can happen in what Buber called the "inbetween," as a consequence of issues shared with a *mushpa*. So I give you a *brukheh* (Yid., a blessing) to keep yourselves aligned and you will do a great good with your life and work in this world.

Recommended Reading

Howard A. Addison and Barbara Eve Breitman, *Jewish Spiritual Direction: An Innovative Guide from Traditional and Contemporary Sources*, Jewish Lights, 2006

Goldie Milgram, *Reclaiming Judaism as a Spiritual Practice: Holy Days and Shabbat*, Jewish Lights, 2004

   Meaning & Mitzvah: Daily Practices for Reclaiming Judaism through Prayer, God, Torah, Hebrew, Mitzvot & Peoplehood, Jewish Lights, 2005

   Living Jewish Life Cycle: How to Create Meaningful Jewish Rites of Passage at Every Stage of Life, Jewish Lights, 2009

Marcia Prager, *The Path of Blessing: Experiencing the Energy and Abundance of the Divine*, Bell Tower, 1998

Zalman Schachter-Shalomi, *Spiritual Intimacy: A Study of Counseling in Hasidism*, Jason Aronson, 1996

   The Geologist of the Soul: Talks on Rebbe-*craft and Spiritual Leadership*, Albion-Andalus Books, 2012

   with Joel Segel, *Davening: A Guide to Meaningful Jewish Prayer*, Jewish Lights Publishing, 2012

   Jewish with Feeling: A Guide to Meaningful Jewish Practice, Jewish Lights Publishing, 2013 (reprinted)

   A Heart Afire: Stories and Teachings of the Early Hasidic Masters, Jewish Publication Society, 2009

   and Ronald S. Miller, *From Age-Ing to Sage-Ing: A Profound New Vision of Growing Older*, Grand Central Publishing, 1997

   with Ellen Singer [Ed.], *Paradign Shift: From the Jewish Renewal Teachings of Reb Zalman Schachter*-Shalomi, Jason Aronson Inc., 1993 with Netanel Miles-Yépez and Robert Esformes, *Gate to the Heart: A Manual of Contemplative Practice*, Albion-Andalus Books, 2013

edited by Rabbi Daniel Siegel, *Yom Kippur Kattan and the Cycles of T'shuva*, booklet from www..org

Rami Shapiro, *Perennial Wisdom for the Spiritually Independent: Sacred Teachings-Annotated & Explained*, Skylight Paths Publishing, 2013

Rabbi Rami's Guide to God: Roadside Assistance for the Spiritual Traveler, Spirituality and Health Publisher, 2011

translated and interpreted; with a foreward by Rabbi Zalman Schachter-Shalomi, *Tanya, the Masterpiece of Hasidic Wisdom: Selections Annotated & Explained*, Skylight Paths Publishing, 2010

Shohama Wiener, *The Fifty-Eighth Century: A Jewish Renewal Sourcebook*, Jason Aronson, 1996

and Jonathan Omer-man, *Worlds of Jewish Prayer: A Festschrift in Honor of Rabbi Zalman M. Schachter-Shalomi*, Jason Aronson, 1993

Part I

How We Listen and Guide:
Techniques of *Hashpa'ah*,
Jewish Spiritual Guidance

Entering the Unknown through the Silence of *Dmama*
by Estelle Frankel

*"Stop the words now. Open the window in the center of your chest
and let the spirits fly in and out."* Rumi

"There is a time to speak and a time to be silent" Ecclesiastes

"For You, Silence is praise." Psalms 65:2

"Be still (and) silent before YHVH and wait patiently...." Psalms 37:7

Estelle Frankel, MS MFT is a licensed psychotherapist and spiritual advisor (*mashpi'ah-maggidah*) who blends the wisdom and healing practices of Kabbalah with insights from depth psychology. She is a seasoned teacher of Jewish mysticism who has taught innovative programs in Israel and throughout the U.S. for over 35, and is currently on the teaching faculty of Chochmat Halev in Berkeley, CA. Estelle has written numerous essays on Judaism and healing, and is the author of *Sacred Therapy: Jewish Spiritual Teachings on Emotional Healing & Inner Wholeness* (Shambhala 2004). Estelle is working on a new book, entitled *The Wisdom of Not Knowing*, which will expand on this chapter. www.sacredtherapy.com

One of the great challenges every spiritual companion faces is knowing when to speak and when to be silent. Words offered prematurely (wise and insightful though they may be) can get in the way and even feel downright trite. It's not just our spoken words, but also "wordy thoughts." This is particularly true in those moments when deep feelings are surfacing or when an inchoate question or thought is incubating in the directee's heart. At these times prayerful silence is what makes it possible to listen for the subtle intimations of God's presence. And though it is not always easy to quiet our own minds and let go of our thoughts and our desire to be helpful, it is the quality of silence we offer that makes room for the unknown and the unexpected. By not hurrying to name or define what is going on, we allow the truth of the moment to be revealed in all its mystery. And in the pregnant pause of silence, new insights and possibilities are born. But in order to create this sacred container of silence, we ourselves need to develop a particular skill — namely, the ability to rest comfortably in the uncertainty of "not knowing" and "not thinking." In this essay I would like to share some teachings from the Zen Buddhist and Jewish traditions that may help us grow comfortable with "not-knowing" and relieve our anxiety in those moments when we are called upon to do nothing, say nothing, and know nothing.

I want to open with a teaching from Zen Buddhism, where "not-knowing" is the central focus of spiritual practice. In Zen, "not-knowing" is considered to be our original nature. It is present in the effortless open-sky-like state of mind that we return to, moment by moment, as we let go of thoughts and thinking and rest in the pre-reflective moment— the moment before thoughts emerge. Paradoxically, it is a state of mind we must never cease trying to reach, yet it is not something we can achieve through our efforts but only as we let go of all striving. Norman Fischer, a Jewish-Buddhist monk, describes how not-knowing allows us to see clearly what is right in front of us, free of the prejudice and distortion that ideas and past experiences can impose on the present moment:

> When we know something and rest in that knowing we limit our vision. We will only see what our knowing will allow us to see. In this way our experience can be our enemy. True, our experience has shown us something about ourselves and about life. But this moment, this situation that faces us right now- this patient, this person, this family, this illness, this task, this pain or beauty — we have never seen it before. What is it? How do we respond? I don't know. I bow before the beauty and uniqueness of what I am facing. Not knowing, I am ready to be surprised, ready to listen and understand, ready to respond as needed, ready to let others respond, ready to do nothing at all, if that is what is called for. I can be informed by my past experience but it is much better if I am ready and able to let that go, and just be present, just listen, just not know. Experience, knowledge, wisdom — these are good, but when I examine things closely I can see that they remove me from what's in front of me. When I know, I bring myself forward, imposing myself and my experience on this moment. When I don't know, I let experience come forward and reveal itself. When I can let go of my experience, knowledge, and wisdom I can be humble in the face of what is, and when I am humble I am ready to be truly fearless and intimate. I can enter into this moment, which is always a new relationship, always fresh. I can be moved by what happens, fully engaged and open to what the situation will show me.[2]

Not-knowing, as described by Fischer, is the state of mind that allows us to get close to what is in front of us, to our actual experience, not our idea about what we are experiencing. This seems particularly relevant to spiritual direction, where holy listening requires an openness and attunement to the immediate presence of the divine. In order to

---

2   http://www.everydayzen.org/index.php?Itemid=27&option=com_
teaching&topic=Zen+Koans&sort=title&studyguide=true&task=viewTeaching&id=text-128-87

hear what is being revealed in any given moment, we must let go of what we already know. Our thoughts and our thinking are already old news. We receive the gifts of spirit only when we come to the table with empty hands.

The Jewish contemplative practice that brings us closest to Zen Buddhism's "not-knowing" is *ayin* meditation. In Kabbalah, *ayin* describes the divine nothingness out of which the fullness of existence in all its many varied finite forms continually emerges. All things are continuously being created anew, *yesh m'ayin*, something out of nothing, and returned to their source in *ayin*, the divine womb of all being. The Maggid of Mezeritch and his disciples taught that in preparation for prayer, for communion with the divine, we must become *ayin*, allowing our separate sense of self to dissolve into the boundlessness of the divine. This practice seems particularly relevant to the inner work spiritual directors can do in preparation for holy listening. *Ayin* meditation allows us to be still (*domem*) and return to the ground of our being. Interestingly, the Hebrew word for stillness/silence *dumiah* or *dmamah*— shares two root letters with the Hebrew word *adamah*, ground. In the silent stillness of *dmamah* we offer those we companion access to *ayin*, the sacred ground of being from which new life and new insights are born.

When I am doing spiritual direction, *ayin* meditation helps me release my thoughts and thinking to make room for God's presence to be felt. When I spend time in *ayin* meditation before a spiritual direction session, I notice it is easier to relax into uncertainty during silent pauses. Sometimes I still do get anxious during prolonged silences, especially on those days when I am too rushed to meditate before each session. At these times I notice that holding the space of silence can be more challenging, so I pay close attention to my body and my breath, releasing thoughts and thinking, noticing fantasies and images that arise, and trusting that, by waiting patiently, what is most helpful will be revealed.

"Not-knowing" and "not-thinking" are themes found in the Zohar, where the highest rung on the Tree of Life (*Keter* of *Atzilut*) is called "the Unknowable Head — *risha d'la ityada* — the Head which neither knows nor is known. This implies that at its source divinity is neither conscious of its own inner being nor is known to any consciousness outside of itself. It is simple absolute unity. At this non-dual level, God becomes the absolute, unknowable Mystery, beyond words, beyond all dualities of thoughts and thinker. Suzie Yehudit Schneider describes how we reach this level on Purim through our intentional practice of inebriation, whereby we reach a state of "not-knowing" (*lo yada*). Through the principle of resonance, our not-knowing allows the unknowable head — *risha d'la ityada* — the highest aspect of the soul that is undifferentiated from divine oneness, to make itself known.

> The highest root of the soul, the point where it is hewn from the pure simple oneness of God... is called *risha d'la ityada* —is the source of pure, simple faith; knowing beyond mind, experiencing beyond awareness the truth of God, and the truth of God's oneness, goodness, and love. On

Purim the lights of this highest root of soul, the Unknowable Head, fill the world. We express this below by entering the state of consciousness defined by the *Code of Law* as "until you don't know the difference between curse...or blessing...This state of 'not knowing' that is accessed on Purim through inebriation, is also accessed by the throwing of lots (*purim*).

Some questions are beyond the rational mind's capacity to fathom all of their relevant factors. One solution is to throw lots, asking for God to make His will known through their outcome. The person throwing lots admits that he doesn't know which option is the right one. *Ayin* means literally, nothing. When a person cast lots he stands in a place of 'not knowing,' aware that he is 'nothing' before God. By the principle of resonance his 'nothing' invokes the Divine "Nothing," the Unknowable Head, the innermost pure core of Divine Presence" [3]

Purim is the holiday when we go beyond "thinking" and enter the state of "*lo yada*" of "not-knowing." We transcend the dualistic story line of the Purim plot where good and evil, heroes and villains do battle, and instead we reach beyond our "minds" for a level of faith where we experience in our *kishkes* (innards) that God is One, and that life, no matter how difficult at times, is an expression of divine love and goodness. In spiritual direction we can reach this same state of mind only through silence, the still silence of *dmamah*. As we surrender our "thoughts" and "thinking" and release all the old "stories" we tell ourselves about our lives, we can begin to construct a new narrative, one in which God's presence is felt. When God's presence is felt, we begin to discover a new set of questions to contemplate.

The Zohar describes how our "questions" change as we develop spiritually and are capable of contemplating higher levels of awareness. According to the Zohar, contemplation of the *Sefirot* below *Binah* (these *Sefirot* are involved in the operational dynamics of this world) stimulates questions of "What" (*Mah*), as in—What is the nature of this universe? In contrast, inquiry into the *sefirah* of *Binah*, (Understanding) the emanation closest to *Chokhmah*, the point of origin of the entire tree of life, can only be formulated with questions of "Who" (*Mi*), along the lines of Isaiah's awestruck words: "Lift up your eyes to the heavens! Who created all these heavenly hosts." [Isaiah 40:26]

Note: In spiritual direction it is interesting to notice when a directee's questions begin to change. The shift from "what" to "who" often suggests a movement towards I-Thou communion, or greater spiritual intimacy. A *midrash* about Abraham suggests that his

---

3   A Still Small Voice—a correspondence course with Suzie Yehudit Schneider, http://www.astillsmallvoice.org.

repeated inquiry into the question of "who?" was the master of the world brought about a revelation from God.[4]

But there is yet a higher level of inquiry, according to the Zohar, that reaches all way to *Chokhmah* and *Keter*, the very Source of Being. Here, questions once more begin with the word "what" (*Mah*), but this is an entirely different kind of "what." It is the "what" of "what do we really know? We really do not know anything!"[5] At this level, "not-knowing" is key. Here, silence is the only way to praise, as Rabbi Shimon instructs his son: "El'azar, my son, cease your words, so that the concealed mystery on high, unknown to any human, may be revealed." Rabbi El'azar was silent."[6]

Aryeh Lieb, a secular Israeli mystic, expands on this teaching from the Zohar, showing how the silence of "not-knowing" provides a passageway into higher levels of knowing, where new questions and new insights can arise:

> An amazing spiral of *gnosis* (*Daat*) is born of the tension
> between "knowing" and "not-knowing." There are fifty levels/gates
> of "Understanding" (*Binah*). The fiftieth level/gate is the gate of "not
> knowing," along the lines of what the mystics meant when they said that
> "the endpoint of all knowledge is to know that we do not know!"[7] When
> a person reaches the outermost limits of his/her knowledge and arrives at
> the point where knowledge originates, a moment of stillness and absolute
> silence is reached. Everything has been said and all thoughts have been
> thought. Everything that one can know about that particular level has
> been understood. All remaining questions, articulated or non-articulated,
> can find no answers from the existing pool of knowledge. From this very
> silence, a new level of "knowing" is born that is connected to an entirely
> new level of understanding. It utilizes all the previous knowledge and
> questions as a vehicle (vessel) to attain a higher level of knowledge. And
> this new level of "knowing" has a ladder (comprised of fifty levels) with a

---

4   A midrash (legend) from *Genesis Rabba* says that Abraham saw a palace on fire and demanded to know who was the owner of the palace. Immediately, the owner peeked out and revealed Himself to Abraham. In this midrash the burning palace is a metaphor for this world which is a palace for the King of Kings.

5   *Zohar Pritzker Genesis Vol. 1*, p. 6. "Once a human being questions and searches, contemplating and knowing rung after rung to the very last rung—once one reaches there: What? What do you know? What have you contemplated? For what have you searched? All is concealed, as before."

6   *Zohar Pritzker Genesis Vol. 1*, p. 7.

7   Rabbi Yedaiah Bedersi, the 14th century ethicist wrote: "The ultimate purpose of knowing is to know that we don't know." (*Bechinat Olam* 13-45)

boundary of its own. It too reaches a fiftieth gate with its own silence and openness to receive an entirely new level of awareness. In this fashion an infinite spiral is created....

The fiftieth gate requires special study, special preparation—inner silence and readiness to let go of the "known," a special attention to a fresh perspective, a faith in the infinitude of wisdom, a depth within a deeper depth, a faith in oneself, a faith in the Godforce (*Elohim*) that graces humans with knowledge out of desire to share its (divine) wisdom and love.[8]

What I understand from this teaching is that our ability to know and understand things at different levels evolves throughout the life cycle. By allowing ourselves to "not-know," we make it possible to learn something brand new. To evolve spiritually we must be willing, at times, to let go of all our prior knowledge and understanding. At these moments we may feel as though we are jumping off a high dive, free-falling into "space" as we wait for our "parachutes" to open—for the words to emerge that formulate the new question we must ask as we enter the next level of understanding. During that "free-fall" the role of the spiritual companion is to hold the space of *dmamah*, of stillness and silence—the silence of not-knowing.

This is perhaps one of the lessons that can be learned from the story about *Aharon* (Aaron) the High Priest, when he responded to the news of his sons' deaths with silence, the still silence of *dmamah*. It says in the Torah, "*Vayidom Aharon*" — Aharon was absolutely still and silent!" [Bamidbar 10:3] Rashi says that he had been weeping, but when he heard Moshe's words, he was comforted and found a way to surrender and express his humble awe through *dmamah*.

These teachings would eventually find their way into my work with Judith, a 52 year old woman who found her way to me after losing her twenty year old daughter in a tragic car accident. When I began seeing her, Judith was, understandably, deeply depressed. She was haunted by regrets and ruminative thoughts. She couldn't stop her mind from asking over and over again the same questions of "What could she have done differently to prevent this from happening?" And —"How could God allow this terrible tragedy to happen?" She cycled, as many bereaved individuals do, between the emotions of anger and grief. Most of the time, her anger at herself was extended to her relationship with the divine, so Judith found it difficult to pray. The God she had believed in no longer seemed to exist, or at least was not accessible. She was too angry. Her life had changed irrevocably since her daughter's death. She was no longer drawn to the activities, people, and interests that had given her prior life meaning. So we sat in silence through many difficult sessions

---

8   *Mibesari Ehezeh Eloha (In My Flesh I See God)* p. 232 "The Spiraling Tree of Knowledge and Tree of Life," translated from Hebrew by Estelle Frankel

of overwhelming grief. I did my best to offer my heart as a place to rest in these silences. Judith began to find comfort in our silent meditations. As she began to deepen in her meditation practice, I noticed that Judith's questions began to change. Instead of "what" and "how" I noticed that she began asking questions of "who." "Who am I really?" and "Who was my daughter?" She also had a new question about God: "Who is this God that creates a world in which love and grief, joy and sorrow exist side by side?"

As Judith was able to take comfort and refuge in deeper states of silence, the silence of *dmamah*, finding answers to her questions became less important than resting in an open-hearted state. Not-knowing was actually far more comforting than any vain attempt to know. Allowing herself to be lovingly held by the divine embrace in the midst of her sorrow and grief helped Judith begin to accept her loss and go on living, loving and experiencing moments of joy without feeling that she was being disloyal to the memory of her daughter. Judith took comfort in the Biblical tale about Aharon, because it inspired in her a sense of deep humility, faith, and surrender, which freed her from guilt and self-blame.

The quintessential biblical tale of spiritual awakening, namely Abraham and Sarah's journey from Padan Aram to Canaan, is essentially a journey into the "unknown." God says to Abraham: "*Lekh lekha*...Go to your Self, to a land that I will show you."[9] Abraham and Sarah answer the divine call by leaving everything familiar behind, their homeland, culture, community and family, to go to some faraway, unnamed, unknown land—a place that will be shown to them some time in the future. No map, no itinerary. They will know they have arrived when they get there. The midrash quoted by Rashi suggests that God intentionally concealed the intended destination in order to give Abraham and Sarah reward for every single step they took on faith, as they journeyed into the unknown. Rabbi Yehudah Aryeh Leib Alter, author of the *Sefat Emet*, reminds us that the journey to the holy land is also an inner journey which takes us from self-will, from what we understand with our own minds, to an alignment with the divine will, which is always beyond comprehension:

> The simple meaning of this is that the land of Israel is the place where one surrenders one's senses and desires (will) to God's will, as it is written (Gen. 12:11) 'Go to your Self, from your land (*artzekha* may be understood here as a pun, *ratzon shelkha*—your will). All externals must be abandoned for the sake of seeing God's will. Only then is it revealed to a person. And the general rule is that we must listen in order to receive

---

9   Genesis 12:1

what we cannot possibly understand, namely knowledge of God's infinite nature. To this end we must continually surrender our knowledge...that which we understand with our minds.

Spiritual companionship, ultimately, involves accompanying others on this journey into the vast unknown terrain of the Divine Mind.

The Lament: Hidden Key to Effective Listening
by Barry Bub

Barry Bub, M.D., family physician, Gestalt psychotherapist and chaplain is the author of *Communication Skills that Heal: A Practical Approach to a New Professionalism in Medicine* (Radcliffe Medical Press).

Simply stated, the lament is an expression of suffering. Since suffering is universal, laments are pervasive everywhere humans are found—from the checkout counter to the workplace to the street corner to the assisted living facility. Laments are particularly pervasive in healthcare settings where patients, their loved ones, physicians, and the staff, all in their own ways, experience suffering. Not surprisingly, the word patient is derived from the Latin word *patiens* meaning "to suffer."

Regardless of where they are found, laments contain elements of hopelessness, helplessness, disempowerment, absence of choice, pessimism, grief, weariness, lack of meaning, isolation—from others, from God, from self—perhaps anger, fear, shame, anguish, self blame, guilt, and cynicism. The chronic lament also includes hope, since when lamenting, the individual is reaching out from a place of isolation, with the hope (often unaware) that the cry will be heard.

Sometimes a lament becomes chronic, seeming to take over the very identity of the chronic sufferer. Like the playing of a tape, there seems to be an endless retelling of the trauma story, In this case, there is little that the listener can say or do that is helpful and this is one instance when interruption may be appropriate. Normally, what is most indicated is listening.

Laments involve the vocal expression of suffering. Good examples are provided in the Book of Lamentations. The Hebrew title is *Eikhah*, meaning "How?!: Like a "howl", the rough sound of this Hebrew word embodies the harshness of the pain. Laments are also found in other books of the Bible, particularly Job and Psalms. For example:

"If so, why me, why me - if so - why me?" Genesis 25:22

"Bitterly she weeps at night, tears upon her cheek. With not one to console her..." Lamentations 2:2

"I am weary with calling, my throat is dry; my eyes fail while I wait for God." Psalm 69:4

"I call God to mind, I moan, I complain, my spirit fails." Psalm 77:4

"I am disgusted with life; I will give reign to my complaint, speak in the bitterness of my soul." Job 10:1

"Why Lord do You reject me, why do You hide Your face from me? From my youth I have been afflicted and near death; I suffer Your terrors wherever I turn." Psalm 88:15-16

"My God, my God, why have you abandoned me; why so far from delivering me and from my anguished roaring? My God, I cry by day, You answer not; by night, and I have no respite." Psalm 22:2-3

"Lord, hear my prayer, let not my cry come before You. Do not hide Your face from me in my time of trouble. Turn Your ear to me when I cry, answer me speedily." Psalm 102:2

The Evolution and Types of Lament

It is helpful to understand the evolution of a lament. Trauma (physical, psychological, spiritual) always results in losses. These losses need to be borne or carried (*suffere* Latin to bear or carry) until the self reintegrates around these losses. In the process the suffering is expressed (lament). When listened to, understood and validated the sufferer is no longer as isolated and healing occurs.

A lament may be considered acute or chronic. The differences are important to recognize so that the proper listening can be provided.

The acute lament

The acute lament is a normal, healthy, integral part of the healing process. Traumas always result in losses. In the face of sudden severe losses, screaming, crying, bemoaning, and wailing serve to generate the energy that frees the individual from the numbness created by the shock of trauma and allows the traumatized individual to adjust and realign to the new reality.

With the lament, it is useful to think of energy being transformed into movement. In the acute lament, movement is vertical: "descent for the purpose of ascent" as Rebbe Nachman of Breslov described it in the 18th century. Sometimes the deep, dark despair is so severe that descending into it feels like death and then, as hope begins to return, ascending into a world of new possibilities feels like rebirth. The poet David Whyte describes this experience as a descent into "the well of tears".

In the usual course of events, trauma is followed by what we term The Healing Sequence. A simple metaphor that illustrates this healing sequence is one of a child falling and scraping a knee. The injury (trauma) results in pain (suffering), which leads to crying (lamenting); the parent hears and comforts the child (listening) and the child runs off and plays again (healing).

In relationship to *hashpa'ah*, let's take the situation where a person has lost her job. The injury (trauma) results in pain (suffering), which leads to lamenting; the person eventually seeks counseling (listening) and as her pain is witnessed, and her ego marinates in awareness and gradual understanding, life energy returns and ascent into a new, even better direction in her life as it comes into focus (healing). With serious traumas, such as a financial reversal, an accident, an illness, a death, abuse and more, the emotional, spiritual or physical (suffering)—which leads to crying, wailing, collapsing, moaning (lamenting), so that when recognized and validated by the self or another (listening), the losses and suffering become integrated (healing) and the individual moves on.

Alternatively, with overwhelming trauma the response may be stunned, numbed, silence, just as Aaron was silent when his sons were burned to death by God [Leviticus 10:1-3], In such a situation, movement is frozen rather than directed. For some, this Acute Stress Reaction (ASR) may eventually lead to Post Traumatic Stress Disorder (PTSD). ASR and PTSD can manifest when patients have been exposed to traumas such as accidents, acts of violence, sudden loss of a loved one, acute myocardial infarction, spontaneous abortion, diagnosis of cancer, or even a serious lawsuit.

The chronic lament

A lament may become chronic when grief following an acute trauma is interrupted, disowned, or disenfranchised and there is no opportunity for complete mourning. It may also occur when the onset of trauma is gradual or trauma or overwhelming stress is unrelenting.

Being denied the transformative power that comes from openly expressing grief, energy, needing to go somewhere, seeps out. The poet Rumi described this in the 13th century: "I spill sad energy everywhere. My story gets told in various ways: a romance, a dirty joke, a war, a vacancy."

The chronic lament is frequently expressed in a flat repetitive way and as such is mostly counterproductive, alienating rather than drawing others closer. This lamenter, needing to be heard, repeats the lament constantly, often unconsciously and in a number of vague ways. It creates a frustrating experience for the listener who may feel helpless and trapped. When the light bulb of awareness goes on and the listener recognizes the repetitions for what they are, a lament, then the listening experience changes. Now the listener becomes empowered and useful, for the lament can be responded to appropriately and sometimes, transformed through the release that yields awareness of desirable change of direction or expression.

The movement of energy with the chronic lament is *circular and non-linear*. It does not lead to healing. Dr Simcha Raphael, psychotherapist, calls this "stuck movement". Like a tape recording played over and over, the lament leads nowhere, although may be responsive to skillful help, as will be described below.

Why is recognizing the lament important?

As already stated, the acute lament is a normal, healthy response to a painful trauma. It is integral to the healing process. Tears have been described as "nature's way of washing a wound" i.e. removing particles that obstruct healing. Appreciating this, the listening avoids the error of interrupting the process by failing to provide a safe place to grieve or by premature comforting.

The chronic lament is important for the opposite reason. It may go unrecognized and like a foreign body in a wound, it draws attention to itself and inhibits healing rather than facilitating it. Only when genuine emotion is felt and expressed can the lament begin to shift into constructive action. In other words, when the chronic lamenter experiences sadness or weeps in the course of talking, this is a positive sign.

Certain groups of individuals are at higher risk for chronic laments—the recently separated, divorced or bereaved, the unemployed, patients, particularly the elderly and nursing home patients. In these groups, lamenting can be anticipated and responded to quickly and effectively.

How to recognize a lament

The acute lament is usually obvious. The chronic lament might be recognizable as a chronic complaint. On the other hand it may also be almost totally masked—the individual with a fixed smile, the always joking physician, the cynic, the intellectual, the loner, the disruptive physician (or patient), the workaholic. Consequently, the lament is frequently missed. Similarly the lament may be expressed as physical symptoms such as chronic backache, fatigue, vague abdominal pain, and headaches.

Anticipate it

Common things occur commonly; therefore expect to hear suffering from certain groups of individuals such as those who are unemployed, nursing home patients, those who are overworked or suffering burn-out, experiencing marital difficulties, recently divorced or widowed, etc.

Listen for clues

All senses are utilized in active listening. Notice the manner of handshake, eye contact, facial expression, body posture, speech pattern, and choice of language. The theme of the lamenting person's narrative is often peppered with disempowering words such as buts, can'ts, shoulds, musts, and if onlys. Notice also: hopelessness, pessimism, weariness, loneliness, and negativity.

Notice your own response:

> Am I finding myself wanting to avoid this person?
> Do I find myself yawning, bored, and irritated by our conversation?
> Do I feel redundant here, as if this person doesn't see me?
> Am I hearing a tape and it doesn't matter if I am in the room or not?
> Were we talking and then the conversation was hijacked by a lament?
> Do I feel stimulated to offer advice, counsel, or fix a problem?
> Do I notice an emotional mismatch? Is the story powerful but the delivery flat and emotionless?

Any of the above suggests one is hearing a lament.

An example of a subtle lament:

> Returning from presenting at a conference, I found myself sharing a cab to the railway station with a young medical fellow. As we pulled up to the station, she commented: "I hope the train is on time. Amtrak is often late."
>
> She sighed and repeated: "Yes, they're erratic".
>
> While we waited for the train, which incidentally arrived on time, she asked what I taught.
>
> "Listening skills—for example, how to recognize a lament." I responded.
>
> "What is a lament?" she asked.
>
> "You just did it, a few minutes ago" I replied.

She looked at me quizzically.

"Remember your comment about Amtrak, that was a lament. You sighed as you said it, and you repeated yourself. You know when a word or a phrase is repeated in the Bible, it's always significant. Same in real life. Neither of us wants the train to be late, but for you it has a special significance."

We seated ourselves across the aisle from one another. She chatted easily about her job. How fortunate she was to have it. It required some travel, but was otherwise a "plum". There were many perks, such as her recent eight weeks maternity leave instead of the usual six. "Yes," she told me, "my friends envy me having a job I actually enjoy, something unusual in this day and age."

"How old is your baby?" I asked. "She's eight months old, the joy of my life. My husband's babysitting. She will be asleep by the time I get home, I guess," she replied, her smile now less pronounced.

"Is it hard for you to be away from them?" I asked.

"It is," she said, her voice now dropped to barely a whisper. "It's been tough. Still, it's too good a job to give up." Her eyes were misty.

Leaning forward across the aisle toward her, in an invisible "bubble" of rapport, I responded that it had to be wrenching having to make the choice between work and baby. Regardless how great the job, her losses were big. She nodded, silent now.

After a while: "What will you do with the next one?" I asked.

"No way will I return to work!" her voice now assertive and strong. She then paused for a moment: "So, I was lamenting, ha? Go figure."
A short while later, when I disembarked at my stop, she flashed a broad goodbye smile. She was sitting straighter. A lightness had come over her.

It is important to note that lamenting, particularly if accompanied by physical symptoms, loss of appetite, weight loss, fatigue, aches and pains may be indistinguishable from, or associated with, a concomitant depression or serious physical illness.

Appropriate response to a lament:

At a recent symposium, the speaker was asked what one does when encountering someone who expresses suffering. His answer was to the point: "Simply listen." He was technically correct – one does listen but he was totally wrong about it being simple. Sure, there are those labeled "born listeners" but the harsh reality is that truly skilled listening, an activity that includes understanding and helpful response requires training, practice and supervision.

Apart from the notion that listening is a passive, simple activity, there are many other misperceptions concerning listening. One prevalent one is that quality listening is motivated by compassion. The reality is that no one is compassionate all the time and for listening to be compassionate, it must emerge authentically. This generally occurs when one offers support and is listening actively and non-judgmentally. Another myth is that listening is time consuming. Good listening actually saves time in the long run.

The acute lament

A quiet supportive presence is helpful, meaningful, and healing. Silence may be an appropriate and active response since space is being created for grief. Here the listener serves as an invaluable witness to the experience. There are different types of silences—icy, cold, warm, intimate, etc. A helpful image of silence here is one in which "You hold in your heart the person with whom you are sitting, creating a warm silence where s/he knows you are not off somewhere else in your thoughts" (Rabbi Goldie Milgram, personal communication, 2003). Attention to "simple" details, such as having tissues on hand and ensuring privacy is important. Often long after the event, the sensitive role played by the attendee will be recalled with appreciation.

The chronic lament

Upon inquiry as to how he responded to his clients who seemed disheartened, pessimistic, disempowered, a hairdresser offered this insight:

> "I do not attempt to fix their problems. I listen, empathize, and focus on improving the client's self image. I remember one young woman who shared her troubles with me. Finally, when I had finished she was thrilled by her appearance in the mirror. Walking to the door now with a bounce to her step, she paused, turned around and blurted: "You done gone and changed my way of walking!"

Once the light bulb goes off as in "Aha! A lament!" then the listener needs to switch to "hairdresser mode" and pay particular attention to:

- Being fully present and demonstrating this with eye contact, body language, and verbal response
- Regardless of the temptation, not responding with advice, critique, or reassurance
- Suspending personal judgment. Each person's suffering is unique. What seems trivial to one individual, may be very important to another
- Offering therapeutic validation (the intentional use of validation in ways that enhance the recipient's capacity to face life's existential moments). It requires identifying the underlying emotions and reflecting back in a way that demonstrates understanding of them
- Demonstrating empathy with phrases such as "I am sorry to hear this" or "What a sad time for you"
- Being very careful not to respond with: "I understand" or "I know what you are going through" because it is impossible to fully understand the suffering of another
- Suspending attachment to outcomes
- Silently acknowledging one's own anxiety at not being totally in control of the length, direction, or outcome of the encounter and reminding oneself that time listening often feels longer than reality

When an individual feels heard and validated, laments tend to fade and the focus of the lamenter's attention may shift from lament to the listener. The listener may notice feeling visible for the first time in this encounter. Even though the listener has not fixed anything, a shift has occurred. This may be enough for most transient situations.

If there is an ongoing relationship, then opportunity for further healing exists. Facilitating a shift in the chronic lament requires a deeper understanding of the nature of suffering. The word suffer is derived from the Latin *sufferre*—to carry. To suffer is to carry, to endure. What is being carried is always an undesired burden. This knowledge provides the listener with therapeutic opportunities.

Name the suffering

Responding: "How do you possibly manage to cope?" or "You have endured so much, what keeps you going?" or words to that effect, raises the lamenter's awareness that he or she is suffering. This awareness alone serves to ease suffering. The renowned philosopher and Holocaust survivor Viktor Frankl articulated it well: "Emotion, which is suffering, ceases to be suffering when we form a clear and precise picture of it".

Identify losses

Asking oneself: "What is this person being forced to carry or endure?" helps identify losses. Reflected back, this helps the lamenter connect to specific losses and to move into a phase of conscious mourning—a precondition for moving forward.

Relieve isolation

Not only is a burden being carried, it feels as if it is being carried alone. The very nature of suffering is separation and isolation. This can be understood from the perspective of a cancer patient. The moment the diagnosis is revealed this person now leaves the community of the healthy and faces an unknown future. As in the three stage "rite of passage" process described by Arnold van Gennep, this person having separated from society (stage 1) is now on a journey as an ill person (stage 2) and upon recovery returns to society (stage 3) somehow transformed by this life threatening experience This entire process of detachment, journey, and return is an isolating and frightening one. Having the lament heard and supported, means that this burden is no longer being supported alone.

Shift perception

The lament tape may be played so often that it is experienced as the reality of the situation. This becomes a fixed image. When the listener reflects back what is heard—for example, "So you feel you have only one choice" this may stimulate awareness that this is a feeling and not necessarily reality. Images may shift. The question: "What do you think you need right now?" may sharpen the focus from lament to specific need. Reflecting the lament back in the form of a metaphor—for example, "You feel you are wandering in the wilderness," may also help reshape the image of the situation.

Empower

Powerlessness, helplessness is the lamenter's present reality. It is rarely absolute. Asking: "What supports or strengths do you have?" may help the lamenter connect with forgotten strengths. Asking "How may I be most helpful to you?" is also empowering because it hands over control to the lamenter. This question presents an opportunity for partnership and collaboration.

Support faith

For some, the lament is a cry to a higher power: Hear my suffering! Get me out of here; this is such a painful place! Clergy and chaplains are seen as messengers of God. Any human can fulfill this role, just by careful listening. Deep listening is in fact the spiritual experience many need from their caregivers. What is heard, the lament, can be reflected back in the form of a blessing, prayer, or affirmation. Listening becomes a powerful and moving experience.

Many will find comfort in reading Psalms, Job and Lamentations because they give voice to feelings of the sufferer.

Support the Best Self

Self-perception is by definition subjective. The lamenter connects with helplessness, loss, failure, and shame. Positive qualities are often forgotten and self-esteem suffers. Just as the hairdresser holding a mirror reflects a beautiful image, the listener can often quite sincerely remind the lamenter of personal strengths that are being overlooked.

Introduce Hope

Without negating the negative perceptions of the lamenter, the listener, through his/her spirit, positivity, humor, and humanity may stimulate some of these same qualities in the person lamenting. Music, poetry, story all can lift the spirit, shift mood, optimism, and perception of the situation.

Touch

Nowadays regarded with suspicion, appropriate touch done with great care and consciousness can be very healing. A simple touching of the hand can mean a great deal to someone who feels isolated and estranged. Sometimes you might ask if the person wants a hug in a way that lets him/her accept or decline with dignity. Very careful listening has the same effect. Dan Bloom, Gestalt psychotherapist, states this succinctly: "I touch by my listening".

Utilize Ritual

When losses have been openly lamented and grief has been expressed, then the time has come to move on to effective action. Recommending or assisting in creation of a ritual can help to support and facilitate this transition.[10]

When an individual feels heard and validated, laments tend to fade and the focus of the lamenter's attention may shift from lament to the listener. The listener may notice feeling visible for the first time in this encounter. Even though the listener has not fixed anything, a shift has occurred. This may be enough for most transient situations. When there is an ongoing relationship with the *mashpia*, then opportunity for further healing exists.

Here is an example of a lament that was written to express grief, and resulted in a return to hope.

The Elderly Woman's Lament
Anonymous[11]

How lonely I am now, in my once-crowded house,
once happily married to a man
whose mind has vacated the premises,
yet whose body requires the hard labor of daily upkeep

Bitterly I weep at night,
my friends either dead or in Florida
or living with children somewhere else

I have withdrawn into my daily habits,
cruel benign slave masters;
my fears assault me
as I refill the daily pill dispenser

---

10   See article on ritual in *hashpa'ah* by Rabbi Jill Hammer, p. 79
11   Reprinted with permission of the author

Friends, family, children
used to stream in for *Shabbos*,
Pesach, kisses and Band-Aids.
Now I listen as the clocks tick down the seconds,
a blessed break while he's at Adult Day Care

My body betrays me,
My husband listens blankly to a blasting TV by night,
My children live in that happy place
of being needed now.

The essence of the lament is that it is a vocal expression of suffering, a prayer seeking the listener. One doesn't go over, under or around it—we go to it and into it, before coming through to awareness and action. In *hashpa'ah* a lament is a prayer that is actually heard and mirrored by the *mashpia* on its way to the Listener beyond and within.

Recommended Reading

David R. Blumenthal, *Facing the Abusing God: A Theology of Protest*, Westminister/John Knox Press, 1993

Barry Bub, *Communication Skills that Heal: A Practical Approach to a New Professionalism in Medicine*, Radcliffe Medical Press, 2007

"The patient's lament: hidden key to effective Communication: how to recognise and transform," *Medical Humanities*, 32: 45-46, 2006

Mitchell Chefitz, *The Curse of Blessings: Sometimes, the Right Story Can Change Your Life*, Running Press, 2006

Estelle Frankel, *Sacred Therapy: Jewish Spiritual Teachings on Emotional Healing and Inner Wholeness*, Shambhala, 2004

Viktor Frankl, *Man's Search for Meaning*, Beacon Press, 1946

David Hartman, *Love and Terror in the God Encounter: The Theological Legacy of Rabbi Joseph B. Soloveitchik*, Jewish Lights Publishing, 2004

Abraham Joshua Heschel, *God in Search of Man: A Philosophy of Judaism*, Farrar, Straus and Giroux, 1976

Man's Quest for God, Aurora, 1998

Anson Laytner, *Arguing with God: A Jewish Tradition*, Jason Aronson, 1990

Michael Lerner, *Jewish Renewal: A Path to Healing and Transformation*, Harper Perennial, 1996

Spirit Matters, Hampton Roads Publishing, 1996

Rabbi Goldie Milgram, *Reclaiming Judaism as a Spiritual Practice: Holy Days and Shabbat*, Jewish Lights Publishing, 2004

Carol Ochs and Kerry M. Olitzky, *Jewish Spiritual Guidance: Finding Our Way to God*, Jossey-Bass Publishers, 1997

John M. Schneider, *Finding my way. Healing and transformation through loss and grief*, Seasons Press, 1994

Embodying Spirit:
Jewish Spiritual Direction Through Movement
by Rabbi Diane Elliot

Rabbi Diane Elliot directs Wholly Present, a center for embodied spirituality, as well as /Ruach Ha'Aretz's *Embodying Spirit*, En-spiriting Body, a two-year movement-based Jewish leadership training, and also maintains a private practice in spiritual direction and other modalities. Ordained by the Academy for Jewish Religion (Los Angeles) after a 25-year career as a dancer, choreographer, and somatic therapist, Diane is an active Bay Area spiritual leader and teacher, who also long-served as spiritual leader for the Aquarian Minyan. www.whollypresent.org

The Challenge of Embodiment

For many of my directees, staying present in and accepting of the body, with its strong, often uncomfortable sensations and unpredictable flows of emotion, is the greatest of all spiritual challenges. The complexity of life, the sheer volume of information that bombards us on a daily basis, pulls us out of ourselves. We flail about, engulfed by tsunamis of stimulation for which our nervous systems and psyches are not evolutionarily prepared. We meditate, do yoga, go to aerobics and cycling classes, climb sheer rock faces, windsurf, zip-line, listen to music, even attend religious services. Still, many of us, unable to settle deeply into our own embodied lives, regularly lose touch with the Beingness that flows through and enlivens and nourishes us, connecting us with one another and all of creation.

Our tradition teaches that we are made *b'tzelem elohim*, in the divine image, and so, all aspects of us—not only our minds and our souls, but also our physical forms—are holy. The truth is that for long stretches of history, it simply hasn't been safe or pleasant to inhabit a Jewish body. But the safety and prosperity with which many of us are now blessed, in this time and this country, afford us the breathing space to come into relationship with our bodies in a new way, the courage to call our soul energies back inside. Gratitude for all we have been given can help us soften and dissolve the old shells of fear and begin to suture painful fissures between body, mind, soul, and spirit.

Moving Spirit

My work as a *mashpi'ah*, a spiritual guide, springs directly from my own instinctive need to befriend and to heal these splits within myself. I began my professional life some 40 years ago as a modern dancer and choreographer, an investigator and teacher of movement. Later as a contact improviser, a student of numerous body healing modalities, a somatic therapist, and a meditator, I gradually grew more able to deeply sense, feel, trust, and enjoy the aliveness pulsing within my own skin, in other beings, and throughout the natural world. This fertile, experiential ground now affords me rich, multi-modal, even ecstatic moments of prayer, study, and contemplation, and naturally informs my companioning of others who seek meaning and connection with the Mystery within and beyond themselves.

In sharing Judaism's core spiritual practices with students and directees, I draw attention to tangible, physical actions embedded in the tradition that support and make manifest movements of spirit. Placing a *kippah* or skullcap on my head may be, on one level, an act of humility, acknowledging that I stand in the presence of Mystery, a vast Ground of Being beyond my comprehension. At the same time, it serves as a tactile reminder that life works better if I anchor my energy inside my body, rather than succumbing to fear's habit of "flying out" through the crown of my head. *Kippah* pinned in place, I'm reminded to remain as present as I can to the movement of soul/spirit/life inside me. Staying "in body" allows me to experience my body as the very stuff of cosmic goodness—once-upon-a-time stardust of which not only I am made, but also dogs, hawks, redwood trees, butterflies, calla lilies, raindrops, cars hurtling down highways, skyscrapers, river rocks, and all other persons.

During a recent group session called "Moving Our Prayers: A Four Worlds Approach to *T'filah*," held at a Minneapolis synagogue, some 35 participants take a moment before donning our *tallit*ot (prayer shawls) to hold them in front of us, visually registering color and size, then to bring them up to our faces, feeling the texture of the fabric against our skin.

Embodiment—the act of fully inhabiting and making tangible a place, an act, a vision, a singular moment—takes time.

We draw the shawls over our heads, blessing the act as we breathe in their woolly aromas, snuggling them around our shoulders like little "prayer cocoons" in which we might gestate, tender and protected, but at the same time connected with others, performing this same action in the room together. Gathering the strings of the *tzitzit*, the knotted tassels tied to the corners of the *tallit*, we smooth the uneven jumble of threads, as if combing out the unruly strands of our thoughts and feelings. We touch and kiss the knots, caressing the lumpy nature of our own minds.

One might say that flesh is solidified soul in the same way that matter is densified energy. A guided movement experience that connects each of the five soul levels identified by the Jewish mystics with particular layers of physicality is designed to help us experience this confluence. As we chant the name for each level of soul to a simple folk melody, I suggest which layer of our physicality, from the densest to the most rarified and sublime, we might move from, each creating our own "soul dance":

- For *Nefesh*, the densest, animal soul, I invite us to initiate movement from our bones and muscles, the densest aspects of our anatomy.
- *Ruakh*, like wind over water, might be evoked as we move with an awareness of the juicy weight of the body's contents—organs, blood, synovial fluid.
- *Neshamah*, the heart-mind-soul, moves through us as the expansion and contraction of breath and the precise lightning flashes of our nerve impulses.
- In *Chaya* we hover like God's Presence over our own body's waters, letting ourselves be danced by our aura, the energetic glow just beyond our skin. Separateness begins to evaporate.
- As we enter *Y'khidah*, the most expansive and dissolved soul level, our individual soul energies merge into oneness with everything around and beyond us. Now all of Creation moves us in a joyful dance of unity.

We pause. We return. Taking time to notice, to feel where we have been, we rest in the present. In Presence. In our bodies.

I now invite the prayer journeyers to trace with their fingertips the four-letter Divine name (*yud-hey-vav-hey* – יהוה – in Hebrew) on their own bodies. We begin with our feet and draw the two verticals of the lower hey (ה) up the front surfaces of our own legs, making the cross bar across the pelvis, leaving a small opening at the left hipbone. The long vertical of *vav* (ו) runs from pubic to collar bone; the *yud* (י) flows in a plane perpendicular to the other letters, from between the eyebrows across the top of the head to the nape of the neck. The upper hey (ה) drapes across the shoulders, leaving that same small opening at the left shoulder, and flows downward as the arms unfurl to the sides of the body. Reaching again toward our toes, we inhale *hey-vav* to standing; rolling the head forward and releasing the arms down toward the feet again, we exhale *yud-hey. Hey-vav-yud-hey* (הויה) *HaVaYah*: this was one of the ways the medieval kabbalists vocalized the Name that was the act of breathing itself.

As we let this divine name soak into our physical structures, we experience it almost as another body system, a kind of spiritual anatomy interpenetrating our physical one. We move through the room, literally becoming God's name in motion, feeling how the Mystery lives in and through us, witnessing one another as the Divine dancing. "*Elohai neshama sheh'natata bi tehora hi*," we chant; "O Pure Soul in you I see endless possibility..." Eyes have softened, hearts have settled, brains have let down their guard, remembering that they belong to the community of the body.

Now, focusing our prayers with *kavannah*, an archery term whose Hebrew root means "to take aim," we move closer to one another, sensing the fellowship of embodied souls that we have become, as we chant, "*Sh'ma yisra'el, HavaYah Eloheynu, HaVaYah ekhad*, Listen: the Divine Creative Force will never give up! The divinity that courses through our very own bodies and the great cosmic force that vibrates through universes—they're the same One!"

On the window ledges at the back of the sanctuary, one of the synagogue's ritual leaders has created little prayer stations designated with markers—one ledge for "wow," another for "help," a third for "thank you," and one ledge left empty for simple remembrance and silence. Some of us gravitate to these stations, filling ourselves with the light pouring in the tall windows and with the particular quality of awareness named on each ledge, using the paper and pens that have been placed there to jot down prayer messages that bubble up from within ourselves. Others flow through the room, moving to inner rhythms that only they can hear. Some sit quietly or lie on the floor, some wrap themselves in their *tallitot*, and a few climb the stairs to the *bima*, tango-ing with the energy of the Torah scrolls peeking out through the sculpted doors of the ark. This is our *Amidah*, our time of personal prayer.

As we finish up our experience of moving prayer and come back together to share our insights, one participant, her eyes brimming with tears, reflects on how rare it is to feel this kind of permission to pray with one's whole self and in the ways that most suit one's own soul. How precious it is, she says, to experience this freedom with the support of a roomful of other embodied souls, all reaching beyond themselves to touch the invisible.

Everything is Movement

The work of embodiment is not only about entering, sensing, feeling, knowing, and moving the body expressively through space, though it includes all of that. It is, more broadly, the work of full presence, the compassionate practice of gradually coming to know and accept and express all the parts of ourselves—the sincere and the jaded, the empathic and the cruel, the passionate and the blasé, the ethereal and the dense. Our embodiment is supported by knowing that, at the most basic level, it is all acceptable to God because it is all God.

It strikes me that, on the meta level as well as the level of daily praxis, our core Jewish practices are all about movement—and stillness. *Teshuvah* ("return"), one of Judaism's most essential practices, is the ever-present possibility of making a course adjustment in our lives, of returning to connection with our own essential nature and with the Truth and Goodness that source the cosmos. *Shabbat*, Judaism's other core practice, speaks to the power of pausing in the midst of movement. Built into the very fabric of our mythic creation story is the cessation of outward-directed activity: on the seventh mythic day, "*shavat va'yinafash*," God stops making and just breathes (literally, "en-souls"). *Shabbat* brings us each week to a temporary, blessed stillness of mind and body that refreshes awareness through the gifts of deep rest and sensuous enjoyment.

Even the phrase "spiritual direction" implies sensitizing ourselves to subtle—and sometimes not so subtle—movements of mind, heart, soul, and spirit as they are expressed, held in suspension, and channeled through our bodies. An important part of our jobs as *mashpi'im*, then, is to include the body, to make space for the body, the felt sense of movement, within our own lives and within our sessions, so as to support the awareness of movement, the openness to and alignment with movement, within the spiritual life of our directees.

My directee rushes into our session 15 minutes late. A single parent, sole caregiver for her young daughter, she is frustrated and angry. Once again she has failed to care for himself, sacrificing part of her own session to accommodate the other families in the childcare coop. "I feel surrounded by people just like my own narcissistic parents and siblings—my co-workers, even my girlfriend! Incapable of respecting or even seeing my needs! I'm always bending and bowing, accommodating to them."

I note these movement words: "bending," "bowing," "accommodating." "What would be the antidote, the polar opposite of 'accommodating'?" I ask. "When I feel my own wellspring, my core strength," she replies. As she says the words, I notice her feet, which are often swollen and painful, connecting with the floor for the first time since she has arrived. Checking in with the sensations in my own body, I notice that her energy seems to have shifted downward and settled into her body. "How do you feel?" I ask. "I feel a sense of power in my hara, in my womb and lower belly," she replies.

But as soon as she returns to describing her discomfiture, her upper body begins to flail, and she reports feeling once again disconnected from her belly and legs. "Where do you feel this disconnect in your body?" I ask. She points to her solar plexus. I invite her to place her hands there and to breathe into and out of that place. Almost immediately, she reports "seeing" a burst of fiery light at her third eye. This surprises her. Energy that was stagnant before is now moving.

I know from my somatic work that the solar plexus area is a kind of energetic "horizon" between upper and lower body. So I suggest that my directee might practice breathing into and out of this "horizon" place when she feels stressed and assaulted by life. This is a kind of embodied teshuvah that, practiced over and over, may gradually begin to encourage the energy that so easily flies upward and out of her body when she is angry, hurt, and disappointed to re-enter, fill, and nourish her. Practiced over time, this might allow her to come back more consistently into connection with herself and with the sense of larger support—God's Presence—that she so often loses touch with.

As a spiritual director, the more parts of myself I "live into," the more experiences I can make room for and embody in myself, then the more fully I can support my directees in inhabiting themselves and in moving into alignment with the truth of their own lives and with the larger truth that we sometimes call God. Taking time to unscroll the texts of our own body-mind-spirits, we become more transparent and at the same time more passionately engaged in life, and ultimately more attuned to the movements of the transcendent within and around us. We become better able to encourage one another to listen deeply for the inner flows of desire and longing, for the sensations of blockage, tightness, and release, that reveal the quality of our relationship with the self and with the wondrous, mysterious, sometimes frightening energy that flows through us, guiding our lives.

Recommended Reading:

Comins, Rabbi Mike. *Making Prayer Real*, Jewish Lights, 2012

Elliot, Diane. "The Torah of the Body," *New Menorah*, 2000 (available from the author, rabbi.diane18@gmail.com)

Michaelson, Jay. *God in Your Body*, Jewish Lights, 2007

Schachter-Shalomi, Rabbi Zalman. *Davening, A Guide to Meaningful Jewish Prayer*, Jewish Lights, 2012

The Gates of Prayer, Albion Andalus Books, 2011

Wolfe-Blank, Rabbi David. *The MetaSiddur*, Self-published, 1995-98. Order from Elaine Wolfe-Blank, weaving@opendoor.com

Spiritual Development in Nature:
Methods of Individual and Group *Hashpa'ah*
by Rabbi Howard Cohen

Rabbi Howard Cohen is a graduate of the Reconstructionist Rabbinical College and the Founding Director of Burning Bush Adventures. His rabbinate involves taking people outdoors and connecting them with God and Judaism through close encounters with the natural world while canoeing, hiking, cross-country skiing, dogsledding or snowshoeing. Like the Dubner Maggid who used to visit a certain pond early in the morning in order to learn the songs with which the frogs praised God, Rabbi Cohen guides families, parent/child units, students from day schools, families from synagogues and occasionally random individuals seeking a Jewish experience outdoors. www.BurningBushAdventures.com

Judaism outdoors is natural. Virtually the entire Torah is set outdoors. Divine encounters and revelations, with few exceptions take place under the moon, stars and sun. The liturgy in the *siddur* is replete with references to towering trees, rivers clapping their hands, mountains singing in joy and life-giving springs of water. Without the frequent use of this metaphorical imagery from the natural world our liturgy would lack imagination, vibrancy and an important element of concreteness. The use of nature imagery also provides a reminder that Judaism is not confined to four walls.

Part of guiding the human spirit when out in nature is appreciation of the importance of shifting out of *mohin d'katnut*, one's preoccupation with personal destiny or life issues into *mohin d'gadlut*, the Bigger Picture. Carl Jung wrote in *The Undiscovered Self*, "You cannot solve a problem with the same level of consciousness that created it". Nothing shifts consciousness and lifts dispiritedness so much as time in nature.

Over the years I have created, adapted and collected many activities and exercises for teaching Torah and Judaism outdoors. Some of my favorites are on the following pages. For the most part, each activity contains everything you need to know in order to do it by yourself or lead it for others. The overall thesis is expressed as follows:

"From the Wilderness: A Gift"—Numbers 21:18

Wilderness is a necessary condition for every revelation; for every true internalization of the Torah's teaching: Whoever would wish to acquire Torah must become ownerless like the wilderness.[12]

---

12 *Bamidbar Rabba*, 1:7-8

Action grows from awareness. As we learn to understand and appreciate our world, so too, does our desire to act in ways that are not harmful to the earth and all of its inhabitants. This awareness/action binary is reflected throughout the liturgy (prayers) in the *siddur* (prayer book). The ancient rabbis describe increasing awareness of the world as *ole malchuyot ha-shamayim*, which literally means taking on the yoke of acceptance of the divine presence, or influence, in the entire natural world. This possibility is advanced when we raise our awareness of the many extraordinary wonders (miracles) in the natural world.

Once we have awareness, it is natural to want specific actions to help show this love and concern for our holy world. The rabbis called this *ole malchuyot mitzvot*, which literally means taking on the "yoke of the commandments." Each mitzvah is a spiritual practice that provides us with specific actions for expressing the love aroused by our deep experience of nature.

What follows are a variety of tools to help you experience and guide your *mushpa'im* in relationship to the divine through nature.

I. In The Woods

> **"The clearest way into the Universe is through a forest wilderness."**
> **—John Muir**

> **But ask the beasts, and they will teach you; the birds of the sky, and they will teach you. Or speak to the earth, it will teach you. The fish of the sea, they will inform you. Who among all these does not know?**
> **—Job 12:7-9**

As you begin your journey into the wilderness, whether it is only for a few hours or the start of multi day trip, think about what you hope to learn or experience. Journal on this, have your experience in nature, and upon emerging read the following tale found in a book by Rabbi David J. Wolpe, and then journal again. These may be reflections to explore in a *hashpa'ah* session.

> *"The child of a certain rabbi used to wander in the woods. At first his father let him wander, but over time he became concerned. The woods were dangerous. The father did not know what lurked there.*
>
> *He decided to discuss the matter with his child. One day he took him aside and said, "You know, I have noticed that each day you walk into the woods. I wonder, why you go there?"*

The boy said to his father, "I go there to find God."

"That is a very good thing," the father replied gently. "I am glad you are searching for God. But, my child, don't you know that God is the same everywhere?"

"Yes," the boy answered, "but I'm not."[13]

II. Awaken Yourself

hit'or'ri, hit'or'ri, ki va oreckh kumi ori—
"Wake yourself up. Wake yourself up!
For when your light comes My light arises."
—Shlomo HaLevi Alkabetz

In this prayer, *L'cha Dodi*, we are asked to awaken ourselves as *Shabbat* arrives. What could this mean? In the 11th Century Rabbi Abraham ibn Ezra wrote:

"Whenever I turn my eyes, around on Earth or to the heavens I see you
in the field of stars; I see you in the yield of the land, in every breath and
sound; a blade of grass, a simple flower, an echo of your holy name."

So, now, take a few minutes and concentrate on receiving input through each of your senses: hearing, taste, sight, touch, smell and it's helpful to also include intuition. Do you go into nature to wake yourself up? How is this different to your usual time in nature? Take this opportunity to journal and/or discuss in *hashpa'ah*.

III. Among All Growing Things

"May it be my custom to go outdoors each day
among the trees and grasses, among all growing things..."
—Reb Nachman of Breslov

Find a comfortable place to sit or stand or just pause and be still. "Listen" for whispered secrets. Record what you "learn" in words or images and then express this in dance, art, prayer, discuss in your *hashpa'ah* group or classrooms. Certain forms of poetry lend

---

13   David J. Wolpe, *Teaching Your Children About God*, HarperPerennial, 1994, page 44

themselves to such experiences. You might create a haiku, a cinquain, or perhaps an acrostic. These reflections these by Emerson and Rav Kook may synergize helpfully.

> The whole course of things goes to teach us faith. We need only obey. There is guidance for each of us, and by lowly listening we shall hear the right word.... Place yourself in the middle of the stream of power and wisdom which flows into you as life, place yourself in the full center of that flood, then you are without effort impelled to truth, to right, and a perfect contentment.
> —Ralph Waldo Emerson, Essays, Series I (Spiritual Laws)

> Rabbi Aryeh Levine recounted: After *Mincha*, my teacher set out on a walk in order to focus his thoughts. I accompanied him. On the way I plucked a flower. He trembled and said to me softly: Believe me, I have always been careful not to purposelessly pluck a blade of grass or a flower which could grow and develop; for there is no grass from below that does not have a *mazel* from above imploring it 'Grow!' Each blade of grass says something, each stone whispers a secret, and each creature utters a song.
> —Rabbi Abraham Isaac Kook

IV. Dendrochronology and The Tree of Life

Trees contain some of nature's most accurate evidence of the past. Their growth layers, appearing as rings in the cross section of the tree trunk, record evidence of floods, droughts, insect attacks, lightning strikes, and even earthquakes. Each year, a tree adds to its girth, the new growth is called a tree ring. Tree growth is affected by many variables, such as rainfall, fire, disease and insects. The study of rings is called dendrochronology.

A tree ring consists of two layers:

- A light colored layer grows in the spring
- A dark colored layer in late summer

Drought, a severe winter, or other factors can inhibit growth and cause narrower rings. If the rings are a consistent width throughout the tree, the climate was the same year after year. By counting the rings of a tree it is possible to determine a reasonably accurate history of the tree and the growing season of each year. Judaism compares a person to a tree in a variety of ways:

- A person is like the tree of a field... (Deuteronomy 20:19)
- For as the days of a tree shall be the days of my people. (Isaiah 65:22)
- [S/He] will be like a tree planted near water... (Jeremiah 17:8)
- But a person whose good deeds exceed his wisdom is likened to a tree whose branches are few but whose roots are numerous. Even if all the winds of the world were to come and blow against it, they could not budge it from its place. (Avot 3:22)

Now find a tree that "calls" to you. Examine it with all of your senses. Using words or images describe some of the ways you are like a tree. If you were to do a "dendrochronological" study of your own core where would you expect to find strong "growth rings" or "weak growth rings"? Consider shaping a prayer for the courage to honor and support this awareness that is part of your spiritual development.

V. Trees as Sacred Space

We spend time in nature. We are suffering rapid climate change. We breathe in what the trees breathe out. How do you stand in relation to the spirit of the trees? Consider these citations when entering into contemplation. Questions for reflection follow.

> Any fool can destroy trees. They cannot run away... It took more than three thousand years to make some of the trees in these Western woods... Through all the wonderful, eventful centuries God has cared for these trees, saved them from drought, disease, avalanches, and a thousand straining, leveling tempests and floods; but he cannot save them from fools...[14]
> —John Muir

> Once Honi was walking along the road when he saw a man planting a carob tree. Honi asked, 'How long before it will bear fruit?' The man answered, 'seventy years.' Honi asked, 'Are you sure you will be here in seventy years to eat from its fruit? The man replied, 'I found this world filled with carob trees. Just as my ancestors planted for me, so I will plant for my children.'
> —Babylonian Talmud Taanit 23a

---

14   John Muir; *Nature Writings: The Story of My Boyhood and Youth; My First Summer in the Sierra; The Mountains of California; Stickeen;* Essays, Library of America, Vol. 92, 1913, pages 186-187

For Further Reflection

Inquire within:

> Am I getting the spiritual food and shelter I need to survive?
> Am I part of a strong forest of support, perhaps a strong Jewish community, providing a warm and nurturing environment?
> Am I looking to future generations knowing that I am providing them with the proper foundation and forests of real trees as well as spiritual food and shelter for their lives?

VI. The Path

> The voice of your thunder rumbled like wheels; the lightning lit up the world; the earth quaked and trembled. Your way was through the sea, Your path in the great waters; Your tracks were not known. *Psalm 77:19-20*

Track, follow=עקב *ayin, koof, vet* to which one adds a *yud* for Ya'acov (Jacob) יעקב

Yaacov/Israel is our ancestor in whose footsteps we follow. It is interesting that his name contains within it the root letters for track and 'follow'. Learning to "track" Yaacov, or to determine the right path (*halacha*) for us is challenging. Some believe that God's "tracks" are those that are left by the myriad of life forms that fill the world.

If you are observant as you walk through the woods you will likely see many different types of animal tracks. These footprints, like our own, can reveal much about us, and the world in which we live.

> "In every walk with nature one receives far more than he seeks."
> —John Muir

> "Many people will walk in and out of your life, but only true friends will leave footprints in your heart."
> —Eleanor Roosevelt

> "Blessed are you, The Way, our God, life of all the worlds, who makes firm a person's steps. *Baruch atah adonay, eloheynu chey ha'olamim hamechin mitzadey gever.*"
> —*Siddur*/Prayerbook

"ha-mechin mitzadei gever - When one's steps follow the divine path, they bring delight along the way."
—Psalm 37:23-24

"Walk in my ways and be blameless."
—Genesis 17:1

When you spots tracks stop and consider them. Who do they belong to? What was the critter that left them doing? Running? Hoping? What kind of critter left them? Can we draw any conclusions from the tracks? For example, if the front tracks are bigger than the back, what does this mean about the distribution of weight of the animal? Which animals would have this pattern? Does the animal place its whole pad down or does it walk on its "toes"? What might this mean?

For Further Reflection

In the Bible, Yaacov's "tracks" leave many stories lines for us to explore. In the woods animal tracks can also tell a story. Study a set of tracks carefully and compose a story based on your observations. For example, perhaps two animals were traveling together from a food source to a den, or two animals encountered each other and there was a fight, and then they retreated in opposite directions. You might consider: How was it moving? Where was it going? With whom was it traveling? Whom did it meet? What might have been its purpose? Record your observations.

And what about you?

> What ancestors are walking beside you?
> How have they blessed or challenged your life?
> What footprints have you left on this world, metaphorically, of your own?
> Who has left a footprint on your soul?
> Do you find spiritual inspiration in the footprints of the animals?
> How does life's trail move forward for you in healthy and holy ways?

VII: Going Solo = *Hitbodedut*

And lo the Lord passed by. There was a great and might wind, splitting mountains and shattering rocks by the power of the Lord; but the Lord was not in the wind. After the wind – an earthquake; but the Lord was not in the earthquake. After the earthquake – fire; but the Lord was not in the fire. And after the fire—a soft murmuring sound.
—I Kings 19:8-13

It is impossible for human intelligence to comprehend God, yet certain places may allow people to experience the necessary risk that opens them, body and soul, to what their minds cannot entertain...liminal places are able, symbolically if not physically, to put people on edge, driving them beyond all efforts to control reality (and even God) by means of the intellect.[15]
—Beldan C. Lane

And Jacob came upon THE PLACE and stayed there for the night because the sun was setting...And Jacob arose from his sleep and said: Surely God is in this Place and I did not know it.
—Genesis 28:16-17

Try Being "Soul-O"[16]:

Find a comfortable place where you can sit undisturbed by others. Leave behind books and other distractions. Limit your possessions to a water bottle, clothing to stay dry and warm. Define your space with a natural border, perhaps by a tree, rock, creek bed or other natural feature. Be still. Read (reread) the passages in this journal.

Consider speaking out loud as though as though you are speaking to someone. Let the words pour out. Any content is acceptable. You can inveigh, praise, plead and muse. If words don't flow freely that is okay too. Record your thoughts, words, feelings and observations (remember to include sounds, smells and other sensations). You may want to share your experience with others or perhaps just with a mentor or trusted friend. Or you may prefer to keep your thoughts and reflections from this *hitbodedut,* private time with God. As Beldan C. Lane teaches:

---

15   Belden C. Lane, *The Solace of Fierce Landscapes: Exploring Desert and Mountain Spirituality*, Oxford University Press, 2007. p. 65.

16   I am indebted to Rabbi Michael Commins of Torah Trek for this spelling of the Solo Activity

Don't think anything about what God is, only that God is. Don't try
to reach into God's inner mystery by subtle reasoning. Similarly, don't
think about what you are, whether focusing on your competence or
incompetence, your weakness or strength. Only be content that you are.
When you put those two things side by side – the naked fact that "God is"
and that "you are" – letting the two exist together in quiet contemplation,
you have entered the deepest, simplest mystery of prayer.[17]

John Muir: "Only by going alone in silence, without baggage, can one truly get into the
heart of the wilderness."

In Conclusion

Rabbi Joshua Ben Korah said, why does the section 'Hear oh Israel'
precede 'and it shall come to pass if you listen...'? So that a person may first
accept the yoke of **the Kingdom of Heaven**/*Ole malchuyot shamyim*
(the physical and natural world) and afterwards accept the yoke of the
commandments (*Ole malchuyot mitzvot*).
—*Mishnah Berachot 2:2*

The *ole malchut shamyim* (awareness) / *ole malchut mitzvot* (action) binary model
provides a simple but powerful strategy for enriching a person's spiritual life out of doors
or even inside in the synagogue. Maimonides said that prayer enables us to create a
wilderness within where we can be alone with God. [Hilchot De'ot 6]

How do we do this? Consider the *Shema* prayer and her *brachot*, blessings. This section of
the prayer book begins with the *Borechu*, the call to prayer, followed by these words:

Blessed are you, Eternal One, our God, the sovereign of all worlds,
who fashions light (*yOtzer or*) and creates (*u'vOrei*) darkness,
maker (*Oseh*) of peace and creator of all (*kOl*)[18]

---

17   Beldan C. Lane, *Solace of Fierce Landscapes*, p. 108

18   Note the onomatopoeia in the liturgy. When we encounter wonders in nature such as the view from
a mountaintop, a cascading waterfall, or eagle in flight our natural tendency is to say Ooo, Wow. After the
barchu we encounter a lot of oo wow sounds like one makes when encountering natural wonders. As the
service moves towards the *Shema*, the love song between Israel and God, the language shifts to more ah
sounds, (ahavah, *shema*, etc) like one makes when responding to love.

And then:

> *Mah rabu ma'asekha adonai, kulam b'chakhmah asita.*
> How great your deeds, Eternal One. In wisdom you have made them all.

First we use words (of prayer) to create a pristine and beautiful wilderness setting full of potential for growth and deep connecting with God. This is *ole malchut* **shamayim**. Then, as Jews, we affirm that this divine love is expressed through Torah and *mitzvot*: Liturgically this is the sequence of the *ahavah rabba*, *shema* and *v'ahavta*, which is the *ole malchut mitzvot*.

> *shema yisrael adonai eloheynu adonai echad*
> Listen, Israel: The Eternal is our God, The Eternal One alone!

Human time in nature can lead to an indivisible, un-dissectible sense of love and being loved. As John Muir wrote: "When we try to pick out anything by itself, we find it hitched to everything else in the Universe."

In Conclusion and for Reflection

Where do you find yourself after all of this time discovering and communing with all that is Divine in nature? How do you "know God"?

Recommended Reading

Robert Barry, *Wilderness in the Bible: Toward a Theology of Wilderness*, Robert Barry Leal: Peter Lang Publishing, 2004

Thomas Berry, *The Sacred Universe*, Columbia University Press, 2009

Martin Buber, O. Marx, *Tales of the Hasidim: The Early Masters*, New York: Schocken Books, 1947

Abraham Joshua Heschel; "Religion in a Free Society," in *The Insecurity of Freedom* Schocken Books, 1966

Beldan C. Lane, *Solace of Fierce Landscapes, Exploring Desert and Mountain Spirituality*, Oxford University Press, 2007

Goldie Milgram, "*Hitbodedut*: Jewish Approach to Vision Quest: " http://reclaimingjudaism.org/teachings/jewish-approaches-vision-quest

Roderick Nash, *Wilderness in the American Mind*, Yale University, 1967

Ritual as Spiritual Direction:
Transition, Transformation, and Revelation
by Rabbi Jill Hammer

Rabbi Jill Hammer, Ph.D., is the Director of Spiritual Education at the Academy for Jewish Religion and co-founder of the Kohenet Hebrew Priestess Institute. A widely published author, her books include *Sisters at Sinai: New Tales of Biblical Women* (Jewish Publication Society), *The Jewish Book of Days: A Companion for All Seasons* (Jewish Publication Society), *The Omer Calendar of Biblical Women* (Kohenet Institute, 2011), *The Hebrew Priestess: Ancient and New Visions of Jewish Women's Spiritual Leadership* (forthcoming, Ben Yehuda Press), and *The Garden of Time* (forthcoming, Skinner Press). Jill lives in Manhattan with her wife and daughter.

> Ritual focuses attention by framing; it enlivens the memory and links the present with the relevant past. It can permit knowledge of what would otherwise not be known at all. It does not merely externalize experience, bringing it out into the light of day, but it modifies experience in so expressing it.
> —Mary Douglas

The ancient mystical work *Sefer Yetzirah* divides the cosmos into three basic elements: space, time, and soul. Ritual brings together a time, a space, and one or more individuals in a frame that invites meaning. One of the important factors is whether and how we understand our experience is framing—whether, and in what context, we are seen and we see ourselves. Ritual provides a frame for spiritual experience. Therefore, ritual can be used as a tool for spiritual formation.

Ritual often has the quality of transition. A ritual may mark a communal transition from a weekday to *Shabbat*, or from the old year to the new. A ritual, such as kissing a *mezuzah*, marks a transition from one space to the next. A ritual may also frame an individual's transition: from being from another tradition to being Jewish, or from being single to being married (or the reverse). Contemporary Jewish rituals may seek to honor transitions that have not been honored in the past. Bat mitzvah is the most celebrated example, but there are many others: rituals designed to mark events such as retirement, miscarriage, menopause, and children leaving home. Transitional rituals may include a conscious element in which the transitioning individual reflects on the meaning of this change and how it affects the individual's relationship with the Divine and with other people. We might think of these rituals as pauses in a doorway, pauses to connect with God.

Another quality of ritual is transformation. A transformation ritual asks for a transformative event (such as healing, fertility, or forgiveness) to take place. A healing ritual asks for healing of body, mind, heart, and/or spirit, in whatever way the individual understands that healing). A ritual of reconciliation invites two or more people to change their relationships with one another. A fertility ritual asks for conception or another transformative change in which an individual is able to take on the mantle of a parent. We might think of transformation rituals as requests for a new doorway to open.

A third quality of ritual is the quality of revelation: a ritual that tells a story that has not yet been told. Revelatory rituals provide space for an individual to tell a story and give it meaning. These rituals empower individuals to frame their own lives. For example, rituals that include stories of surviving the Holocaust, or sexual abuse, are rituals of revelation. We might think of revelation rituals as doorways into a story. Transitions, transformations, and revelations are central to an individual's spiritual life and we develop ourselves spiritually when we are present for them.

One ritual I witnessed contained all three of these components. At the Kohenet Hebrew Priestess Institute, a program in Jewish women's spiritual leadership that I co-founded, we often mark important life-cycle moments with ritual. This particular ritual began as a ritual to mourn and heal from a hysterectomy. A woman designed, with three other women, a ceremony in which she told of the frightening experience of surgery to remove her womb. As she told of this experience, the celebrant described the abuse both she and her mother had survived at the hands of the same family member— abuse she had been silent about. The hysterectomy had re-awakened this experience and she felt she had to tell of it. During the ritual, she chose and named a new role in her life: "I am my mother's *goelet*/redeemer." She used a Jewish concept, that of *ge'ulah* or redemption, to transcend her prior relationship to her past. By engaging the transition of the hysterectomy and the revelation of the abuse, this woman was able to reach toward self-transformation.

As a sign of this transformation, two ritual companions wrapped the celebrant in a prayer shawl. She fell backward into their arms, showing her trust that the community could support her. She relates

> I still think about that moment. I had absolutely no concern about falling backward. I had absolute trust. That was the experience of the hysterectomy, having to surrender.

A friend and co-participant had knitted this woman a womb out of red yarn to use in the ceremony. At the end of the ceremony, she sprinkled rose petals into this womb and offered her words of blessing, encouragement and healing. She danced holding the womb, radiating joy. She later said: "Something real happens in ritual. There is a liminal space that you go through; then you are transformed."

In my twelve years as a rabbi, I have had the privilege of watching ritual exert its extraordinary potency in the lives of individuals. I believe in the efficacy of carefully crafted ritual to help people be conscious and present to the rhythms of their lives. I want to provide a variety of examples of these rituals, to show what is possible. Then, I want to offer some thoughts on how to create rituals so that they are safe and effective containers for all present. This article will consider contemporary Jewish rituals and how they can be crafted as instruments for spiritual reflection and formation.

Transition

Lifecycle ritual can be part of a spiritual reflection process that brings the individual into a new understanding of his/her life and relationship to spirit. Rituals for aging, moving from one place to another, relationship beginnings and ends, and other important events, can give people grounding and a sense of being loved and accompanied as they shift from one place in life to another. As reflected in the bibliography, a number of helpful books have emerged on this topic.

For example, in a private ceremony for a friend, I created a ritual for transition from one gender to another. After guiding her down a narrow hallway and into the ritual space, we sat her in a special chair and she read poems that told the story of her transition from man to woman. We read blessings we had written for her. We took stones and put them on a scale until the scale tipped, honoring the many small and large actions she had taken to live as a woman. We gave her the Hebrew name she had chosen and offered naming blessings of the kind one would give a child, enacting her rebirth as a new person.

A ritual of this kind provides the individual with an opportunity to fully feel and face a life transition and open to its meaning. This particular person has a deep, intense relationship with God, and chose to address the nuances of that relationship by writing poems/psalms to God and to her new self. While there is no traditional model for such a ritual, we drew on traditional ritual elements such as the chair of honor for a newborn, and the blessing for one being named. We also provided ample opportunity both for the ritual journeyer to speak, and for the witnesses to share their visions of her and for her. In this way, the celebrant could tell her own story, and those who listened could reflect it back to her: two important components of spiritual work.

Transformation

We often have trouble accepting illness, dealing with anger, or coping with abuse or violence in our past. We may have trouble asking for help as we approach, or recover from, a difficult process like surgery, the end of a relationship, or fertility treatment. Ritual can provide a context for individuals to transcend the normal social restraints on deep feeling, and find the space within to ask for witness and compassion.

In one healing ritual, utilizing a traditional Jewish healing blessing, my community prayed together with a woman with brain cancer. We invited her under a *huppah* during the Torah service. We gave her a new name, a traditional practice to ward off someone's fate. In another, a prayer group spontaneously gathered with a man who was seriously ill, at sunset on Friday night, and prayed with him at the center of our circle, inviting him to speak about his illness and his wish for healing. In a third ritual I attended, a group of women seeking to conceive immersed in a river together, using the traditional ritual of *mikveh* or ritual bath. In a fourth, I created a sacred space for two people in my community who were angry with one another to reconcile, using the model of *sulha*, an Arab/Muslim ritual of reconciliation.

Rituals of transformation often use the elements as a tool for change. Fire can serve as an elemental catalyst: using a havdalah candle or a *Lag b'Omer* (festival) bonfire, we can burn words on scraps of paper, releasing rage or grudges or bad habits. Earth can serve as well: placing hands on the earth is a way of letting go, releasing into the larger whole. The traditional ritual of immersion after menses (a biblical tradition carried on in traditional Jewish life), or prior to *Shabbat* (a mystical tradition of cleansing and union with the divine) can often be adapted for individual purposes. Places like Mayyim Hayyim, a non-denominational *mikveh* and spirituality center in Boston, and the Isabella Freedman Jewish Retreat Center, which has a lake often used for immersion, encourage such rituals.

One powerful transformation ritual I attended was a repentance ritual performed for the month of *Elul*. The group, led by Jay Michaelson, Shoshana Jedwab, and myself, descended into an underground river within a cave. We shared in pairs about what we needed to let go, and then each went into the darkness of the cave to cry out to God by ourselves, a practice known as *hitbodedut* in Hassidic tradition. We then gathered in a circle to cast stones into the river, representing our desire to release all that was not right for us. Finally, we each received blessings from the group, and immersed in the water one by one, readying ourselves for the new year. Emerging from the cave into the sunlight felt like being reborn.

Revelation:

Rituals of revelation are relevant to spiritual direction because they name the truth. Rituals in which survivors of abuse or trauma tell their stories, or rituals where other usually unspoken things are spoken, fall into this category. For example, at the Kohenet Institute, a group of women walked in silence to a moon lodge, a structure built in the woods for women's use, and then shared a ritual to tell their stories of trauma related to fertility and infertility (abortion, miscarriage, childlessness, painful fertility treatment, sexual violation, etc.). Rituals like these break the strong social taboos around speaking of certain topics. These rituals can be an important component of spiritual direction because they help individuals to share deeply about what is in their hearts, and speak things they may be afraid to say.

At the Academy for Jewish Religion, a non-denominational seminary where I work, we conduct a Sacred Arts Institute twice a year. One year, I taught a four-day liturgy-writing workshop to rabbinical students and laypeople. As part of the workshop, Nathaniel Berman, a scholar of kabbalah taught us a saying from the Zohar: "The roots of the dragon [dark side/*sitra akhra*) are in the supernal realms." In other words, the "light side" and the "dark side" both come from one place. Berman also quoted for us the teaching that the dark part of the soul has its own name, a name we must discover throughout our lives so that we can seek to heal it. I wanted to invite the writing group to consider their dark, hidden, or shadow sides: whatever this meant to them.

The six of us went into the meditation room, which is a small chamber painted to look like an ocean, to conduct a ritual in which we would speak of our "dark" sides as we understood them: the parts of us that we never spoke of, or were afraid of, or were ashamed of, or the parts of us that evoked a sense of mystery. We did not set out to demonize or remove these parts of ourselves (and did not want to assume that darkness implied evil). Rather, we wanted to see these aspects of ourselves clearly for what they were. Each person had brought an object or a part of a life story representing his or her dark side, and spoke about the object or the story and what it meant. The rest of the group witnessed this sharing.

After each person had spoken, the group and I gave the person a name for her or his dark side. This name both described the dark, hidden, or mysterious part of that person's soul, and offered a *tikkun*, a way of thinking about that part in a positive way. Some of these names came from biblical characters, and others from elements of the natural world. After the name was suggested, the individual was asked if he or she wanted to accept that name. Sometimes the name was renegotiated after discussion. We then brought the person into the center of the circle and laid on hands and offered blessings.

This ritual offered the possibility of sharing, with a small group of trusted people, truths that had not been shared with anyone. We surprised ourselves by speaking these truths. We became fuller, and more present, to ourselves and to God. As Mary Douglas said, our ritual permitted "knowledge of what would otherwise not be known at all."

How to Create a Ritual

If you are thinking of using ritual in a spiritual direction context, you will want to create a sacred space where reflection and connection are possible. This means providing a container within which there can be a kind of spiritual alchemy: where different components of the ritual can awaken new associations, insights, and feelings in the individual or individuals at the center of the ritual. The ritual must speak specifically to the spiritual journey of the person or persons involved. You may be able to find a Jewish ritual that already exists that meets your needs. However, if you need to design a new ritual, here are some steps to consider.

> **Think about goal:** A ritual needs a clear purpose. An individual can only do strong spiritual work if the goal of the ritual is clear. Generally, the purpose of a ritual must be determined in conversation with the individual or individuals that the ritual serves. The ritual structure may be co-created, or it may be created by a ritual leader, but it should clearly provide a path toward the goal of the ritual.

> **Think about structure**: It may be helpful to consider the categories of transition, transformation, and revelation as you are deciding the goal of your ritual. Is this ritual marking a change in someone's life? Is it invoking a transformation: a healing or a blessing? Is it providing a space for someone (or multiple someones) to tell a truth that needs to be told? Or all three?

What ritual action will fulfill the goal that you have set? Donning a *tallit*? Immersing in a ritual bath? Writing a contract or covenant, or tearing one up? Don't be afraid to write down your most radical ideas as sometimes they turn out to be the ideas that work. Keep in mind that simple actions and images are best: good rituals don't have more than three or four components. You want to allow feelings and insights to arise in the celebrant(s) and witnesses; keeping them busy following an elaborate ritual is probably not the best path. One ritual component for the beginning, one for the middle, and one for the end is a good way to go.

Another question about ritual structure: will the ritual involve participation from everyone, or mainly focus on one person? How much will you do as a leader, and how much will you ask the group to do? If there is group sharing or action, do you as group leader plan to participate, or just to hold space? Consider these questions in light of your chosen goal and structure.

You may find it helpful to think in terms of a ritual container: that is, a beginning and end to the ritual that creates "spiritual safe space." This could be participants naming themselves in a circle and/or invoking a name of God at the beginning of the ceremony, and then each person sharing a name, word, or blessing at the end. It could be a ritual action that is done at the beginning and undone at the end (i.e. building a cairn of stones and then unbuilding it, or vice versa). Or, it could be a prayer of invocation, echoed at the end with a prayer of devocation. Such ritual containers help "enrole" the gathered community and keep them focused on the goal of the ritual, and they also help individuals to feel protected, included, and clear about what is happening. Within the container, the main ritual event can unfold.

> **Think about symbols**: What texts, stories, symbols, poems, objects, or songs most fully represent the individual's journey? Interview the ritual recipient(s) and think about this yourself. Does the story of Abraham or Miriam resonate? What about a staff, bowl of water, pomegranate, spice box, candle flame, Torah pointer? What about a doorway, or a lake? What about a favorite song or reading? What symbols and senses can you powerfully involve in the ritual?

What traditional Jewish elements can you bring into the new ceremony so that it feels ancient, authentic, real? Think about music, about rituals that seem related in theme, about blessings that would work in this context. Having a link to tradition is important for many people.

> **Think about space:** An intimate ritual often may allow for more spiritual work than a large ritual— but, there may be times when a large ritual is called for. Do you want a home? A sacred space such as a synagogue or *mikveh*? An outdoor space where you can connect to nature?

> **Think about time**: a night ritual provides more mystery; a daytime ritual more clarity and wakefulness. Is there a sacred time such as *havdallah* (the end of *Shabbat*) or *Rosh Chodesh* (the new moon) that would be appropriate to this ritual? Is there an anniversary or date particularly important to the individual or group in question?

Think about person: Consider with the ritual recipient what kind of witnesses are needed for this ritual to be effective. Family? Friends? Spiritual mentors? Women? Men? People with whom you meditate or study Torah? There are times when others are not available and a ritual might only include the celebrant and the Divine, e.g. writing a journal about a difficult event, tearing it up and burning or burying it.

Think about safety: How can you make the ritual not only effective but safe? How will you hold the space and make expectations clear? How will you make sure any offerings by participants are appropriate (in terms of content, amount of time, etc.)? And, will the ritual be too long, or uncomfortable in any way (i.e. the space will be cold or there will be too much standing)? If there are any safety concerns, make changes and corrections.

Is the person at the center of the ritual safe? Is the ritual emotionally and spiritually appropriate to the person's beliefs and needs? Is this person someone who wants some or all of the ritual to be a surprise, or who wants to okay all the parts of it? Are you making sure not to put the celebrant on the spot in ways not agreed to? How will you process the ritual afterward? If the ritual is focused on a group, how will you deal with the differing spiritual needs of participants? Again, make sure to take all of these questions into consideration when you plan.

However, you will want to allow for some spontaneity. Rituals that are too heavily scripted may fall flat. Celebrants or participants will sometimes have ideas that can be implemented in the moment. You may have a sudden insight as things unfold. Make sure you leave yourself some space to deviate from the plan if it seems necessary to do so in order to achieve the goal of the ritual.

Think about sealing: A ritual needs a good ending to be effective. One end that often works well is to offer blessings suited to the celebrant(s): spontaneous blessings from individuals, or a group blessing such as the priestly blessing. You might consider physicalizing the blessing with a gift: beads strung onto a necklace as each blessing is offered, ribbons tied onto a tambourine, notches made in a staff, etc. Or, give each participant a stone or bit of string as a reminder of the ritual and a way of remembering this ritual community and the work you all did together. Another possible end is for the group to close the ritual with a chant, offering, seed-planting, or other ritual action that provides a formal end to the ritual's work. Again, think about ritual container: if your end echoes your beginning, that will often make the ritual feel complete.

Make a plan: For example, the ritual you design might be to give someone a new name that expresses a shift: a new stage of life, a new spiritual calling, a new sense of identity. Shape the ritual to achieve the goal of bestowing the name and effecting the desired transition. Let's say the name is *Erev*, evening.

In keeping with the meaning of the name, let's say that you choose the time of *havdallah*, Saturday evening, the end of *Shabbat*, for this ritual. This time signals transitions and beginnings, and fits with the meaning of the new name. You may choose to weave a naming blessing in with the traditional blessings over the candle, spices, and wine. You can connect the meanings of these symbols— light, fragrance, abundance, etc.— with the qualities and hopes of the individual you are naming. You can also invite the person receiving the name to share what the name means and reflect on how their relationship with self, community, and God is changing.

The naming blessing should take place in front of significant people in this individual's life. Let's say you are the director of a spiritual direction group, and this group will be the witnesses for the ritual. You may want to ask the guests to each prepare and offer an interpretation of the name, or a blessing regarding the name or the new stage in life. You might want to ask each guest to bring a spice, and have each person put the spice into a new spice box as he or she speaks. As a naming gesture, you give the individual the spice box to use on Saturday nights, to honor and remember the new name— and since the spice box is always used at evening, it will remind of the name's meaning as well. You seal the ritual with songs to Elijah and Miriam, the prophets who accompany transitional moments.

If you can imagine yourself guiding such a ceremony, you may want to consider ritual as one component of your spiritual direction work.

Conclusion

Not all rituals are spiritual direction. Ritual that can serve as spiritual direction must address the spiritual needs, gifts, and truths of individuals and make space for them to share, reflect, and make offerings. The ritual must provide safety, intimacy, and a sense of spiritual companionship. It must have a clear purpose related to a community's sacred times, and/or to individuals' life-paths. And, the ritual must have preparation beforehand and processing afterward, so it is integrated fully into real life.

Rituals that do take into account these needs can be powerful tools for spiritual growth. The frame that ritual provides for spiritual experience can allow for astonishing things to happen, movements of the soul that might not have seemed possible. Ritual can be a channel for Divine presence. It is a way of providing a space for the Holy One to work.

We may think of ritual as a *mikdash*, a kind of sanctuary, one that occurs at a specific moment in space, time, and soul. The sanctuary provides a frame: an invitation to holy experience. If we build the *mikdash* with intention, what happens within it is a gift, for us and for the Divine.

Books for Further Ritual Exploration:

Jewish:

Goldie Milgram, *Living Jewish Life Cycle: How to Create Meaningful Jewish Rites of Passage at Every Stage of Life*, Jewish Lights, 2009

Irwin Kula and Vanessa Ochs, *The Book of Sacred Jewish Practices: CLAL's Guide to Everyday Holiday Rituals and Blessings*, Longhill Partners, 2009

Vanessa Ochs, *Inventing Jewish Ritual*, Jewish Publication Society, 2007

Debra Orenstein, *Lifecycles: Jewish Women on Life Passages and Personal Milestones*, Jewish Lights, 1998

Jill Hammer and Holly Taya Shere, *The Hebrew Priestess: Ancient and New Visions of Jewish Women's Spiritual Leadership*, Ben Yehuda Press, forthcoming 2014

General:

Catherine Bell, *Ritual Theory, Ritual Practice*, Oxford University Press, 2009

Tom Driver, *Liberating Rites: Understanding the Transformative Power of Ritual*, Booksurge, 2006

Ronald Grimes, *Deeply into the Bone: Re-inventing Rites of Passage Life Passages*, 2002

Additional Website(s):

www.Ritualwell.org
    A profoundly useful collection of contemporary rituals, as well as essays on ritual-making.

www.Reclaimingjudaism.org and Bmitzvah.org
    Offers rituals for meaningful Jewish living

www.Mayyimhayyim.org
    The website of Mayyim Hayyim, the *mikveh* and spirituality center in Newton, MA that encourages contemporary ritual usage of the ritual bath.

www.Kohenet.com

The Hebrew Priestess Institute trains women as ritual leaders and offers resources related to embodied, feminist, earth-based ritual, including *Siddur* haKohanot: A Hebrew Priestess Prayerbook

Telshemesh.org

Resources related to nature-based Jewish ritual.

Peelapom.com

More resources related to nature-based Jewish ritual.

Encompassing the Four Worlds in Spiritual Direction
by David Daniel Klipper

David Daniel Klipper received *smicha* as a Rabbinic Pastor from the Aleph Ordination Program and trained as a spiritual director in the Morei Derekh Program. Currently, he works as a Clinical Pastoral Education Supervisor teaching pastoral care to seminarians, clergy and committed laypeople as well as providing direct chaplaincy services. He is a senior faculty member of the Hashpa'ah Training Program (the Aleph Ordination Program in Jewish Spiritual Direction) and serves as an individual *mashpia* (spiritual director) as well as a supervisor of group spiritual direction.

Much of my time is spent in intimate discussions with patients and CPE students. Yet intimate as those discussions are, I have found that the most intimate interactions I have are those I have with *mushpa'im* (directees). There are a number of reasons for this: Chaplaincy visits tend to be one-time or limited in frequency, and it is important to keep an educational focus in my interactions with CPE students. But I think there is another reason for this – in spiritual direction, the directee is trusting me with sharing what can be the most intimate relationship we have—the one with the Holy One of Being. As a privileged onlooker of this relationship, I find myself even more careful about what I say than I am in my chaplain or CPE (Clinical Pastoral Education) Supervisor role.

In Jewish thought, there are four worlds or levels of consciousness–the world of materiality, the world of emotion, the world of intellect, and the World of divine connection: *Assiyah*, *Yetzirah*, *Beriyah* and *Atzilut*. It is important for me to understand which world my *mushpa* (directee) inhabits at the moment. However, as a *mashpia*, I try to be aware of all Four Worlds, and utilize the perspective that each offers in formulating a response to my *mushpa*.[19]

Situations appear different depending upon the level of consciousness with which we approach them. As I write these words, it is during the *Yamim Noraim*, the "Days of Awe" between Rosh Hashanah and Yom Kippur. During this time I am very conscious of my need for *teshuvah* (repentance, as in turning back to God) and it is central to Jewish experience and liturgy. It is a time when I am urged to not only confess my shortcomings to God, but also to go to those people I may have harmed and ask for their forgiveness. I try to take this principle seriously, particularly during this time of year.

But life can be complex. What if a *mushpa'at* (f.) who was sexually abused in childhood by her father comes to me filled with fear that her abuser will come to her and

---

19   Editor's Note: The Four Worlds are further explicated in useful ways in the Introduction by Zalman Schachter-Shalomi and Anne Brener's "Configuring Grief in Spiritual Terms" in this volume.

ask her forgiveness? This is an issue in which my response could vary depending on which level of consciousness I use to inform my response.

At the level of *Assiyah*, the *pshat* (literal reading) of our tradition could be interpreted to mean that we are supposed to forgive.[20] As it is stated in the Talmud, "The Day of Atonement absolves from sins against God, but not from sins against a fellow man unless the pardon of the offended person be secured." [Yoma viii. 9] There are other passages that deal with the nature of the obligation to pardon, but I think it is fair to say that there is an implicit presumption among many (if not most) Jews that it is a Jewish value to grant forgiveness. I have personally experienced the strength of the expectation that I forgive someone when that person asked me for such forgiveness face to face. From this level of consciousness, therefore, the right answer could seem to be clear–if someone comes to us looking for forgiveness we are supposed to grant it.

On the other hand, if I look at the issue from the level of *Yetzirah*, feeling, I might have a totally different perspective. I will have great respect for how my *mushpa'at* feels. I may well identify with her feelings of hurt and/or anger, especially if I have sensed her difficulties in being able to access or express them. I will be highly conscious of the damage that premature forgiveness might do to her. I will be sensitive to the concern that this situation could in fact be recreating the abuse if the *mushpa'at* again felt she had to comply with what she experienced as inappropriate demands of her abuser. Thus, from the world of *Yetzirah*, the answer might also seem to be clear–if the *mushpa'at* is not emotionally ready for contact from her abuser, she should refuse to see him or allow any communication from him. The thought of forgiveness should not even be considered.

What if I look at the question from the level of *Beriyah*? At the level of the intellect, I as *mashpia* might have yet a third perspective on the situation. Perhaps I am aware from the *mushpa'at* of the factors in the father's childhood (perhaps his being sexually abused as well) that led him to recreate his abuse on his daughter. While not condoning this behavior, I might have sympathy towards the father based on my understanding of the factors that helped cause it. I might want to encourage behaviors that could help the father's potential *teshuvah*, not only for his benefit but perhaps ultimately for hers as well, since his healing may well make him more receptive to hear his daughter's concerns and anger. From the perspective of *Beriyah*, intellect, therefore, I might approach this situation in a more nuanced way, trying to balance and reconcile many different interests.

Finally, what about the perspective on this issue from the level of *Atzilut*, Divine connection? At the level of pure soul consciousness, I may intuitively know that the part of each person that contains the spark of God can never be harmed. At the level of *Atzilut*, I might find myself experiencing the boundless Divine love that embraces all of us, saint

---

20   This example and those following are given for illustrative purposes only. I am well aware that alternative interpretations through the lens of each of the four worlds could be derived regarding this situation.

and sinner alike. I may feel the love that comes from experiencing the certainty of the Oneness of all beings. From the level of *Atzilut*, how can one not forgive? Or perhaps more accurately, from the level of *Atzilut* is there even harm or simply another aspect of the wonderfully intricate tapestries that we weave of our lives for the benefit of our soul's learning within God's beneficent and magnificent universe?

The point of these illustrations is not to say that any one of them is the right answer, or any one of the four levels of consciousness is always appropriate as a place to come from in response to a *mushpa*'s issue. What I hope to convey is my sense of how important it is for me as a *mashpia* to do my best to comprehend all of these perspectives. Issues brought up by a *mushpa* have many "right" answers, depending on the *mushpa*, the specific circumstances, how the Holy One is operating in the *mushpa*'s life and the *mushpa*'s and *mashpia*'s lived experience of this.

I believe it is this aspect of spiritual direction–this simultaneous accessing of each of the four worlds of consciousness—that gives this work its enormous richness. It is also what makes me so careful of what I share and why I seek to have a keen sense of self-awareness in knowing what I am saying and why I am choosing to say it. I call the wisdom that comes from the ability to access and weigh all four worlds' soul wisdom.

For me, soul wisdom is deeper than things I perceive, things I feel, or things I know intellectually, although all of those knowings are included. My process of developing soul wisdom usually includes having lived with something, prayed over it, suffered with it and possibly rejoiced about it as well. Soul wisdom usually manifests for me as multi-faceted and complex knowings rather than simple solutions. Soul wisdom rarely is the first thought that wants to leap from my lips in response to a *mushpa*'s comment or question. Soul wisdom in spiritual direction may be transformative and profound, but these qualities are by-products of soul wisdom as soul wisdom is sufficient in itself.

Finally, I find that living in the experience of soul wisdom is both grounding and uplifting at the same time. I experience the awe of accessing what is only a fraction of the infinite depth of the Divine within, the terrible and wonderful delicacy of the human spirit and the profound tenderness within which the Holy One of Being holds us all. It is truly a privilege to be honored with the opportunity to do this work.

Recommended Reading

Joseph Dan, *Kabbalah: A Very Short Introduction*, Oxford University Press, 2006

Rabbi Dale Friedman, Ed. "PaRDeS: A Model for Presence in Hitlavut Ruchanit" in *Jewish Pastoral Care: A Practical Handbook from Traditional & Contemporary Sources*, Jewish Lights, 2001

Daniel Matt, *The Essential Kabbalah: The Heart of Jewish Mysticism*, Harper One, 1996

Additional Website(s):

Goldie Milgram, "Principles of Rebbetude" http://reclaimingjudaism.org/teachings/spiritual-formation-jewish-clergy-principles-neo-Hassidic-*rebbe*tude

CD Set: Rabbi Zalman Schachter-Shalomi, *Advanced Kabbalah*, http://www.elatchayyim.org

CD set by Rabbi Simon Jacobson, *Spiritual DNA: Advanced Kabbalah*, http://www.meaningfullife.org

Helping Holiness Happen: Focusing™ and *Hashpa'ah*
by Rabbi Goldie Milgram

Rabbi Goldie Milgram, DMin., founder and Editor-in-Chief of Reclaiming Judaism, Reclaiming Judaism Press and Jewish Spiritual Education (JSE), a distance learning certification and/or ordination for those serving youth and families. A widely published author and long-time Jewish communal service professional, she has been honored by the Covenant Foundation, and her volume co-edited with Ellen Frankel, *Mitzvah Stories: Seeds for Inspiration and Learning* was honored by the National Jewish Book Awards. "Reb Goldie" was ordained by the Reconstructionist Rabbinical College and also by Rabbi Zalman Schachter-Shalomi as *rabbi, maggidah, mashpi'ah* and *shlicha*. She often serves as a scholar-in-residence and retreat leader for communities worldwide. www. ReclaimingJudaism.org

This article teaches a method that Reb Zalman recommends for all *mashpi'im.* He brought it to my attention in the 1990's when he sent Dr. Eugene Gendlin, who discovered this human capacity, over to our home. Over the course of my relationship with him, a fusion emerged of his methodology and what I learned from my many teachers has become a form of *hashpa'ah* that I find works well with virtually everyone

Focusing™ provides a way to enter into one's own life with awe, respect and hope for the future. It greatly amplifies the traditional Hasidic approach by adding a bioenergetic way of working, a way of "knowing God" and being guided by the "Still Small Voice," that arises within our embodied souls from underneath all of life's traumas.

Focusing has six formal steps;[21] here is a way to customize Focusing in my work as a *mashpi'ah.*

I. Clearing a space

Do you know the aphorism: "The presenting problem is rarely the real problem"? The first step towards an effective session of *hashpa'ah* is "clearing a space". While those who come to us often arrived troubled about something or someone in their lives, skillful *hashpa'ah* begins with different sense of starting *makom,* "place". We know this from scripture where we read: "*asu li mikdash, v'shokhanti b'tokham*—Make Me a sacred space and I will dwell within you." [Exodus 25:8]

---

21   http://www.focusing.org/sixsteps.html.

"Letting God in," as we say in *hashpa'ah*, begins with having a process for clearing a space within. A simple prayer is rarely sufficient when the "Kiddush cup" of a person's life is clogged up with stressors, holiness and happiness rarely happen. The Passover Kiddush prayer teaches: "*z'man heiruteinu, mikra kodesh*—times we are free, holiness happens", so tools for freeing up soul space for a healthy and holy *hashpa'ah* process are vital. Let's begin with how a *mashpia* might guide a Focusing session.

a. "We are going to clear a holy space within for this time together. The 'Cliff Notes' for our process are that I'll have you take a specific sequence of breaths, and then you will invite your soul to show you, one by one, what between you and feeling good in your life. We will honor each in a particular way, and when you are 'emptified' and more centered and relaxed, I'll invite you to scan your body for a sense inside that can now call for your attention and we will stay with it and get to know it the way a best friend might visit another friend and listen deeply. After that process the session will finish with a prayer. I have found this to help many people, are you open to give it a try? Great. Let's begin."

b. Please place your feet on the floor and plant your tree of life on the earth. Align your head with the heavens and open your shoulders. Take a short breath, a long breath and another short in-breath of life. [Note : We are aiming for cleansing and presencing in the body and not a meditative state, hence the importance of bracketing the long breath with the short breaths.]

c. Now place your attention in the center of your body. Invite your body to relax…Inquire of your soul as to "What is between me and feeling good in my life?" Or, "What is on the plate of my life?" Or, "What is gumming up the '*Kiddush* cup' of my life?" There will be a number of things that arise to consciousness in answer to these questions. Welcome each of them as your guests one at a time without going inside it. Stand back a respectful distance, knowing "Yes, that's there. I can feel that, there." Let there be a little space between you and that."[22] Name it and place "it" on your hands and look at it as though you are a best friend coming to visit it.

d. Shape your hands to the weight and size of it. If this is a phone session, then kindly describe its size and weight to me.

<hr>

22   http://www.focusing.org/sixsteps.html

e. See if "it" is willing to wait out the rest of our session by allowing you to honor it by placing it upon a shelf of honor beside an imaginary ark containing a Torah, or upon an "altar of higher consciousness." If "it" is not willing, you can let it know you will come back to it refreshed and shifted in ways that will make you better able to relate to it. That often helps "it" to be willing to sit out.

> *Note to mashpia: This process of emptying while honoring what arises leads to spaciousness within is so that what arises from underneath "all of that" which has been cleared from the inner sanctuary can find "its voice," which is often composed of sensations and imagery.*

f. "After these concerns (usually 3-6 of them) are put down (i.e. placed out of the body) it is sometimes useful to also put down your "background feelings" as well. Your background feeling is the feeling that you carry around all the time and don't notice any more, such as feeling constantly pressured, hurried, tense, a little sad, a little resentful, etc.

When you've put down your current concerns (i.e., the ones you can actually feel in your body right now) and you've put down the "background feeling", see if you are feeling O.K. If another concern pops up at this point, place that outside of your body as well. ... Notice that there can be a cleared space" in you in which you are safely distanced from your current concerns and worries. A sense of relaxation and well-being is often contained in the "cleared" or "all fine" space."[23]

Clearing A Space: From a Session in Progress

"Oh, the first thing that comes up for clearing isn't what I thought I came here to talk about. It's, yes, it's that my fourteen year old daughter is going out on her first date tonight."
"Your fourteen year old daughter is going out on her first date tonight. Can you place that awareness onto both of your hands and look at it like a best friend coming over to visit this awareness?"
"Yes."
"There are more matters that will arise underneath of this one. Can you hold your hands in the shape of a gem stone, rock or boulder to indicate the size this awareness occupies in your life?"

---

23   Joan Klagsburn, *Focusing: A Healing Practice for Care of Yourself and Others*, training manual, 2004

"Yes, it's not huge, more of a combination of a doorstop size rock with lapis lazuli gemstones coming out of it." [While the symbolism seems obvious, let it pass. Our destination is deeper.]

"Door stop size, with lapis lazuli gemstones coming out of it. Would you ask if "all that about your daughter's upcoming first date" is willing to sit out the rest of this session in a place of honor, say on a shelf next to an imagery Torah in an ark? It's certainly a valuable to address later in the day. (I also demonstrate by looking at my cupped hands, as though such a rock is upon them, then lifting it up and placing up on the imaginary altar of higher consciousness, as sometimes I call it.) 'Let it know that you are doing something good for yourself right now, and if it is willing to sit out in this place of honor during this session, you will be able to return to it in a personal place to attend to its needs…Is it willing? Yes, great.

The next point that came up in this session went like this:

"There's the situation of not knowing if our division is going to be closed by our company; they've closed most of the similar ones here on the east coast and relocation offers to the Midwest are being provided to some, pink slips to others."

"Your division may close, your job is uncertain, relocation or unemployment may result…do I have that right? (pause) Can you place 'all that' about your job onto your hands and visit it like a best friend coming over? (Pause, tissue) What size rock or boulder is this?"

"It's huge (she moves her hands the width of her chest and down as if the boulder is very heavy). "Everything is so uncertain right now."

"Uncertain (I echo) There may be more underneath. Inquire of this huge boulder in your soul if it will let you set it in a place of honor and return to it later."

She says, "It will. I'm surprised, and yet it will." [We continued with this approach until she reported feeling clear and ready for the next stage of our process.]

This approach to *hashpa'ah* underscores the truth of the Hassidic saying: "The body is the instrument upon which the soul plays life for God." The body will be of even greater assistance in our next step:

II. Felt Sense

"Now just be with yourself. [Give a nod of honor, but do not stay with pre-existing conditions like a full bladder or toothache; sense for a place that is subtly or overtly calling for attention.] Your body will speak to you, maybe via a glow of happiness, or you could feel like dancing or purring, or sense a tugging, hurt or turmoil somewhere inside. Pick one sense, it might be murky, unclear right now, and rather than thinking about it, feel its effect on your body and spirit. Gently sit with the sensation and where it is within you, gradually become curious about it."

III. Finding a "Handle"

"What is the quality of this unclear felt sense? Let a word, a phrase, or an image come up from the felt sense itself. It might be a quality-word, like *tight, sticky, scary, stuck, heavy, jumpy* or a phrase, or an image. Stay with the quality of the felt sense till something fits it just right."[24]

Handle: From the Session in Progress

"So heavy and tight around my heart. You are so thick, concretish, gray."

Mashpia: "Heavy and tight around your heart, gray, thick, concretish..."

IV. Resonating

"Go back and forth between the felt sense and the word (phrase, or image). Check how they resonate with each other. See if there is a little bodily signal that lets you know there is a fit. To do it, you have to have the felt sense there again, as well as the word. Let the felt sense change, if it does, and also the word or picture, until they feel just right in capturing the quality of the felt sense."

"It" may seem murky and unclear at first and gradually become more available and open up with new imagery as you describe it to itself. Most find "it" really appreciates being allowed to be known, heard and understood. "You are a hot jabbing pin...no, that's not right?...oh, I see, you are a hot shard of broken glass...yes...how did you break?...Oh... you were..."

---

24   Ibid.

Note: The person serving as mashpia needs to be careful to avoid direct questions or the person may lose contact with "it". Suggest: 'See if you can sense what this might need.' rather than 'So, what are you planning to do about it?' 'Check and see what this might mean to you.' rather than 'What do you think that means?'"[25]

Resonating: From the Session in Progress

"Rocks, not concrete, rocks are around my heart."

Mashpia: "Rocks, not concrete."

"You are such sharp, heavy, big rocks now...oh, you are changing...now shifted, you are only one huge rock."

Mashpia: "One huge rock."

V. Asking

Note to Mashpia: Now invite the person to ask of the "makom," the place where the "felt sense" is: "What is it, about "all this"? "What is in this sense?" "Or what does the sense need or want?"

"If you get a quick answer without a shift in the felt sense, just let that kind of answer go by. Return your attention to your body and freshly find the felt sense again. Then ask it again. Be with the felt sense till something comes along with a shift, a slight "give" or release." [Focusing.org]

Mashpia: "[perhaps noticing that Rock is a name for God in Judaism, "*maoz tzur* - Rock of Ages," and *tzur mi shelo akhalnu*—The Rock from which we have eaten" and "*tzur hevli b'eit tzarah* [from the *Adon Olam*] – the Rock which anchors me in times of distress", i.e., the Rock as umbilical cord.

"Does The Rock want something?"

"Rock, do you want to be climbed?...Or to have a garden to rest in? No, you say you don't. What do you want? Why are you here? Do you need something?...Oh. You wants tears; to be softened

---

25   Klagsburn, op. cit.

Mashpia: "The Rock wants tears, you left your husband and you have not cried, since; it asks for softening."

…(long silence) I have not cried since leaving my husband." She tears up and begins weeping deeply, perhaps for five minutes and then after a long silence says: "Rock, you are no longer sharp; you are rounder and growing larger, and you have a glow now.

Mashpia: "Growing larger, a glow. Isaiah teaches God will sprinkle pure water on your heart of stone and give you a heart of flesh."

"Yes. It wants me to finally release my sharp stony resentments. To soften my heart with tears." She burst out weeping again, then sobbing.

Mashpia: "Tears are watering your parched heart."

She cries and cries becomes quiet. [Inside this *mashpia* weeps in empathy and may have tears dripping down and yet, in this approach does not bring her own feelings into the room audibly.]

VI. Receiving

"Receive whatever comes with a shift in a friendly way. Stay with it a while, even if it is only a slight release. Whatever comes, this is only one shift; there will be others. You will probably continue after a little while, but stay here for a few moments."

Receiving: From the Ongoing Session

She comes out of her silence to say, "I sense a fluttering."

Mashpia: "A fluttering."

"A small bird is there with its wings folded, right against my sternum."

Mashpia echos and guides: "A small bird. Perhaps see if the bird has a meaning."

"Small bird, are you my soul?…(silence) then: It says 'more than your soul.'"

Mashpia: "More than your soul."

Suddenly she becomes radiant and declares. "It is *Shekhinah* (God's presence); I had not known She is within me! And the stones, they are gone!"

Mashpia (softly, staying steady): 'The bird against your breast is *Shekhinah* and the stones are gone."

We hold the awe-filled silence.

Mashpia: "It is time for our closing prayer of *hakarat ha-tov*, 'gratitude' to the Source of Life. It might begin, Holy One, thank you for..."

She understands quickly and begins: "*Shekhinah*, thank you for revealing yourself to me. I promise never to forget you want, you need me to feel, to cry, to release resentments and begin to heal. Thank you for being inside loving me, just as I realize how much I need and love you."

Note to mashpia: On the Focusing website there is a note at this point about the process: "If you have spent a little while sensing and touching an unclear holistic body sense ...then you have Focused. It doesn't matter whether the body-shift came or not. It comes on its own. We don't control that."

While the classical approach to Focusing does not use the process of imaging what comes up as a rock as a Jewish spiritual guide, I deliberately embed this metaphor from Torah into my sessions. Later I discovered that Rav Kook, [19th century chief Rabbi of Israel] taught in the prayer book he edited, *Olat Ra-aya*:

> "The perpetual prayer of the soul continually tries to emerge from its latent state to become revealed and actualized, to permeate every fiber of the life of the entire universe...Sudden spiritual clarity comes about as a result of a certain spiritual lightning bolt that enters the soul... when many days or years have passed without listening to this inner voice, toxic stones gather around one's heart, and one feels, because of them, a certain heaviness of spirit. The primary role of spiritual clarity is for the person to return to him[her]self, to the root of one's soul."

Further Applications

Focusing is also wonderful way for a *mashpia* to teach preparation for prayer or to deepen in relationship to an ethical quality, or piece of text. For example, in the morning blessings, we read a blessing of gratitude for "freeing those who are bound." Focusing helps us explore "Where am I currently 'bound?'" The prayer implies that I could be free — ah... there is my longing to be free — what would it be like to be free? Can I "taste" it? It would be right for me to be free — it says here that the Universe (or whatever All That should be called.....) could free me — Without any particular shape or answer I am relating to this promise of no longer being so bound — (in that way I know myself to be bound, that I felt at the start). [paragraph composed with Gene Gendlin]

Focusing is as an inherent capacity of all humans and a gift the *mashpia* can offer to liberate the soul towards healing, spiritual development and a meaningful connection to Judaism. When the intellect is by-passed, a more comprehensive and accurate pre-conscious knowing that comes from the soul connection to Beyond emerges. When someone says "I think," we are not yet at the level of Spirit that is the core of *hashpa'ah*. A great deal of time can be spent at the "thinking" level in psychotherapy because it is here that defenses get their best purchase against the unknown. When the *mashpia* or spiritually oriented psychotherapist moves the client from thought into embodied knowing, holiness and happiness truly may happen as the God experience becomes possible. As we read in *Etz Hazman*:

> Subtly, in a moment, in stillness, and in contemplation, we are able to hear the echo (*bat kol*) of "that which I command you this day." Being that the "sound" of the "*Bat Kol*" comes in the subtle stillness, tenderly, it is more difficult to hear it if there is a denser stronger *Kol* (voice) which is overcoming and forcing it aside; polluting it. Therefore we must quiet the senses and expand beyond our immersion in the three garments of the soul: Thought, Speech and Doing. Then, as in "Let the whole earth be still before God," will "God be found in God's holy sanctuary" and in the soul, which is the meaning of "seek God where God can be found."...If you consider that by means of this *bittul*, (literally self-annihilation — *bittul ha yesh*) you become a vessel for blessing, then you will achieve that level of clarity called "transparency" — it is only the sense of the reality of the self which disappears and you won't avoid experiencing the consciousness which is beyond the self. Whoever merits this clarity and concentrates inner vision on that which is arising...is close to the Holy Spirit (*ruach ha-kodesh*).

Recommended Reading

Anne Brener, *Mourning & Mitzvah: a Guided Journal for Walking the Mourner's Path through Grief to Healing*, Jewish Lights Publishing, 1993

Mitchell Chefitz, *The Curse of Blessings: Sometimes, the Right Story Can Change Your Life*, Running Press, 2006

Estelle Frankel, *Sacred Therapy: Jewish Spiritual Teachings on Emotional Healing and Inner Wholeness*, Shambhala, 2004

Gene Gendlin, *Focusing*, Bantam Books, 2007 re-issue

Shefa Gold, *Torah Journeys: The Inner Path to the Promised Land*, Ben Yehudah Press, 2006

Lynn Gottlieb, *She Who Dwells Within: A Feminist Vision of a Renewed Judaism*, Harper One, 1995

David Hartman, *Love and Terror in the God Encounter: The Theological Legacy of Rabbi Joseph B. Soloveitchik*, Jewish Lights Publishing, 2004

Anson Laytner, *Arguing with God: A Jewish Tradition*, Jason Aronson, 1990

Michael Lerner, *Jewish Renewal: A Path to Healing and Transformation*, Harper Perennial, 1996

Spirit Matters, Hampton Roads Publishing, 1996

Goldie Milgram, *Reclaiming Judaism as a Spiritual Practice: Holy Days and Shabbat*, Jewish Lights Publishing, 2004

Leah Novick, *On the Wings of Shekhinah: Rediscovering Judaism's Divine Feminine*, Quest Books. 2008

Carol Ochs and Kerry M. Olitzky, *Jewish Spiritual Guidance: Finding Our Way to God*, Jossey-Bass Publishers, 1997

Zalman Schachter-Shalomi, *Spiritual Intimacy: A Study of Counseling in Hasidism*, Jason Aronson, 1996

Joseph B. Soloveitchik, *The Lonely Man of Faith*, Three Leaves, 2006

Adin Steinsaltz, *The Longer Shorter Way*, Jason Aronson, 1994

    The Strife of the Spirit, Jason Aronson, 1996

    The Sustaining Utterance: Discourses on Chassidic Thought, Jason Aronson, 1996

Joel Ziff, *Mirrors in Time: A Psycho-Spiritual Journey through the Jewish Year*, Jason Aronson, 1996

Additional Website(s):

http://www.caroladevriesrobles.nl/
    Teaches numerous methods of *hashpa'ah* via a wide integration of methods and images.

http://www.focusing.org
    Offers free teaching partnerships and numerous resources, programs and trainings.

Chant in *Hashpa'ah*
by Shefa Gold

Rabbi Shefa Gold teaches on chant, devotional healing, community building and meditation, and trains chant leaders via Kol Zimra, a two-year program for rabbis, cantors and lay leaders. Shefa combines her grounding in Judaism with a background in Buddhist, Christian, Islamic, and Native American spiritual traditions to make her a spiritual bridge celebrating the shared path of devotion. She is the author of many works such as *Torah Journeys: The Inner Path to the Promised Land* (Ben Yehuda). Her newest release is *The Magic of Hebrew Chant: Healing the Spirit, Transforming the Mind, Deepening Love* (Jewish Lights). www.rabbishefagold.com

When someone comes to me for guidance, coaching, comfort, inspiration, encouragement, support or spiritual friendship, I listen with a heart that has been informed by my own powerful chanting practice. Chanting is the melodic and rhythmic repetition of a Hebrew phrase drawn from our sacred text. It is a practice that allows for the exploration of the deeper levels of meaning and experience that lie beneath the surface of our religious lives. For many, chanting has become an important method of opening the heart, connecting with community, quieting the mind and viscerally embodying our liturgy and scripture. In the context of *hashpa'ah*, the practice of chant can be used as a method of inquiry and as a vehicle for expanding our capacities to receive and integrate the vast mystery and wisdom of our souls.

It's important to bring our sustained and loving attention into building and refining our inner lives. Chant is a practice that connects the outer dimensions of sound with the inner dimensions of awareness. As we grow and nurture our inner lives, it is important to have ways to express and share with our community the gifts we have received in the solitude of our personal practice. Chant is the bridge between the inner life and the outer expression; between the solitary practice and the shared beauty of fellowship. When we chant we are using the whole body as the instrument with which to feel the meaning of the sacred phrase. We study the meaning of the words and the context from which they are drawn. We explore the range of our feelings so that they can be dedicated to the purpose of the chant. And we use the power of the practice to enter into the silence and stillness at our core. Thus the practice of chant integrates our spiritual, intellectual, emotional and physical energies. The practice of chant takes the words of prayer and uses them as doorways into deeper meanings and into the spaces of our own hearts. It does this through the clarifying and refining of our intention. Sometimes the sheer volume of prayers collected over the centuries becomes an obstacle to delving more deeply into their meaning or using their power for transformation. The practice of chant allows us the luxury of exploring one phrase at a time, igniting the fire of our enthusiasm and pouring our passion into those particular words. Our prayer-life will start to reflect the personal and passionate experience we have had with those words. Chanting wakes up our liturgy and brings it to life within us.

The practice of chant allows us to begin to approach the text from an expanded understanding – from our hearts, bodies and experience as well as from what we know intellectually. In addition to preparing us for text study by expanding our perception of the words in front of us, chant may also be used in the comprehension of a text. We take a phrase from the text that holds some power or mystery for us and experience it with melody and rhythm and repetition until it unlocks its secrets for us.

Often during the ongoing practice of chant the complexities of our inner lives are brought to the surface. In the context of a counseling relationship, the seeker can acknowledge the mysteries and challenges that are called up by the chant and begin to appreciate the complexities of the inner life as they are revealed by the practice.

One facet of *hashpa'ah* is support for the work of cultivating *middot* (qualities) such as: the conscious awareness of God's presence, compassion, wisdom, love, open-heartedness, justice, spiritual community or humility. Chanting can be an effective and powerful tool in this work. In the practice of chant, we choose a phrase that expresses or embodies a quality that we wish to cultivate. As we chant, we can step inside that quality, feel its beauty and also explore the obstacles that arise in response to its presence.

Chant Prescriptions

1. Richard asks me to help him learn about patience. We chant from Psalm 37:7, "*Dom l'Yah v'hitkhollelo*" (Be still and wait for God). As we repeat and embody that phrase, he experiences both the feeling of patient waiting AND his rising impatience. Through the practice of chant, Richard works on strengthening and appreciating the stillness of waiting and he has the opportunity of exploring the roots of his impatience. This exploration can be done with compassion and understanding as he directs the beauty of the chant to soften hard places in the heart and melt his defenses.

2. Laura comes to me filled with anxiety about getting old. We explore her fears and see that she has ignored some of the gifts of aging. I sense that these gifts might be important in strengthening her sense of wholeness as she faces the challenges of getting old and frail. Together we study the words from Psalm 92: "*Od y'nuvun b'sayva d'shaynim v'rananim y'hi'yu* — They will be fruitful, even in old age. They will be juicy and luxuriant." The intention that I bring to this chant is to get in touch with the kind of fruitfulness, luxuriance and juiciness that emerges from my depths after many years of experience. This is a fruitfulness of wisdom and subtlety and it's not always obvious if you're only attuned to the surface of things. Even as our outer skin dries and wrinkles, there is an inner softness

that can be cultivated from years of rubbing up against the Mystery. Even as outer sight dims and hearing falters, there are inner senses that can become fine-tuned as we age.

As we practice together, I ask her to use this chant to bless the elders who have been models of aging and saging as they continue to blossom, burgeon and flourish in full-hearted glory.

I send Laura home with this practice, with instructions to chant these words daily, and use them to open up to a new vision.

3. Paul has been through a devastating divorce. He is just beginning to see glimmers of hopefulness again, but he feels weighed down by the past. He would like to examine and eventually heal the wounds that he has suffered through this painful time, but he feels overwhelmed by anger, shame and remorse. Together we study the word of Isaiah 51:3, *vayasem midbarah k'eden, v'arvatah k'gan adonai* (He transforms her wilderness into Delight, her wasteland into a Divine Garden.)

I ask Paul to remember another time in his life when he came through a period of devastation and found himself again filled with hope and beauty. I ask him to remember the feeling of miraculous rebirth. We use the chant to call up the possibility of Transformation and of Miracle. In the silence after the chant I instruct Paul to breathe this possibility into his broken heart.

4. Susan comes to me because she's feeling overwhelmed and afraid. She is starting a new job, entering into an intimate relationship, beginning to know her own strength and calling... but she is plagued by self-doubt. Together we look at Psalm 112:8, *samukh libo lo yira*. We sing this in the feminine as *samukh liba lo tira* and I translate it for her as "Heart supported, fearless." This practice opens up a new way of approaching the cultivation of courage. "What if we became fearless," I ask, "by allowing our heart to feel completely supported? Can you imagine what that would feel like?"

With Susan's permission, I place my right hand gently over her heart and put my other hand at the back of her heart. I ask her to close her eyes, dance gracefully and notice what it feels like to have her heart supported as I chant to her. She moves tentatively at first, but then as Susan's body relaxes into the sensation of being held as I follow her movements with my hands gently supporting her heart, her dance becomes more deliberate and beautiful. When the dance is completed, I remove my hands but ask Susan to remember what it felt like to receive support, and to breathe into that feeling until it is anchored in her bodily memory. The chant itself becomes a tool of remembrance. I suggest that every time the old fears come up, that she bring this chant to mind as a reminder to open her heart to the sensation of receiving support.

Discerning the Medicine

As I study a text, I read with a sensitivity to subtle shifts in my own energy. A certain phrase will intrigue me or disturb me or make me curious. And so I'll begin to explore that phrase through melody, rhythm, or gesture. My exploration also takes me to the dictionary and concordance so that I can learn the nuance and meaning of these powerful words. I experiment with tempo, tonal quality, movement or visualization. At some point in my exploration, the sacred phrase begins to emerge as a distinct "medicine." I discern and experience its particular power and transformative quality by noticing its effect on me.

Sometimes the medicine of a chant shows me a "disease" that I didn't even know I had. Here's an example: One Friday afternoon as I was getting ready for *Shabbat*, I came across the line from Isaiah: "*ki malah tz'va'ah* — Her time of service is fulfilled." [Isaiah 40:2] In exploring the power of this phrase I allowed myself to receive its message as a practice of receiving Divine congratulations. God was chanting to me and saying, Shefa, in this very moment, you are complete; you have done enough and you are enough. Tears began to roll down my cheeks, and something in me relaxed that I hadn't known was tense. The chant was delivering to me a contradiction to a very deeply ingrained belief – a belief that was so a part of me that I just experienced it as "normal." It was the belief or way of being in the world that said that "you're never done… you'll never finish… your to-do list keeps getting longer and you'll never keep up with it." Underneath that voice lay a dreadful accusation that whispered, "You'll never be enough (smart enough, beautiful enough, good enough). As I chanted the words of Divine congratulations, I suddenly became aware of a low-level anxiety about ever getting things done; this feeling had been with me for as long as I could remember. That anxiety had become the fuel for my accomplishments. As I let the power of the chant in and that newly revealed anxiety dissolved, I experienced a vision of a completely new way of being. In this vision, each moment was completed in joy and I could rest in that joy. The work of the next moment was given to me and the fuel that helped me rise to the new challenge was not my anxiety about getting something done, but rather my joy for the work.

At the end of the chant, I brought all of the power of the observer to this new way of being, to this clear vision of switching fuel tanks from anxiety to joy. That moment has become the compass point that guides me in my work now.

Before I ever teach or prescribe a practice to someone, I have worked with it first in my own practice in order to make its "medicine" my own. As a healer/shaman/rabbi I am continually practicing my art and adding to my "medicine" bag so that I will be able to tune in to the need or challenge of the one who sits before me, and find just the right treasure from the vast store of my inheritance that might bring beauty and power to the holy process of transformation, purification, healing and renewal.

Recommended Reading

Jalaja Bonheim, *The Hunger for Ecstasy: Fulfilling the Souls' Need for Passion and Intimacy*, Rodale Press, 2001

Brother Lawrence, *The Practice of the Presence of God*, Xulon Press, 2007

Yitzhak Buxbaum, *Jewish Spiritual Practices, Jason Aronson, 2nd edition*, 1999

Rabbi Moshe Cordovero, *The Palm Tree of Devorah*, Targum, 1994

Mitchell Gaynor, *The Healing Power of Sound, Shambhala Publications*, 2002

Shefa Gold, *Torah Journeys: The Inner Path to the Promised Land*, Ben Yehudah Press, 2006

Jonathan Goldman, *Healing Sounds: The Power of Harmonics*, Element Books, 1996

Bachya Ibn Paquda, *Duties of the Heart*, Feldheim, 1996

Kabir Helminski, *The Knowing Heart: A Sufi Path of Transformation*, Shambhala, 2000

Rabbi Abraham Joshua Heschel, *I Asked for Wonder*, Crossroad, 1997

Aryeh Kaplan, *Jewish Meditation: A Practical Guide*, Schocken, 1995

    Meditation and Kabbalah. Weiser Books, 1989

    Meditation and the Bible. Red Wheel/Weiser, 1989

Thomas Keating, *Intimacy with God*. Crossroad Press, 1996

    Open Mind, Open Heart, Element Books, 1991

Lawrence Kushner and Kerry Olitzky, *Sparks beneath the Surface: A Spiritual Commentary on the Torah*, Jason Aronson, 1993

Moshe Chaim Luzzato, *Messilat Yesharim (Path of the Just)*, Feldheim, 2004

Randall McLellan, *The Healing Forces of Music: History, Theory and Practice*, Authorhouse, 2000

Henri J.M. Nouwen, *Life of the Beloved: Spiritual Living in a Secular World*, Crossroad Publishing, 10th anniversary issue, 2002

On Ecstasy, a Tract by Dov Ber of Lubavitch, Translated by Louis Jacobs, Rossel Books, 1963

Rabbi Mendel of Satanov, *Cheshbon HaNefesh*, Feldheim, 1996

Gabrielle Roth, *Maps to Ecstasy: Teachings of an Urban Shaman*, New World Library, 1989

Rabbi Zalman Schachter-Shalomi with Robert Esformes, *Gate to the Heart: An Evolving Process*, : Alliance for Jewish Renewal, 1993

and Joel Segel, *Jewish With Feeling*, Riverhead Trade, 2006

Brother David Steindl-Rast, *Gratefulness, the Heart of Prayer*, Paulist Press, 1984

Llewellyn Vaughan-Lee, *The Paradoxes of Love*, Golden Sufi Center, 1996

Rabbi Rami Shapiro, *Minyan*, Belltower, 1997

How to invite God in: *Hashpa'ah* after the *Shoah* (Holocaust)
by Carola de Vries Robles

Carola de Vries Robles is a social psychologist, body-oriented psychotherapist, visual artist and *Mashpia'ah Ruchanit* ordained by Rabbi Zalman Schachter-Shalomi. A resident of the Netherlands, she is among the founders of Jewish Renewal in post-war Europe. Her professional career has primarily involved working with Holocaust survivors and their children. Carola's documentary "To Remember to Return" along with companion retreats, programs and website teachings demonstrate the healing power of art-making and reveal Judaism as a transformational force. www.caroladevriesrobles.nl

Despite a dominant, defensive and self-centered Judaism in the Netherlands, one can invite God in after the *Shoah*. One can re-discover one's true nature deep inside and learn to deal with tragedies and existential suffering. One can learn to move through a traumatized Jewish identity into a creative joyful "Jewishing". This article shows some of the methods that I have experienced to be effective and continue to use with those whom I serve.

Discovering a "Spiritual Body" inside the Physical Body

During my psychotherapy training, I discovered there was a state or space in me that was not wounded, that was not affected by the suffering of being a social/historical Jew, not even affected by the misbehavior or lack of love from my parents. At a certain moment in my training, I refused to "work" and "go back" to childhood traumas. I had the feeling I was falling in a gap/trap/bottomless pit that I knew all-too well by then. Finally, I had a "seeing through," and became unattached and calm. Bearing witness. This was a very new, strong experience. I did not have words for being "not-wounded."

I found through Viktor Frankl's Logotherapy that the spirit IS. Just IS. The spirit cannot be infected, affected, or corrupted by life experiences. However horrifying they may be, the spirit just IS. This became my inner push to turn to soul-oriented practices, including Psychosynthesis, Jungian depth analysis, and Sufi practices.

In the field of psychotherapy, spirituality was used as a concept, an idea, an ideal and as an addition to the existing analytic, expressive or creative therapies. I have had a hard time in my professional life integrating "spirituality" as a living, down-to-earth experience. Including an expanding sense of "depth," "width," "height" and "through."

For these reasons I left the transpersonal association in 1995, committed myself to the Jewish Renewal movement and teachings and teachers in deepening Jewish Spirituality through me. I started offering spiritual guidance in my private practice at home, and on request in retreat centers. And at the same time I began co-leading a *havurah* and Jewish meditation classes.

This shift from being self-absorbed and ego driven to opening/surrendering to the One — one's soul and God-connection — is a very fundamental shift. Not a one-time thing, rather an ongoing challenge and process.

When one shifts one's center of identification from the physical body, its needs and reactivity to the soul and its longings and potentialities, the sense of one's body changes and one can direct the mind differently. Warren Kenton describes these shifts as shifts on Jacob's ladder, one of his interpretations of the *Sefirot* (the aspects of the kabbalistic Tree of Life):

When one's sense of fate is externally influenced, that corresponds with a centering in the ego, the lower part of the tree, body/mind dynamics. When one's sense of fate becomes more self-willed, that corresponds with a sense of self and having a connection with inner desires, responsibilities and responsiveness. (*Tiferet*, "beauty" and *neshamah*, "soul" coming into awareness)

The challenge here is being invited into wisdom and mastery through letting go of self-control and self-centeredness. When one's sense of fate becomes more internally influenced, that corresponds with contact with spirit and what in Jewish tradition is termed the lower upper and upper realms. Unconditional love and discriminative awareness become available as the center from which to do and be. The soul becomes the container for spirit development in body/mind/soul. The ego becomes transparent. One truly becomes a vehicle for Presence — *merkavah la'Shekhinah*.

When one becomes centered in "inner knowing, *Daat*," and connected with the influx of higher qualities (*Chokhmah* — wisdom, *Binah* — understanding), one is living one's spiritual destiny, and possibly called to work at this level of destiny.

Shifting one's motivation and direction towards coming closer to *HaShem*, doing things *l'khvod HaShem* (for God's sake) will build this spiritual body inside or through the self, mind, and physical body dynamics. I believe that what a person did in past lives is stored in the soul and lays hidden or sleeping in the present life, needing to be kissed to life, reawakened, to be cultivated or released.

One of the first things I learned from Reb Zalman was the Four Worlds song: "It is perfect, you are loved, all is clear and I am Holy." Over time this chant unfolded its layered meanings. At first I took it to refer to the Four Worlds themselves ("outside" me). Next, it invoked doing, feeling, thinking and being, so it was all about my doing, feeling, thinking, and being. Gradually, the song referred to my life and history and all peoples' lives — potentialities, ideals, strivings, and healings. Thereafter, the song reminded me of states of consciousness. Now, the words are pointers to ways of embodying God's presence.

Knowing that human beings contain the possibility to realize "I AM HOLY and therefore have "a spiritual body" inside their personalities and physical body, forms the basis of my way of seeing and relating to people. I assume God's indwelling presence. I build an environment and container for the person with whom I am working so that she or he might see, feel, hear and imagine God's presence. I offer support to build and cultivate his or her spiritual body.

I rarely speak about God as though God is not already present. Thus, I often begin a session with "*Hineni osah et atsmi, merkavah l'sh'khinah* – Here I am making myself a chariot for the *Shekhinah*," chanting this in Rabbi Shefa Gold's melody either silently or sometimes as an attunement with my client. At the same time I/we address God "*ki imkha mekor chayyim, be orkha nireh or* — For with You is the source of life — in Your light we see light." Psalm 36:10

The First Steps in Teshuva: A Process of Deep Return/Rebalancing/Centering

I developed a centering exercise that has basic steps that can be reformulated or modulated for different circumstances. Certain "steps" need more practice, yet all the steps together keep the *Shekhinah* alive. "When *ahavat Yisrael* (love of the people of Israel) is in the hearts of the Jewish people...the heart of God, the *Shekhinah*, is also healthy." *Tanya, Iggeret HaKodesh* (The Holy Epistle), Chap. 31

Step 1. Here we ask: "Where do you go inwardly, to be your self, to be safe, at home, at peace, whole? What is your safe-space, your refuge?"

Exploring this "realm of consciousness" is often very revealing. Childhood memories, unrecognized preferences, loves and secrets become conscious.

Offering images, verses and stories from the tradition, from liturgy, psalms, TaNaKH, *Shabbat* and holiday practices, brings alive the sense of a safe space, a sense of God's Presence, where one can "taste and see that God is good" [Psalm 34:9]. With this wisdom, the invitation is to create your own centering image/words, an abiding in God's Presence.

Suggestions for words to chant are: "*Atah seter li* – You are my refuge," [Psalm 32:7] "*Adonai li, v'lo ira* – You are my God, so I will not fear," [Jewish liturgy, ff. Psalm 118:6] "*ruakh* – Spirit," breathing; meditating on the Tetragrammaton, the four letter Name; the "*Adon olam* – Threshold of Eternity," "*Ribbono shel olam* – Master of the Universe/ Eternity," "*Ad olam atta el* – Forever You are God" [Psalm 90:2], "*Barukh shem kevod malkhuto l'olam va'ed* – Blessed be the Glorious Name of [God's] Domain for ever and ever," etc. [Jewish liturgy]

To make a safe space, sometimes we chant or sing these lines, but sometimes we search for a *shiviti* (art which includes or invokes the Tetragrammaton) for contemplation, or make a *shiviti* for ourselves, or find a another representation of our sense of Beauty/ Truth/Goodness.

Finding an uncontaminated space, a place of safety is not an easy thing for people who identify with trauma. Finding an ideal parental archetype is not self-evident either, surely not with European Jews or with others who have so many broken family relationships. Sometimes a person's God-ideals or ordinary pleasant experiences in nature have to be re-created in order to make the God-field real.

Step 2. Here we ask: What is the Face of unconditional love?

Do you know a Jewish person who embodies unconditional love for you? How does it taste to receive unconditional love? If there is no experience in real life with Jewish heroes or a mensch, search for one in your past, in Torah, in books, among historical figures, teachers, special people you have known, and in stories of *tzaddikim* (righteous people)— bring them alive, loving you.

It was a shocking experience for me to find out that many, many soul searchers have not have had a personal connection with unconditional love from a Jewish parent or person in their lives.....so I had to help them find the face of unconditional love coming from within a Jewish source. Why be part of a tribe, if one is not lovingly seen and welcomed??? "You are Loved!" It may take a while to be able to receive and absorb this, to trust it and later contain it.

When a client has a weak love flow, I suggest they learn practices to receive comfort, to feel oneself as forgiven, to work on increasing a healthy self-love in order to say "no" and stay true to oneself.

Step 3. Here we ask: What needs to be seen and relinquished?

We carry the past in our cells and genes. The historical dimension, including many pasts with traumas, sufferings, exiles and liberations, are all imprinted in us. The past can imprison us. We are born in a historical setting and marinated in unfinished, incomplete, unspoken dramas. We are sensitive to dynamics of events, circumstances and the behavior of people we ourselves in fact may never have experienced. Fear and brokenness reinforce the building of false-selves. That is not who we really are.

"Being a Jew" is so much interwoven with rejections and humiliations. These come from inside the Jewish world and own complicated families, as well as from the dominant Christian culture and countries. Layers of shame and shaming "otherness"/"uniqueness" need to be taken off as garments holding the soul enprisoned. The ongoing vicious circle of the drama-triangle (attacker/propriator-target/victim—rescuerer/helper) needs to be unmasked, stopped and transcended.

Love and longing for wholeness and goodness bring us back to a deeper, more truthful Self. Along this soul journey, we allow "karmic cleansing" to happen. That can take many forms, e.g., a trip to Auschwitz, watching Claude Lanzmann's *Shoah* television series, visiting the Jewish museum built by Daniel Libeskind in Berlin, going through immersions in a *mikveh* (ritual bath), daring to open the locked box with letters and photos of our family who did not return from the *Shoah* and other traumas, too many to name here, can become a healing element in the soul's development and spiritual guidance trajectory.

Discriminative awareness needs to be developed and a quality of bearing witness cultivated. One helps the client to discern what needs to be seen, what needs to be released, what needs to be set free, what needs to be stopped, and to be dis-identified from. A learning is "to be human against all odds." (Frederick Frank)

Step 4. Know you can touch your Jewishness from the inside out.

However lost, broken and disconnected you may seem, however far away from tradition and transmission you may be, you can return to the Source and let the waters of life bring you alive!

"Seeds of holiness are nurtured with joy, not despair"
—Reb Nachman

"Do not forget to water the Tree," says a father on his deathbed to his son in a story from Reb Nachman. Become active, remain connected to your inner path, nourish your soul, question and learn, keep going. Develop a personal discipline of "watering the Tree of Life."

Step 5. Find your soul's purpose. What does your heart know?

Now. Can you say "*Hineni*, here I am!?" Do you have a Jewish name or want one? Where do you come from? Where are you going? May you be blessed with fellow travelers on your journey. And, "Let the future pull you" (to invoke Reb Zalman's saying).

"As we bless the Source of Life, so are we blessed"
—Faith Rogow

Step 6. Find a name or metaphor for God you can work with, live with and be grounded in. And let us answer: "*na'asseh v'nishma*— let us do and listen."

May the longing for wholeness be kept alive! Dream, imagine and bring about justice, love, beauty, truth, etc., in your doing, feeling, thinking and being. May Goodness live through you. May God be with you...and may we, the larger we, have the courage to act. It is through our choices and deeds that we come closer to God and the God-field.

Discovering a Spirituality without the Old-time Religion

It is not important to believe or not believe in God. I think it is even healthier to trust the questioning process and dare to not-know, to delve deeper into the innermost realms of the inner.

In Holland, some who have made a commitment to a trajectory of spiritual guidance and learning Jewish spirituality have dared to commit themselves to synagogue life and have become members of Jewish communities. Some chose to become fully accepted Jews and have started to go for a *giur* (conversion), to become officially Jewish. Holland today offers four main religious approaches to Judaism (Ashkenazi Orthodox, Portuguese/ Sefardic Orthodox, *ChaBaD*, Progressive Judaism), and two relatively new synagogue communities: *Masorti* (equivalent to the American Conservative movement) and a Jewish renewal-minded congregation called "*Beit HaChidush*" (House of Renewal).

Some have dared to explore their Jewishness through artistic and expressive means. Some grandparents have become bat- and bar mitzvah together with their grandchildren. Some have discovered that Torah study and building up a prayer life and a personal practice of meditation and self reflection is not a matter of "religion" or "tradition," but is about personal transformation, ethical behavior and being human in this world. In that sense, Judaism has become a source of wisdom and healing instead of trauma and darkness. Jewish religion, in the sense of denominations and organized Jewish communities, has not necessarily become more attractive for many soul searchers, who have told me, "I was searching for where to belong. Now I belong to my true Self, my Jewish soul. It is not an issue any more that I do not belong to the Dutch-Jewish world around me. I accept myself as a Jew."

May there always be someone around who remembers and re-activates the soul. May future generations find the wisdom and skill to create a spiritual home (community-synagogue) together. May "the House of Renewal" be turned into "a House of Renewing Life." Again and again..........

Recommended Reading

Ben Zion Bokser, Ed., Abraham Isaac Kook, The Lights of Penitence, The Moral Principles, *Lights of Holiness, Essays, Letters, and Poems* (Classics of Western Spirituality), Paulist Press, 1978

Martin Buber, *The Way of Man According to the Teachings of Hasidism*, Kensington Publishing Company, 1995

Avraham Burg, *The Holocaust Is Over, We Must Rise from Its Ashes*, Palgrave MacMillan Publishing, 2008

Frederick Franck, *What Does It Mean to Be Human?* St. Martin's Press, 2000

Viktor E. Frankl, *Man's Search for Meaning*, Beacon Press, 2006. Original edition, 1960

Zev ben Shimon Halevi (Warren Kenton), *Kabbalah, Tradition of Hidden Knowledge*, Thames and Hudson, 1979

Judith Lewis Herman, *Trauma and Recovery: The Aftermath of Violence—from Domestic Abuse to Political Terror*, Basic Books, 1997

Louis de Jong and Simon Schama, *The Netherlands and Nazi Germany*. Harvard University Press, 1990

Stephen Levine, *Unattended Sorrow: Recovering from Loss, and Reviving the Heart*, Rodale Publishing, 2005

Donald Kalsched, *The Inner World of Trauma, Archetypal Defenses of the Personal Spirit*, Routledge Publishing, 1996

Bob Moore, *Victims and Survivors: The Nazi Persecution of the Jews in the Netherlands 1940-1945*, Oxford University Press, 1998

Zalman Schachter-Shalomi, *Spiritual Intimacy: A Study of Counseling in Hasidism*, Jason Aronson, 1996

Simon Schama, The Story of the Jews: Finding the Words 1000BC-1492AD. Vol 1. and Vol 2. "When words fail—Present" Publisher: Ecco 2014

Holy Stories and Spiritual Direction
by Marcia Prager

Rabbi Marcia Prager is a teacher, storyteller, artist, and therapist. She is Director and Dean of Ordination Programs for Aleph: Alliance for Jewish Renewal and rabbi of the P'nai Or Jewish Renewal Congregation of Philadelphia. She is the author of *The Path of Blessing* (Jewish Lights), *P'nai Or Siddurim* and other innovative approaches to Jewish liturgy. Her work as a teacher of Jewish spiritual practice includes developing and co-directing DLTI – the Davvenen' Leadership Training Institute and teaching for EAJL – the European Academy for Jewish Liturgy. She travels widely to teach in an array of Jewish and interfaith settings. www.rabbimarciaprager.com

The great Seer of Lublin was walking in the town one winter night, on a route which took him near the synagogue. As he got closer to the building, he saw a fire burning in the *beit midresh*, the study hall – a room filled with priceless holy books. *Gevalt*! A fire in the *shul*! Maybe a spark or a coal from the stove had gone unnoticed, or a candle left to burn unattended... Hurry, get help! Sound the alarm. What if the fire were to burn the holy scrolls? His heart leapt in panic, as he raced in the cold to the *shul*. Others began to follow him calling out "Fire! Fire!" But when they got to the *shul* and peered in the window, there was no fire, but a room filled with a luminous glow and a group of *Hasidim* making a *l'chaim* (toast, to life!) and telling holy stories of the *tzaddikim* (holy teachers and role models).

Holy stories! What is a holy story? And what is it about holy stories that can fill a room with light? I write to remind spiritual directors of the value of stories! What kind of stories? The kind of stories we can perhaps call "holy stories," because they lift us up and open our hearts to God. These are the stories that touch our soul's longing to be our best selves, to rise beyond despair, alienation and exile into the most hopeful vision of what is possible – into wholeness, connection, purpose, compassion, love, generosity, curiosity and a rededication to living a joyous and meaning-filled life. These are only some good ingredients of that state of grace-filled affirmation we might call holiness. This rededication to a joyous and meaning-filled life does not gloss over adversity, pain, loss or tragedy. It is not saccharine or shallow, glib or superficial. Holiness can, most desirably, be a reaching of the soul for that of God that is present in every moment, and then in discovering God-ness as truly present, holiness becomes a gift of courage to swim through turbulent circumstances into the deeper waters of faith.

Reb Nachman of Breslov, the great Hasidic master, rebbe and maggid (sacred storyteller), teaches us that stories awaken the highest and holiest levels of our imagination. We enter a story and find ourselves, like in a dream, traveling in landscapes at once familiar and new. We enter a holy story and emerge with a renewed capacity to grasp the purpose of our own lives. We are lifted beyond our small selves into a larger sense of what is possible.

The Holy Seer of Lublin taught us that when we tell holy stories we bring the Divine Presence, the *Shekhinah* with all Her light, into the room with us. Why does a room fill with light when we tell holy stories? It fills with light because our hearts light up, our souls light up. Our limited view opens to a more expansive vision of our selves and our possibilities. Our perspective shifts, and suddenly new meanings emerge out of the tangle of our too-often confused or anxious narratives.

As spiritual directors, or as directees, haven't we all known those moments in which a numbing or even terrifying spiritual fatigue lifts because a new insight has redefined the very circumstances that held us trapped? At those moments the sense of the Divine Presence can be very strong. There are many different ways in which this can happen during spiritual direction. It can be in the silence, in the shared prayer, in the simple gift of hearing our own voices tell our own stories. It can emerge from the gift of trusting a lovingly compassionate listener, or it can arise from the director's gentle questions and the way in which one might be led to re-examine or reframe a set of circumstances.

One further tool in the *mashpia*'s toolbox is the wealth of holy stories that our tradition offers. In *Lamed Vav: Collection of the Favorite Stories of Rabbi Shlomo Carlebach*, Tzlotana Barbara Midlo quotes Rabbi Shlomo Carlebach, of blessed memory, one of the greatest *maggidim* (pl) of our generation: "A good story," Reb Shlomo says, "increases our knowledge, but is deeper than that knowledge. It comes from beyond our consciousness, but flows into our conscious awareness. The power of a story reaches beyond our minds, penetrates even deeper than our hearts, it *mamash* (above all) touches our souls...When we seek knowledge or information, it is because we want to learn something we don't already know. But with a story, it is just the opposite. What we want is to know what we already know, the knowledge that is already hidden in our hearts."

This short chapter is designed to inspire *mashpi'im* to embrace the art of holy storytelling, and integrate that skill into your practice. It is full of stories, for all kinds of readers as well.

First: A Story for Spiritual Directors

One Friday afternoon, a few hours before sundown, when *Shabbos* would begin, a man came into the study of a rabbi in a small village. He brought a question. "Rabbi," he asked, "is it permitted to make *Kiddush*, the sanctification blessing for *Shabbos*, over milk?"

"Hmmm," said the rabbi, thoughtfully shaking his head. "No," he replied, "it is not, but I must tell you, it is an interesting question, I'm glad you asked because a strange thing happened this week. Early on Sunday, a wealthy man stopped here and had a difficult question for me. When he left, he gave me seven rubles and told me to award them to whoever brought me the most intriguing question during the remainder of the week. It is Friday afternoon, almost *Shabbos*, and the week is over. I believe these seven rubles now belong to you."

No sooner had the amazed man left with his seven rubles, then in burst the rabbi's wife and several of his students. "Why," they demanded, "did you give all that *tzedakah* to him! Surely you know that while it is preferable to make *Kiddush* over wine, it is perfectly permissible to make Kiddush over milk. And that story about the rich man! You made that up!" "Ahhh," said the rabbi. "What you say is true, but you are missing the point. In his question I heard his need. He had no money to buy wine, or even a chicken for his family's *Shabbos*. In his poverty he would have had to make his *Kiddush* solely over milk. Now he will buy wine and food, and his *Shabbos* will be joyous!"

Why am I offering this tale to spiritual directors? Of course because it elevates the high art of listening! How often is it that the presenting issue brought into spiritual direction is not the real issue? When we are overly hasty or listen through the filter of our own assumptions, we can easily miss the point. Sometimes a questioner appears to be seeking information, but a holy listener must be careful. The real concern that the questioner may long to reveal (or even discover!) may ripple below the surface of the question. "In his question I heard his need," responds the rabbi.

When we welcome another person to come to us for spiritual direction, we enter into a sacred trust that calls us to offer our most alert and sensitive soul-capacities in the service of that seeker's spiritual growth. Our ability to listen deeply, to make gentle inquiries, and thus to discern deeper layers of possible meaning than might be immediately apparent, is the holiest skill we bring to this work.

This story is my gift to you for use whenever you wish to be reminded that your personal capacities for holy listening and creativity are two of your best tools.

Stories! It is a famous quip that Jews will answer a question with a question, but an even older practice is to answer a story with a story. When a friend tells me a story, don't I often respond with one of my own? But when someone comes to me for spiritual direction, it is generally not my own personal story that I would share, but drawing from the well of holy stories – when the moment is appropriate and the story a compelling fit – I will tell a holy story!

How does one acquire a reservoir of holy stories, learn to tell them, and discern how and when? Well there is a story about that too:

A certain Hasid was walking on the road on the way to town when he saw off the side of the road a grey weathered barn. Not so unusual, except that its side was covered with painted bull's eye targets, each with an arrow in the dead center! He had to stop and ponder it in amazement. *Gevalt*! What an archer! What skill, what perfect aim! Who might imagine that here on this rundown rural road there might live a master shot of such skill? Just then he saw a boy run past. Calling out to him, "*Shalom*, you, yes, you young *bokher*," he asked, "Do you know the man who shoots these arrows?" "Of course I do!" said the boy. "It's Mendele. He's right on the other side of the barn. Do you want to speak to him? I'll get him." Mendele ambled over and the two men stood side-by-side staring at the barn wall. "How do you do it?" the hasid finally asked. "I mean, how did you get to be such a master... every one a bulls-eye! It is awesome!" Silence again. "Weeeell" Mendele finally replied (in Yiddish of course). "You see, it ain't all that hard, 'cause you see, I shoot the arrows first and then I paint the circles around them afterwards..."

Which is to say, that you have to be ready to wrap your story around any "arrow" that gets shot. If you are going to introduce stories into your practice of spiritual direction, you need to have many stories, stories that you remember because they have already wrapped themselves around the "arrows" of your life. You must read and re-read all the great anthologies of holy stories. But reading alone will not do the job. You must practice telling these stories until they become part of whom you are, for a story told in a clumsy and amateurish way will not be very effective.

Learn BY HEART the stories of TaNaKH (all the Jewish canonical texts), rabbinic *midrashic* stories, mystical stories of the Kabbalists, and most of all, immerse in the wealth of soul-upifting Hasidic stories as these were crafted especially for our purposes. You will find contemporary stories too, as the spinning of modern "chicken-soup for the soul" stories clearly has no end. You will come to know which stories feel right to you because of how you yourself light up when you read or hear them. They will become part of you and emerge as tools for insight or healing when they are exactly what are needed.

A Story of the Baal Shem Tov

You may know that it was not infrequent that the great master, the Holy Baal Shem Tov, would call his *talmidim* (students) to him, and then call his coachman to harness the horses and prepare for a journey. On this fall night, as on many others, as the coach picked up speed and the town receded into the distance, the coachman would drop the reins letting the horses run free. Through the night the coach would fly, as if beyond the reaches of ordinary time and space.

On this journey the coach came to rest just after dawn at the fence gate leading up to a modest farmhouse. The sun was already filtering into the yard and the chickens were cackling as the mistress of the farm threw out the feed. She looked up to see a Hasidic rebbe in full garb and then a throng of *yeshiva talmidim* spilling out of the coach. Flustered at suddenly having unexpected but obviously holy and important guests, she ushered them inside, called her husband, and offered them refreshment. The couple was honored further when it became apparent that the rabbi and his students hoped for hospitality under their humble roof!

That afternoon and night they fed their guests the best meals they could create. But you can imagine the horror of the *talmidim*, when their teacher and master loudly announced that he was the famous Baal Shem Tov, then gorged himself with food and passed the platters to them urging them to enjoy and eat more! Clearly the farm couple was poor, even if modestly comfortable as poor goes, yet winter was coming. They were suddenly feeding a dozen men from what they had stored.

Embarrassed, the *talmidim* looked on with horror as their rebbe ate platter after platter, not only for lunch, but again at dinner, and again the next day. With each meal the nervous students ate less and less, while watching their supposedly holy rebbe feast as if a never-ending river of food would flow. To their greatest shame, he showed no sign of leaving. By the time he announced that they would stay though *Shabbos*, the sweet farm couple had already *shechted* (slaughtered) their chickens and used up their eggs, milk and much of their flour.

Yet the holy rebbe showed no sign of concern. He laughed, joked and ate. Meanwhile the poor couple was at their wits end. To host a great rabbi and *yeshiva* students...a great honor for simple people like themselves...but how to feed them? As the days went by, the horrified students watched the couple sell their cow and then even take out another loan on their poor farm.

Still the Baal Shem Tov laughed, joked and ate. The students meanwhile could barely come to the table. Among themselves they swore that when they left this place they would abandon their rebbe, for clearly he had lost his mind and was not the master they believed him to be.

The day came when they did leave, but not before the poor farmer had mortgaged his farm beyond redemption and faced winter to starve with an empty pantry. The coach ride back to Medzhybizh (Ukraine) was silent and tense.

The farmer, distraught out of his mind, staggered out of his house into the nearby woods. A light dusting of snow fell as he wandered among the trees, crazed with grief. "My God, my God? What do you intend for me? What do you want for me? I have nothing left. I am ruined. All I have is You. What do you want of me? God help me."

Hearing his cries, the other wanderer in the woods drew close to him. Who could that be, but Shmoykl the town drunk, drunk on cheap vodka as usual. But who cares? The farmer and the drunk cried together. In each other's arms they wept, and the farmer prayed. "My God, my God! What do you intend for me? What do you want for me? I have nothing left. I am ruined. All I have is You. What do you want of me? God help me!"

When Shmoykl the town drunk, began to babble at him he barely could listen. Something about money, a lot of money, hidden in a rotten tree, and wanting him to have it if anything ever happened to him. "You are the only one I've ever told. You are the only one who has ever comforted me, cried with me. Over there is the tree, that one with the rotten hole in the side and a rock up against the hole…"

The farmer staggered home late that night, opening the door to a hysterical wife sobbing in fear for him. Into the night, as the snow fell, they held each other by the stove, sobbed and prayed.

It was afternoon before the farmer made it into town, He had nothing to sell and nothing with which to buy, but he could not sit at home. That was how he heard that Shmoykl the town drunk had been found dead of frost and drink at the edge of the woods. *Oy gevalt*. Shmoykl dead. Shmoykl dead. But wait… Maybe…

The destitute farmer walked calmly past the village and then raced to the woods. Where was the tree? Could it really be so? Which tree, which tree? Holy God. Which tree?

The snow was already deep when, a month later, another coach pulled into Medzhybizh and stopped at the *yeshiva* (school) of the Baal Shem Tov. The *talmidim* watched with stunned amazement as the farmer and his wife emerged, dressed in warm furs and clearly well to do.

The Baal Shem Tov greeted them with pleasure and took them for hours into his private study. Then as mysteriously as they arrived, they left.

Finally, calling his bewildered *talmidim* around him he explained: "You see, in one of the soul ascents that you know that I make, I learned that this couple had a much different destiny intended for them. They were really *tzaddikim*, intended to make an important contribution to our people, to Torah learning and to help the poor, but they had become comfortable with their small lives and their ordinariness. They had, in a way, fallen asleep. The farmer knew how to *davven* but had forgotten how to pray. You have no idea how hard it was for me to do what I knew I had to do. I had to steal their comfort and force the farmer to pray, even though I knew that once he prayed from the deepest depth of his soul, the gates of Heaven would crack open for him. Know this: there is no deeper place from which to pray than to cry out to God for help; to cry out for what we desperately need and beg to understand what God wants us to do.

I offer this story because it has helped me pray for myself in a way that I never thought I could. One day, in a spiritual direction session convened more spontaneously than expected during a retreat I led, this story became the bulls-eye around an arrow. A deep and kind man sat with me to pour out his anguish about his woes. My heart was moved for him. But when I asked him if he ever felt able to cry like that to God, he said, "Oh, no! That would be so selfish. People shouldn't pray for themselves! I don't think that God would pay attention to prayers like that". We sat quietly together for a few minutes, and then I told this story. That was all. Then we looked at each other, sat quietly again, and ended. Months later he told me of the profound shift that had happened for him that day, and the hopeful directions that had opened again and again for him because of the permission he had to pray from the deepest depths of his heart. I smiled.

There are so many extraordinary holy stories. Fill your bookshelves with collections of not only Jewish stories, but also the best stories from all traditions. You can find stories that touch on every aspect of the human condition and speak to every striving. Sometimes you'll even find the same story told in the literature of different faith paths, which attests to the power of those messages.

Perhaps I can end with two stories. One is about imperfection and one about joy in the face of adversity. Both subjects come up in spiritual direction.

A poor Jew in an equally poor *shtetl* had two large pots. When he needed to get water from the stream at the edge of the town, he hung them on the ends of a pole, which he carried across his neck. One pot had a crack in it, while the other pot was perfect and always delivered a full portion of water. At the end of the long walk from the stream to the house, the cracked pot arrived only half full. For a full two years this went on daily, with the water carrier delivering only one and a half pots full of water to his house. Of course, the perfect pot was proud of its accomplishments, perfect for which it was made.

But the poor cracked pot was ashamed of its own imperfection, and miserable that it was able to accomplish only half of what it had been made to do. After two years of what it perceived to be a bitter failure, it spoke to the water bearer one day by the stream...

"I am ashamed of myself, because this crack in my side causes water to leak out all the way back to your house." The bearer said to the pot, "Did you notice that there were flowers only on your side of the path, but not on the other pot's side?

That's because I have always known about your flaw, and I planted flower seeds on your side of the path. Every day while we walk back, you've watered them. For two years I have been able to pick these beautiful flowers to decorate my *Shabbos* table. You have given me and my wife so much joy. Without you being just the way you are, there would never have been this beauty to grace my house."

I resonate with this story because I grew up in an environment in which being perfect seemed to be an important goal. Now, being perfect was never more important than being a *mentsch*. Yet even *mentchlichkeit* was something at which you could be strive to be perfect! Alas, there have been many times in my life in which striving for excellence became so difficult that I froze, unable to try any more because the fear of mediocrity was too paralyzing. This story has helped me feel valuable for my imperfections, not in spite of them (an honorable person).

There are stories like the next one from Yitzhak Buxbaum's *Daily Maggid* email stream, that are like the best health-food store energy-bar, a quick and invaluable booster when a situation is bringing you down.

Rabbi Mordechai of Chernobyl often praised the quality of being joyful. He once told a parable: There was a king, two of whose subjects rebelled against him, and he had them both thrown into prison. One of them sat in the jail cell miserable and broken. The other one acted like the happiest man in the world; he was singing and dancing and jumping around like a crazy person. The jailer complained to the king that he can't stand it any more, "He's jumping around and dancing in the jail!" "Throw him out," said the king. "Why should you suffer?" So the jailer kicked him out, and the man was free. Rabbi Mordechai concluded, "That's the way it is with joy."

Maggid Yitzhak Buxbaum says that Rabbi Shlomo Carlebach, *z"l* (of blessed memory) would call this a "cash story," meaning that it's not a "bank story" that you need only once in a rare while. Reb Shlomo said "You need a story like this often so it has to be like cash, ready in your pocket." Remember this story the next time you're sad or depressed and follow its teaching!

So holy friends, learn stories! Use them to inspire, to enlighten, to heal, to encourage, to uplift and to teach. Find ways to use the stories that touch your own heart in the service of others. When you find a story that wraps itself around the core issues of your own life, tell it often so that you will really own it. Then it will be like cash in your pocket, ready for you whenever you need it. Yes, there will be stories that are powerful, but needed less often. You still must tell them many times in order to make them really yours, so that you can put them securely in your story bank for use when needed. Eventually you may find yourself with new stories emerging from within, try them, refine them and share them to enrich us all! Yours are holy stories too.

Recommended Reading

The foundational text is the Torah, the primary Jewish translations are:

_____, *Hebrew-English Tanakh*, Jewish Publication Society of America, 2000

Everett Fox, *The Five Books of Moses: Genesis, Exodus, Leviticus, Numbers, Deuteronomy*, Schocken, 2000

Aryeh Kaplan, *The Living Torah: The Five Books of Moses and the Haftarot - A New Translation Based on Traditional Jewish Sources*, Maznaim Publishing, 1981

Nosson Scherman, *The Stone Edition Chumash, The Torah, Haftaros, and Five Megillos with a commentary from Rabbinic writings*, ArtScroll, 1993

David E.S. Stein, *The Contemporary Torah, A Gender-Sensitive Adaptation of the JPS Translation*, Jewish Publication Society, 2006

Compilations of Major Jewish Stories and Legends

Hayyim Nachman Bialik and Y.H. Rawnitzky, *Book of Legends/Sefer Ha-Aggadah: Legends from the Talmud and Midrash*, Schocken, 1991 (also available on CD via Davka.com).

Martin Buber, *The Tales of the Hasidim*, Schocken Books, 1991

> with Maurice Friedman, *The Legend of the Baal-Shem,* Princeton University Press, 1995

Yitzchak Buxbaum, *Storytelling and Spirituality in Judaism*, Jason Aronson, 2005

> *The Light and Fire of the* Baal Shem Tov, Continuum, International Publishing Group, 2005

> *Jewish Spiritual Practices*, Jason Aronson, 1999

> *Jewish Tales of Mystic Joy*, 2002

> *Jewish Tales of Holy Women*, Jossey-Bass, 2002

Shlomo Carlebach and Tzlotana Midlo, *Lamed Vav: A Collection of the Favorite Stories of Shlomo Carlebach*, Israel Book Shop, 2004

Mitchell Chefitz, *The Curse of Blessings: Sometimes, the Right Story Can Change Your Life*, Running Press, 2006

Avraham *Yaakov* Finkel, *The Great Chasidic Masters*, Jason Aronson, 2004

Ellen Frankel, *The Classic Tales: 4000 Years of Jewish Lore*, Jewish Publication Society, 1998

Louis Ginsberg, *Legends of the Jews, Jewish Publication Society*, 2003

Aryeh Kaplan, *Chasidic Masters – History, Biography and Thought, Mo Publishing*, 1991

Paysach J. Krohn, *The* Maggid *Speaks: Favorite Stories and Parables of Rabbi Sholom Schwadron shlita,* Maggid *of Jerusalem*, Mesorah Publications, 1987

Lawrence Kushner, *The River of Light: Jewish Mystical Awareness*, Jewish Lights, 2000

Jiri Langer, *Nine Gates to the Hasidic Mysteries*, Behrman House, 1976

Meyer Levin, *Classic Hasidic Tales*, Penguin, 1975

Yitta Halberstam Mandelbaum, *Holy Brother: Inspiring Stories and Enchanted Tales about Rabbi Shlomo Carlebach*, Jason Aronson, 1997

Susan Mesinai, *Shlomo's Stories: Selected Tales*, Jason Aronson, 1996

Goldie Milgram and Ellen Frankel, (Eds.), *Mitzvah Stories: Seeds for Inspiration and Learning*, Reclaiming Judaism Press, 2012

Rebbe Nachman of Breslov, Chaim Kramer, and Aryeh Kaplan, *The Seven Beggars & Other Kabbalistic Tales Of* Rebbe *Nachman Of Breslov*, Jewish Lights Publishing, 2005

Joachim Neugroschel (Ed & Transl.), *No Star Too Beautiful: A Treasury of Yiddish Stories*, W.W. Norton & Company, 2002

Louis Newman, *The Hasidic Anthology*, Jason Aronson, 1987

David Rosenberg, *Dreams of Being Eaten Alive: The Literary Core of the Kabbalah*, Three Rivers Press, 2001

Peninnah Schram, *Jewish Stories One Generation Tells Another*, Jason Aronson, 1987.

   Tales of Elijah the Prophet, Jason Aronson, 1991

Zalman Schachter-Shalomi and Howard Schwartz, *The Dream Assembly: Tales of Rabbi Zalman Schachter-Shalomi*, Gateway Books and Tapes, Santa Cruz, CA: 1998

Kalman Serketz, *The Holy Beggar's Banquet*, Jason Aronson, 1998.

Rami Shapiro and Andrew Harvey, *Hasidic Tales Annotated and Explained*, Skylight Paths Publishing, 2003.

Adin Steinsaltz, *The Tales of Rabbi Nachman of Bratslav*, Jason Aronson, 1994

   Beggars and Prayers: Adin Steinsaltz Retells the Tales of Rabbi Nachman of Bratslav, Basc Books, 1985

Aryeh Wineman, *Ethical Tales from the Kabbalah*, Jewish Publication Society, 1999.

Mystical Tales from the Zohar, Princeton University Press, 1998

Elie Wiesel, *Souls on Fire: Portraits and Legends of Hasidic Masters*, Simon & Schuster, 1982.

Additional Website(s):

http://www.breslov.com

http://rebshlomo.org/

http://www.sholom-aleichem.org/

http://www.chabad.org/library/article_cdo/aid/109851/jewish/Stories.htm

http://www.folklore.org.il/

http://www.storyteller.net/

http://www.reclaimingjudaism.org/stories.htm

Using Imagery in *Hashpa'ah*
by Joyce Reinitz

Rabbi Joyce Reinitz, ACSW, splits her time between Bainbridge Island near Seattle, and Palm Beach Gardens, Florida. She trained in the techniques of imagery with Mme. Colette Aboulker-Muscat, *z'l* (of blessed memory) in Jerusalem and with Dr. Gerald Epstein in New York. She has worked as a psychotherapist for over 30 years and was ordained by The Academy of Jewish Religion. She led a monthly *Rosh Chodesh* group, Spiritual Journeys at the 92nd St. Y for many years. She currently utilizes imagery techniques in her Torah Study classes and private spiritual guidance sessions.

Imagery and the imagination provide a way to access the deepest parts of ourselves. They transport us beyond the day to day "knowing" of our intellect and put us in touch with the "wisdom of the heart," the intuitive, mystical, "knowing" which awakens our spiritual selves and allows us to connect to the greater Whole. Imagery reveals to us our profound inner wisdom and helps us to experience—to see, sense, feel, what is sacred, rather than merely contemplate it.

The use of the imagination within Jewish tradition has a long and rich legacy. The imagination has been considered a vital feature of the soul and credited with the capacity for allowing us to envision the Invisible and perceive the formless Divine. It was through the faculty of imagination that our biblical patriarchs and matriarchs encountered and experienced God's Presence. We are told that God "appears" to Abraham in visions, but it is clear that these are not ordinary experiences of sight since Abraham "hears" the visions. His encounters, as well as the encounters that other biblical characters have with God, indicate a perceiving of a different sort, an experience of a different consciousness, which involves the faculty of the imagination.

The imagination is not to be understood as "the unreal" or as fantasy. The imagination is the faculty of perception that stimulates a real experience and response through the creation of a mental image. The imagination is the uniquely human quality that allows us to transcend the physical limitations of time and space permitting us to have a true sensory experience regardless of the presence of an external stimulus. This sensory experience is not only real but is extremely potent. It brings a shift in our perception which essentially changes us from the inside out. In this regard, imagery is a powerful instrument for promoting self-growth and personal transformation and can be an important tool to use in *hashpa'ah*.

A Little Shock to the System

Hashpa'ah helps us find a new path by turning from our habitual ways. Of course, this sounds much easier to do than it actually is. We all know that as much as we may say we want our lives to be different, as much as we seek a new path; it is not so easy to change. Old habits, like old beliefs, are not easy to surrender. My teacher Colette, as Mme. Aboulker-Muscat was affectionately called, was masterful at helping people to change. She did it by bringing balance where she perceived imbalance. She carefully observed and listened to whoever came to see her and then helped them discover a way to shed old patterns. She used the power of imagery to push open the gates of resistance and clear the way for change.

Her intent was always to deliver what she called "a little shock" to the system. "The shock" has the purpose of interrupting or overwhelming a habitual pattern by stimulating a quick internal shift. When the habitual is interrupted an opportunity for new possibilities is created. The inner-directed work of imagery interrupts our habitual, linear way of thinking and activates the non-linear, intuitive, creative potential dwelling within us. The use of imagery is not a coping strategy; it is a way to disconnect from old patterns and create new experiences, which can lead to lasting change.

The language of imagery reveals resources deep within us that have eluded our awareness. Once these resources are revealed to us we can begin to draw upon them. Simply by closing the eyes and going inward, we can quiet the mind and interrupt the habit of focusing on the external world. When we allow ourselves to trust the process of going inward, and begin to surrender to the non-linear way of thinking, the images we discover can, in the twinkling of an eye, open us to a whole new world and a whole new sense of self.

The experience of one of my congregants demonstrates the change that can occur when we let go of our habitual mode of logical, solution- oriented thinking and surrender to the world of image; the realm of non-linear thought. Her experience, which she calls "an epiphany that changed" her life, is especially informative and inspirational because she works as a courtroom judge. Her logical, habitual mode of thinking and gathering information is her bread and butter so to speak. Her orientation in the world is one of attempting to determine objective reality.

Her life-changing epiphany occurred during the following guided imagery based on an exercise learned from Colette that I call "Turning towards the Light:"

> Gently close your eyes and exhale slowly through your mouth.....take a
> short inhale through your nose...then exhale and inhale two more times...
> now breathe easily and effortlessly.....

Imagine that you are in a dark forest. See a light coming from the right. Sense yourself moving toward the light until you find yourself in a clearing. In the clearing see a circle of light coming from above........

Stand in the circle of light and offer a prayer...speak your heart...............

When you are finished......Sense yourself in the hands of God being lifted up.........Breathe out once.......................

Now, feel yourself placed down gently. When you are ready, slowly open your eyes....noticing how you look and how you feel.

Here is her description of what happened to her in relation to this session:

You know those moments when you see the light go on...? I had one of those moments last week during an imagery exercise. I am usually quite resistant to any suggestion of closing my eyes to the rational world and am extremely skeptical about the concept of a "greater power" calling the shots, but this time, for some reason, I pushed my resistance away and followed the instructions. ....

I actually envisioned placing myself in the hands of "God." Within seconds, the most amazing thing happened! My body began to disappear. I could sense the presence of my mind, but there was no body attached to it. Suddenly, I was transported to an ineffable place of peace, calmness and wellbeing.

I felt no pain because there was no body and my mind was floating in a glorious and beautiful location. I had finally achieved the peace and calm that I had been looking for in my life. And I got that peace by **NOT** searching for it. All those years of intensely and diligently seeking the pinnacle of peace were focused in the wrong direction. The results were more immediate and more certain when I let go. I got the message, loud and clear. For the first time, I understood the power of faith!

The first question that Colette would ask anyone who came to her was, "What do you want?" This is a deceptively simple question which, in an instant, accomplishes several very important things. First of all, it conveys the message that the seeker is being taken seriously and that time is of the essence. It validates the person and his or her quest and quickly establishes the tone of the relationship. It also recognizes the seeker as an active participant in the process and empowers him or her to become one's own authority.

This question interrupts the seeker's narrative, which is very likely a retelling of a chronically repeated lament of victimhood and immediately propels him or her in a new direction. In order to answer the question, "What do you want?" we have to stop and take stock of ourselves and our situation. We have to make contact with our inner selves and listen to our inner voice. It requires making a shift in perspective from looking backward to looking forward. We become oriented to the present and open to new possibilities. This question stimulates the creation of an image in the seeker's mind which then informs and shapes his or her behavior toward achieving the designated goal.

The Function of Imaging

Images are basically pictures of our emotions. Given that images represent the mental form of how we are feeling, images give us an authentic and direct reading of a person's emotional situation. When we communicate through images, we are connecting on a deep emotional level. This is, of course, invaluable in doing the work of *hashpa'ah*.

We all spontaneously use imagery in describing our situations. When we listen carefully to language and let the images speak to us, we can become very effective in responding to what people need because the images perfectly express and reveal their emotions. "I feel like a caged bird," "I feel like a ship that's lost its rudder," "I feel like a lost soul." Each of these statements gives a vivid picture of the person's emotional experience and the imagery provides us with a key to help us respond. To the person who feels like a caged bird, I might say, "see yourself in that cage...... now, find a way to open the cage and see yourself flying free. What happens?" To the person who feels like a rudderless ship, I might say, "Find your rudder, attach it securely and see yourself steering your ship...... Where are you going?" To the person who feels like a lost soul, I might say "Dig into the ground with a golden shovel....find a map......see where it is leading you." Intervention of this kind immediately goes to the heart of the situation and reveals a new possibility. It often brings an intense emotional release and a welcome change.

Because every emotion can be expressed as an image, imagery is a useful tool for exploring and dealing with feelings that are particularly painful or disturbing. If someone is overwhelmed or paralyzed by fear, we can ask him or her to see an image of their fear: Is it a color? a shape? a form? What does the fear look like? The image that emerges will be unique and reflect the true picture of the person's emotional state. Once the image is formed, we can help the person find a way to alter the image, a change which will bring relief and sense of liberation. If he sees his fear as a "tiger about to eat them", I might suggest that he turn it into a kitten and tame it. If the image of the fear is "total darkness," I might suggest that she quickly turn on the light. This type of intervention is done quickly, as is all imaginal work, because we want to minimize the possibility of the rational mind intruding upon the process.

Position and Breath

It is best to do imagery in a seated position, with feet flat on the floor. To aid in turning the attention inward it is useful to keep the arms and legs uncrossed and to avoid letting the hands touch each other.

Breathing plays an integral role in any methodology that aims to integrate or balance the mind and body. Breath is the starting point that allows for the turning inward away from the external world. Imagery exercises always begin by directing the "imager" to emphasize the exhale. This has the physiological effect of quieting the vagus nerve, which relaxes the body and enhances the inner-directed work. As practitioners we always need to pay close attention to the breathing of clients, for the breath gives us an excellent indication of someone's emotional state. An experience I had with Colette gave me an important insight regarding the impact that our emotional state has on our breathing and how by altering our breathing we can alter our emotions.

During 2001 my husband and I spent the year in Jerusalem and I visited with Colette as often as I could. Just after the 9/11 attack, I found myself feeling very frightened and anxious. I went to see Colette. She had a few people visiting with her in her garden but as soon as she looked at me, she must have seen the tension in my face. Without a word, she signaled for me to come and sit right next to her. She continued her conversation with the person she was addressing and without missing a word or blinking an eye, she quietly put her hand on mine and began to breathe along with me. She at first matched my anxious shallow breaths but within a short amount of time she slowed her breaths and before I knew it or even realized what was happening, I found myself to be breathing in sync with her, exhaling slow even breaths and inhaling gently. Before too long I was feeling calm and grounded and present and enormously grateful. Without saying a word she had managed to restore my balance and help me regain a sense of normalcy. I'll never forget this invaluable lesson about the use of breath.

Imagery Exercises

The following imagery exercises offer additional examples of the way that imagery can deepen self-awareness and illuminate a path of change. The exercises bring us to a different place of "knowing." They ask us to briefly turn down the volume on the outside world and have us listen, for a change, to our inner voice. They bring us beyond the limitations of our logical mind and connect us with "the wisdom of the heart" by awakening us to the fact that there is more to life than meets the proverbial eye. The images we form and the experiences we have when doing these exercises alert us to our potential and open the door to new possibilities. We return from the inner experience with a fresh orientation and a new sense of self, which we can then integrate into life with eyes wide open.

It is important to remember that everyone images in their own unique way. Some people respond with vivid images, others have kinesthetic responses, i.e., physical sensations. Some people sense colors or shapes, and some have auditory responses. We want to be careful not to judge or compare and it is essential not to analyze or impose meaning on the experiences that people have. The process is one of pure and exhilarating discovery.

Each exercise has a specific intention or possible *kavannah* (intention), which its title reflects. My hope is that these exercises will be useful in enhancing the work of *hashpa'ah* and that they will give you the opportunity to experience the healing, transformative and sacred power of the imagination. These can be done individually or in a group setting. It is recommended that people report their imagery so that the inner experience takes on another dimension. Verbally reporting is valuable in helping to concretize the images as is drawing or illustrating an image. When appropriate, it may be beneficial for someone to replicate an object of special significance that is revealed in an imagery experience.

Imaging takes some getting used and some practice. It is not easy for any of us to surrender to a new experience. The fear of losing control may interfere with the process of closing the eyes and it is not so easy to stop the mind from its incessant habit of thinking. We need to be patient with others and ourselves. The exercises are designed to be done rather quickly, which helps to deter the "thinking mind" from intruding.

Discovering Life's Journey

Close your eyes and exhale slowly through your mouth.....take a short inhale through your nose... then exhale and inhale two more times.....now breathe easily and effortlessly.....

Within the quiet depths of your heart......Listen...........Listen for the still small voice calling your name........Hear a soft sweet voice singing the song of your soul........Dance to the melody.......move to the beat.......Sense how this song is uniquely your own.....Breathe out....

Now....listen and hear what you need to hear about yourself.......

Breathe out.....

Listen and see what you need to do to fulfill the essence of your being.........
See yourself being true to yourself.......See yourself living the life you are meant to live......
Breathe out and slowly open your eyes......

Sparkle and Grow

Close your eyes and exhale slowly through your mouth.... take a short inhale through your nose... then exhale and inhale two more times...now breathe easily and effortlessly.....

Recognize a part of yourself whose growth or expression has been thwarted......Now.... Look up in the sky and find a twinkling star.

Sense yourself jumping up very, very high.....touch the star and gather some stardust.....

Sprinkle half of the stardust over yourself....and mix the rest into a glass of water........ Slowly drink the sparkling mixture......sense it nourishing you and supporting your inner growth. Feel yourself sparkling both inside and out...How do you feel.......how do you look? Breathe out and open your eyes...remembering to drink this potion whenever needed.

Weaving the Tapestry of Your Life

Close your eyes and exhale slowly through your mouth.....take a short inhale through your nose...then exhale and inhale two more times...now breathe easily and effortlessly.....

Carefully examine the fabric of your life...Observe the many colored threads....note the textures and the varied patterns ....
Notice which patterns please you and see which ones you'd like to change. Breathe out..... Now, see yourself sitting at a loom....weaving your life.....add or eliminate threads as you wish.......

Weave a tapestry of the life you want........wrap it around you and see yourself living that life... Breathe out and slowly open your eyes.

Illuminating the World

Gently close your eyes and exhale slowly through your mouth.....take a short inhale through your nose...then exhale and inhale two more times...now breathe easily and effortlessly.....
With a golden shovel dig deep into the earth and find a crystal. Hold the crystal in your hands and see each facet reflecting light.

Take the crystal and place it in your heart........Sense what is happening.... Feel yourself filled with light...and life....

Breathe out.......Now see everyone you know radiating light......See yourself and the world in a new light.

Breath out and slowly open your eyes.....keeping your newly illuminated awareness.

Jacob's Dream: Turning Fear into Faith
(for facing difficult transitions)

Close your eyes and exhale slowly through your mouth.....take a short inhale through your nose...then exhale and inhale two more times.....now breathe easily and effortlessly.....

Like Jacob, see yourself setting out on a new path...What are you feeling?...You are alone in the desert at night.........dream Jacob's dream: See a ladder reaching up to heaven.....see the angels climbing up and down....

Hear God tell you, "Remember, I am with you....I will protect you wherever you go......."

Breathe in these words...let them fill your being....

Sense yourself turning fear into faith.

Breathe out and slowly open your eyes.

The Power of a Smile (a remedy for sadness)

Gently close your eyes and exhale slowly through your mouth.....take a short inhale through your nose...then exhale and inhale two more times...now breathe easily and effortlessly.....

Sense yourself quiet and very still........Now feel a smile forming deep within you.....smile with your heart.......smile with your mind.....sense yourself smiling with every cell of your being...Hear a chorus of giggles........ Feel yourself grinning........ See smiles on every tip of your toes....... Do a tippy- toe dance with laughing feet.......How do you look...how do you feel?

Breathe out and slowly open your eyes....

Recommended Reading

Gerald Epstein, *Healing Visualizations, Bantam Books*, 1989

   Climbing Jacob's Ladder, ACMI Press, 1999

   Healing Into Immortality, Bantam Books, 1994

   Kabbalah for Inner Peace, ACMI Press, 2008

Catherine Shainberg, *Kabbalah & The Power of Dreaming: Awakening the Visionary Life*, Inner Traditions, 2005

Additional Website(s):

http://www.reclaimingjudaism.org
  Sound files of free guided meditations by Rabbi Joyce Reinitz

Let Her Own Works Praise Her
(A tribute to Mme. Colette Aboulker-Muscat)
by Carol Rose

Carol Rose is a spiritual counsellor, author, educator, and award-winning poet. She holds an MA in Theology and certification as Mashpi'ah, Minister, Spiritual Director, Maggid and Preacher as granted by Rabbi Zalman Schachter-Shalomi. She has five children and fourteen grandchildren. Among her books in print are *From the Dream* and *Behind the Blue Gate*. Her essays appear in Canadian and American anthologies.

For several years our family spent summer holidays and sabbaticals in Jerusalem. We did so in order to help our children become fluent in the language and culture of Israel. During one of those sabbaticals (1979-80) I enrolled in Pardes, a gender-inclusive, *yeshiva*-like Judaic studies program. Since this was our sabbatical year, I also allowed myself to enjoy some of the treats that were specific to Jerusalem, like the women's *hamam*, old Turkish bath house no longer in operation today.

On one of those luxurious afternoons at the *hamam* I met a therapist who told me that she had come to Jerusalem to study "with the only true teacher she had ever met." Thinking that she was referring to one of the new *b'aalei t'shuvah yeshivot* (schools for Jewish religious studies) that attract newly religious students, I asked who her teacher was. She said, "Madame Colette Aboulker-Muscat, an Algerian therapist and wise woman who teaches a form of imagery work that is truly spiritual." She invited me to see for myself at one of Colette's soirées that were held on Wednesday or Saturday evenings. As it happens, Reb Zalman had just spoken to me about Colette, suggesting I might find her work compatible with my interest in psychology and religion.

I also visited Moshav Modi'in, an Israeli form of collective living and resource sharing, several times that year. One *Shabbat* I shared a guesthouse with Elfie Goodman, a Jerusalem teacher who currently lives and teaches in Germany. After a short conversation Elfie said, "You know, you really should come to meet Colette. Do you know who she is? I have a feeling that you'd enjoy her work. Why don't you meet me there this Wednesday morning? She's offering a special class for therapists from the US, and I think you'll fit right in!" By now I had heard about Colette three times and, as our tradition teaches, when one receives the same message three times, it should not be ignored! I felt certain that I was being directed to this unusual woman, but I had no idea why.

So instead of going to my Pardes class that Wednesday morning, I went to Colette's house on Shimoni Street. Although much has recently been written about her home behind the blue gate, there was nothing to prepare me for the transformation that would take place once I entered. The front hall was saturated, from floor to ceiling, it seemed, with photos of students and loved ones. Suddenly I knew that I was in a holy place... a sanctuary. Much prayer and healing had taken place here, I sensed.

I quietly moved from the outer room into an inner sitting area where Colette and her students were gathered. The house was tiny. Every nook and cranny held objects of beauty. Once inside, I noticed that several blue globes hung from the ceiling, and that they cast a remarkable light. Everyone in the room was bathed in it, as were the many paintings, colorful cushions, and unusual wooden window dressings that ornamented the room. At the far end was an ivory carved headboard supporting a large bed. Seated on the bed was the teacher, Madame Colette. She was regal and, at seventy, she was one of the most beautiful women I had ever seen! I tried to slip in unnoticed, but there was no chance of that. Colette's eagle eye spotted me! In quite a stern voice she called out "What are you doing here?" a question I could barely answer myself, but one I knew I had to respond to. Just then Elfie spoke up, "It's all right, I invited her," and then Susan, the therapist I'd met at the *hamam*, piped in, "So did I." For the moment, at least, I was safe!

The students were discussing an exercise. Each person offered a lovely, detailed, account of the journey that they had taken under Colette's guided image. I was enthralled as I listened to each carefully worded description. Then it was time for another exercise. Colette said, "You may do this, but do not speak," which, of course, was not difficult in the face of such beautiful articulation. I, who never lacked for words, felt mute... and keeping silent was something that I actually welcomed. Again the students offered their images and Colette commented on each. I found myself "seeing" each image as though it were my own. After a few more exercises Colette said to me, "And you, what did you see or understand?" and suddenly my anonymity was gone! I had to share my image, whether I understood it or not. As it turns out, the image shook me! What I saw was a large golden breast (and although I worked with Colette from that day until her death, in 2003, I have never forgotten the power of that first exercise). Shyly, very shyly, I described my image and the accompanying sense of awe that I experienced. I said that I felt protected and cared for. There was an uncomfortable giggle from some of the male therapists, but the women in the room looked at me tenderly. Today I might not have found the image as revelatory as I did, but in 1979 there wasn't much talk about El Shaddai, the Nurturing Presence that I had just experienced in such a profound and immediate way. When I finished describing my experience Colette said, "Come to see me tomorrow morning at eight" and that was the end of my Pardes studies, and the beginning of my work with Colette.

I continued studying with Colette (three or four times a week) for the rest of that year. Sometimes I'd have a private session before a class. Other times there would be two or three of us who came for those early morning sessions. Often I would return at five in the afternoon for a gathering in the garden. Although these were not classes, in the usual sense, there was always something to learn. Mainly I observed how Colette helped her visitors rediscover the meaning and purpose of their lives. Along with a cup of herbal tea, a mixture of rose petals and jasmine from her own tree, there was a sense of deep spiritual companionship. Colette learned about the outer world from her guests, the world of travel, of scientific research, of contemporary literature and art, of new trends in psychology, or current theological thought. In exchange, her visitors were offered opportunities to journey inward and, with a simple image or idea, they learned to shift perspective instantly. We never left the garden quite the same as when we entered!

I returned to Colette every summer until her death, sometimes returning during winter break, as well. I came because she was, most assuredly, my *mashpia'ah*, my spiritual teacher! I always refer to her as the third member of my *beit din* (religious court) the third individual who initiated me into the work of Jewish spiritual teaching and guidance. Certainly, Rabbi Shlomo Carlebach *z"l* and Rabbi Zalman Schachter-Shalomi were influential spiritual guides, and they have remained my lifelong companions. Each encouraged my learning, and each nurtured my creativity. They directed me to follow our holy teachings, guided by my own insight and intuition. But it was Colette's work that would become my own; her work colored by my own temperament and personality. She gave freely of her exercises, and she gave totally of her wisdom. Her example encouraged each of us who were her students to become, in her words, "authors of our own lives," or "our own authority."

All of this is background to the ways in which I have come to use Colette's work.

Creating Visibility for *Hashpa'ah* Offerings

Generally, private *hashpa'ah* sessions take place in our counseling office. The individuals I work with are best described as women in transition. I've also worked with the occasional couple. Since our office is located in a Catholic church, those who come for spiritual direction come from diverse backgrounds. They either hear about imagery work from those who have taken my classes, or they've taken classes themselves and want an opportunity to deepen their work, or they've been referred by a clergy person, or a therapist. Some come because they've received a health warning and have been advised to try imagery work for healing. I usually suggest that we work together for three sessions (about 1 1/2 hours per meeting) for three consecutive weeks. Then we re-evaluate and decide if further work is desired. This is based on Colette's observation that it takes three weeks to break a habitual pattern, and to begin to integrate a new behavior, belief, or attitude.

Although I really enjoy journeying with individuals, my primary work has been teaching imaginal exercises in small classes, similar to the group work that Colette conducted in her garden behind the blue gate. It is also important to remember that Colette called those who came to her students, rather than clients, since she believed that we are all here to learn; to gain greater facility and access to Spirit.

Classes have been offered at the University of Winnipeg within the Certificate in Theology program, as well as at synagogues, JCC's, various wellness institutes, and for retreat centers that cater to a broad spectrum of seekers. Generally courses are described in the following way:

> Imagery is a Jewish meditative practice for contemporary seekers. Exercises are based on biblical, midrashic, liturgical and kabbalistic sources. Students learn to "harness the imagination," to increase their ability to relax and release daily concerns, and to turn inward in order to discover the stillness and wisdom within. This work is based on the teachings of Jerusalem psychologist and spiritual teacher, Madame Colette Aboulker-Muscat, and it combines modern psychological insight with ancient mystical teachings. Classes are experiential in nature. No prior Jewish or meditation training is required.

Those in the midst of life changes, whether challenges or blessings, frequently choose to engage in spiritual work. Some may be considering conversion, or may have recently converted to Judaism. They come looking for the spiritual promise of Judaism; the experiences that their teachers and rabbis have assured them are at the heart of Jewish practice, which they have been unable to access in their newly chosen families or communities.

Since I also work with multi-faith groups, students may come in search of what they call their "roots." They seek a Jewish interpretation of the stories that were part of their spiritual formation; stories that still reside, vividly, in their imaginations. They want to know about prayer, about the psalms, about what it is that Jesus might have experienced as a Jew. They are curious about Jewish wisdom, but they are not looking for a new religion, only for a sense of the origins of their own. Often what is most desired is an articulation of Judaism's encounter with the One.

Imagery exercises can awaken that sense of encounter, often in rapid and immediate ways. With guidance, the exercises (some crafted by Colette, others inspired by her technique) permit an individual to cultivate that connection and to return to it in the midst of daily living. A *mashpia* can deepen experiences by attending to the language, visual cues, or felt sensations that have provoked this shift in consciousness. The *mashpia* can then offer a Jewish spiritual context for the images that have been awakened by the exercise. I call this phenomenon "contextualizing awe."

Imagery classes meet for six weeks, each session lasting about two hours. The depth of shared spiritual experience creates a feeling of community, and groups continue to journey and meet together for years.

Recently I designed a local spiritual outreach program for one of the larger Conservative synagogues. Together with Rabbi Alan Green, I offer imagery and kabbalah courses to those who have expressed an interest in spirituality, but who are not (yet) comfortable in a synagogue setting. Classes are held in private homes. Experience leads me to believe that the mini-communities that evolve as a result of doing spiritual work together create a safe arena in which the group can begin exploring other Jewish spiritual practices together, including communal prayer and study. Naturally, individual *hashpa'ah* is a significant component of the outreach program. It is available to congregants and to synagogue staff, as well as to unaffiliated members of the community who seek companionship and support in discerning their own spiritual direction. As part of a team, the spiritual outreach person recognizes the need for reciprocal referrals between clergy and teachers.

Conducting an Imagery-based *Hashpa'ah* Session

Since this article is called "Let Her Own Works Praise Her" to honor the imagery techniques created or inspired by Colette, and written during the period of her fifth *yahrzeit* (the anniversary of her departure from earthly life), this paper concludes with sample exercises, student responses, and additional instructions or interventions that may be used. Student privacy has been respected.

We begin a session sitting in straight-backed chairs, feet on the ground, arms resting on thighs, diaphragm relaxed and moving freely. Students are invited to formulate a private *kavannah*—an intention which they set prior to the exercises, (much like turning a dial to a particular frequency). Some will jot down their *kavannot* (pl) for future reflection.

As in all spiritual work, simple breathing techniques are used. Students close their eyes, breathe out slowly, and inhale slow, shallow breaths. This is generally repeated three times in order to break habitual breathing patterns, and to alert the system to a new rhythm. Once the body and mind are in a receptive mode, a cleansing exercise is introduced.

In the Beginning

The following cleansing exercise that I created begins our sample session:

- Breathe out slowly 3 times. Hear the Hebrew word *b'reisheet*.
- Know that although it is translated as "in the beginning," our sages have suggested that it can also mean "with beginnings."
- Hear the word *b'reisheet* as a call to your own beginnings. What do you see, sense, know and feel in a world created with beginnings?

L: "I see the horizon; the start of a new day. I sense that I live between the sky and the earth. I feel myself touching the "hem of heaven." I imagine Frank Lloyd Wright's work, full of light."

D: "I see growth and learning; physical growth in my garden (and in my children). I feel personal growth."

JM: "I feel a jolt, like when two opposing forces mix... a sort of chemical reaction. On the one hand I have a sense of exhaustion (oh, no, not again), on the other excitement about new possibilities."

J: "I came in feeling gray. It is nice to be reminded of beginnings. I check in and I am suddenly feeling on the upside."

C: "I didn't see anything. I feel myself waiting."

G: "I see words, words, words. And then I remember how God creates the world over again each day. This is comforting to me."

This simple cleansing exercise has set the tone. Students have removed daily concerns, and they have turned inward.

I might then ask **L** what it feels like to touch the hem of heaven... re-entering her image for an instant, feeling the hem (she used the word "touch") and then holding the image and its message with open eyes.

In **D**'s case I might suggest that she identify what is growing for her, that she "see" this when she enters her image again. (She used "see" for the growth of others, but "felt" personal growth.)

JM's jolt is a wonderful, concrete sensation! She is surprised by her image (Colette called these "shocks". In this system, "shocks" are a way that body/mind/emotions and spirit are called to attention. The individual can then choose to reconfigure around the new image, idea, feeling or sensation. It is an opportunity for change. I might then invite her to consider how she will keep this awareness alive in her daily life.

This is also true for **G**. Now that she knows that God creates the world anew every day, now that she knows this from the inside, how does she choose to sustain this new awareness?

For **C** the challenge might be to hold the feeling of waiting... to live in the void or emptiness... to return to it welcoming what she feels is beginning to open for her.

And **J**, who has had a spontaneous mood shift - who moves upward, leaving grayness behind–she has discovered a useful tool. How will she use this image to "lift her spirits" at will, whenever this is needed in life?

As a teacher of Jewish spiritual awareness, I would then laminate the experiences to prayer, creating a new daily practice. For example *modah ani*–"I am grateful", which is a simple prayer that can be recited every morning. I would ask students to experiment with the prayer at the start of their day. I would encourage them to be aware (or mindful) of how reciting this helps them recall their own image of living in a world of beginnings. And, although some class members do not follow the Jewish path, I'd invite them to try the prayer in translation and to extract from it what is helpful. Or I might encourage them to find a prayer, (or a psalm or a song) which they can use daily to help keep their inner work conscious.

In Your Light

The next exercise draws on an image from Psalm 36:9, which reads "*b'orkha nireh or*, in your light we see light."

- It is an exercise intended to provide students with the opportunity for a unitive experience, an instant when connection with Source is possible.
- Frequently we have experiences like these spontaneously, in the natural world or when we hear music or see great beauty, but imagery exercises help us transcend ordinary consciousness, at will.
- When we return to our images and harness their power we remember how intimately connected to Spirit we really are.
- For Colette, remembering is the key to all spiritual progress.
- Re-membering ourselves, putting our selves together in a new way, remembering who we are and what we are created to become is the task of imaginal work.

The exercise begins again by breathing out slowly, 3 times.

- Imagine yourself as a being of crystal.
- Hear the words "*b'orkha nireh or*... In Your Light 'I' See Light."
- What do you see, sense, feel and understand as you listen to the words of the psalm?

W: "I see myself with my daughter. She becomes transparent and the light is refracted through her. I experience (and there simply is no other way to say this) revelation!"

T: "I see a globe of light and a silhouette inside. I am inside the light and the light is inside me. I feel a sense wonder and reassurance."

KS: "I am in the presence of enlightened teachers and I am receiving new ideas that enlighten me. I am enlightened and enlivened."

R: "In Your light I AM light. There is a blurring of seeing and being."

KM: "The light is coming from inside, at first. It is like stage lights, and the light adds color to the outside. Then it becomes Northern Lights, and I am surrounded by the light."

P: "I exhale darkness and inhale light that becomes sunlight. I feel bright. I go inside the house and I blend with man made light. Suddenly the contrast is so great. I see a tunnel and I see that there is light at the end of the tunnel."

It would be irreverent to comment on, or evaluate these responses. They are an internal shorthand...a code...tiny nuggets of truth. They are revelatory experiences as powerful as any that have been recounted by the mystics of old. The responsibility of the *mashpia*, in this instance, is to witness, to silently affirm the power of the encounter and to help the student return to waking reality enriched by the experience. It may be helpful to concretize the image, and encourage the student to draw or create a collage using the images of what that they have seen or sensed or felt. Some may select symbols of what they have learned from the experience, such as a globe, a crystal, a photo of teachers or wise ones they have known. The task is, as Colette continually reminded us, to re-member; to hold the image, to keep it alive and to draw upon it when we loose our way or forget our purpose. In truth, images have the power to alter lives.

Recommended Reading

Simcha H. Benyosef, *Empowered To Heal: Therapeutic Visualizations Drawn for the Lunar Months*, Devorah Press: 2008

Gerald Epstein, *Healing Visualizations*, Bantam Books, 1989

    Climbing Jacob's Ladder, ACMI Press, 1999

    Healing Into Immortality, Bantam Books, 1994

    Kabbalah for Inner Peace, ACMI Press, 2008

Carol Rose, "Harnessing The Imagination" in *SPIDER WOMEN: An Anthology of Creativity & Healing*, J. Gordon Shillingford, 1999

Catherine Shainberg, *Kabbalah & Dreaming*, Inner Traditions, 2005

Kabbalistic Wisdom and Meditation as a Foundation for Jewish Spiritual Therapy and Direction
by Melinda (Mindy) Ribner

Melinda (Mindy) Ribner is a spiritual psychotherapist (LCSW) in private practice using meditation and Judaism as part of her treatment with clients. Ordained as a *mashpi'ah* and *maggidah* by Rabbi Shlomo Carlebach, *z"l* (of blessed memory) and Rabbi Zalman Schachter-Shalomi, she is also a teacher of Jewish meditation. The founder of Beit Miriam, she is also author of *Everyday Kabbalah, New Age Judaism, Kabbalah Month by Month* and the award winning *The Secret Legacy of Biblical Women: Revealing the Divine Feminine.* www.kabbalahofheheart.com.

Professionalism requires a therapist to be value free, neutral, and of course not an advocate of belief in any religion. Yet I know from my own life that it is opening to the experience of God that healed and heals, and transforms me. Many years after social work graduate school, and after being a Jewish meditation teacher for some time as well, I started my own private practice and began to help people access and strengthen their relationship and experience of God, especially when they could not access this soul dimension within themselves.

My clients generally are open to Judaism, but are not necessarily "believers." Most of them have spent several years in psychoanalysis and other traditional talk therapies prior to working with me. They have been Buddhist or Hindu Jews, non-religious Jews, converts, atheists, angry and rebellious Jews, observant Jews and even non-Jews. Their concepts of God have very often been tainted by their negative experiences of Judaism in childhood as well as by their relationships with their parents, who were their first representatives of God. If a person grew up with inconsistent, ambivalent, or critical parenting, it might be hard for them to believe in a god they can trust. Toxic parent-onto-God projections make it difficult for them to turn to God for support.

My work as a therapist incorporates my knowledge and experience of meditation, prayer, Torah and kabbalah, as well as body-centered and transpersonal psychotherapies. I comfortably wear many different hats with my clients: therapist, Torah educator, meditation teacher, spiritual guide, friend and even rabbi (though I am not a rabbi).

Being a therapist is part of my spiritual calling and spiritual practice. My clients know this and may even choose to come to me for this very reason. It is powerfully centering to pray and meditate in preparation before each session, and often during the session with the client. When working with a client, I imagine myself as God's representative. Love is the foundation for my work. Underlying all the various techniques that I may employ in my practice, my basic and primary commitment is to love the person who is coming to me for therapy, and to help them to love themselves and others.

Serving as a therapist can be viewed a little like being a priest of ancient times privileged to enter into the Holy of Holies of the Holy Temple. In many ways, in our modern times, the therapy room today is a place of revelation, one of the most holy and sacred places available to many people. It is here that people share their secrets, their deepest feelings, their fears, resistances, their hopes, their dreams, and their fantasies. It is here that they discover and experience aspects of themselves they did not or could not previously acknowledge.

As a spiritual kabbalistic therapist I symbolically and often literally hold the hand of the client as he or she enters into the deepest places, the most inner chambers, to experience the most holy, the most hidden, the most real, the most beautiful, and the most wounded and dark places within the human soul. Through the therapeutic process, the hold of the *yetzer ha-rah* (the negative inclination), the judgmental inner inclination, is released and the hidden sparks of the holy soul are redeemed. In opening to the truth of our inner essence, we open to the Inner Essence of Reality, which is what we call God and we become vessels able to receive greater love and joy than we had previously allowed.

Inherent in my work is the belief that God is the healer. A person cannot heal with the power of his/her mind alone. Understanding does not equal transformation. Though it may be healing and interesting to understand and find some justification for one's suffering, it alone does not change a person in the ways that s/he wants. To effect real change, we need to go beyond the mind, because the mind cannot understand or heal the spirit or soul. Using the mind to solve the problems of the soul may be compared to using a bicycle to fly to the moon. The bicycle may have been adequate to travel in Freud's time, but now in this accelerated time of science, technology and social change, we need technologies that are more potent.

Through various breathing techniques and guided meditation on verses of prayer and Jewish concepts, clients access their own souls and receive Divine support. They learn how to let go, surrender and allow God to be present in their lives. The concepts and images of God that they had prior to therapy are replaced with a new, more mature and deeper experience of God as well as themselves. The practice of meditation enables clients to go beyond the analytical mind of trying to figure life out to be able to listen to the needs and wisdom of their inner souls.

Opening with Attunement

Helping people to breathe and attune to their body is the first thing that I do in sessions. It is simple, but profound and powerful. Our life begins and ends with the breath. We say in the morning prayers in the *siddur* (prayer book): "The soul You placed within me is pure, You created, You fashioned it, You breathed it into me." The quality of our lives is related to how we breathe. It is through the breath, and the spaces between the breaths, that we glimpse and touch our soul.

Most people who come to therapy breathe rapidly, shallowly and unevenly. People can talk and talk about their problems, their pain, their fears, but when they slow down to breathe and breathe deeply, they can begin to feel and be present with themselves in a deeper more loving and accepting way. That presence on their part begins the healing process. The use of meditation along with breathing practices is a particularly effective treatment modality for people who are verbal and analytical, and who use words in therapy to avoid internal expression of feelings.

In addition to the one-hour experiential counseling session, it is valuable to give clients specific meditative, prayer, affirmations and bio-energetic practices as homework between sessions that is individually tailored to them. Some of my clients are encouraged to avail themselves of additional spiritual strength and support by taking on certain mitzvot (Jewish spiritual practices), such as putting on tefillin (prayer boxes worn with straps to facilitate meditation), wearing a *tallis* (the Jewish prayer shawl), lighting *Shabbat* (Sabbath) candles, and also keeping *Shabbat* on some level, etc. Over time, they begin to understand that it is through nurturing their own souls, strengthening and deepening their relationship with God that they will find the healing and transformation that they seek.

Though everyone can benefit from having a spiritual guide, those who come for therapy and stay in treatment generally do so because they are in great psychic pain. They are often experiencing intense anxiety, panic, phobias, addictive behaviors, depression, a terminal illness, extreme isolation, loneliness or marital instability. As they introduce their reasons for coming to therapy, pay attention to what they say, how they say it, and also how they are breathing as they speak. So much can be learned by paying attention to how people breathe. From there we move to other important psycho-spiritual, skills, especially meditative, to secure attunement to current body sensations and feelings, as well as learning to observe repetitive thoughts without judgment.

Healing Early Wounding

An important challenge for the spiritual psychotherapist is not simply to appeal to the reasoning powers of the person, nor solely to connect him or her spiritually to Judaism, but also to heal the early wounding and the defenses that s/he developed to protect against the tremendous vulnerability and precariousness of childhood. Too often the ego defenses that people develop in childhood continue to run their lives as adults even though they are self-defeating, inappropriate and illogical for their current life circumstances.

In the beginning of therapy much of my work is to teach people how to re-parent themselves, how to be the loving parent to themselves by first modeling to them unconditional love, honest reflection and complete acceptance. The initial step is to help my clients to identify, express and accept the negative emotions that are overwhelming or paralyzing to them that have their source in the wounded child within themselves.

Helping them to feel compassion for this part of themselves rather than the usual self-criticism, guilt, or fear is an important component of healing and transformation. It is helpful to know when we are feeling overwhelmed that we are no longer the three or five year old even though that part of ourselves, the inner child, cannot be simply dismissed through denial, or rationalization.

For example, Susan, a woman in her third year of residency as a resident in pediatric medicine, came to me many years ago, suffering anxiety attacks of such severity that the successful completion of her residency was in jeopardy. When she was in the pediatric intensive care unit, she would identify with the critically ill infants to the extent that she would cry uncontrollably and become distraught and so extremely anxious that she could not function effectively as a doctor. Because of her unusual sensitivity, she could not be a real team player on the unit and she felt estranged and persecuted by the other doctors and interns. She was even hospitalized by the medical staff for this condition. A friend referred her to me, after her hospitalization.

Upon first meeting Susan, I was surprised by how petite and frail she was. With a childish body, looking quite pale and malnourished, her shoulders were caved in, her head bowed; she looked as if she would fall down if you blew at her. Susan surely did not look like doctor material. Inwardly, I wondered how such a person got through medical school and the first two years of residency. As Susan began to share in the beginning of our first session about all the problems she experienced at work, all the ways in which she had been mistreated, all the symptoms of her anxiety, I knew that our hour of time together would soon be over and she would not have learned anything to help herself. I did not want to waste her time or mine. I wanted to give Susan real tools to effect an immediate change within her even during our first session.

Helping her to manage her anxiety through meditation, prayer, and visualization was my initial focus in treatment with her. I had Susan lie down on the floor and simply guided her lovingly in deep breathing. She literally had to learn how to breathe. It was actually quite hard for her to take a deep breath. Like so many people, she was so disconnected from her body that she had to be reconnected and grounded through the breath and meditation. Initially, there were areas in her body that she could not even contact and there was pain and tension in other areas that she was previously not aware of before she learned to breathe deeply. The body talks to us in the form of sensations and it is important that we decode its message to us. As she learned to breathe correctly and experience herself in her body, she also learned how to be with feelings in her body with God's help rather than defend against them with anxiety or numbness.

Susan's initial symptom was anxiety. Anxiety, I have found, is interestingly enough often a cover-up for earlier and deeper feelings of the child within. Through extended counseling, Susan learned how to honor and be compassionate with that frightened and wounded child within her and she also gained the capacity to choose when her child could be present and when she as an adult had to be present. She understood quite clearly that the five year old child within her could not be the doctor in the emergency ward. During those times of being a doctor, she learned how to connect to a higher part of herself, and draw strength from her relationship with God, while still honoring and loving the child within. Though this woman was not a Jew by birth, she was very spiritual and connected to Judaism and found comfort and strength from Jewish practice. She, on her own, took on the practice of praying from a Jewish prayer book daily as well as meditating in prescribed ways. Over the years of treatment, she was successful in completing her residency, got married, and established a general medical practice of her own.

Further Integration of Meditation into Treatment

In using meditation as a part of treatment, the therapist employing meditation must know when to use meditation to help the client to experience a transcendent state of consciousness and when to use meditation as a tool to help the client access the feelings within, to release and transform them. These are very different experiences. Many people use meditation and prayer as a form of medication to repress or deny feelings. Meditation may offer temporary relief but if used exclusively in this way, it will not help in ego functioning. For example, a person may feel himself filled with negative thoughts, self-criticism, feelings of unworthiness or shame and the constant repetition of these thoughts makes him feel depressed. He may use meditation as a way of replacing the negative chatter of the mind with positive thoughts, such as affirmations, prayer, or even the simply watching of the breath. Though he may experience some relief from anxiety or depression from this practice, it is usually not sufficient for transformation because the deep feelings within the heart and soul of the person remain buried, unheard and unacknowledged.

This was very clear in my work with Lillian, offered now as an example of the use of meditation as a way into the release and expression of feelings. Lillian complained of extreme fatigue in her position as a chaplain. It was enjoyable and comforting for Lillian to meditate, to pray, to connect with her soul and experience herself outside of her body, but these practices alone would not be healing for her. To help Lillian, I had to guide her to feel the feelings that were underneath the presenting symptom of fatigue. "It takes a lot of energy to cover up feelings," I told her. "This is what is tiring you out so much." Lillian, like Susan and so many of us, was not connected to her feelings or to her body. It took much encouragement and gentle guidance to facilitate her access to her feelings. I always tell my clients, "It is safe to feel your feelings," since most people in therapy received messages to the contrary when they were younger. With Lillian, the fatigue was a cover-up for anger so I guided her to feel what was there for her while in a meditative and somewhat altered state.

Underneath the anger was a deeper feeling of sadness. As I encouraged her to stay with these feelings and express them, she cried, "I am not being heard. I have no voice." She learned that the fatigue she was experiencing at work was a cover-up for the anger and sadness of feeling that she was not being listened to by her supervisor and colleagues. This was a trigger of deep early childhood wounding where she also did not feel heard.

As she made contact with her inner child who did not feel heard, who did not have a voice, she was initially critical of herself, feeling that her opinions or needs were not worthy of the attention of others. She hated that she had this deep need to be heard. This kind of self-criticism is also quite common, unfortunately. People often identify with the ego defense (*yetzer ha-rah*) and are their own worst critic, taskmaster and even abuser.

As she was guided deeper into her feelings, and given permission to feel her vulnerability, she contacted the deep need that is within the inner child of each of us. She let her inner child have a voice and express what she needed. "I want to be cared for, I want to be loved," she cried in a child-like voice. "Does little Lillian have the attention of her parents?" I asked her. She replied, "Nobody's around."

Most of my clients will say something similar. We all have a need to be unconditionally loved, honored, heard and cared for. This is inherent to who we are as human beings, yet for many of us these basic needs for love and attentiveness were never adequately or completely met. For many of my clients, the vulnerability of childhood was magnified by a divorce, an emotionally volatile parent, another parent who was not so present or who even left the home, a disabling illness or even the death of a parent. Children may secretly or even unconsciously blame themselves for their parents' unhappiness or departure. Intellectually as adults, we know and understand that we are not responsible for our parents, but knowing something emotionally is something totally different from knowing it intellectually. Our ego defenses come to protect us from the lack of love, safety and even feelings of terror of abandonment or fears of annihilation that we felt as infants and young children. When we can safely feel those feelings in the therapeutic context, the defense is no longer needed and there is now freedom to choose how to respond to life rather than react from fear or guilt.

When I asked Lillian how she felt about her parents not being available to her as a child, she contacted feelings of anger, but she cried that she would die if she expressed anger. She explained that her mother, a Holocaust survivor, was always angry and she grew up terrified of speaking to her. Her father, also a survivor, was a weak passive man who offered her and her siblings little protection from the rage and angry outbursts of her mother. Emotional orphans, she and her siblings parented each other. As a child, she would pray, "If only I could run away, I would take my sisters and brothers, but there is no hope and no one to help us." She never expressed any anger to her mother as a child or even as an adult. She felt that her mother was so emotionally broken that it would not have made a difference. Furthermore, she felt even guilty saying bad things about her mother. Her mother's emotional state was a family secret.

In subsequent therapy sessions, Lillian was able to express her feelings, and even forgive her mother. This deep feeling release work in therapy restored her energy and enabled her to be present and appropriate with her supervisor, colleagues and friends.

Interestingly enough, Lillian had been raised Jewishly observant as a child. Part of her rebellion was to separate herself from her Jewish practice and she even married a non-Jew. During the therapy, she made a commitment to return to Jewish observance and share this with her loving and supportive husband. The two case examples of Susan and Lillian provide a taste of the use of meditation as a treatment modality.

My work with clients also draws on the themes within Jewish holidays, the kabbalistic energies of the months, and even specific Torah portions. The Bible is full of stories, rituals and motifs outlining the path of personal transformation for people of all eras that I have adapted as therapeutic interventions. For example, the Jewish people's journey out of the bondage of Egypt is an enactment of the universal journey to freedom and liberation that every person in and out of therapy can relate to. The Hebrew word for Egypt is *mitzrayim*, which kabbalistically means "narrow constraints," and represents all psychological, emotional, physical, and spiritual boundaries and constraints. The journey out of Egypt to the Holy Land may be viewed as the therapeutic process of freeing oneself from one's internal and external constraints to a life of great authenticity, inner wholeness-physical, emotional, mental and spiritual- as symbolized by the Holy Land.

Prior to therapy, Rachel was a very harsh critic of herself, having spent most of her adult life on anti-depressive medication. Although she is beautiful, brilliant, witty, and a real joy to be with, she constantly complained that she didn't earn enough money, she was not passionate about her work, she didn't read enough, and basically felt that she was simply "not enough." Rachel constantly experienced herself in comparison to how she imagined others experience her. I call this tendency, "living from the outside in." Although people often gave her much positive feedback, she did not believe it and could not accept it. So many people with negative self-esteem and little sense of self have difficulty accepting and absorbing the positive feedback they receive from others.

As much as Rachel wanted to change and free herself from this inner critic, she was so identified with it that she mistook it for her true self. The idea of letting this critic go was frightening. "If I let go of this inner critic, who would I be?" She felt she needed the inner critic to keep her alive. Like a taskmaster, she believed that it was this critical judgmental part of her that enabled her to function. A Type A personality, she was constantly busy doing many things, rarely giving herself time to rest and relax. Without this harsh critic, she confided, "I would be a blob, a couch potato."

"There is another way to be in the world," I told her. "You can be creative and productive without the inner critic and that is what we will discover through meditation." If she could relinquish the hold that the harsh critic had on her, she could actually recover and experience her true self and gain the capacity to be truly creative.

In one session Rachel was guided through a powerful visualization of leaving Egypt to wander in the desert prior to entering the Holy Land. As I guided her in this journey, Rachel reported all the feelings she was experiencing. My presence provided a safe container for Rachel to stay with and release the feelings that arose for her. The image of wandering in the desert was for Rachel, and is for everyone, a powerful invitation to find true inner order, to be in the "not knowing," not judging, not comparing, and listen to one's inner guidance.

There was considerable fear on Rachel's part. Even though this experience was only occurring on a psychic and soul level, it felt very real and exciting as if it were really happening. In the quiet of this desert meditation with nothing to hold onto, Rachel experienced the aloneness that she had feared and found that it was actually exhilarating and liberating. During the entire journey, Rachel was guided to turn inward to do the deep inner listening, to cultivate faith and trust and to go forward. Though I was guiding her the whole time, she had to be with herself in a way that she never had been before.

As a result of this meditation and all the intense work she did in therapy, Rachel gained a freedom and joy to be herself in the way that she always wanted. She began dating and entered into a serious relationship with a man. In previous relationships, she felt inadequate, not enough, afraid to reveal her true self, afraid to commit or be intimate; now she was able to be present and loving. Several women I have worked with were able to go on to marry and have good marriages because they did this deep inner healing transformational work prior to marriage.

Working with Couples, Sexuality and Intimacy

In recent years, I have offered workshops titled Kabbalah of Intimacy and Kabbalah of the Feminine and have applied my knowledge from kabbalah about the nature of masculinity and femininity in much of my private practice, particularly with clients who are married. Most of the married people who come to me for therapy are having problems in the sexual arena of their marriage. They either are not having sexual relations or not fully enjoying them. It is preferable to work with both people simultaneously, though therapy has been helpful when only one spouse has been in therapy.

Most of my clients, whether as individuals and couples, have a goal of improving their relationship with their spouse. If they have not identified improving their sexual relationship as a goal, I may encourage them to make that a goal as well. Even today in our time of sexual permissiveness, some of my clients feel guilt and fear around their sexuality. According to the Ramban, Nachmanides, the bedroom in Judaism is considered the Holy of Holies. It is a mitzvah to have sexual relations on *Shabbat* and holidays. Judaism may be the only religion that affirms that sexual relations in marriage bring a person to a higher state of holiness than abstinence. The sexual relationship is the most intimate, holy and important foundation for the marriage. In my work with couples, it is often necessary to rekindle sexual attraction for the couple by restoring the inherent polarity in their relationship with each other.

Many of us today in our post-feminist world need to relearn what it is to be masculine and what it is to be feminine. Kabbalah and Judaism in general offer us important guidance that is traditional and yet still relevant to modern people today. Generally speaking, the feminine energy, *nukva* (*Shekhinah*) in kabbalah, is the energy of receptivity and the masculine energy, *zer anpin* (*ha-Kodesh Barekhu*) is one of bestowal. Without a giver, there can be no receiver. And vice versa, without a receiver, there can be no giving. The feminine (vessel) needs the masculine (light) and vice versa. Men and women contain both masculine and feminine energies within them. Each of us may demonstrate the feminine in one aspect of our life and demonstrate the masculine in another. It may appear that the masculine energy is higher than the feminine in this perspective; it is important to emphasize that the feminine energy is not passive; the feminine actually arouses, limits, and shapes the influx of Divine blessing coming from above. Without the feminine to enliven the masculine, the masculine would be dormant.

As a rule, women who are primarily embodying the feminine energy in the relationship need to learn better how to become a vessel, how to be receptive, how to arouse, how to beautify, how to ask for what they need lovingly, how to surrender, and how to trust. As Marion Woodman states in her book, *Conscious Femininity*, "To receive a penis takes trust and surrender." By radiating her love and the feminine energy of receptivity, the woman stimulates and attracts the man to give to her. When a woman appreciates and honors her husband, he is empowered, happy and wants to give to her. Most of the married women in my practice were wounded in childhood and have issues of trust that make it difficult to trust their husbands. They tend to engage in critical, judgmental, controlling and withholding behaviors towards their husbands that create distance rather than the intimacy they really want. My work focuses on helping them to learn to trust, love and honor themselves. When the woman can take responsibility for her own issues with trust, and not blame her husband, the healing has started and the relationship improves.

For several women in my practice who became more observant than their husbands and felt that there is a rift in the marriage because of that difference, I developed the strategy that I call the "*Shabbos* Seduction Program" that has successfully uplifted their husbands' level of Jewish observance as well as improved the quality of sexual intimacy at the same time.

Men, on the other hand, represent the light, according to kabbalah, and they need to learn how to give, how to shine, how to expand, and how to show leadership. In learning how to demonstrate the power of *hesed* (lovingkindness), the man will have to contact, develop and strengthen his inner warrior to overcome feelings of rejection so he can provide vision and leadership. Many men in my private practice often acknowledge that they sometimes relate to their wives as mother surrogates. They try hard to please their wives, "to be good enough" but they also become resentful and act in passive/aggressive ways to her as well.

Within the therapeutic context, all my male clients are given an arsenal of spiritual tools including traditional ones like tefillin and prayer as well as specific meditative practices to draw down the light from above to reclaim their masculine power and become powerful givers and warriors for love. When a man experiences his strength, his direct connection to *HaShem*, he becomes masterful and able to penetrate his wife with his consciousness and love. He gains his own self respect and that of his wife's as well.

When the sexual polarity between the couple is restored through kabbalistic teachings, meditations, and exercises they practice with each other, it has been frequently reported that sexual intimacy is better than it ever was, even in the early days of marriage. When sexual intimacy is restored, the couple may perform the greatest unification of *ha-Kodesh Borekhu* (the Divine Masculine) and the *Shekhinah* (the Divine Feminine). Marital relations, according to Nachmanides, bring wholeness and healing not only to the couple, but radiate blessings and healing to the world.

Recommended Reading

David A. Cooper, *The Handbook of Jewish Meditation Practices: A Guide for Enriching the Sabbath and Other Days of Your Life, 2nd. Ed.,* Jewish Lights Publishing, 2000

Avram Davis, *Meditation from the Heart of Judaism: Today's Teachers Share Their Practices, Techniques and Faith,* Jewish Lights Publishing, 1999

Estelle Frankel, *Sacred Therapy: Jewish Spiritual Teachings on Emotional Healing and Inner Wholeness,* Shambhala, 2004

Nan Fink Gefen, *Discovering Jewish Meditation: Instruction & Guidance for Learning an Ancient Spiritual Practice,* Jewish Lights Publishing, 1999

Shefa Gold, *Torah Journeys: The Inner Path to the Promised Land,* Ben Yehudah Press, 2006

Aryeh Kaplan, *Jewish Meditation: A Practical Guide,* Schocken Books, 1995

> *Meditation and the Bible,* Weiser Books, 1998

> *Meditation and Kabbalah,* Weiser Books, 1989

> *Inner Space: Introduction to Kabbalah, Meditation and Prophecy,* Moznaim Publishing Company, 1990

Melinda Ribner, *Everyday Kabbalah: A Practical Guide to Jewish Meditation, Healing and Personal Growth,* Carol Publishing, 2000

> *New Age Judaism: Ancient Wisdom for the Modern World,* Health Communications Incorporated, 2000

> *Kabbalah Month by Month: A Year of Spiritual Practice and Personal Transformation,* Wiley Publishing, 2002

Jeff Roth, *Jewish Meditation Practices for Everyday Life: Awakening Your Heart, Connecting With God,* Jewish Lights Publishing, 2009

Additional Website(s):

http://www.inner.org

http://www.awakenedheartproject.org/

http://reclaimingjudaism.org/meditation.htm

Part II

Hashpa'ah
in the Cycle of Life and Death

Opening the Dialogue with God
in *B'nai Mitzvah* Preparation
by Hanna Tiferet Siegel

Rabbi Hanna Tiferet Siegel has been talking to God since the age of three. She has recorded eight albums of original liturgical music. In 1977, Hanna co-founded Or *Shalom*, a Jewish Renewal Synagogue in Vancouver, BC. In 1982, she was the first woman to receive the title, "*Eshet Chazon*"/Woman of Vision and Midwife of the Soul. She is currently the rabbi of B'nai Or of Boston and a member of the *mashpia* faculty for the Aleph Ordination Programs. www.HannaTiferet.com

An anxious pre-teen enters tentatively into my home for the first day of *b'nai* mitzvah training. We begin by chatting to learn the basics about each other. Listed below are some of the questions I ask and some of the responses I receive.

"What's your name in English and Hebrew?"
"Tell me about your family. Do you have brothers and sisters?"
"Do you have two parents? What is their work? Are your grandparents living?"
"Where do you go to school?"
"What are your favorite subjects and activities?"
"When and where were you born?"
"Would you like to find out your Hebrew birthday and birth *parasha*?" (weekly reading from Torah)
Yes.
"What is the scheduled date of your bar/bat mitzvah?"
"What is the Torah portion of that week?" I don't know.
"Have you attended other *b'nai mitzvah* ceremonies?" Yes.
"When and where was that?"
It was my cousin's bar mitzvah.
"How was it for you?"
I didn't understand what was going on.
"What do you think of synagogue services?"
They're boring.
"How's your Hebrew?"
Not so good. I feel really stupid in Hebrew school.
"What does bar/bat mitzvah mean to you?"

Not much yet except a lot of work with presents at the end for my reward.

"Is this something that you want to do?"

No, my parents expect me to do this.

Or, Yes, and my parents can't understand why.

I listen very carefully, noticing how the child speaks and relates. Then I share some aspects of the story of my own Jewish journey and why I have found that preparing for bar/bat mitzvah is an important moment in one's life. I confirm that this will be a year of intense study and that the rewards will be far greater than s/he could ever imagine.

As a *b'nai mitzvah* tutor, I consider myself a "personal spiritual trainer." Amazing breakthroughs in learning and comprehension can take place in this one-on-one relationship. It has been my joy and responsibility to encourage the uniqueness of each student and to nurture his/her soul. I have been called upon to teach a wide variety of children. Some excel in school and social skills while others are challenged by ADD, ADHD, dyslexia, Asperger syndrome, and depression. I have taught children who are angry, distracted, resistant, nervous, shy, and curious. And with each one, I have found that the assignment is the same - to establish trust and then open the heart, open the mind, and open the gateway to the soul.

For many years, I taught in communities of disenfranchised and assimilated Jews. I prepared my students with basic synagogue skills, each one according to his or her ability, but there was something lacking. It was too predictable. I sought a different model. It was clear to me that the power of the bar/bat mitzvah passage could last a lifetime if it were a meaningful experience for the student. I knew that our brief time of study together had to be relevant and creatively grounded in tradition. I saw it as a precious opportunity, when the window of wonder was still open for these children-becoming-adults.

As I looked at the traditional framework of the liturgy, I felt that it was important for the students to explore and understand the words of the *Shema* (the prayer that expresses the Oneness of God and our relationship with God). As the essential message of Jewish religious practice, it holds within it endless mysteries and countless interpretations. By studying the three paragraphs of the *Shema* and also the accompanying *Barukh Shem* verse, I sensed that we could tap into the student's personal theology and philosophy of life and bring the relevance of these ancient words alive today. Although the students weren't necessarily able to express the depth of their wisdom in written form, they could speak it. As a result of that realization, I developed a dialogical process in which I asked questions of them and they were able to free-associate and tell their stories, while I wrote them down.

At first there is often a stiffness and resistance because they are straining their brains to come up with the right answer. But once they settle into a level of trust in me, the process, and their own inner wisdom, the heart opens and their insights flow freely. I also have to trust the student to find the truth within him or herself and be courageous enough to express it. Embarrassment is a common condition of that age and I want to reassure the student that a revelation of his or her true feelings and insights is part of becoming a bar/bat mitzvah. After all, how can we take on the responsibilities of a tradition if we do not understand our personal relationship to it?

I divide the *Shema* into five sections. Each part has specific questions which arise from the nature of the words. That is the starting place, but where it goes, no one knows. That is the excitement of the spiritual journey. I want to be surprised by what the students uncover for themselves as they go to new places of personal discovery in the telling of their own story. The goal is to find the entryway into the child's experience and then let the telling begin. The response is not always positive. I do my best to leave room for questioning, cynicism, resistance, and even anger. It is my hope that we can engage in a dialogue that allows them to grow up in their relation to God and the tradition as they wrestle with its quintessential teachings.

Shema – Listen

We begin by looking at the six words of the *Shema* and try to translate them. It's not an easy task. What are these words trying to say? What does it mean to listen? We talk about the custom of covering one's eyes while saying the *Shema*, so that one can truly listen. What are we listening for? To whom are we listening?

As we move on to the second word, *Yisrael*, we ask, who is Israel? It can mean the people, the land, and the literal translation of "God-wrestler." We talk about the biblical story of Jacob who wrestled with an angel and received his spirit name of *Yisrael*. Translating *Yisrael* as "God-wrestler" also allows us to read this verse in a more universal way, since most people we know are searching for the meaning of life and are engaged in a relationship to a power greater than themselves.

Is our God Jewish, or is there one God who manifests in many different ways for all of creation? We look at the three consecutive God words - *YHVH Eloheynu YHVH* - and talk about the transcendent qualities of God and the immanence of God. We discuss compassion and karma (cause and effect), and the idea that the great power of God is also personal for each and every one of us.

The last word, *ekhad*, evokes a lot of questions. There are many different ways to understand the meaning of "one"—alone, unique, above in heaven, a part of everything. This is an interpretation that evolves as we, as humans, evolve, from childhood to adulthood, and through every new wave of conscious awareness. We look at the enlarged Hebrew letter *ayin* in the word *shemA* as well as the enlarged dalet of *ekhaD* that together spell *AyD*/witness and discuss what it means to be witnesses to something that we cannot see.

After defining and discussing the nature of these words and coming up with our own translation, we begin to talk about God in his/her life. Who is God for you? We talk about God's gender and all the names we have for God in Judaism. Have you ever felt or experienced God in your life? Maybe you don't call it God, but you feel a presence, or a tingling in your spine. Have you ever prayed to God? What do you pray for? When do you pray? Can you pray in the synagogue? Why or why not? Can you pray to God in nature? This is when the storytelling begins. It's often difficult to talk about God if the student's family is not spiritually attuned, but it is my belief that each of us has a relationship with God. Sometimes children will relate a story of a time they prayed to God to pass a test or to win a sports game. Sometimes they have experienced an illness in the family, or a death. Some are more articulate than others, but each one has a story. Here are some examples of the inner wisdom that they are able to articulate as a result of our dialogue.

Hana

"There have been times when I wasn't so sure God existed and I felt that people made him up because they wanted to feel like they had a Higher Power. I used to think that God made the world a happy place where people liked each other. But there are wars and that's because people don't like each other. Also, I thought people he made were supposed to have long, happy lives. But good people, like Mark, have died because of diseases, because of war, and because of accidents. They are too young and deprived of a good life that could have happened.

"People say God is everywhere, but I'm not quite sure if I believe them. If God was everywhere, he'd control what we say and how we act. He'd be inside of us. If he did control everything, then wouldn't there be peace in the world? Wouldn't bad people - murderers, thieves, etc., not exist? I think God doesn't want to control us. He wants to see how we manage on our own. God doesn't stop us from doing the wrong thing. We have to do that ourselves. But he's there in case we need him and that's why we pray to him. I think he's almost everything: flowers, rivers, trees, the winds. That's how we know he's beautiful. Nature is part of him. So, in a way, he does have a physical form, but we don't recognize him until he has passed us by."

Ben

"We say that God exists and God created us, but what if the big bang theory is true and God doesn't exist? What if nobody believed in God, would God still exist? Is God the essence of life, or does God depend on our believing in Him?

"There are so many ways of perceiving God and everyone says that they're doing something in the name of God, whether it be good or bad, but good or bad is an opinion. How can you believe in God when He doesn't intervene? We seem to be doing all the work. People have said that God is there, but where is He? What if the messiah can't come until it's peaceful enough for him to stay alive?

"To me, God is the idea that can bring peace. To me, God is the idea and feeling of inner peace. To me, God is the universal idea that there is a greater power that can help us. The way I experience God is when the people around me are kind and give off a feeling of love. They know you have your troubles and they have theirs. They know how to let you be, without trying to change you or make you feel bad. The only exception is your parents who have the right to make you feel bad for doing something wrong, so you'll feel guilty and you won't do it again.

"When someone is mean, they take away from your connection to God and they make you feel like you don't deserve to be there. I see God through other people because you can't see God. When others are around you, they show you the part of God that's in them and then you can see the piece that's in you. Everything you know and learn comes from someone else. That's why I experience God through other people."

Noah

"When I say the *Shema* at school in *minyan* (prayer services), I feel closer to God and I can communicate with Him in a special way. I feel like He can help me and when I'm talking to Him, nothing can go wrong. God definitely helped me when I was a baby. I was very sick and they thought I would die and then I got better. My twin brother wasn't quite as sick. My dad videotaped a lot of me in the hospital and it's very sad and emotional to see how I was, but it's amazing to see how far I've gotten.

"When I'm scared at night, I say the *Shema* to relax myself. Sometimes when I'm overwhelmed and I don't think I'll get all my work done, I know God will help me and He almost always does. He does make people suffer, but it usually turns out okay. And when it doesn't, it's usually for a good reason."

Matthew

"At home, when I'm alone, I sometimes ask myself what God is. Sometimes I don't even believe in God, but sometimes I ask God to help me when life is hard. I don't feel that anyone responds, but something hears me and knows and understands what I am feeling. God likes to be heard and so do we because we share the respect of listening and understanding each other.

"When my mom had cancer, I really hoped that nothing bad would happen to her. When I was alone, I would tell myself and God that she would be okay and not die. The night after she had the operation, I was scared. I was at home in bed, trying to go to sleep. Silently, I said to myself, 'Please God, don't let anything happen to her.' We went to visit her, and although friends assured me that she was going to be all right, I really couldn't believe it until I saw her and she told me herself. Another time I prayed was when the year

2000 began. My uncle is a pilot and he had to fly that night, so I prayed that he wouldn't crash and that I would be able to see him again.

"Thinking of God can help us feel more safe and comfortable. It helps to think of God because you say to yourself, 'Oh, there's God. Maybe He can make things better or just comfort me.' When we're talking to God or praying, we're really talking to everyone around us in our community. Sometimes I think of God in the goodness and helpfulness of human beings. Everything and everyone is part of God, so if the community is helping us, then God is helping us too."

Rachel

"*Shema* is an announcement reminding people that YHVH is our God. 'Listen, Everyone who wrestles with God, YHVH, the God of Being, is part of this Earth. YHVH is One with everything else and there is only One, even though there are so many things.'"

"Nature's kind of like God for me. There are a lot of things that aren't explained like, why are we the perfect distance from the sun so that we can live here on earth? Sometimes I pray, but not usually, at little times when I feel scared or sad or really happy. When something really good happens, I think of God.

"A lot of times, even when there's something bad, there's something good with it. When I was ten, my great aunt's funeral was on my birthday. All my aunts and uncles on her side came from around the country. It was really sad, but in the evening, we all went out to dinner for my birthday, which was fun because we are rarely all together. That was when I realized that every cloud has a silver lining. Sometimes people can bring kindness in a bad situation. When people help each other, it's like God is there."

Josh

"It's almost like I have two parts to me. One part is scientific and I don't believe in God at all. Everything has a scientific explanation. Love is just chemicals in the body. At the same time, I totally believe in God. I believe in seeing things from past lifetimes. I believe in asking God for help and sometimes He helps you along the way. It doesn't matter whether some guy made up the Torah and the Bible; it's just another way of connecting to God. I always have two perspectives on life. When you vote, you can either be a Republican or a Democrat. I'm like an Independent. I don't choose one side over the other. I always hold two different views at the same time.

"When I say the *Shema*, I feel like I'm a part of Israel. In that one moment of saying the *Shema*, we are taking in all the things that have happened to our people and accepting them. We are telling God that we are Israel too. It's not just Moses and the people who left Egypt who went through the Exodus. Even though we're not them, we feel their pain and happiness. This also includes the Holocaust and what happened to our ancestors there.

"People pray at the Western Wall in Jerusalem that those who suffered in the Holocaust have a good afterlife because they didn't deserve all that pain. Putting a letter in the Wall is like putting a letter in the canister at the Science Museum. It shoots up through the tubes that run along the ceiling, and you can send messages back and forth. With God, you don't actually have to write a letter. The words in your heart are enough to travel through the invisible gateway to God and He sends it back to you."

Barukh Shem – **Blessed Name**

The six words of the *Barukh Shem* are not found in the Torah, whereas all the other words of the three paragraphs are. Why was this verse inserted into the morning and evening prayer service? What does it add to the *Shema* and where does it come from? We learn several midrashim (pl, legends) regarding the origins of these words. There is one *midrash* that says that when Moses ascended to heaven to receive the Ten Commandments, these are the words that he heard the angels saying. From their vantage point, they were looking out and declaring the great glory of creation. Another *midrash* says that when Jacob was dying, his children gathered around his bed and declared their allegiance to his path of faith. They said, "*Shema Yisrael* (Jacob's other name) *YHVH Eloheynu YHVH Ekhad.*" And Jacob responded with surprise and gratitude, "*Barukh shem k'vod malkhuto l'olam va'ed.*"

We then begin the process of translating these words, which are somewhat vague. *Barukh* indicates blessing and *shem* refers to the name of God without saying it. *K'vod* is honor or glory and *malkhuto* is God's kingdom, which is this world and the way that God manifests in every part of it. *L'olam va'ed* means forever. The question is, how do you experience God in this world? Is there a place that you have been that had such awesome beauty that you felt God was there with you? Describe the details of that place — the sunlight, the air, the water, the trees, the birds, the snow, and the feelings inside of you. Sometimes the kids are awed by the perfection of nature, sometimes by the seasons, and sometimes by animals or birds. The most important thing is for them to connect an experience that they have had in the natural world with the creative presence of God. The *Shema* takes us to a private place of unification with the God of being and the *Barukh Shem* brings us into God's presence in every detail of the world. The *Barukh Shem* serves as a bridge to the *V'ahavta* ("and you will love").

Allison
"*Barukh Shem* is awareness of more than yourself. This verse says, not only do I love myself and God, but I have to love the rest of the earth and its creatures. If we don't think of each other, then it's just every person for him or herself and that doesn't seem right. The *Barukh Shem* is also about appreciating the beauty of this world and working to preserve it.

"One of the most moving and beautiful experiences I've ever had was when I went scuba diving with dolphins in Eilat during our trip to Israel a few years ago. Each person in the group was given an instructor to guide us. We strapped on our oxygen tanks and dove in. It was incredible to be "in" the water, to be still and have it move around me. The color of the water was aqua, so different from here in Massachusetts. And on the bottom, there was beautiful coral and fishes. We were in their home, observing their environment.

"The first dolphin I saw went by and didn't stop. We kept moving and another one came and I was hesitant to pet it. By the time I decided to reach out, it wasn't within my arm range anymore, but I still got to see it. I didn't want to scare the dolphin because I'm used to cats, and if you make a sudden movement, they run away. By the time I made up my mind, it was gone, but just the experience of seeing it was incredible.

Even if there weren't any dolphins, fish, or coral, just scuba diving would have been amazing. When we came out, the realization hit that I wasn't floating any more and I had an oxygen tank on that was really heavy, but I still had the feeling of being in the water. I felt so happy to observe and be a part of something so beautiful. The whole experience was breathtaking. Dolphins have had a special meaning to me since then."

Erica

"The *Barukh Shem* tells us to bless everything because everything was made by God and is holy. Being human is sometimes difficult, but when we stop to think about it, there is so much to appreciate. Through our senses we experience the wonders of the world. I am grateful to be able to see all the beauty of nature and all the things that human beings have made, like paintings, movies, and books. I am grateful to be able to hear peaceful birds chirping and school bands playing music; to taste delicious foods like butterscotch ice cream, fresh salads and watermelon; to smell the air outdoors after it rains, the sweet aroma of cookies and cakes from the bakery, and the fragrance of wild honeysuckle in the summertime. And I am grateful to be able to touch soft silk fabric, to pet furry animals like a bunny, to feel soft fluffy snow as it falls gently on my shoulders, and to be able to hug people and feel comfort and understanding without talking."

V'ahavta – You Will Love

How can you love God with all your heart, soul, and strength? Is this possible? It's a pretty tall order, especially if God isn't a part of your daily vocabulary. How can you be told to love someone if you don't even know him or her? Most kids don't feel connected to God in such a deep way, so I ask them what their passion in life is, what they truly love. It can be sports, music, rock collecting, drama, camping. Many say it is family and friends. This is an opportunity for them to describe what calls them and shapes their internal life. I ask them to tell a recent story about their passion and why it is important to them.

Then, focusing on the words, *v'shinantam l'vanekha* (and you shall teach your children), I ask them about their parents and what they have learned from them. At first they might be a little shy. I reassure them that this is not an exposé, but a deep way of appreciating what their parents have taught them and the best way to say "thank you." We talk about each parent separately and I ask if there is a phrase that the mom or dad repeats that encourages them or guides them. I ask about the work that each parent does in the world and what they admire about their parents. I ask them to open their hearts and describe the influence each parent has had on their lives. This is often the most touching part of the *Shema*. It is a profound way of acknowledging what the parents have given to the child. This can also include grandparents and siblings. Family is the most influential part of a child's life and they have a lot to say about this. I am always sensitive to family dynamics. Sometimes a child is adopted and has only one parent, sometimes the parents are divorced and there may be a blended family, and sometimes there may be financial or emotional problems. I do not want to be invasive, but I want the child to be able to affirm his/her inheritance and know that s/he will take this with them into their adult lives.

If appropriate, we look at the teachings on *tefillin* and *mezuzah*, both being Jewish awareness tools that contain scribed manuscripts of the section of Deuteronomy that contains the *Shema*. I ask why someone would want to put the words of the *Shema* on the arm, the head, and the doorpost of their home. We talk about the sanctity of body and home and how we humans need reminders to stay connected to the Holy One of Blessing.

Leila

"I have many passions in life. I love to read books, write stories and poems, and play my violin. When I write, I enter another world. It's a place where anything can happen. I can make the sun bloom off a butterfly's wings or catch starlight on the water. Images of color fill my mind, spilling out onto the page. I create brilliant pictures that flash into the sky.

"I also love to ride horses. It gives me a sense of togetherness. I love to ride through the lush Vermont forest, the wind rustling the leaves, accompanied by the muffled sound of trotting hooves. The feeling of galloping through a wide open space, the horse and me almost as one, is like a dream. It's like flying though the sky.

"Playing my violin also gives me a wonderful feeling. I can feel the music all through my body as the notes burst into the air. The low ones, rich and deep, swirl around my head, echoing their glorious sounds over and over. The high ones are like birds singing. They can be blossoming flowers or snowflakes softly falling. I play songs that go on and on, but I do not mind. I love it. After I play the last note, stand still listening. The piece is over, but still I can hear the silence. It's like the silence after a spring rain."

Aliza

"It's hard for me to think about loving God with all my heart, soul, and strength although I will probably understand it as I get older. Writing poetry is my real passion, as well as traveling to other places and cultures. Sometimes when I get wrapped up in a poem, I feel like the words are coming from somewhere beyond me. I'm not thinking about what I'm writing down. The words are just flowing out of my pen. Poetry is the best way for me to interpret an event in my life. When I write poetry, I feel like I have understood a new aspect of the time, or even opened a new door for understanding myself.

"I also love my family. My mom is always there for me, organizing her life around my brother and me, always being there in the morning to get us ready for school and make breakfast for us. She has taught me to never give up. I remember when I learned how to play the piano, at the age of seven, I had trouble on a piece of music, and she told me to keep on trying. When I'm really lost on a school project, she supports me and tries to help me. She encourages me to be the best that I can be. My mom grew up Catholic and when I was little we tried out both a church and a synagogue to see what was best. It was obvious that the synagogue was going to be the best place for us. She worked very hard on her conversion and has made time to go to services and make holidays really special for us. She's a mediator and I've learned from her that it is very important for everybody to feel that they are treated fairly and that they have worked out their problems for themselves. As I grow older, she has told me that there will be people who will be prejudiced, but that I should just keep on being myself.

"My dad is always interested in what is going on with me, even if he comes home late from a meeting and we have already had dinner. I feel from him that I matter and that I'm important. Through his love of trying to preserve the environment, I've learned how much his work means to him and how much enthusiasm one can have in their job. Both of my parents have taught me that spirituality is a big part of their life. They try to make the synagogue a good place for everybody."

David

"To love with your heart means to be thankful. To love with your soul means to be aware of the godliness of every person. To love with your might means with every aspect of your being. This is a goal that everyone should strive for, but it's pretty much impossible to accomplish. I think this means not to take things for granted like food, being alive, and living in a free country. It's good to be appreciative. If you see someone less fortunate, you realize how much you really have and how important it is to use it in the best way possible.

"One of the ways that I love God is through the many things I like to do. My main sports are basketball, soccer, and baseball. I play the saxophone in my school's band and jazz band. I enjoy acting and singing and last year I was in a musical for my school. I also like writing for my school newspaper and I draw comics for that. I am grateful to be able to do all these fun activities. But I couldn't do these things without the help and support of my parents.

"My mom has taught me to be brave when facing new things. When I was little, she would always tell me that when I was scared, I should take a deep breath and keep repeating, "I can handle it. I can handle it." During the first day in kindergarten, this really came in handy. I was very scared walking up the steps of the school, so I kept saying those words in my head and it got me pumped up to face this new experience. When I encounter a new scary situation, I think, "You can do it, David," and I cheer myself on.

"My dad is my alarm clock. He wakes me up at 7 o'clock every morning and sets up breakfast for my sister and me. I'm grateful for his kindness because I'm really tired and he helps me to get going and gives me the extra boost for starting my day. He got me interested in musical instruments. He plays clarinet and saxophone and when I was little, he would let me try out playing with the instruments for fun. My sister is an important part of my life. Even though we fight a lot, we forgive each other in the end. Its fun to play together and I would be lonely without her."

V'haya Im Shamo'a — It Will Happen If You Follow Through

In the *Barukh Shem*, we talked about the beauty of this world. Now we have an opportunity to discuss ecological concerns and ways in which the child chooses to take action and work for healing the planet, *tikkun olam*. As we study this paragraph from Deuteronomy 11:13 we see its similarities to Deuteronomy 6:4 - loving God, passing it on to our children, *tefillin* and *mezuzah*. What stands out in this paragraph is how our actions affect the world around us. If we live in harmony with the laws of nature and care for the world that we have been given, then it will provide all that we need. But if we worship false gods, then the heavens will close up, there will be no food, and we will die.

I ask the kids about false gods. At first they respond by saying that false gods are idols, but then I ask them about what people really worship today and they name money, power, and fame as some of our modern idols. From here we begin to see how human greed is destroying the earth and that we need to return to the natural harmony of God's rhythms. They list their concerns and the causes that they have worked for including recycling, hunger, abuse, and pollution. It is very important that they see the connection between the concerns of the Torah and their modern day concerns for the survival of the planet. Many of the kids have done projects in school or have particular concerns that can be expressed here. The description of the heavens closing can represent acid rain or the hole in the ozone layer. As genetically engineered seeds are used, there is a concern that the earth will no longer be able to naturally bear fruit and that all the neighboring plants will be harmed by the effects of human manipulation. There is a delicate balance which we must honor and we must not be afraid to speak up.

Marissa

"My *opa*, which is German for grandfather, was a part of the Kindertransport that saved children before the Holocaust. He came to America when he was only 13 and got adopted by a family in Indiana. A year later, his brother and parents came and they all lived together again, but the rest of our family died in Germany. He has passed stories of that time on to my mom and me and his other grandchildren.

"When I was writing this, the war with Iraq was about to happen and I was scared. Because we didn't know what was going to happen next, it made me live in fear instead of just living life. When I read Anne Frank's diary and learned about the Holocaust, I wondered what it would be like to live with the burden of war. Now I have a sense of what it feels like because we would wake up every day with the fear of a terrorist attack and we knew that in Iraq, people were dying. When I think about September 11 and the war with Iraq, I think about how in the future I'll be able to tell my children and grandchildren that I lived during this era. If we all got along, there wouldn't be war. I don't think there would be as much conflict in Iraq and other places in the Middle East if we weren't so dependent on oil. We need to find other ways to satisfy our needs for energy. I hope it's not too late."

Molly

"This paragraph says that if we care for the earth and protect it, then we'll have what we need and be happy, but if we waste and pollute, then there will be consequences. I'm concerned about all the trees that are being cut down and the land that is being used for cities instead of left to be natural and wild. We need trees because they provide the oxygen that we breathe. And we need the land to grow our food, to be a home for wild plants and animals, and because it is beautiful. There are some things we ourselves can do to help. We can recycle our paper, plastic, and clothes, not waste the food we eat, and not buy more products than we need or use. On a larger scale, we can join organizations that help to buy and conserve land and protest the exploitation of the earth. If we don't work to save the land, the creatures and beauty of the earth will not survive."

Aaron

"We need to learn how to get along and stop having petty disputes over land, religion, wealth, beliefs, and power. We have to stop, or we will set an example for future generations that war is the way to live, like they did in medieval times. Back then it was pure butchery. How can we stop? That's the hard part! We need to learn how to negotiate and make life worth living. For that, people need the basic necessities of life - freedom, food, shelter, medicine, clothes, tools, and safety. We have to share our wealth and help people who are in need. We have to give *tzedakah* (charitable donations), vote for honest representatives, and participate in rallies and campaign movements so our voices are heard."

Va'yomer HaShem—God Said

The third paragraph of the *Shema*, Numbers 15:37, is different from the other two. Rather than *tefillin* and *mezuzah*, it refers to the *tzitzit* (symbolically knotted fringes) of the *tallit* (prayer shawl) as a reminder of the mitzvot. Many of the kids have learned to tie *tzitzit* or made their own *tallit*, so I ask them to talk about that process. We talk about the nature of mitzvot, what their purpose is, and which ones they know about and fulfill in their own lives. Usually the kids say that mitzvot are good deeds, or they mention the Ten Commandments, but they rarely understand the concept of mitzvot as guidelines for holy action in the world. We talk about the *brakhah* (blessing) formula that says, "asher kidshanu b'mitzvotav" (That Which makes us holy through Its sacred instructions) and question how the observance of mitzvot is connected to holiness. I ask them what it means to be holy, and that is perhaps the hardest question of all to answer.

It is a subtle concept to comprehend how we draw close to God through the way that we act. The end of the paragraph is reminiscent of the Ten Commandments and we discuss how the Children of Israel left Egypt to serve God rather than other masters. We question the meaning of freedom and how it is more than the ability to do whatever we want, but it comes with the responsibility and the desire to help others and to act kindly in the world.

The kids, of course, have their own words for all of these concepts and I encourage their fresh approach and individual interpretations. It is my job to open their hearts and minds and it is their job to be themselves. Since I do the writing and read it back to them, it allows them to get in touch with deep feelings and insights that might otherwise be lost in the writing process. This is an effective approach to preparing a d'var Torah, (interpretive teaching about the Torah portion keyed to the day of their ritual) no matter what the physical or mental limitations of a child. By the end, the students are amazed by the wisdom that has come through them and there is a sense of awesome delight as they share their stories with the community on their bar/bat mitzvah day.

Micah

"We respect God a lot because He let us get out of Egypt and be free. To thank God, we do mitzvot, which are good deeds and commandments. The purpose of mitzvot is to help us be holy. When you help somebody, they feel better and so do you. When you light candles on *Shabbat*, you feel happiness and you feel the light of God around the people you are with. To be holy is to remember that we are from God. Just in case we forget, God told us to tie the fringes of the *tzitzit* on our *tallis* (Ashkenazi pronunciation of *tallit*). When we look at it, it helps us to remember God because it spells out God's name. To everybody who is wearing a *tallis* today, take a minute to look at your *tzitzit*. Maybe you never noticed them before. It's traditional to kiss the *tzitzit* during the third paragraph of the *Shema*. When you kiss the *tzitzit*, it's like kissing God and appreciating life."

Isaac

"God reminds the people that S/He led them out of slavery in Egypt so they could be free. Then they got the Torah at Mount Sinai, including the Ten Commandments, which gave them basic laws for living. But God knew that they would need reminders, so God told them to put *tzitzit* (fringes) on the four corners of their clothes, which were like tunics.

"What does it mean for a person to be holy? God is holy. The Torah is holy. Jerusalem and the Western Wall are holy. Every person has the potential to be holy because God is part of everyone. We just need to do certain things to bring it out. In the Jewish tradition, doing mitzvot is the way to holiness. But even if a person follows all the mitzvot and studies all day long, if s/he is not kind and doesn't help people, s/he is not holy. Holiness is not just about observing the laws and rituals of Judaism but also about helping others."

Jesse

"Sometimes when I have a problem, I picture myself walking down a narrow pathway with a dim light up ahead. There are feelings that are trying to pull me off the path, making me want to give up, but the light keeps me moving forward. I don't know what lies ahead, but I do know that it's good.

"The *tallit* is our prayer shawl. It has *tzitzit* (fringes) that are tied on to each corner to spell out God's name. When we put on the *tallit* and see the name of God, we are reminded not to stray off the path. The *tallit* reminds us that we want to be holy in our lives. It symbolizes that I am now a full member of the community even though I'm only 13. Well, almost 13. Now I can lead prayers, be called up to the Torah, and be counted in a *minyan*.

"The *tallit* I am wearing today, I picked out by myself. It's unusual because it has a black background. The color black is strong and solid. It means that I won't give in easily to being pushed around and that I will have the courage to be my own person. The white stripes are the light at the end of my dark path. I hold them close as I step further and further down the dark road, unafraid."

Adina

Tzitzit
blue through your
heart and eyes
holds you back from temptation
remember the Faithful One
who freed us from
bondage,
and bonded us
to truth
love is holy

What a great honor it has been to serve as witness and guide for this process of spiritual revelation. The students can hear the voice of truth ring inside of them and it establishes a foundation built upon courage and trust in oneself. Many of these students are in college or working in the world now and they have shared with me how important it was to have someone take the time to listen deeply, to respond thoughtfully, and to celebrate their human and divine wisdom.

Recommended Reading

Penina Adelman, *The J Girl's Guide: The Young Jewish Woman's Handbook for Coming of Age*, Jewish Lights Publishing, 2005

Barbara Diamond Goldin, *Bat Mitzvah: A Jewish Girl's Coming of Age*, Viking, 1995

Eric A. Kimmel, *Bar Mitzvah: A Jewish Boy's Coming of Age*, Viking, 1995

Rabbi Goldie Milgram, *Living Jewish Life Cycle: How to Create Meaningful Jewish Rites of Passage at Every Stage of Life*, Jewish Lights Publishing, 2009

> *Mitzvah Cards: One Mitzvah Leads to Another*, Reclaiming Judaism Press, 2013.

> *Reclaiming Bar/Bat Mitzvah as a Spiritual Rite of Passage*, Reclaiming Judaism Press, 2014

> "Choose Life: Identifying and Addressing the Spiritual Needs of B'nei Mitzvah Students and Their Families" , in "Sacred Teaching and Spiritual Learning Symposium Issue", *CCAR Journal: The Reform Jewish Quarterly*, Winter 2014, pp 83-97

Rabbi Jeffrey K. Salkin, *Putting God on the Guest List, 3rd edition: How to Reclaim the Spiritual Meaning of Your Child's Bar or Bat Mitzvah*, Jewish Lights Publishing, 2005

Zalman Schachter-Shalomi, *Jewish with Feeling: A Guide to Meaningful Jewish Practice*, Riverhead Books, 2005

Additional Website(s):

http://www.bmitzvah.org
Extensive b'nei mitzvah resources developed by Rabbi Goldie Milgram

Sharing an Inspiring Story in *Hashpa'ah*
by Shulamit Fagan

Rabbinic Pastor Shulamit Kate Fagan is the founding and current Director of the Aleph: Alliance for Jewish Renewal Rabbinic Pastor Ordination Program; she also serves all the Aleph Ordination Programs as a *Mashpia* (Spiritual Director) and teacher of Pastoral Counseling. A storyteller, spiritual director and hospital chaplain, she teaches nationally and locally on ethical wills, decisions at the end of life and the art of compassionate listening.

Storytelling is a Jewish tradition. It is one of the ways that we remember the past and pass it on to future generations. It is part of our culture, perhaps even a force in shaping our culture. Rabbis often use stories in sermons to make a point, and, if we listen carefully, even politicians use stories!

I've been wondering about the use of stories in spiritual direction as well as pastoral counseling and grief counseling. How do we use them? Are there effective methods of story telling in our practices? Let me tell you a story and you can decide for yourself.

I first met John (a name I have chosen for this retelling) at a function sponsored by a local Unity church, where he was drawing caricatures of the attendees. His tall, thin body was propped up behind a sketchpad as his twinkling eyes and brilliant smile lit up the room. I met his wife Marie a few weeks later at the hospital where I work as a chaplain. John was having the first of many surgeries which took place over the next few years. I spent many hours in his room listening and talking about his life, God, Spirit, and what life means or might mean. Marie began to visit my office for a series of sessions talking about God in her life, and what she saw as the imminent ending of John's life.

About six months before he died, as he was regaining whatever strength he could find after his last surgery, I visited him at home. John asked "What do you think happens when you die?"

In good chaplain form I asked: "What do you think happens when you die"?

"If I knew I wouldn't be asking you!" was his fast answer. Marie, sitting on his bed, replied, "Our bodies are buried, but our Spirits leave the body and reside with God."

"I hope you're right," he said, "but I'd like to know what the chaplain thinks."

It took me only a moment to ask if I could tell them the following story.

My parents were married for 53 years. Saul was a big strong man with a soft heart who drove a truck all his life. My mom, Sandy, was a little woman with a miniature mouse collection, who would ask for a small juice glass for her Coca-Cola, and the tiniest fork I owned whenever I offered her something to eat.

Some years before their death I was introduced to Five Wishes, a living will and health care surrogate form with some added flourishes. I don't remember thinking a lot about how to present it, but just knew automatically that I needed to approach them separately. The conversation happened first with my dad, and the question that was not on the form just rolled off my tongue:

"What do you think happens when you die, Dad?"

"What do you mean what happens when you die? Nothing. Nothing happens. You die, you're dead, that's it."

"Really," I said. "What about God?"

"I don't know about God. I just know you die and that's it."

"Well, just in case you're wrong," I said with a little laugh, "and there is something after this life, would you send me a sign?"

"Oh for Pete's sake," he said after a pause, "you'll hock me a *cheinick* (talk off my ear, or demand attention like a whistling tea kettle) if I don't say yes."

The conversation with Sandy came a few days later. We sat on the sun porch where she often played solitaire. As I got to the end of the form questions, I asked her the question that had jolted my Dad.

"What do you think happens when you die?"

"What do you mean what happens when you die? If you've been good, when you die you go to heaven. I've been good, I'm going to heaven."

"That's great, Mom" I said, the tears close to the surface. "When you get there, would you send me a sign?"

"Sure," she said. "Sure I will."

Saul died first. My Mom called about 10 AM on a Sunday morning to tell me that he didn't feel well but he wouldn't let her do anything about it. I spent several hours at their independent living apartment, watching his lungs fill up with fluid until he finally let me call an ambulance and take him to the hospital. About three days later the doctor came to the ICU to tell him that his kidneys had stopped working, and that he needed to go on dialysis.

"No, it's time for me to die now." Pointing at me he said, "She has her instructions, just ask her."

He died about 24 hours later, with my brother, my son and me sitting by his side as his breathing became irregular and then stopped.

I lived on the second story of a large house. The front steps ended on a small covered porch facing the front door. The morning after his death I opened that door and found a large white feather directly in the middle of the doormat. I'd never found a feather there before and I felt certain it was the sign I'd requested. Everywhere I went in that month of *shloshim* (the first thirty days after burial) I found feathers. I'd look down, see nothing, and a feather would just appear. For once, my father was wrong, and telling me so in beautiful plumage.

Sandy, my mom, died 357 days later. I believe that the almost year after her husband's death was a good year for her. She found her independence again, realized she really could do anything she wanted with her time, and somehow missed my father's criticizing voice. The paramedics brought her into the ER at the hospital where I work. I was busy with a trauma, and although she said I looked right at her on the stretcher, it took about a half an hour before I realized she was there. Her heart attack and the two that followed it took her life about two weeks later. There were decisions to be made in that time span, and my brother and I made them with a sense of inevitability and peace, knowing what she had told us she wanted. We opted for the heart catheterization with her permission.

"But remember," she said, "no open heart surgery. I'm too old."

My mother never really came back from that procedure; her mind seemed to have already traveled to the other side. She died a few days later after a night in which I lay next to her listening to the irregular rhythm of her breathing, waiting for it to stop completely, giving her permission to go as soon as she was ready.

I still lived in the same rented house, with the same covered porch. As I tried to come to terms with being an orphan I opened the front door for a breath of fresh air. There, on the doormat, was a tiny white feather. My mother had sent me a sign of life after death in her own, love of the small, way. Baby feathers began to appear everywhere I went. Thanks, Mom. I love you too.

A few years ago I went to Jerusalem to celebrate my 60th birthday. On the sixteenth of July I went to the *Kotel* (Western Wall) early in the morning. It was very warm. I waited a while and was able to get a white plastic chair and pull it up so that my knees touched the wall and my forehead could rest there as well. I prayed, meditated, and tried to squeeze all the *kvitels* (small written message or petition to God) into the spaces already stuffed with paper. I looked around on several occasions, seeing that there were black birds occasionally passing overhead. After several hours I decided I needed to get out of the sun and go somewhere cooler. I walked backwards away from the wall trying not to trip over the many women asking me for *tzedakah* (charity). As one of them was tying a red string around my wrist and I was dropping shekels into upturned palms, I looked up. There were no birds to be seen, but there, falling in a clockwise swirl, was one medium-size white feather. I put up my right hand and it fell right in. Happy Birthday from your parents!

I continue to see feathers, and often wonder if they are sent as messages. But there was only one more time, about a year ago, when I was sure it was a sign of intervention from my parents. I was late leaving the hospital with a plumber waiting for me at home. I stopped to get cash to pay him, and went home a slightly different route then normal. I was stopped at a traffic light with a few cars ahead of me when I looked in the rear view mirror and realized that the car approaching in the next lane was going too fast. It hit the car in front and to the right of me with so much force that the car lifted straight up in the air. I saw the entire underside of the vehicle and, in that flash of time, wondered where it would hit me and how badly I would be injured. The car landed on all four wheels about half an inch from my car. It took only a moment for me to get out of my car to see where help was needed. Fortunately there were no terrible injuries, and the police arrived shortly thereafter. I was able to get out of the traffic jam and headed back to my house in short order. When I arrived, the plumber needed to remind me of how late I was and how valuable his time was. I was explaining the circumstances as we headed to my door. I live in a different house now, but when I first saw it, there in the middle of the doormat, right in the middle of the doormat, was a large white feather with a smaller white feather attached to it.

I will always be grateful, I told John, that I questioned my parents about life after death, and that they sent me answers so clearly.

Marie turned to John and asked: "Will you send me a message when you get to heaven?"

"Of course I will," he replied.

"What kind of message will you send and how will I know it is from you?"

"You'll know, dear one, you will know."

Marie tells me that she receives many messages from John. He was a very talented artist, and had no talent whatsoever for cars. He never drove one and had no idea how they worked, so when the hearse broke down on the way to the church for the funeral Marie was sure that was the twinkle in John's eye coming through. He loved to whistle and Marie reports that a particular bird lands on her windowsill periodically, singing its particular brand of bird song. But mostly she tells me that she just feels him, knows he is watching her, and that my story brought them both a comfort they had not found anywhere else.

This brings me to a story of the Baal Shem Tov, the great hasidic master of long ago who, our stories tell us, had "magical" powers.

When the Baal Shem Tov was troubled and in need of an answer, a miracle, it is said that he would go to a specific place in the forest, light a fire, say a prayer, and the miracle would happen. The problem would somehow be averted.

Later, after the Baal Shem Tov died, the Maggid of Mezeritch had learned from his master where this special place in the forest was located. He would go there and say, "Master of the Universe, I don't know how to light the special fire, but I know the prayer and I know this place and I ask for this special favor" and again events would happen in what appeared to be a more favorable way.

Moshe Leib of Sasov had followed the Maggid to the magic place in the forest and years later he would go there and say, "Holy One, Creator of All That Is, I know this holy place, but I don't know the prayer, and I don't know how to light the fire, please help us." And help would arrive.

Now, when we do not know even where the special place in the forest is, perhaps we can find a special place in our heart where we can offer the prayer: "Creator of All There Is, Wonderful *YaH* (one of the shortest Hebrew names for God, from YHVH), I no longer know where the place is in the forest, or what the special prayer is or even how to light the fire, but I do know the story of what happened long ago, and I promise to pass it on. May the passing on of the story bring us the help that we need."

Recommended Reading

Anne Brener, *Mourning & Mitzvah: A Guided Journal for Walking the Mourner's Path Through Grief to Healing*, Jewish Lights Publishing, 1993

Barry Bub, *Communication Skills that Heal: A Practical Approach Towards a New Professionalism for Medicine*, Radcliffe Medical Press, 2007

Yitzhak Buxbaum, *Storytelling and Spirituality in Judaism*, Jason Aronson, 1996

Rita Charon, *Narrative Medicine: Honoring the Stories of Illness*, Oxford University Press, 2006

Goldie Milgram, *Living Jewish Life Cycle: How to Create Meaningful Jewish Rites of Passage at Every Stage of Life*, Jewish Lights Publishing, 2009

> and Ellen Frankel with Peninnah Schram, Cherie Karo Schwartz and Arthur Strimling, *Mitzvah Stories: Seeds for Inspiration and Learning*, Reclaiming Judaism Press, 2011

> and Ellen Frankel with Arthur Kurzweil, Batya Podos, Peninnah Schram, Mindy Shapiro, Danny Siegel and Shoshana Silberman, *New Mitzvah Stories for the Whole Family*, Reclaiming Judaism Press, 2014

Simcha Paull Raphael, *Jewish Views of the Afterlife*, Jason Aronson, 1996

Rachel Naomi Remen, *Kitchen Table Wisdom: Stories that Heal*, Riverhead, 1997

> *My Grandfather's Blessings*, Riverhead, 2001

Elie Kaplan Spitz, *Does the Soul Survive: A Jewish Journey to Belief in Afterlife, Past Lives & Living With a Purpose*, Jewish Lights Publishing, 2002

The Spiritual Director as Midwife to the Dying
by Nadya Gross

Rabbi Nadya Gross has developed a program to train end-of-life doulas, and serves on the faculty of the Anamcara Project of the Sacred Art of Living, Center for Spiritual Formation in Bend, OR, where she was awarded an Honorary Anamcara. Reb Nadya also serves as *mashpi'ah* with individuals, couples, and clergy, and is the Director of Hashpa'ah: The Aleph Ordination Program in Jewish Spiritual Direction. http://www..org/hashpaah_program.htm

As a young child, my *savta* (Heb: grandmother) taught me how to tell my story, as a tool for becoming self-aware and examining the meaning of the life I was living. She was my first *mashpi'ah* (f.): she listened closely, and guided my story telling with probing questions and loving instruction.

At 25, I faced the loss of my father. Daddy had always been my source of strength, the well of confidence I could dip into whenever I needed some. As it became clear that the disease that had spread throughout his body was going to take his life, he began to tell me his story. I listened closely, with an open – and breaking – heart, and received the right questions that encouraged his self-examination and made it possible, in the end, for him to surrender to a gentle death.

Years later, having forgotten the majestic awe that surrounded my father's dying, I turned to birth to feed my longing to experience the miracle of God. I became a labor doula.[26] I learned to open to the moment, to allow the truth of each moment to be determined by the mother's experience while facilitating, in the best of circumstances, the collective experience of all who were present. I learned, once again, to listen to the stories. I listened for the clues to the fear that might impact the labor, for the needs and wishes that could be supported. Mostly, I listened for God, in order that I might help guide the mother to a deep, intimate experience of her co-creative power.

Almost a full decade after choosing to work with birthing mothers, and more than 20 years after my father's death, while I was facilitating a spiritual support group for people coping with catastrophic illness I received a call from the husband of a group member. We expect and hope that she'll live a very long time, but just in case...we want to know if you will be willing to be with us through the end. Our conversation at that meeting focused

---

26   Dana Raphael first popularized the word "doula," a Greek word meaning "woman caregiver," in her 1973 book *The Tender Gift*. She used it to describe women who provided help and support to women after childbirth. However, the researchers who first studied the effects of female labor-support companions used the same term. Today, women who offer postpartum home-care services and women who do labor support both call themselves doulas, and some women do both.

on her fear of death, and her perception that my acceptance of death as a part of life would help her face whatever awaited her. I became her "end of life doula," drawing on my experience with mothers in labor, the lessons learned through my father's dying, my early training with my *savta*, and my growing experience as a *mashpi'ah*. She died less than a year after that meeting, and her gift was my new "calling."

In time, I developed a program to train end of life doulas,[27] and the first class of 27 volunteers joined in creating the End of Life Doula Association in Boulder, CO, dedicated to the memory of the woman whose question set me on the path. The work, as it unfolded, was an integration of *hashpa'ah* skills, understanding the dying process and making peace with one's own mortality.

The critical role that spiritual direction can play at end of life is not a new discovery. The Celts, in ancient times, created the role of the *anamcara* (Gaelic: "soul friend"), who served as a life counselor and spiritual guide. The tradition was carried into the Christian world, and for centuries these *anamcara* became mentors and companions to persons from all walks of life who yearned for a deeper relationship with the Divine. By the 11th century, their work extended to hospices that were being established across the European continent. *Anamcara* were known for their extraordinary skills as spiritual midwives to the dying, especially in diagnosing and relieving spiritual pain related to the values of forgiveness, meaning, relatedness and hope.[28]

The questions that are central to *hashpa'ah*—questions of the meaning of the life one is living, the relationships that inform the purpose of that life, and "Where is God in this?" become more acute as one approaches death. When the answers don't come easily, or are troubling, or point to unfinished business, the spiritual pain that results can present an obstacle to the dying process. If dying well is our goal, then the role of the *mashpia* as end of life doula is a critical component of palliative care.[29][29] Common guidelines for supporting a dying person always include the importance of Presence. Consistency and frequency of visits are discussed in terms of helping to create a sense of safety and comfort, so that the dying person can share her thoughts, fears, feelings, wishes, dreams, and hopes. Listening more than talking, and following the dying person's agenda are essential elements of the support to be offered.

---

27   My gratitude flows to the Boulder JCC for supporting the funding and development of this ground-breaking program.

28   I was introduced to this ancient tradition, and the 21st century revival of the work, by Richard Groves of The Sacred Art of Living Center for Spiritual Formation in Bend, OR. For more information, see: www.sacredartofliving.com

29   Palliative care (pronounced pal-lee-uh-tiv) is the medical specialty focused on relief of the pain and other symptoms of serious illness. The goal is to prevent and ease suffering and to offer patients and their families the best possible quality of life.

In our work as *mashpi'im*, we learn to cultivate the skill of being truly Present; to "meet" the *mushpa* in the truest sense of the word. This is what Martin Buber termed an I-Thou encounter, meeting on the level of spirit that which resides at the core of one's being, or what we might term a God encounter. When a person faces death, when there is no choice but to recognize that life is finite, s/he is catapulted into an acute awareness of the preciousness of life, and how the remaining time is to be used. This is what I learned as I watched my father prepare for his death, and as I have been privileged to accompany many others on this path. There is a natural reprioritizing that takes place, and the list of what's important shrinks. It almost always includes ~appreciating the natural world ~deep encounters with family and friends ~contemplating the meaning of things and sharing ideas ~choosing to be rather than do. When the *mashpia* accompanies the dying process, the skills s/he has cultivated of simple Presence, deep listening and reflecting or affirming the Truth as experienced by the *mushpa* are the most important tools in her/his toolbox.

Often, as previously mentioned, the deep sharing – telling the story of one's life – brings to the surface memories and relationships that need healing. Our task becomes one of encouraging the full story with all the details, and listening for the clues to the unresolved issues that may lie just beneath the surface of the fear of dying. We fear: leaving before we've completed our life; being forgotten because, in the end, our life was without purpose or meaning; or that those we leave behind may have lingering hurt and anger. We fear dying alone and in pain.

When acting in the capacity of end of life doula the *mashpia* must become more proactive than at other times, guiding and facilitating the healing of relationships and the work of *teshuvah* (forgiveness) with family and close friends. I often describe the role as seeing the situation through a wide-angle lens, watching the family dynamic and noticing who or what may be falling through the cracks. Helping the child sitting alone in the corner approach the dying grandparent, or gently inviting an overwrought spouse to take a walk so you can hear them out is also part of the work. Because we know that death is not an end, but an opening to another state of awareness, there are unparalleled opportunities for healing and hope at the end of life.

While attending to forgiveness and cultivating loving relationships are key factors in the process of dying well, we ultimately turn our attention to finding meaning in one's life. Viktor Frankl, who wrote one of the most significant books of the 20th century, *Man's Search for Meaning*, said, "Man's main concern is not to gain pleasure or avoid pain but rather to see a meaning in his life." He believed that the search for meaning was a drive in all of us. The desire for one's life to have had meaning is perhaps more acute when one realizes one is near the end. Here, again, we invite the stories: helping the dying person share her accomplishments, express the things he's proud of, and transmit her values and blessings to those who will be left behind.

The most powerful tool that I've used in the end of life work is the process of writing one's own *vidui* (deathbed confession). *Vidui* is the means through which we may consciously come into the Presence of the Holy One as death approaches. Whether read by the infirmed, a chaplain or clergy person, or the entire family, this is a method to provide meaning and purpose at this critical moment.

One form reads as follows:

My God and God of all who have gone before me, Author of life and death, I turn to You in trust. Although I pray for life and health, I know that I am mortal. If my life must soon come to and end, let me die, I pray, at peace.

If only my hands were clean and my heart pure! I confess that I have committed sins and left much undone, yet I know also the good that I did or tried to do. May my acts of goodness give meaning to my life, and may my errors be forgiven.

Protector of the bereaved and the helpless, watch over my loved ones. Into Your hand I commit my spirit; redeem it, O God of mercy and truth.[30]

Writing one's own *vidui* is one way to "make meaning" as the end of life approaches, and to derive the comfort that allows one to surrender to the Will of the Creator. Expanding on the traditional *vidui*, mine will contain the following:

Address to Whom I am presenting myself. The opening phrase names my relationship with God – the One to whom I am entrusting my soul as I transition from this life into the next. Is this the "God of my ancestors," the "Source of Life and Breath," the "Beloved," or something other? Naming the relationship with or the image of God that is true for the writer at the moment of facing one's death or mortality is often the primary work of *hashpa'ah*, and will open the path to the healing that yet needs to be done, or provide clues to the spiritual pain or dissonance that stands in the way of dying well.

Who I am; the accomplishments of which I am proud; the relationships that are meaningful in my life. Completing this part of the *vidui*, with the personal content that is missing from the traditional form, makes me real – makes my life a real experience that was filled with

---

30   From the *Reform Rabbis' Handbook*

meaning and purpose, and allows me to rest in the comfort of knowing that there will be a residual trace of my life left in the world.

What I have left undone; what I regret. Whenever life comes to an end, there are always regrets and a sense of tasks not completed, 'conversations left in the middle of a sentence.' Naming these makes it easier to "let go and let God."

A statement of surrender, and my prayer/wish for those I leave behind. In all my [limited] experience, I have watched the final surrender come within weeks, days or even hours of death – no matter how much fear there was, or how much the person fought to live. The day before my father's death, he shared with me that he was ready to go – that he had completed his work, and was ready to accept his death. He said: *I'm really OK with this, and I want you to be OK, too.* In his surrender, there was also the wish that I could accept his truth, and go on living a good life.

Traditionally, the *vidui* is said by the dying person, as the end approaches. Rabbinic manuals instruct that if the person is unable to recite it herself, then it is to be said by the rabbi or chaplain present. The process of writing one's own *vidui* helps to arrive at the closure and surrender that make way for a "good" death. It is not uncommon that the dying person stops communicating verbally for some time before death comes. Someone else will almost inevitably be the one to read his words aloud and "announce" her at the threshold.

A few years ago, I assisted a dear friend, dying of ALS, in writing her *vidui.* The disease had already stripped her of her ability to speak, but her typing fingers were strong – as were her mind and heart. She wrote a beautiful tribute to her life and her loving family. She wasted no words in asking for and offering forgiveness. She acknowledged that she didn't understand why God caused this disease to take her life, and yet she surrendered to the mystery. When she completed it, she shared it with her family and friends in her *havurah* (a more intimate form of Jewish community than a formal congregation).

On the day before her death, my beloved husband and I visited with her for the last time. She was quiet and uncommunicative when we arrived. Medication was helping her stay calm, and she was more gone than present. We sat on either side of her, stroking her arms and face, whispering our farewell into her ears and allowing the tears to flow unchecked. She began to clutch at my hands, and her daughter suggested that she was becoming anxious and perhaps needed more medication. I felt that she was trying to communicate something to me. I asked her soul, and opened my heart to hear what she wanted me to know – and then I remembered. Just before leaving her home, I suggested to her family that they should read her *vidui* to her. I had promised her that her own words would be the last thing she'd hear as she crossed the threshold into the next world. They asked me when it should be done, and all I could say was that it was their decision, but I felt it should be soon.

When her brother called me early the next morning to tell me that she had died peacefully just hours before, he shared with me that they had read her *vidui*, while sitting around her bed, and that she became peaceful and calm from that moment until she took her last breath.

Supporting the dying is among the most holy and satisfying work I am blessed to do. I consider it a privilege to be there, and when I am able to help a family arrive at a place where they can lovingly let go, and be fully present to the dying person, I know I have contributed to *tikkun*, the repair of this world. The lessons I've learned and the miracles I've witnessed could not have come in any other way. Death is our teacher. It teaches us about God's Presence; about human goodness, as it awakens our compassion; about courage, hope, faith – as we encounter both those who struggle to live in the face of suffering and pain, and the ultimate surrender to the will of the Creator and courage in the face of loss and grief. It teaches us to believe in things we can't see.

The day before my father's death when he assured me that he was OK with dying and wanted to know that I'd be OK, I knew that he was asking me to let him go. When your parent asks your permission to die – you give it…even when the voice inside you is screaming: "How can you be OK when you're leaving me!" But, of course, my father being so close to the threshold, already knew that he wasn't leaving me at all. We were just going to have to get used to a new way of being in relationship.

Our Torah teaches that God formed Adam out of clay and breathed into his nostrils the breath of life and Adam became a living soul.[31] In Hebrew, the word for breath, *neshimah* and soul, *neshamah*, are of the same root; breath has the addition of one letter, a *yud*, which is the first letter of God's name. When we are placed in this realm, the soul is breathed by God, and when that letter is returned, the breath ceases, and the soul remains.

My father has emerged in my dreams and waking reveries when I've needed him. While nothing makes up for the bear hug that I've longed for these past too many years, I know with certainty that death does not put an end to our relationships.

One more personal story: Two years after my father's death, our second son was born. I knew, without benefit of tests and images, that I was carrying a son, and that he would carry my father's name. As our child was emerging into this world, my father's presence became palpable. I knew he was there with us, and a look into my husband's eyes confirmed that he knew it, too. Nothing was said – we just held the awareness between us. Moments after the birth, when our doctor had finished his task, he turned to us and asked, "So who was that who came to bless this birth?"

---

31   Genesis 2:7

Often, in the days or weeks before death, the dying person will report having been visited by dead relatives and friends. I have heard "one-sided" (that is I can only hear one side of it) conversations that the dying person is having, often buying a little more time because he's waiting for a relative to arrive and say good-bye, or asking why so and so isn't also coming to accompany her to the other side. Many a *mashpia* knows the experience of being guided in his or her work by angels, long-dead *rebbe*s or other entities/energies in the spiritual realms. We often don't share this guidance with our *mushpa'im*; we may not always consider it crucial to the relationship with the directee, but more a part of our own relationship with the Divine. At end of life, speaking about the relatives and guides who may come to assist is often critical. It can provide comfort, and more often serves to affirm experiences that the dying person is already having, and may not know how to articulate. One person, whose dying process I accompanied for over two years, found my belief in these things to be quaint and unconvincing. On the day of her death, she had been semi-comatose for more than a day, when she suddenly sat up in bed, pointed to a far corner of the room and winked at me. I understood that she was letting me know that "they" had indeed arrived.

This work is equal parts holy and satisfying, and difficult and challenging. Death may not be the end of existence, and we may learn afterwards to be in relationship with the soul that has transitioned, if we are so blessed; but it is still the end of the life and physical presence as we know it. We are material beings, and thus are very attached to physical form. Whether or not we make peace with the fact of our and our loved ones' mortality, the loss that death brings is very real. Grief is a factor that the *mashpia* as end of life doula must face and know how to manage – both for the dying person and his or her circle of intimacy, and for her/himself.

When I become the end of life doula for someone, just as when I serve as *mashpi'ah* for someone for any length of time, I open my heart to that person and take him or her in. I can say that I love all my *mushpa'im*, and have loved all those whose death I have accompanied. I grieve their loss, and feel deeply the grief of their circle of intimacy. I have learned that it is not only OK, but often very important that I don't hide my grief – my tears affirm the sadness that the family and close friends are feeling, and give them permission to express theirs. That I feel the loss too is comforting, and confirms the value of the life that is no longer. Still, one must be able to recognize and honor the boundary that rests between sharing in the grief and loss and becoming one of the mourners. Crossing that boundary, fusing with the dying person or their family, will damage both the family and the *mashpia*.

During End of Life Doula Training, I had each doula form a "spirit buddy" team of three. I had learned, in my time of working alone in this, the importance of having someone with intimate knowledge of this holy and difficult work there to catch me when I came home from a visit. My husband, who is my partner in so many ways, saw me falling into dark spaces, having difficulty separating from the families and re-entering my blessed life. He counseled me to call on my friends who were serving as Jewish chaplains around the country. The relief and return to a clear perspective on life was, and is, immediate, once I have been able to "debrief" an encounter with someone who simply knows what it's all about. This is where we turn to express our grief, our sense of loss or failure, the fears that emerge out of the experience of so many difficult or painful deaths, so that we can continue to turn back to face the needs of the dying and their families.

Even as the skills that are most necessary are already part of the *mashpia* toolbox, one must prepare well to accompany a dying person. It is critical that you do your own work: that you face your own unresolved fears and painful early or recent experiences with dying, that you engage in the exercises that are offered in Reb Zalman's book *From Ageing to Sage-ing*, that you write your own *vidui*. I have been writing my own and teaching the practice to others for many years, as a way to clarify the meaning of my life right now and acknowledge that it may end at any moment. Every year, as I update my *vidui*, I must face that truth again. That encounter helps me approach each new dying person with the greatest empathy that I can know without having my own "death sentence" pronounced by a doctor. Again, our tradition offers us wisdom: Rabbi Eliezer declared: "Repent one day before your death." Whereupon his disciples asked: "How does one know which day that is?" "Exactly," answered the sage. "For that reason, we ought to live our lives each day as though it were our last."[32]

It is also important to understand the dying process, and to be aware of the end of life choices that one may be faced with. As the spiritual director supporting the dying person, one will inevitably be asked the tough questions. How I may wish to die, and the intervention I may or may not think I will choose, is not relevant to the person whose death I am supporting. Once again, we face the challenge of getting out of the way, and allowing the truth of the moment to be determined by the patient. Still, we must be well enough informed to be able to guide with appropriate questions, and to know when fear or rumor is clouding the truth. Knowing what it looks like to die, and how different treatments and interventions affect the body, will help the *mashpia* remain present to the person and not be distracted or distressed by the patient.

Finally, when you say yes to the privilege of accompanying the dying process, you learn to make each moment of your life count. This is what our Sages knew when they bracketed our day with *modeh* (*modah* f.) *ani* (prayer said on awakening) and *Shema al ha-Mitah* (prayer said before going to bed). Each day, as I awake, the first prayer uttered is one which expresses my thanks to the Source for returning my soul breath to me, and at

---

32   Babylonian Talmud, Shabbat 153a

the end of the day, the bedtime prayer ends *"b'yado afkid ruhi* — I entrust my soul to the One."* Imagine how we might live differently, if we all actively cultivated awareness of the precious gift of this day

> *R. Yaakov said: This world is like a passageway before the world to come.*
> *Prepare yourself so that you may enter the main banquet room.*[33]

---

33   Pirkei Avot 4:21

Recommended Reading and Listening

Ira Byock, *Dying Well: The Prospect for Growth at the End of Life*, Riverhead Publishing Co., 1997

Maggie Callanan, and Patricia Kelly, *Final Gifts: Understanding the Special Awareness, Needs and Communication of the Dying*, Bantam Books, 1992

Carmy, *Shalom*, ed. *Jewish Perspectives on the Experience of Suffering*, Jason Aaronson Inc., 1999

Elliot N. Dorff, *Matters of Life and Death: A Jewish Approach to Modern Medical Ethics*, Jewish Publication Society, 1998

Wayne Dosick , *When Life Hurts: A Book of Hope*, Harper San Francisco, 1998

Viktor Frankl, *Man's Search for Meaning*, Beacon Press, 1946

Dayle, A Friedman, (Ed.) *Jewish Pastoral Care: A Practical Handbook from Traditional and Contemporary Sources*, Jewish Lights Publishing, 2001

Richard F. Groves and Henriette Anne Klauser, *The American Book of Dying: Lessons in Healing Spiritual Pain*, Celestial Arts, 2005

Stephen Levine, *A Year to Live: How to Live This Year as If it Were Your Last.*, Bell Tower, 1997

Rabbi Goldie Milgram, "Chapter 8: Leaving Life" in *Living Jewish Life Cycle: How to Create Meaningful Jewish Rites of Passage at Every Stage of Life*, Jewish Lights Publishing, 2009

Rabbi Kerry M Olitzky and Debbie Friedman, *Jewish Paths Toward Healing and Wholeness: A Personal Guide to Dealing With Suffering*, Jewish Lights Publishing, 2000

Timothy E., Quill, M.D., *A Midwife Through the Dying Process: Stories of Healing and Hard Choices at the End of Life.* The Johns Hopkins University Press, 1996

Jack Riemer and Sherwin B. Nuland, (Ed.), *Jewish Insights on Death and Mourning*, Syracuse University Press, 2002

_____, Behoref Hayamim, *In the Winter of Life: A Values-Based Jewish Guide for Decision Making at the End of Life*, Reconstructionist Rabbinical College Press, 2002

Rabbi Zalman Schachter-Shalomi and Ronald S. Miller, *From Age-ing to Sage-ing*, Warner Books, Inc., 1995

Rami M Shapiro, *Last Breaths: A Guide to Easing Another's Dying*, Temple Beth Or, Miami, 1993

Michael Stillwater and Gary Malkin, *Graceful Passages: A Companion for Living and Dying*. Book and CD Set *A Wisdom of the World Production* (www.wisdomoftheworld.com) New World Library www.newworldlibrary.com) 2003

Configuring Grief in Spiritual Terms
by Anne Brener

Rabbi Anne Brener, LCSW, a spiritual director, psychotherapist, and frequent "scholar-in-residence," assists in creating caring communities and speaks on the therapeutic impact of Jewish ritual and practice. She teaches at The Academy for Jewish Religion/CA, Hebrew Union College/CA, and and is a founder of the Morei Derekh Jewish Spiritual Directors program. Rabbi Brener authored the acclaimed *Mourning & Mitzvah: Walking the Mourner's Path* (Jewish Lights) and many other publications. Ordained at HUC/LA, she is on the steering committee of HUC-JIR's Kalsman Institute on Judaism & Medicine and the Board of the Southern Clifornia Jewish Burial Society.

So many people come to spiritual direction after a loss. Very often their sense of God has been shattered. They may feel betrayed or abandoned by the God that may have been their bedrock in the past. It is the privilege and challenge to the *mashpia* to serve as midwife as a new spiritual identity is birthed and with it, perhaps, a new understanding of God.

It is appropriate to add the spiritual dimension to our understanding of grief. The fact that Jewish law exempts mourners from certain religious obligations during the early days of grief indicates an assumption that a death provokes a spiritual crisis. In addition, the search for the Holy Presence can be perceived at the core of the practice of saying the *Kaddish*, Judaism's primary tool for mourning the death of a close relative.[34] That our doxology for mourning centers on praising God as the principal balm of comfort is another indication that the intention of the Jewish mourning rituals is to focus the mourner on loss as a spiritual journey. The ritual involved in saying *Kaddish* (prayer) holds and guides the mourner's journey through the wilderness of grief.

Kabbalistic Caveat

To describe the spiritual journey of grief, this article borrows vocabulary and metaphors from Jewish mysticism. Teachings from kabbalah help to clarify the variety of places those in pain must stand in for healing. They allude to possibilities for healing that are beyond the known world. They provide a map that delineates the tasks of healing in ways that make healing more accessible and directs one to the higher purpose of grief-work.

This article describes the process of grieving within the framework of the kabbalistic concept of the *arba olamot*, the Four Worlds. The Four Worlds concept is taken from the

---

34   http://www.jewfaq.org/prayer/kaddish.htm

kabbalah of Rabbi Isaac Luria of Safed (16th C.), who saw the flow of Divinity through four worlds or dimensions of reality. In recent years the concept has been further interpreted through a psychological lens. It is from this latter understanding that the following theory regarding grief as a spiritual process is derived. The thesis to be presented below articulates the path of grief as a spiritual journey through all four worlds, from the physical pain of a world bereft of one who has died, to the apprehension of that person's spiritual presence and the presence of the Holy.

Kabbalah and Kaddish

When we mourn, we strain our ears, listening for the voice of the deceased —until we hear that voice coming from our own hearts.

As mourners, we yearn to continue the conversation. We search for the unsaid words to resolve the unfinished issues. The *Kaddish* can take us there. *Kaddish* parts the curtains and forces open the space between the worlds, breaking open the crevices where the voices still come through and where all the worlds are one. For the price of our yearning, our anger, and our tears, the *Kaddish* will carry us beyond the edges of the world we know. It takes us to a place of wholeness- *shalom* - of peace-where all the polarities dissolve, where life and death, black and white, male and female, God and not-God are revealed as one, *Adonai Ekhad*. God is one, the words of the *Shema* become the reality of the world. *Kaddish* ends exile. It suffuses the most profane regions with the holiness of God's name and wrests an Amen from the place where it has not yet been forthcoming, the Amen we have been listening for our entire lives. That Amen sustains the world.

Grief-Work in the Four Worlds

When people grieve it feels as if the world in which they live has been damaged. Holiness seems to have exited from the world; the world feels flat and without its spark. Saying *Kaddish* allows the mourner to breathe God's Great Name, the Tetragrammaton, the *Sh'mei Raba* as it is called in the prayer, back into the world. The *Kaddish* is a prolonged exercise in purgation, cleaning, and purification understood to be a tool for cleansing the soul of the deceased. It can also be seen as a way to polish the world to make the world once again a fitting vessel for holiness, despite the taint of mortality. Saying *Kaddish* can strip away the details of the stories that bind the mourner to what is past. It can open them up to an as yet uncharted experience of Holiness. Standing for *Kaddish* provides the mourner with a means to clear him or herself of the struggles associated with the material aspects of being human. *Kaddish* delineates a path for striving to perceive the Holiness, which seems to have exited from the world when a death has occurred. The mourner stands at that precipice between life and death, between matter and spirit. S/he becomes a vessel for aligning the portals of the worlds and creates a conduit through which holiness can enter the world. This effort fulfills the promise made by the words of the *Kaddish* as those who recite it become channels fit to fill the world with the *Sh'mei Raba*—God's great name.

Said simply, Judaism is about making God, a.k.a. Holiness, present in the world. When a loss occurs, it feels as though the Divine Spark, God's Great Name, has departed. It is the task of being human to keep the channels clear and open so that the flow of holiness can return to the furthest reaches of the created world

This is the goal of spiritual practice. Standing to say *Kaddish* is such a practice.

Kabbalah charts the created world as four successive worlds that emanate from God or from the etheric *Ein Sof* (a name for Divinity that means "without end"). Each world manifests with increasingly concrete dimensions. The worlds extend down the ladder of abstraction from the highest world, the World of *Atzilut*, the world of the spirit, to the World of *Assiyah*, the physical world in which action takes place. The world of intellect (*Beriyah*) and the world of emotions (*Yetzirah*) are the intermediate steps between the two. Human beings live simultaneously in all four of these worlds and when they mourn, they mourn in each of them. Each of these worlds has tasks, which is part of the process of grieving. The *Kaddish* can facilitate that work.

Those who stand for *Kaddish* do so, quite literally in the world of *Assiyah*, but the *Kaddish* has the potential of taking them all the way back up the ladder of creation, through all the worlds to the highest point in the World of *Atzilut*...almost to the *Ein Sof* itself. Standing for *Kaddish* brings all three kabbalistic dimensions (world – *olam*, time — *shana*, and soul — *nefesh*) together. Time and place converge to create an opening for soul. The place one stands for *Kaddish* marks a place in time and space where human bodies can be conduits for bringing the Holy Soul down to earth. Standing for *Kaddish* creates a nexus of the worlds, a place where time and space intersect and create a target coordinate through which holiness can enter the world.

On the horizontal axis, the *Kaddish* is a coordinate in space. It connects the one who mourns to all the other earthlings across the face of the planet who join him or her to say *Kaddish* at any one moment. They stand together to recite the words on behalf of all those who have died recently or for whom a *yahrzeit* (anniversary of a loved one or great teacher's death) is being observed.

On the vertical axis the *Kaddish* provides a coordinate in time. Each *Kaddish* is said not only for the one who is mourned. It is also said for everyone for whom that person said *Kaddish*. Thus each *Kaddish* reaches back in time to all who have preceded us. It passes through their *Kaddish*es to the *Kaddish* said for the primordial soul of the being called *Adam Kadmon* (the kabbalists' conception of a first earthling) the androgynous being who was the first created human and from whom all humankind is descended. As such, the *Kaddish* begins with an immediate personal loss (*katnut*) but heralds standing before the ancient mystery of human finitude that goes all the way back to the beginning (*gadlut*).

When a person stands for *Kaddish*, this intersection of time and space is unique. The individual soul becomes a lightning rod through which the force of holiness, the *ruakh ha-kodesh*, can enter the world. Through the work of "doing *Kaddish*" a person becomes more and more transparent to this Holy Spirit. This enables him or her to give life to the dead (*mekhayeh ha-metim*) or enliven the material world with the sparks of God's name. Following this practice ultimately fulfills the exhortation of the words of the *Kaddish*, "to bring the holiness of God's name to the furthermost reaches of creation." It is ironic that this is done at a time when the individual standing for *Kaddish* may feel furthest from faith in God. This is a reminder of the first act of mourning: to tear a cloth and praise God at the same time.

This healing task works on many levels. According to the mystical understanding, it cleanses the soul of the deceased. It clears a channel through which the holiness of God's name can reach to the furthest worlds from the source of holiness. It repairs the damage to God's name that occurred with each level of creation and repairs the broken worlds in which humans live as they work their way back up the ladder of holiness through grieving the loss.

The words of the *Kaddish* petition for holiness to be returned to each of the worlds. In saying *Kaddish* from each of the Four Worlds, those who grieve heal themselves. They heal the deceased. They heal the world. And they heal the *Sh'mei Rabba*, the Great Name of God. We will walk through each world and then explore the tasks of grief in each of them, as we see how the *Kaddish* can be used to bring healings and creates a paradigm that extends beyond grief for the dead to mourning life's other losses as well.

The Four Worlds of Creation:
A Meditation for Making God Tangible

Imagine God, the Unimaginable Great Name, the *Sh'mei Rabba* (Great Name) of the *Kaddish* or the *Ein Sof* ("Without End") of Kabbalah. Imagine God as a great wind in an inchoate world of holiness. In this world before the worlds, God is a breath that pervades the universe before there is any created thing. That God-Wind (which is all there is), yearns to be manifest. It wants a dwelling place for Holiness — a venue for the enactment of Holiness. From God's yearning God embarks on the experiment of creation. And so unfolds four successive worlds with each world less subtle and more perceptible than those, which preceded it.

To be palpable Holiness must be caught and formed. It must be condensed into something tangible. Imagine a garment being woven of fibers of wind and as the breath of the Unimaginable Great Name blows through it, a world of spirit is captured in its folds. This first world, the world of *Atzilut*, (derived from the word "*etzel*" which means "nearby" and refers to its proximity to God) emanates directly from the *Ein Sof*, the source. Holiness begins to be manifest in a more tangible, but still very abstract, world: the World of Spirit.

But Spirit also wants to be perceived. It yearns for further manifestation. So the *Sh'mei Rabba*, God-Wind blows another breath. This one is directed into a diaphanous fabric of woven light rays, and what is formed is the World of *Beriyah*, (from the Hebrew Word "*bara*" "to create" as in "in the beginning God created…" [Gen. 1:1]. This is the World of Conception, a world of intellect and ideas in which the blueprints for the construction of the less abstract crystallization of being are conceived.

In the World of *Beriyah*, the intention for further creation is asserted. The God-Wind blows again, this time into gossamer strands of interlacing ideas. With that breath emerges the World of *Yetzirah*, (from the Hebrew word "*yatzar*" "to form" as in "God formed man of the dust of the ground"). [Gen 2:7] Ideas, from the World of *Beriyah*, give birth to feelings and emotions as the World of *Yetzirah*. These, in turn, interact, and a breath into the translucent cloth born of that interaction creates the World of *Assiyah*. *Assiyah* (for the Hebrew word that means "to do" or "to make"), is a world of tangible substance and action. It is the material, physical world in which human beings and the things that they do are planted.

A twenty-first century corollary of the Four Worlds points to the emergence of a fifth succeeding world, which derives from the yearning of the World of *Assiyah* to also manifest itself. But there is danger. With each of these successive emanations, as more and more corporeality is achieved, there is damage to the Holy Name, the *Sh'mei Raba*. The initial spark becomes hidden. It becomes harder and harder to contact the pure name of Holiness. Because of its distance from the source, from the *Ohr Ein Sof* (Light of the *Ein Sof*), there is concern that creations in the world which I will call the World of *rakhokiah* (from the word "rahoke" which means "far away") are completely devoid of Holiness. The stuff of this fifth world comes from the combination of material strands of this world, which are the manifestations of the World of *Assiyah*. These creatures could be completely lacking sparks of holiness. The fruit of the World of *Assiyah*, in the World of *rakhokiah* may be too distant from the world of pure holiness to retain the essence of *Atzilut* or the intention of *Beriyah*. These are the substances that do not biodegrade. They choke the planet and they choke the mourner. In the darkest times of mourning, this distance from God is likely to be experienced. The world feels devoid of holiness. This time it is the human who contracts. And in a reversal of the process of creation, it is human yearning from the depths of loss that summons God to descend.[35]

---

35   Brener, Anne. Personal Journal. September, 1997 (unpublished)

Mourning in the World of *Assiyah*

My father's humor, control, and patriarchal generosity made the world predictable. With his death, everything was different. I walked with unsure feet. The world reflected this uncertainty. After his burial came a deluge that his city of New Orleans had not seen in 500 years.[36] I mourned my father in a community of people whose living rooms were filled with mud, whose cars were under water. The world became unpredictable. It was dangerous to walk. In that world, I was a solitary mourner. His only remaining next of kin, I was his *Kaddishele* (*Kaddish*-sayer).

Members of my father's synagogue community came, three times a day, with food and prayer shawls to support me as I began the work of mourning my father. Struggling to learn the words of the *Kaddish*, I leaned on the voices of his community, as they recited the words of the *Kaddish*. These voices, accustomed to joining my father's voice in prayer, surrounded me. Strong at first, they softened as the week wore on and I made the words my own, finding my way once again to the Mourners' Path.[37]

The World of *Assiyah* is the world in which humans spend most of their time. It is the world of action. The most tangible of the worlds, *Assiyah* is the physical world in which mourners wake up each morning to the fact of loss. Here, they remember that someone or something that has been central to their world is no longer present. This is the palpable and practical "real" world in which people live. It is the world in which they feel the physical pain of our broken hearts. In *Assiyah* there is action that must be taken— things to do. This is the world in which the tasks involved in getting through the day can be overwhelming. Funeral arrangements must be made. Possessions must be sorted through. Condolences must be acknowledged.

Mourners may have to learn new skills; skills that might have been performed by someone who is gone. To learn them, it will be necessary to accept the absence of the dead and so mourners face the challenges in the World of *Assiyah* with great ambivalence. *Assiyah* is the world in which mourners miss what is gone. In this world of the physical, they feel the "skin hunger" of longing. They yearn for the touch of those gone. Longing to hold them again, they search for sensual memories. They wrap themselves in their blankets or their sweaters or sniff their coats. Their skin yearns for their touch. They yearn to hear their voices. In the World of *Assiyah*, they must face the memories of what is gone and the stark reality of physical and emotional suffering.

---

36   This took place ten years before the levees broke following Hurricane Katrina in 2005. This flood was an act of God as opposed to the flood that followed Katrina, which was the result of a failure of human engineering.

37   Brener, Anne. Personal Journal. September, 1997 (unpublished)

Physical Care: Creating Order in a Time of Chaos

In the stunned, early phases of loss, mourners need physical caretaking. In the World of *Assiyah*, because they are vulnerable to the high stress and confusion of raw grief, they are likely to neglect themselves. The Talmudic injunction that mourners must be fed by the community guarantees that mourning begins under the watchful and caring communal eye. People bring food to the house of mourning in the week following the burial. After the week of *shiva*, the nourishment becomes emotional as the traditional mourner moves to the synagogue to continue the struggle to inhabit the words of the *Kaddish*. As the voices of the community surround the mourner, punctuating the prayer with a strong "amen," he or she is held in a communal embrace.

At a time that is so often shattering to self-esteem, the unconditional acceptance of the *minyan* (prayer community of ten or more) can be a strong palliative. The meaning of the words at this point is almost incidental as those who recite the prayer claim its sounds as their own. In the World of *Assiyah* mourners can learn to inhabit the *Kaddish* one letter at a time. The words become a lifeline reeling them in from the anxious vastness of uncertainty in which they are lost. Sometimes just focusing on the ink on the page as they try to get through the prayer word-by-word, letter-by-letter is the salvific work.

The words of the *Kaddish* provide those who suffer with a place to go, people to see and something to do—they create regularity in a world of chaos. Sometimes the simple act of surviving from the beginning of the prayer until its end can be a triumphant sign of hope. The *Kaddish* is a vessel in the World of *Assiyah*. It gives a structure to the world and provides a place to stand at a time when mourners are beset by the anguish of struggling to find balance in a world that has lost its moorings. The *Kaddish* in the World of *Assiyah* is a place to show up each day. Since the *Kaddish* must be said in a *minyan*, it surrounds those in pain with the circle of community. This guarantees a consoling embrace at a time when mourners are most likely to feel alone. The *Kaddish* guarantees a place to go when one is at loose ends. To say *Kaddish* the mourner must show up, stand, and recite formulaic words in the midst of a community. In this world of *Assiyah* all that the mourner has to do is to show up and stand for *Kaddish*. Nothing else is required.

In the physical World of *Assiyah*, the absence of what is gone is most palpable. It is a lonely world of yearning where the mourner must learn to walk again and to trust that there will not be an earthquake. This will have to happen despite the fact that it is often a challenge just to place one foot in front of the other. Saying *Kaddish* in this world anchors the mourner to the ground.

The World of *Yetzirah*:
Continuing Communication with What Has Been Lost

The Jewish mystics tell us that the living play a part in the redemption of the dead, by reciting the *Kaddish*...they believe [that mourners] can continue to polish the souls of people who have died...this [suggests a continuing] ...dynamic contact with those who are gone. It [provides] ...the opportunity to say the things that need to be said and signifies that death does not end the relationship...[and that] a relationship can still grow and change and issues can still be explored.

The *Kaddish* can be the vehicle for continued communication, a line between the living and the dead. Over the years, I have learned to use *Kaddish* as a way to communicate with the people I have lost. When I say *Kaddish*, I focus on the person I am remembering and think about what I would like to tell him or her. Through saying *Kaddish*, I have watched my relationships continue to evolve. I have watched as, over time, what I need to say changes, as I move from the painful efforts to voice what I did not say to the bittersweet comfort of once more basking in the presence of the ones I have lost.[38]

In the World of *Assiyah*, so informed by physical activity and material concerns, there is no question that what is lost is gone. In the World of *Yetzirah*, this certainty is a painful challenge. But there is a balm in the possibility this world offers for maintaining the connection.

The World of *Yetzirah* is a world of feelings and interactions. It provides those who suffer with a place for the emotional work that is so essential to *Kaddish*. Here the *Kaddish* is a tool for continuing the conversation with the past and working out unfinished business. This enduring connection is based on kabbalistic understandings of the dynamic ties between souls. This tie with the deceased is especially strong during the first year of mourning and on days of *yahrzeit* and days of *yizkor* (communal remembrance) in the subsequent years. At these times, it is believed that souls are affected by the actions of those remaining on the earth. By saying *Kaddish* on their behalf it is believed that the soul is cleansed of misdeeds and is given the opportunity to rise to become closer to God. The words of *Kaddish* on the lips of those below, this thinking asserts, can affect the destiny of the soul above.

This mystical understanding of loss provides a powerful metaphor for confronting the past in search of a healing and positive connection with what is lost, no matter what the loss has been. This understanding promotes the effort to remove any lingering negative charge from the past.

---

38   Adapted from Brener, *Mourning & Mitzvah: a Guided Journal for Walking the Mourner's Path through Grief to Healing,* Jewish Lights Publishing, 1993, p. 137-138.

As the numbness begins to wear off, those who mourn need emotional caretaking. Here the words of the *Kaddish* change from being the holding place they provided in the World of *Assiyah*, to being a medium—an invisible line of connection between the living and the dead. The words of the *Kaddish* enable the emotional work essential to grieving. They can be the vehicles for the next task of mourning: repairing the severed communication with what has been lost, in order to harvest blessing and purify memory.

In the World of *Yetzirah* purgation occurs. It is here that mourners scrub the past from their eyes until it no longer blinds them to the present. The goal is to erase the constrictions of personal history in such a way that memory is a blessing that propels into the future. ....On the wings of the *Kaddish*, those who suffer express their concerns for what is gone. As they struggle to find peace in the relationship with that which is being mourned, they discover the opportunity they need to confront the past and its lingering emotional issues.

It is in the World of *Yetzirah* that the window is opened on previous losses. Mourners may inventory other difficult times to explore their impact on the current situation. They can harvest past learning and apply it to the current challenge. In addition they may face what was not fully confronted at earlier rough places, identifying the growing edge left hanging in the past. The new experience of pain thus becomes a double-edged sword. Not only does it call for grief-work concerning the fresh low but it also forces the mourner to deal with the unfinished business of past suffering as it provides an opportunity to re-visit an old wound with the gift of healing

All losses occur in the middle of a conversation. The suffering that comes in their wake forces an effort to recover that conversation with the past in order to work through unfinished business, bring healing with the past, and make peace with the current circumstances. Mourners must find the honest voice for their guilts, regrets, angers, and love. Loss must not silence these voices, for they bring healing to the severed relationships and return those who suffer to their own developmental issues. The World of *Yetzirah* invites those who grieve to come to more nurturing connections with their past, as they resume their individual journeys

The World of *Beriyah*

Stephanie stood in the room stamping her foot as we said the *Kaddish*. Her voice was angry and each time she reached a point of punctuation in the prayer, she read it as if it were a question mark. Finally she turned to me and shrieked, "These words are an insult. They were put here to torture me. 'God's Great Name?'" Sarcastically, she asked me, "I should want it Praised beyond all the other praises?" The *Kaddish* challenges our relationship with Holiness. It inserts a question mark as mourners ask, like Stephanie, "What kind of God would do that to my brother?"[39]

Beriyah is the intellectual World. This is where mourners ask the existential questions about life on a planet where people die, and about the nature of God, justice and the universe. In the world of *Beriyah* mourners consider how they want their lives to change in light of these questions: If, after a loss, a person gets back to his or her regular path immediately— what has he or she learned? A significant loss is likely to call into question each assumption that is held about life. The mourner, who is on the path to becoming an elder, is not likely to retreat to familiar rhetoric, bromides and explanations about the meaning of life. In all of these situations the one who grieves has lost, not only a significant person, situation or object, but may have lost the foundation of his or her world.

From the depths of grief, the mourner may wonder what the purpose of suffering must be or, to broaden the question, if life itself has any meaning. Often, after a loss, people no longer are satisfied with the answers to these profound questions that may have served in the past. This is especially true for those whose image of God may have been of a benevolent protector who rewards good and punishes evil. But this existential earthquake of meaning is essential to loss. If a person is not lost following a loss, they may not yet have experienced that loss as a teacher, prompting the mourner to examine the human condition and his or her own mortality. With all the anguish and difficulty that come with suffering, what a shame to feel that the experience had no impact on the way in which life is viewed. In the World of *Beriyah*, meaning is sought. Mourners must write a new contract with life, God, and the Universe.

Finding Meaning: A New Contract with Life, God, and the Universe

The cauldron of mourning is a place to question everything. Here meanings of the words of the *Kaddish* begin to come into focus, however sometimes they are less of a balm and more of a challenge. The words of the *Kaddish* praise God's Great Name so highly and express the desire to see the entire universe infused with Its Holiness. Rallying behind these words can be an outrageous expectation of an anguished person. Suffering is likely to provoke a profound spiritual crisis. Loss is likely to cause one to question the nature of

---

39   As with all clinical vignettes presented in this work, this is a composite constructed from my work with many clients and does not describe any one individual or situation. All names are changed and stories rendered so as to make identification impossible.

God, justice, and the universe. It raises suspicion regarding the meaning of life on a planet where people suffer and mortality is guaranteed.

According to traditional Jewish mourning practice, the *Kaddish* is repeated over and over following a loss. This repetition is an opportunity to confront the forces that run the universe with all the questions about a world that metes out pain and justice in what appears to be an arbitrary manner. Here the *Kaddish* can act as a crowbar, forcing open a belief system that has suddenly become too small to hold the great paradoxes of Holiness and Horror that dwell together in the universe. By daring, like Job, to perseverate on God's injustice, mourners ask the questions over and over again, hammering at the limits of their understanding until they break a hole in it and crawl through a wormhole into a new universe of meaning. Their world gets larger. They come to embrace the paradoxes of being human, and somehow move to a new plateau on which it is possible to make peace with a God and a universe they cannot totally comprehend.

This theme of hiddenness pervades the book of Job as Job seeks to reveal Justice, Truth, and God, all of which are buried in mystery. Early on Job depicts the non-linear and confused thinking of one who has been stricken by grief. His disjunctive statements reveal the chaotic quality of the thoughts of those who grieve. Lost in their internal ruminations the lines of logic are also lost. The thought processes are disordered. Job is hidden from himself.

Later Job's words become one long question addressed to an unidentifiable force in the universe. In subsequent chapters, he begins to find his voice. This question is particularized and directed to Job's friends and to God. This indirect, rambling and nonlinear challenge of the cosmic order is a preparation for the later questions, which will directly accost God. It is the inchoate rumination of the world of *Beriyah*, in which those who suffer gain courage. They rise from stunned grief and premature spiritual acceptance to be energized for the healing journey. With powerful images, the words of Job hammer on the psyche as do the repetitive string of words of interrogation and resistance. This unremitting perseveration is the tool of grief through which it "knocks on heaven's door"[40] in an effort to find an opening which will reveal the secret passage to a wisdom and peace which can shatter the old world and give shape to the new.

The World of *Atzilut*

> Dream: My mother was calling from far, far away, perhaps from another world. The telephone was a model from the time of my birth: black, heavy and with a rotary dial. But its chord was shimmering: translucent,

---

40   Bob Dylan. "Knocking on Heaven's Door." Pat Garret and Billy the Kid. Musical album, 1974.

somewhat metallic and pulsating—filled with veins and blood — an umbilical chord, connecting us after her death.[41]

Finally there is the Spiritual world in which those who suffer make a new peace with what is holy. Often coming through a crisis of faith demands a completely new experience of Divinity. Here the task is to come to trust in the presence of God, the presence of the deceased, and the presence of the parts of ourselves that have been surrendered in the wake of our struggles and to know that they are all one.

As the old assumptions of faith and/or meaning are shattered and a larger worldview emerges, the mourner enters a spiritual domain, which can slowly bring a new peace with what life has brought. This peace, which Elizabeth Kubler-Ross calls acceptance, recognizes that mourning never entirely comes to an end and that healing does not mean the cessation of grief. Rather healing delivers an ability to integrate pain and find a bounded place for the grief in our lives— a holy place where it is neither denied nor idolized but can be nourished, attended to, and recognized as one of many parts of an individual's history. The great achievement, experienced in the world of *Atzilut*, is in ceding the physical connection to the person who is gone and coming to a comfortable peace with a spiritual relationship.

Mourners ricochet between the four worlds. They are propelled by their yearning and their heartbreak and also by their hope. A dead end in one world may reveal a gateway to work that must be done in another. As they move back and forth in their explorations, they find unexpected comfort and answers. Over time, with attention to the grief work and the process of healing as framed by the *Kaddish* and its understanding, those who suffer come to terms with the words of the *Kaddish*. Creating a world filled with God's name now seems a reasonable goal, despite the fact that one may have been cursing God's name just a few minutes earlier. Out of the darkness in which the old concepts of faith have ceased to serve, a new theology emerges. The words of the *Kaddish* match the mourner's experience as he or she comes through the crisis of faith to articulate a new experience of what is Holy. Perhaps God's name can no longer be spoken, but paradoxically, the mourner may hold a renewed sense of what is sacred, embracing life and its sanctity all the more tightly. The difference between the World of *Beriyah* and the World of *Atzilut* are clear here. They parallel the differences between belief and faith and between theology and encounter. In the world of *Beriyah* the mourner struggles intellectually to come to terms with God. In *Atzilut* he or she simply dwells in Holiness.

Let us return to the Jewish law which bids the mourner, upon hearing of the death of someone close, to tear his or her garment and immediately recite a phrase in praise of "God the true Judge." This challenges the mourner to trust God's truth despite his or her

---

41   Anne Brener, *Meaning & Mitzvah*, Jewish Lights, 1993. pp 138-139.

ruptured feelings. It can be a long journey from the initial moment of brokenness caused by the news of the death through the emotional work of grieving to finally being able to praise God, according to the formula of the blessing: *Barukh dayan emet*, blessed is the true Judge.

So I ask again, what is the purpose of that teaching which bids mourners to tear and praise in one act? It might be seen as an offensive instruction deliberately designed to challenge the mourner. The words seem to force an immediate confrontation between the bereaved person and the force that runs the universe. Such an outrageously provocative assertion could pierce the initial numbness and re-kindle the mourners' passion. That passion is the life-giving fire with which one begins the process of healing. Such a line can also leave the mourner speechless. It emphasizes that humans are not in control, reminding us that very little is known about the larger questions in life: what it means to be human, the journey of the soul, why we are on this planet, and what causes life and death. Like Job, in the final chapters of his book, mourners are silenced in awe at the mystery that is life. Perhaps this practice is simply spiritual guidance, designed to provide an answer to those questions and to direct the mourner to the challenge of coming to peace with that verdict. As Job said, "I relent, knowing that I am dust and ashes."

By attending to the tasks of grief that are present in each of the four worlds, mourners can work their way up the ladder to proximity with what is holy. Their human *tzimtzum* (contraction) could summon God back into the world. In the process, it is likely that they will change and that the world in which they live will cease to resemble the world they knew before the events occurred that propelled them on this journey. They may encounter new feelings, new ideas, and new faith. They may make new friends. As was said above, it is likely that they may not be able to call the Divine by the name they used before. To climb the ladder to the World of *Atzilut*, it will be necessary to battle, like Jacob, some unknown force and to come out victorious. Like Jacob, who walked with a limp after his confrontation with the being, they are likely to continue to show signs of the scrimmage. And like Jacob when he dreamed of angels, they may come to recognize what can be said about the profound journey through this wilderness that is grief, "God is in the place and I, I knew it not." [Gen. 28:16]

Recommended Reading

Anne Brener, *Mourning & Mitzvah: a Guided Journal for Walking the Mourner's Path through Grief to Healing*, Woodstock, Jewish Lights Publishing, 1993

> "Taking the Time You Need for Mourning" in Nancy Flam (Ed.) *Life Lights*, Jewish Lights Publishing, 2000

> "Spiritual Companionship and the Passages of Life." in *Jewish Spiritual Direction: An Innovative Guide from Traditional and Contemporary Source*, Howard Avruhm Addison & Barbara Breitman, (Eds.), Jewish Lights Publishing, 2006

Stephen Levine, *Who Dies? An Investigation of Conscious Living and Conscious Dying*, Anchor Books, 1982

Rabbi Goldie Milgram, "Chapter 8: Leaving Life" in *Living Jewish Life Cycle: How to Create Meaningful Jewish Rites of Passage at Every Stage of Life*, Jewish Lights Publishing, 2009

Yosef Yitchak Schneersohn, *The Four Worlds*, Kehot Publication Society, 2003

Leon Weiseltier, *Kaddish*, Knopf, 1998

D. Zlotnick [ed. & trans], *The Tractate: Mourning (Semahot)*, Yale University Press, 1986

Additional Website(s):

Ascent-of-Safed. "Dictionary of Terms"
http://www.kabbalaonline.org/staticpages/glossary.asp#M.

http://www.jewfaq.org/prayer/*kaddish*.htm

Opening to God in *Gehinnom*: Issues for the *Mashpia* in Being Fully Present to Suicide Survivors
by Chaya Gusfield

Rabbi Chaya Gusfield has served individuals and groups as a Spiritual Director since 1999 and was the Assistant Rabbi for Beth Chaim Congregation in Danville, California for seven years. She currently serves as a chaplain and works extensively with grief and mourning in the Jewish tradition as a path to healing. She was the interim rabbi for Temple Beth Ora in Edmonton, Canada and has a long association with Kehilla Community Synagogue. She is passionate about engaging in Jewish practices to celebrate the joys of life and to assist us in our day to day heartbreak.

Gehinnom can be considered the liminal space between this life and where we hope to be after death. The Rabbis traditionally view *gehinnom* as a place where people are punished for up to twelve months for their errors made on earth. By doing mitzvot, we can lessen the time in *gehinnom*. During this time, the soul goes through a period of atonement and purification as she prepares to go on to *gan eden*, the World to Come. Kabbalistic philosophy discusses *gehinnom* as a place where impurities of the soul are cleansed in a process of fire, representing passion.

I associate *gehinnom* with places that are beyond our understanding. Being in the shadow of the suicide of a child or a loved one can feel like being in *gehinnom*. It is beyond what our minds and hearts can comprehend. *Gehinnom* is any place where my primal woundedness meets another's, before it has gone through the healing and purification needed to be able to be fully present to myself or the other. When we are in our own *gehinnom*, how do we open to God?

It was the evening after the end of Yom Kippur. I received the call in the middle of the night, but my ringer was still off from my practice during the *hagim* (holidays), so I didn't hear the message until morning. By the time I returned the call, another spiritual leader from our community had responded to the emergency. A 14 year old boy had attempted suicide and the family needed our support. Although I was a rabbinical student and had been serving as a spiritual leader and *mashpi'ah* for several years, I still had work to do on my own history and pain about suicide to be fully present to others experiencing the earthquake of attempted or completed suicide. In this case, the boy tragically died. I was relieved I had missed the call and that I didn't have to officiate at the funeral. When the funeral was held, I didn't go. I was not ready to serve in this context.

When I explored my response to this tragedy with my *mashpi'ah*, I realized that my turning away from this family was a turning toward myself. God was inviting me to pay close attention to my own experience, history, and responses before serving others touched so closely by suicide. Several weeks after the death of this young boy, I took an important step toward healing. I attended a gathering called by therapists at the synagogue for anyone in the community who wanted to talk about the experience and how it had affected them. During this intimate gathering, I shared my history with suicide in my family, my reluctance to respond to this family, and my prayer that one day I would be able to serve families who had survived the suicide of a loved one.

Later that year, I had the chance. I had moved forward in my own process and when I received a call from the mother of this boy who had suicided, I was more ready and able to respond. She didn't know me, but wanted to join my annual Spiritual Direction group for mourners called "May Their Memory Be a Blessing." In those groups we focused on our relationship with the Divine/Sacred and how that relationship moved through our grieving process. She wanted to meet me in person to make sure we would be a good fit. We met, we connected, and she joined the group.

The groups of five or six mourners were very healing. We included mourners of all kinds of loss (parent, child, spouse, sibling) and we met six times over four months. The groups were reflective, unlike a regular "grief group." With each two-hour session, we shared with one another after very specific guided reflections that focused on some aspect of our connection with the Divine and with our mourning process. Woven into the groups were Jewish teachings and liturgy on mourning and healing, and practices to try in between sessions.

A *mashpia* drawn to work with survivors of a family member's suicide is likely, like myself, to have such a history in one's own family. The issues I faced on the journey from my own teenage trauma as a survivor of suicide to becoming able to serve as a healthy *mashpi'ah* for others, are likely to prove instructive for those doing similar work in *hashpa'ah*. How does one open to God during *gehinnom*? How did I become able to be present to this mother who called me and to God's guidance in this tragedy as a *mashpi'ah* and spiritual leader/rabbi?

There are so many factors that can contribute to the lifelong healing journey from the family tragedy of suicide. When my 21-year-old sister took her life as a result of her struggle with schizophrenia, I was almost 14. Receiving individual, group and family therapy from a Suicide Prevention therapist skilled at working with survivors, attending 12 Step meetings for Co-dependents (Al-anon), and learning about death, dying and mourning with experts like Stephen and Ondrea Levine helped to frame the journey, but these tools just began to scratch the surface.

It wasn't until I immersed myself in our tradition and directly faced the legacy of judgment and shame of suicide embedded in Jewish law that I stopped turning away when faced with tragedies that touched that deep open wound.

Even as a teenage secular Jew I felt the reach of our tradition's intolerance to those who suicided. I felt shame about my sister's death and somehow I learned that Jewish tradition also shunned the survivors of suicide. I later learned that Jewish law taught that survivors of a suicide were not allowed to access the full spectrum of Jewish mourning rituals. (*Shulkhan Aruch, Yoreh Deah* 345) Modern *halakhic* thought has eased this restriction. The restrictive law for mourners of a suicide discussed in *Yoreh Deah* 345 now is only applied where the person suicided intentionally. Now, almost all suicides are determined to be unintentional because we understand that no one in their right mind would take their life. Even with the easing of the law for mourners of a suicide, I was deeply affected and hurt by what I experienced as a legacy of shame, judgment, and lack of compassion towards those who suicided and their survivors.

Yet, in the same Jewish tradition that I was so hurt by, I found healing that broke through this legacy of shame, with two simple words. In our tradition, we say of loved ones who have died, "*zikhronam livrakha*" "May their memory be a blessing." Sometimes we say, "*alav or aleha shalom*...May peace be upon him or her."

This is one of our most precious spiritual practices. When we mention the dead and stop to say *zikhronam livrakha*, or *aleha ha-shalom*, we have the opportunity to continue our conversations with them, to receive blessings, and to offer them blessing, through the process of remembering them.

One day, I received an unexpected call from someone I didn't know from New York. She was trying to reach someone else at our synagogue and stumbled on my name and number in the process. She told me that she knew my family from when I was a child. My whole family. And then she said, "I knew your sister Julie, *zikhrona livrakha*." She said that they were the same age. The fact that she said her name and then followed it by *zikhrona livrakha* took my breath away. I don't believe I had ever heard anyone say Julie's z'l name with that blessing before. I asked myself, what was the blessing that I was supposed to receive by remembering her in this moment? I thought about it for many days. What is the blessing? My sister died a tragic death and for most of my life remembering her did not always feel like a blessing. It was a difficult memory. Her memory brought great pain and suffering to our family.

And yet, our tradition asks us to remember those who have died as a blessing every time we mention their name. I believe this practice offers us a profound opportunity. Rabbi Marcia Prager (building on the work of Rabbi Joseph Gikatilla) invites us to see a *brakhah* as the process of humbling ourselves by bending the knees (*birkayim*), reaching into the pool (*breykhah*) and experiencing the fountain of blessings as endless possibilities.

Another way to think about *zikhrona livrakha* is "May her memory be for endless possibilities." Whether you are the survivor of someone who experienced a tragic death, whether you have only difficult feelings about the person who died, or whether all you can remember are sweet moments, by saying *zikhronam livrakha*, we open the door to endless possibilities; to anger, radical amazement, deep grief, a softening of the belly, the warmth of our heart, deep humility. The key is that there are endless possibilities. The door is open to those who have died, and the door is open to our own healing process.

In addition to feeling embraced by our tradition of remembering for a blessing, I notice that in every aspect of my healing I find the concept of companionship and witnessing a primary experience. Even our intellectual study takes place in an environment where ideas are discussed, debated, and struggled about with another person, eventually being integrated into the framework of the healing journey.

This companionship and witnessing is also found in the Jewish experience of *hevruta*, partner study of our sacred texts, which often includes bringing one's own life experience through the lens of the text. The central experience that allowed me to fully engage in healing and find my way to being present in the midst of my *gehinnom* of suicide was the committed *hevruta* (study partner) I am blessed to have. We have similar patterns of family wounding. We speak the same language. We both sit in the shadow of mental illness and suicide in our lives and the avalanche that comes after it. We remember together. We witness together, cry together, and laugh together. We study Jewish law together and we outrage together. We support one another to speak openly and without shame about suicide and we think creatively about healing rituals.

As we are present with one another's life experience and pain, we serve as a place to learn how to be present to ourselves and to others in need. We call upon the preciousness of our experience with one another as we are called to serve as rabbis, chaplains, and *mashpi'ot* to those touched by tragedy.

The Slonimer Rebbe teaches us an important lesson regarding *dibuk haverim*, the connection or clinging to friends or those in your community. [*Chassidut, Chevruta*, essay 4, page 307] He teaches that through cleaving with friends that love/fear God, the entire community raises itself up. Through this path of cleaving with a friend, they are considered as one person watched and guarded by God. When we are in a place that makes it difficult for us to find our way to God by ourselves, maybe because we can't pray or we haven't prepared properly for *Shabbat*, if we bind our heart to another who can, their prayer or their preparation will bring us to God.

Pirkei Avot (Ethics of the Fathers) teaches, *kaneh l'kha chaver*, find yourself a friend. The Slonimer suggests that we should hold on tight and let our friend raise us up when we are in our personal *gehinnom* and need help opening to God. In my experience of my *hevruta*, we understood that at the beginning, we could only witness each other's woundedness and raise each other up for short periods of time. There was no pressure between us that we had to show up or serve. We did it slowly, at our own pace, and only when we felt completely ready. We learned how to be still with one another. We knew that by rushing in too close, too fast, we might cause ourselves to turn away. By taking this care and time to raise up my friend in her time of need, and allowing myself to be raised up in my time of need, I slowly developed a strong intuitive sense of connection with God in the midst of tragedy.

This work in *hevruta* over time has helped me develop my "muscles" for being present in the midst of *gehinnom* so that my first instinct is no longer to turn away. It helped me learn how to be still and open to God with those who seek me for counsel as rabbi, *mashpi'ah* or chaplain in the midst of their deepest tragedies.

When I received the call from this bereaved mother months after the death of her son, I called my friend, and told her that God wasn't letting me turn away this time. I knew I was ready. And we cried.

Recommended Reading

Sidney Goldsten, *Suicide in Rabbinic Literature*, Ktav Publishing House, 1989

Chaya Gusfield, "May Their Memory Be for a Blessing: A Report on Jewish Spiritual Direction Groups for the Grieving," *Presence: An International Journal of Spiritual Direction, Vol. 14, No. 1*, March, 2008

Goldie Milgram, *Living Jewish Life Cycle: How to Create Meaningful Rites of Passage at Every Stage of Life*, Jewish LIghts, 2009.

Marcia Prager, *The Path of Blessing*, Jewish Lights Publishing, 1998

Simcha Paull Raphael, *Jewish Views of the Afterlife*, Jason Aaronson, 1994

Additional Website(s):

http://www.reclaimingjudaism.org/life_20cycle/suicide.htm

Part III

Accessing Guides and Advocates

Guidance from Other Dimensions of the God-Field: Ancestors, Angels and Guides

by Shohama Wiener

Rabbi Shohama Wiener, DMin., is founding Director of The Aleph Ordination Program in Jewish Spiritual Direction, and also serves as Rosh Hashpa'ah, Director of Spiritual Development for the Aleph Ordination Programs and ReclaimingJudaism.org. A widely published author and composer of healing music, she also serves as rabbi for Temple Beth-El of City Island, NY. Shohama was the first woman in Jewish history to head a seminary; she served as Dean, President and Rosh Hashpa'ah of The Academy for Jewish Religion from 1986-2001. www.ReclaimingJudaism.org

Author's Note: The people whose experiences I have reported have specifically given permission for me to use their names.

Ayn od milvado, "There is nothing other than God," is at the core of the Hasidic approach to *hashpa'ah,* Jewish spiritual direction. Everything that we experience in life contains messages from God. Even so, there are many dimensions to experiencing the Divine. All of these may be called the God-Field.[42] Those of us who work as *mashpi'im,* spiritual directors named after the Hasidic tradition of spiritual mentoring, know that God speaks to us through our sacred texts, our experiences, and our intuition. And yet it is also part of the Hasidic tradition to know that God has provided us with messengers of light and learning who assist with the great work of Guidance. The Jewish heritage supplies us with an abundance of examples of Biblical heroes and prophets, as well as sages throughout the generations, whose lives were enhanced by guidance from God's messengers. (For a short review of the literature, see the internet articles by Rabbis Geoffrey Dennis and David Wolpe.[43]) The first Jews, Abraham and Sarah, received an announcement of the miraculous birth of Isaac when three angels in the form of men visited their tent.[44] Their grandson Jacob had his name changed to Israel after wrestling a blessing from an angel.[45] Famous teachers such as Joseph Karo (author of the guide to Jewish law called the *Shulkhan Arukh*) and Rabbi Moshe Chayyim Luzzatto (author of

---

42   Thanks to Rabbi Zalman Schachter-Shalomi for introducing me to this expression.

43   Rabbi David Wolpe, http://www.beliefnet.com/Faiths/Judaism/2002/04/Angels-In-Jewish-

44   Gen. 18:10

45   Gen. 32:29

many books on spiritual and ethical practice) reported being taught by a spirit teacher called a *maggid*.[46] The Baal Shem Tov, the founder of Hasidism, was said to have been taught by a spirit guide named Ahijah of Shiloh (I Kings 11:19f).[47]

Closer to home, tradition teaches that Elijah the Prophet is still able to be present to us in spirit form. Accordingly, it is customary for Jews to invite him to every circumcision, and to place a cup of wine for him on our Passover *seder* tables. We invite him in as a *seder* guest in hopes that this will be the time he will announce the coming of the Messiah or messianic age. Judaism has a long lineage of spiritual guides who are available to those who seek them. In synagogues and at home, when *Shabbat* begins, it is customary to sing a song of greeting, "*Shalom Aleikhem*," written by the medieval Kabbalist Shlomo Halevi Alkabetz. This liturgical piece welcomes the special angels it depicts as joining us on *Shabbat* as guests at home and in synagogue. In addition, the traditional prayer for travelers, called *Tefilat ha-Derekh*, calls in angels to guard and protect us on our journeys.

Note: See Appendix B for a musical version by Rabbi Hanna Tiferet Siegel.

Mushpa'im (seekers) who come to us will likely have had subtle or not so subtle experiences of the presence of beloved relatives, of angels that rescue and heal and nudge, and of guides in spirit form who were rebbes or prophets or teachers. Our *mushpa'im* may not bring these experiences into the *hashpa'ah* session unless we ask.

If we ask, doors may open. This is what happened when I first met with Adalah Caplowe (then a *hazzan*, now also a rabbi and *mashpi'ah*) in the Summer of 2005. Intuitively, I felt the need to ask her if she felt the presence of any guides in spirit form. She writes, "My opening to my spiritual guides, who had been waiting, began when I first met Reb Shohama…I felt that Reb Shohama's soul and mine were communicating from the beginning, and the sheer joy of being able to connect with someone in this way began my journey to awakening my spiritual soul-self."

Since that time, Adalah has engaged in what she perceives to be regular communication with her guidance team, which includes the Baal Shem Tov, her grandfather, *Sarah Imenu* (our Mother Sarah, the Biblical matriarch), and a number of angels. These guides, all servants of the Holy One, have served her well in discerning how to lead her congregation, to flower as a poet and composer, and to serve as a *mashpi'ah* to those drawn to work with her.

---

46 Louis Jacobs, *Jewish Mystical Testimonies*, Schocken Books, 1976, pp. 122 and 169.
47 Ibid., p. 189.

Ancestors

Many people have told me stories of how they received messages from relatives who have departed this realm. I am by nature a skeptic — I only believe something once I have experienced it. But I believe them. Let me share the story that convinced me that the soul remains alive after death.

In 1993, I was a guest rabbi for High Holiday services in Florida, and stayed at the home of a deeply spiritual woman, Laurel Freeman, who was a trained massage therapist. After Yom Kippur, she asked if I wanted a massage, and I eagerly said "Yes." What I didn't then know was that she was also skilled at connecting with spirit beings. At the end of the massage she turned to me and said:

> "This is very strange. While you were on the table my guide began a conversation with your guide, and said, 'I have to get a message to Shohama.' So I said, 'Give me a password so Shohama will know that you are real.' "

> "Tell her 'Hims'," said my guide.

> Replied Laurel, "Well, that's strange. Give me another password."

> "Tell her 'cigar'," said my guide.

> "OK. What's the message?" asked Laurel.

> "Tell her that her grandfather is here with her father, and her father wants her to know he thinks she's on a good path."

When I heard this I felt spiritual chills run up and down my spine, a feeling I sense even now as I write this. My grandfather Saul, for whom I am named, was an atheist, and my father an agnostic. I knew two stories about Grandpa Saul, that he called my sister by the pet name "Hims," and that he was usually seen with a cigar. There was no rational explanation I could find for Laurel Freeman knowing these stories about my grandfather.

That unexpected connection provided emotional healing for me. I felt that two important men in my life, who would not have understood fully my spiritual calling during their lifetime, now gave their wholehearted loving approval. In working with my own *mushpa'im*, I have often found that connecting these seekers with their loved ones on the other side has led to new forms of understanding and healing.

Angels

I used to think that angels were mere folklore, a literary device found in tall-tales. My shift began in the mid 1980's, when I joined the Manhattan congregation of the great musical rebbe, Shlomo Carlebach, of blessed memory. In addition to the music being gloriously uplifting, his theology challenged and inspired me. My favorite song was *b'Shaim HaShem* (in the name of God) — The Angel Song, which contained the text asking for blessing, in the name of God, from the four Archangels *Micha-el*, *Gavri-el*, *Uri-el* and *Rafa-el*, as well as the *Shekhinah* (God's presence in rabbinic literature, which evolved into God's feminine side in Judaism).[48] This text appears in traditional prayer books as part of the bedtime *Shema* prayer. I made it a practice to chant the song or say the words morning and night, as well as at other times when I needed protection.

I wasn't sure initially whether the angels were "real" or just a name for energetic qualities of love, strength, vision, and healing. After studying the tradition and realizing that they appear in many places in the Hebrew Bible, as well as in the Talmud and mystical Jewish literature, I was able to suspend my doubts.

One day in 1994 I was lying on my bed, in a meditative frame of mind, when a huge, loving wave of energy swept through my body. In my mind's eye I saw a large, loving man with huge wings, and felt intuitively that he was an angel. A name came to me, which I hold close to my heart. As I called out this name, my body became swept up in waves of ecstatic energy. That is how this angel made his appearance known. Since that time, I connect regularly with his presence, which feels like a loving and wise guide. I sense that he is the specific angel that God has sent me to help with my work as a *mashpi'ah* and teacher of *hashpa'ah*.

Our sister religions, Christianity and Islam, also teach about the significance of angels as agents of God. M. Ibrahim Baha'uddin Farajaje, a professor, Sheikh and spiritual director in the Sufi tradition, shared with me his life-changing encounter with an angel. A couple of years ago he was in the hospital, at death's door due to a serious lung infection, feeling as if he were drowning. Finally he dozed, and saw an enormous Archangel place his hands on the left side of his chest and pull out "something." The Archangel communicated without words that all would be well, and that this was his initiation so that he could help others through the passageway to the Divine Light.

The following day chest X-rays were taken, revealing only healthy tissue. The pathology in the left side of his lung had vanished. Professor Farajaje experienced this as a miracle sent by God through the Divine messenger, the Archangel.

---

48   A number of websites, such as http://www.rhapsody.com/shlomo-carlebach/haneshama-shel-shlomo, will let you play this song for free.

Not all encounters with angels bring about miracles; but they always serve a function or bring a message. For example, in the spring of 2008, while in meditation, I wrote down the following, which I felt came from the angelic realm:

> Dearly Beloved, I come to you today with a message of hope. Be not fearful for your future. We here stand ready to assist you in the evolution of your planet. **But we must be asked**. You have been given a great and difficult task, to raise the energies of your bodies and of your planet to a level where peace and love will prevail. It begins with you, each one of you.
>
> Know that the force of light can banish darkness whenever it is directed in sufficient strength. Your strength lies in numbers. It says in your Talmud, "Every blade of grass has its angel that bends over it and whispers, 'Grow, grow.'" How much more is it true for every human.
>
> We bless you to grow, grow.

Guides

Jewish opinion generally holds that angels are a form of guide sent by God. These angels may appear temporarily in human form, but have not lived incarnated lives. However, there are other guides that a person may see, sense and/or feel that have lived in a bodily form. How these guides manifest can vary greatly; some report animal guides, or visitations from people from other centuries and/or other traditions. Others feel like they are receiving clear information from a spirit teacher known in Jewish mystical literature by the Hebrew word *maggid*, referring to an angelic spirit, the soul of a sacred text, or even the *Shekhinah*.[49]

It would not have occurred to me to seek a guide who was once a rebbe until my second visit to Israel, in 1980. In that visit I saw that it was the custom for people to visit the graves of famous rabbis and *rebbe*s, and to light candles there and pray for their help with all manner of problems ranging from illness to finding an apartment. Unlike what I was taught growing up, it was clear to me that Judaism does have a tradition of asking for intercessory prayer from *tzaddikim* (righteous ones), those known to have especially strong connection with the Divine.

My sense is that all of us who are called to serve as *mashpi'im* have at least one rebbe guide. It probably is someone whose teachings we admire greatly. Over time, a guide may change. There are some who experience one or more of their guides as archetypal messengers from aspects of their own souls. This interpretation is also echoed in Jungian psychology.

---

49   Thanks to Rabbi Elliot Ginsburg, Ph.D., for this definition.

Meeting Your Guides

If you wish to connect with one of your ancestors, angels, or guides, go into a deep contemplative prayer state, and ask to meet him or her. It may be easier if you have your own *mashpia* or spiritual teacher lead you in a guided visualization, or if you record a guided visualization that you can play back to guide yourself. The exact form doesn't matter; what matters is that you get into a waking dream state where you are in touch with your soul level of guidance.

For a guided visualization see Appendix A.

Precautionary Measures

1. Directing Prayers to God

Jewish tradition holds that we pray only to God, but that we may request help from God's messengers.[50]

2. Protection

In your opening prayer, it is important to ask God to align you with only the "highest guidance" and "guides" for you at this time. A helpful practice is to visualize your self filled with and surrounded by sparkling white light. In your closing prayer, thank these highest sources of guidance, and ask that your energy be grounded so that you can function well in your daily activities. It is important to eat well, connect with nature, and get sufficient exercise. There is also a custom, which I follow, of wearing a *kameya* (amulet)—a piece of specially designed religious jewelry that lies over the heart, and has spiritual meaning for you.

---

50   Rabbi Judah [sic.] teaches in the Talmud that God wishes to be directly addressed: "If trouble comes upon someone, let him cry not to Michael or Gabriel, but let him cry unto Me (*Jerusalem Talmud Berachot* 9:12)." Rabbi David Wolpe at http://www.beliefnet.com/Faiths/Judaism/2002/04/Angels-In-Jewish-Tradition.aspx?p=3

3. Discernment

Hearing voices and seeing images can be either the sign of a mystic or a psychotic, and can come from a high and holy place or a dark, ethically challenged and often dangerous realm sometimes referred to as the *sitra akhra* (the Other Side). How do we tell the difference? As we all have blind spots, it is essential for all of us to be in *hashpa'ah*, to be supervised by our own *mashpia*.

What will we and our *mashpia* look for? First of all, are the messages and guides loving and kind? Do they suggest actions that are ethical, that would serve not only our highest good but that of others as well?

Secondly, does the advice lead us in the direction of our highest dreams? Does the message repeat in different ways? Do doors open for us that seem beyond coincidence? Does it feel like Divine energy is powering our path?

I conclude with thanks to the Holy One, the Source of All, for inspiration and guidance, and for giving me the courage to go public with my experiences of Divine messengers and guides. May this be for the highest good of all creation.

APPENDIX A

Visualization for Finding Your Guide(s)
by Rabbinic Pastor David Daniel Klipper

Editor's Note: This visualization was written with the guide (which the author calls an angel) providing unconditionally positive and affirming responses. It is a visualization akin to the approach of Roberto Assagioli, the Jewish founder of Psychosynthesis. Followers of the imaginal methods of Mme. Colette Aboulker Muscat would more likely listen for the directee's discernment/experience of his/her angel's nature and response.

Instructions

Read the instructions slowly, and allow some time to pass after each one. For the person facilitating the guided meditation, you might want to go along with the process in your imagination, provided that you don't get so absorbed that you forget to give the next instruction. However, this should give you a sense of when to give the next instruction.

The Meditation

- Please sit in a chair, legs on the floor, hands on your legs, back straight, eyes closed. Make sure you are in a comfortable and open position.

- Imagine that you are taking a walk in a beautiful place. It could be anywhere you want, real or imaginary, as long as it is a place where you feel safe and good. Imagine seeing the place where you are walking in your mind.

- Now listen for the sounds that you can hear in this place.

- Now experience what it feels like to be in that place. Are there body sensations that you have? Smells that you experience?

- When you have a good sense of being in this place, imagine that you walk a little further and meet an angel in your path. Somehow you know immediately that this angel is only there for your good and you feel very safe.

- As you are with the angel, somehow it communicates with you. It might be that you have visual images, or you hear its voice, or you sense its communication inside of you. You can decide how you are able to know what it is communicating, but you know with absolute certainty that you can understand what the angel is trying to communicate.

- The angel tells you that God is very pleased with you and your efforts to grow into the person God wants you to be, the best person and your highest self. The angel says that it is there to assist you in your growth and development.

- Now take a little time to say anything back to the angel that you want to say.

- The angel then tells you that it is here to help you attain your deepest yearning. It invites you to tell it what your deepest truth is in terms of who you are and who you want to become. Prepare to tell this to the angel, but make sure that you look deeply within yourself to ensure that what you tell the angel is your deepest truth. Be conscious of how you know that what you are going to say is your deepest truth.

- When you are ready, tell this truth to the angel.

- After you tell this truth to the angel, the angel tells you back that it is very pleased with your response and that it will be helping, guiding and supporting you. The angel then gives you a blessing, and then leaves.

- Imagine yourself continuing to walk along a little bit, and then you come to a place to sit down, and sit.

- Give yourself a minute to allow yourself to experience what this encounter felt like.

- Now, as you are sitting in this visualization, become aware of the chair you are sitting on in this room. Feel your bottom against the chair, your feet against the floor, and your hands in your lap. Don't open your eyes, but let your consciousness return to this time and place.

- Now, using your memory, remember how it felt to tell the angel your deepest truth. How did you know? Was it where it came from in your body? Was it how it sounded to you? Be able to articulate to yourself how you know when you are speaking from the place of your deepest truth. Sit with that for a minute until you are quite sure that you know what it feels like.

- When you are ready, open your eyes.

APPENDIX B

Tefilat Ha-Derekh, Prayer for going on a journey
by Rabbi Hanna Tiferet Siegel

"This melody came to me as I was saying Tefilat Ha-Derekh during liftoff in an airlane. When we are on a journey, we feel vulnerable, so we call on God and God's angels to protect us and to clear the way."

Yehi ratzon Yah Eloheynu
Shetolikheynu v'tatzideynu
V'tadrikheynu l'shalom
V'tagi'eynu limkhoz cheftzeynu
L'chayim ul'simkha ul'shalom

God who hears our prayers, guide us on our journey
Send your angels of peace, to guard us on our way.

Recommended Reading

Dr. J.H. Hertz, Ed., *The Pentateuch and Haftorahs, 2nd edition*, Soncino Press, 1973

Louis Jacobs, *Jewish Mystical Testimonies*, Schocken Books, 1976

Simcha Paull Raphael, *Jewish Views of the Afterlife*, Jason Aronson, Inc., 1994

Additional Website(s):

Rabbi Geoffrey Dennis, http://www.pantheon.org/articles/a/angels.htm

http://www.hannatiferet.com/tapes.html, from the CD Olamama

Rabbi David Wolpe, http://www.beliefnet.com/Faiths/Judaism/2002/04/Angels-In-Jewish-Tradition.aspx?p=3

Co-Creating the Sacred Container
by Ellen Kaufman Dosick

Ellen Kaufman Dosick is a Licensed Clinical Social Worker with degrees from the University of Chicago. She has been a practicing psychotherapist for over 35 years, served on the faculty of the USC School of Social Work, and directed offices of the Jewish Family Service. She is the Master Practitioner of the psycho-spiritual modality, Soul Memory Discovery, and trains Soul Memory Discovery facilitators around the world. With her husband, Rabbi Wayne Dosick, she is the co-author of *20 Minute Kabbalah*, and *Empowering Your Indigo Child*, and channels a bi-monthly Internet publication, *The Cosmic Times: Spiritual News You Can* Use. www.soulmemorydiscovery.com

The high purpose of spiritual direction is to support the spiritual seeker in opening to greater clarity and connection with God, and to release anything that could hinder a total embrace of that Divine "trans-mission" — so that the seeker can be in ever-finer alignment with the Divine Design. In any *hashpa'ah* session then, there are always at least three participants: the spiritual director, the seeker, and God.

If God's presence is a requirement, then spiritual direction is an extremely powerful modality, and the possibility for life-altering transformation is very great indeed. Given this potential, the spiritual director must be an impeccable expert at inviting God in and at invoking the time-space that can perfectly invite holiness, hold holiness, and enable the transmission of holiness — both externally, in the place of the *hashpa'ah* session, and in the relationships of all involved, and internally, within the beings of the director and the seeker.

How does one prepare oneself for the Presence of the Divine? How does one establish a container suitable for holding the Divine energy? How does one open the way for the awesome holiness to emerge? And in that great Light, what can be?

When two people come together with the deliberate intention of furthering the true essence-expression of one of them, and God is not explicitly invited, (hopefully) helpful counseling takes place. The good counselor uses him or her self to make the appropriate space in which the client can find the way into his or her own heart.

In the *hashpa'ah* session, the spiritual director takes on the additional mantle of priest, whose role it is to explicitly invite in the Presence of the Divine. With this invitation, mundane time-space is transformed into sacred space, so that the seeker can find his or her way into God's Heart.

What is "sacred space"? It is a time-space in which Heaven and Earth meet and are connected. That space is holy, that is, it is *kadosh*, set apart, and differentiated, from the regular world. It becomes a *mishkan*, a sanctuary, in which one can more easily become aware of the Divine Presence, in which one can purposefully encounter God.

Just as the primary tool of the good counselor is the use of the self to enable the client's journey in therapy, so the primary tool of the "priest" is the use of sacred ritual, to enable the seeker's journey in sacred space.

What is "sacred ritual" that it is such an important tool for the priest-become-spiritual director? Sacred ritual is always deliberate, conscious, and formulaic. It always uses the power of language, movement, sound, symbol, or a combination of these, in a formulaic manner, meaning that these are used with order and sequence. These formulae subtly, yet powerfully and significantly, shift and alter the vibrations, lifting them, so that those who are present can become more clearly aware of God's Presence in this place. Of course there is no place that is not filled with the Divine, and of course God resides in all time-space, but in the general level of vibrational density that is the norm in our world, we are, for the most part, woefully unconscious, unaware of the Divine Presence much of the time.

To understand sacred ritual, we need go no further than any religious service of any of the world's religions. Words, movement, sound, and symbol are all used in deliberate order and sequence to connect Heaven and Earth so that the participants may encounter God. There is a clear *matbeah* (structure), to the service, whose function is to build the energy and construct a container that is strong and responsive enough to hold the Divine encounter as it progresses. Sacred ritual is used in similar ways to insure the impeccable integrity of the structure, or container, of the *hashpa'ah* session.

If the seeker wished simply to explore the self, s/he would contact a counselor. But the seeker wishes to explore the relationship with God and the self and the path of service, and so finds the spiritual director. The seeker has "hired" you, because you are an expert in guiding the seeker in sacred space. The seeker counts on you to do this, and pays you for this. Therefore the spiritual director works for the seeker. But the spiritual director, as priest, represents God and if you are God's representative, you carry an awesome and enormous power.

The seeker comes to you, the spiritual director, because you know how to find God, you are familiar with the paths that lead to the Divine, you have immersed yourself in the both sweet and harrowing intimacy with Spirit, and you are able to lift the lamp and say, "I am familiar with a way... I have gone in similar directions... I have witnessed others' journeys...I have a familiarity with the lay of the land."

You are a way-show-er, a knowledgeable guide, the expert in connecting Heaven and Earth, and it is incumbent upon you, the spiritual director, to come to the spiritual direction session empowered with a full and complete expectation and certainty, that today, in this time, in this session, it is the whole and sole/soul purpose to find God, to encounter the Divine, to engage in sacred wrestling, and to emerge, bathed in Holy Light.

Obviously, the spiritual director needs to have done his or her own work, and must continue to do the work, in order to be a worthy guide. And it also takes a great deal of spiritual energy to open sacred space and maintain it for the course of a session.

How do you, as the spiritual director, find the power to do this? Where do you begin? It is necessary that before a *hashpa'ah* session you step into the role of God's representative, and mantle yourself in the power inherent in that role. Just as any priest bathes and purifies and carefully dresses and garbs him/herself before making sacred space, so you, the spiritual director, can do this.

You can prepare yourself by taking five or ten minutes before your session to make sure you are in a balanced place, inside and out — that your energies, and the energies of the space in which you are working, are aligned with Earth's energies. Tune into yourself for a moment, and you will be able to feel this. Although meditating or praying before a session are normally activities you might wish to engage in, balancing your energies with Earth's requires physical movement. A quick polarity balance, a few yoga postures, *T'ai Chi*, twirling, dance, chant, or even listening to a few measures of Bach will restore or enhance your balance. Make sure the space in which you will be working is clear and light.

Once you are in balance, stand, and in prayer, call in all the great Holy Beings you would like to be with you during this session. Let them show themselves to you. Invite them to be with you, to surround you, to fill you, to come through you. Invite in all the attributes you would like to embody in this session — wisdom and compassion, strength and integrity, love and joy, gratitude and peace. Acknowledge and appreciate each energy as it comes in and stands with you and mantles you.

Still in prayer, state your intention for yourself for this session, ask all the energies present to enable this, and thank them for having already provided this for you. You are now connected, Sourced, and flowing with Love and Light. You are now in a holy place within yourself, and have the capacity to make sacred space in which to work.

To begin your session with the seeker, use your holy empowerment to connect Heaven and Earth, to make sacred space. Surely, you can go forward without this, and it will be a great counseling session that can be extremely helpful. But you have not done what the seeker has hired you to do until you make this a three-way conversation by inviting God in.

There are a number of ways to connect Heaven and Earth. Probably the easiest and most straight-forward is to invite in the seeker's guides, and ask that all of you be surrounded with Light. Immediately, you will have sacred space.

But your hope and your intention is that in this session the seeker will derive the greatest possible benefit from a most amazing connection with God. To enable the clearest, most powerful Divine encounter in this session, you want to go beyond the basics and carefully construct a prayer or sacred ritual that invokes the presence of an array of great Beings of Light, who are always available to assist and enable *hashpa'ah* sessions to fulfill what has been requested.

Judaism has always prided itself on the idea that when Jews come before God, we can have direct access. We believe that we do not need any intermediaries, any intercessors, any priests to make the connection. Each of us is in covenantal I-Thou relationship with God, and there need be no one to overhear this intimacy. So why would we invite great Beings of Light to join us in the sacred space of a *hashpa'ah* session?

There are many reasons. First of all, the God-energy is a very great energy — so great, that even *Moshe Rabbeinu* (Moses our teacher) could only see God from the back, through God's *middot*, or attributes. All carry the Divine-energy — some, more clearly and purely than others. For that reason, we seek out wise and powerful teachers and models for ourselves, because we see them capable of transmitting more God-Light than we currently do, and we wish to learn from them how to become ever-clearer vessels and channels of that Divine Light. All of the great Beings of Light, whether they are in body on this Earthplane or in other dimensions are "stepped-down" expressions of the infinite God-Energy. We are so grateful that these Beings, these "stepped-down" energies, are available to us, because we can only handle so much Divine Light, without being *saraf* (incinerated), or as we would say, "fried."

A second important reason to invite in the great Beings of Light is that the way to God, whether we journey up or down, is a tremendously intense way. It is wonderful, comforting and helpful to find Holy Ones stationed all along the way who can walk with us a bit, hold our hands, interpret, translate, guide, and provide sustenance for us.

And a third reason is that every Being in Creation is a unique expression of the Divine, who carries specific wisdom expertise, experience, knowledge and knowhow. Each Being in this Creation fulfills a unique purpose, walks a unique path, carries a unique function, serves a unique mission. When we invite in great Beings of Light, we bring in amazing experts in specific areas, to enlighten us, broaden our perspectives, and inspire us to *esa aynai*, to lift our eyes.

Many of the great Hasidic masters had particular master guides whom they invited in and called on in all their holy work, to guide them and teach them and show them the way. And so can we.

In a *hashpa'ah* session then, listen to what the seeker is seeking on this day, hear what the seeker's life is, and then in the making of sacred spacc, invite in those who can be most useful in helping provide the seeker with a clear connection with the Divine. It may be that you wish to invoke the presences of particular teachers or *rebbe*s, patriarchs or matriarchs, prophets or kings or leaders. It may be that you wish to invoke the presences of particular family members, or ancestors in the spiritual or genetic lineages, or even a group of beings who have served as guardians or keepers of a Divine Intention.

It is suggested that you always invite in the seeker's guides and master guides. These know and love the seeker better than anyone can possibly imagine, and are intimately acquainted with the personal Divine Design that the seeker and God have co-created.

It is also recommended that you always invite in the four great archangels —*Micha-el*, *Rafa-el*, *Gavri-el*, and *Uri-el*. These are known as the four great Archangels because they stand at the semiordinates (compass points), to protect and ensure that the sacred space remains pure. You can ask them to surround the session and hold all of it absolutely sacred and inviolable both from within and from without. You can invite in the *malakhim*, those of the angelic realm, who serve as messengers of God. Certainly, invite in the *Shekhinah*, and ask that Her profound compassion envelop all of you, so that the love for self, and others, and the One, grows and grows in the session. And most certainly, invite in God or Source by the naming terms *Hashem* or *Ein Sof* or any of the Aspects of Source — and ask that the Holy Presence is felt and that all present are touched by the Divine.

With the room filled with these amazing presences, when you and the seeker now state the intention for this session, it is not just the two of you who are dedicating yourselves in a certain direction, but an entire host of powerful Beings who are now working for this, with their whole hearts. You can imagine how focused the intent is to "hit the mark," and how high are the vibrations and the levels of awareness and consciousness in which both you and the seeker are now sustained throughout the session!

The Importance of Permission

And so, you have prepared yourself for the Holy Presence, and you have established a suitable container for Divine encounter. How do you open the way for the "magic" to happen?

As the spiritual director, you ask permission. Sometimes, when we think about the concept of "asking permission," a decidedly uncomfortable image appears, in which we are groveling and begging at the feet of some strict authority figure. To hand over to someone else the ability to give the "go-ahead" is to give up some control. And, rather than do this, it can feel a bit safer to simply surge forward and get on with the session.

The word "permission" is an interesting word. If it is broken down into its parts, the word actually is "per"-"mission," that is, "for this"-"mission," or "in accordance with"-"mission." When you ask permission, you are asking, "Is it per this seeker's mission to focus in these directions in this session? Is it in accordance with this one's mission that we use this session in the ways we have just intended? Does this agenda support this person's mission right now?"

When this is your first question, you as spiritual director, have now not only balanced, purified, set and opened sacred space, and intended and enabled the Divine encounter, but you have also aligned the totality of the session with the larger wholeness of the seeker's mission and purpose. You have lined yourselves up with the great Divine Design, and in so doing, opened the channels to receive from God not what you are intending for today, but what God intends for you today. And that is always so much bigger than anything you could ever, possibly, make up or imagine or hope for yourselves in any given moment. And so, indeed, "magic" occurs!

Aligned and receiving in this way, both you and the seeker find that you may as well let go of any preconceived notions you may have had about how this session is going to go, about what the "issue" is all about, about what anyone may come away with. You find that you know nothing, and that that is a good place to be. And you find that no matter the depth of your insight or the extent of your love, you will be taken to deeper levels, and your heart will open further.

Lest you fear that you and the seeker will get all "puffed up" as a result of "hobnobbing" with the Divine, rest assured that sitting in this amount of Love and Light is the most humbling experience of your life. And, as you sit in this overwhelming Love and Light, the Glory shines and shimmers around you, reflecting in your faces and covering both of you in a grandeur which lets you see yourselves as you truly are — the most beloved and precious of God.

And it is this new-found sense of preciousness which allows your beloved seeker to perceive the tendril of Truth that for him or her, in this moment, is the way into greater alignment with God — and to re-dedicate him/herself to this sacred path.

In this kind of sacred space, the *hashpa'ah* session has been incredible and powerful and significant and life changing — and you believe that the seeker will hold the fullness of this session with him/her forever. And yet, because of the "altered" consciousness that makes this space holy, it is sometimes difficult to remember all that occurred in the session after closing the sacred space. It can therefore be very helpful to record what takes place so that it is available to the seeker following the session.

At the end of your session, it is as important to carefully, systematically, thank everyone and close the sacred space, as it was to construct it. You have just been in a very rarefied time-space. It has been *kadosh*, differentiated, from "normal" time-space, because at this point in our evolution, it is not possible for most of us to have enough energy to function adequately in this world while maintaining that kind of purposeful Divine connection.

Yet you, the spiritual director and the seeker, can come together again and again to open in this way and partake of the Light. What a blessing is this field of spiritual direction! And what a blessing the spiritual director is for humankind! And what blessings emerge for the world through this great work! And we all say, "Thank You!"

Melitz Yosher – The Practice of Intercession
Introduction, Ruth Gan Kagan
Guest Teacher, Zalman Schachter-Shalomi

Rabbi Dr. Zalman Schachter-Shalomi, better known as "Reb Zalman," is the father of Jewish Renewal and founder of the spiritual eldering movement. He is an active teacher of Hasidism and Jewish mysticism, and a participant in ecumenical dialogues throughout the world, including the widely influential dialogue with the Dalai Lama, documented in the book, *The Jew in the Lotus* by Rodger Kamenetz. One of the world's foremost authorities on Hasidism, and a widely published author, his works are now often also available as audio and video files including *Heart of the Soul* & *Seasons of Life* (Better Listen)

Rabbi Ruth Gan Kagan is founder and spiritual leader of Nava Tehila, a Jewish Renewal community in Jerusalem. She co-authored, with Rabbi Zalman Schachter-Shalomi, the Hebrew book *Jewish Renewal — Integrating Heart and World* (2006). Ruth works as a *mashpi'ah* in Israel, trains rabbinical and cantorial students from all the denominations and serves as a *mashpi'ah* for the Aleph Ordination Programs.

Introduction

As *mashpi'im* and clergy we often find in our hearts the call to pray for people and situations. Sometimes we are even asked to pray for others. Such prayer, called intercession in English, is an important part of Jewish spiritual practice. Jewish scriptures are full of role models of the practice of intercession. Starting with *Avraham avinu* (Abraham, our father) praying for the people of Sodom, *Moshe Rabbeinu* (Moses, our teacher) and the numerous times he goes up to God to pray on behalf of the people of Israel, Queen Esther and the prophets; through the great intercessors of the rabbinic area: Meir, Yohanan, Hanina, Honi and Beruria. Then there are a number of Hasidic masters who are known for their intercessory practices, the Baal Shem Tov, Rabbi Nachman and the greatest of them all, Rabbi Levi Yitzhak of Berdichev, fondly called the Advocate of Israel.

Melitz yosher is a classic Hebrew term for a spiritual defense attorney, one who brings up our merits before heaven. The advocate is indeed the primary metaphor used in Jewish sources for an intercessor. The *melitz yosher* goes before the heavenly court and pleads cases; s/he hears the heavenly call for someone who is ready to *la'amod ba-peretz* (to stand in the breach) and overturn Divine decrees. Just as *teshuvah* (the capacity to restore damaged relationships) is built into the infrastructure of creation so is the role of a defense attorney built into the theological system that seeks to balance Divine judgment with Divine mercy.

There are many paths suggested in the Jewish tradition for intercession. The major prayer recited three times a day, the *Amidah* with its nineteen blessings, is in itself a petitionary prayer for *kol ha-tzibur* (the whole community), as are the practices of reciting *Tehillim* (Psalms) and special petitionary prayers written through the ages to be recited in the synagogue (the various *mi sheberakh* {"may the One who blessed"}prayers) or to be recited at home, in private (including the vast literature of women's supplications, known in Yiddish as *tekhines*). At the same time there is a call for those who are ready to step up, above and beyond the regular petitionary prayers, and receive upon themselves the yoke of intercessors for particular cases, people or situations. This is a spiritually demanding path that calls for careful preparation, a life of aligned spiritual practice, self-care and knowledge of spiritual protection. Many of the teachings of the path of *melitz yosher* are better shared orally between students and teachers and so are not included. Still, some can be revealed in writing.

Following the guidance of my oral intercession teacher, Hadassah Ben Shmuel, I offered a Melitz Yotzer Training Program in 2007. Rabbi Zalman Schachter-Shalomi, the *zeide* (founding elder) of Jewish Renewal, graciously agreed to visit with the graduates of the program and answer questions about his own practice of intercession. This is an edited version of his conversation with the class.

The class began with Ruth dedicating the merit of the study to the healing of a friend going for a get, a Jewish divorce document and ritual that very day.

Q: What are Some Examples and Types of Intercession?

Reb Zalman: A great deal depends on the available time and the setting. Sometimes you find yourself in a situation where, *has v'khalilah*, (Heaven forefend), you come across someone hurt in a traffic accident. Then you aren't going to say I have to go to the *mikveh* (ritual bath) first (in preparation for sacred service). In this kind of emergency you are directly and immediately involved and offering your prayer. It always depends on the available time and the setting. There are some times when I'm not in the greater mind and then I resort to Psalm 119 in *Tehillim* (Psalms). Psalm 119 is where you have eight sentences per letter of the Hebrew alphabet. So I would then recite the verses that spell the name of the person in need. For instance, if someone's name is *Yaakov* (Jacob), I would do first the eight verses starting with the letter *yud*, then the *ayin*, then the *kuf* and then the *vet* (per the spelling of *Yaakov* in Hebrew), as a preface to the specifics of the healing or whatever else is needed.

Sometimes there isn't any time for it, as I was explaining in the situation of an accident, *chalilah* ([God] forbid). Then I say an arrow prayer, such as when I'm driving and I hear an ambulance or a fire truck or the police. This might be an *Ana b'Koakh* ([God] Please

Respond with Strength), the prayer for such a situation, par excellence, which is important to know by heart. You may use my translation (next page) of the *Ana b'Koakh* if Hebrew is difficult for you.

There's this wonderful story how Reb Nachman was sick and the *hasidim* were standing around him and he turned to his grandson and says, "I want you to pray for me." And the grandson says, "I won't pray for you unless you give me your watch." Reb Nachman takes his watch and gives it to him. And he begins and says: "*Ribbono shel Olam* (Master of the Universe) my *zeide* (grandfather) is sick, please send him a *refuah shlema* (complete healing). Amen." The *hasidim* were standing around and they were sort of smirking and so Reb Nachman says, "What do you think I do?" So you get the idea pretty clearly, the straight way of coming from the heart is important. There are more involved methods and we'll get to some of them later in this session.

Forms of Preparation

In some dire cases I used to go to *mikveh*, when a *mikveh* was available to me; when that's not possible I take a shower and then meditate. If I know the person I am praying for as a friend or a member of the family then I bring up in my mind all the appreciation and love for that person and hold this all up to God. So I can then say, look, *Ribbono shel Olam*, this is how I see that person with my *a'yin tovah* (ability to see the good) and I'd like You to see with Your *a'yin tovah*. "*Na gibor dorshei yihudkha k'vavat shomrem*—honor him or her as if this person was the apple of your own eye.

On the other hand, you have to be clever when praising a person to the Heavenly Court. Sometimes not concentrating on the good parts of the person would be better for them. There's a hasidic story about the mother of Avremaleh (he became later the son–in–law of the Kotzker Rebbe). Avrahamaleh fell terribly ill. His mother comes and cries to the Kotzker to pray for him and says, look, he's such a *lamdan* (learned man), it would be such a pity if a person with such a great mind and such accomplishment and learning would, *chalila*, not get better. And the Kotzker says, "What are you talking about? He hasn't learned anything yet. He's still unlettered." And so she gets so upset, she doesn't know what to do. Why should the Rebbe take this terrible attitude? As she goes out crying, Reb Hershele Tomashover, who was the Rebbe's right hand man says, "What's the matter with you?" And she answers, "The Rebbe says my son is nothing." And he smiles and says, "Of course, because he's trying to say he isn't accomplished yet. He has to learn a lot more, so he needs to live a lot longer." So sometimes you have to use that ruse in order to be able to say that person still has more to go and that's how the Kotzker did it in the service of that person.

Ana b'Koach
translated by Rabbi Zalman Schachter-Shalomi

Source of Mercy!
With loving strength
Untie our tangles.

Your chanting folk
rise high, make pure.
Accept our song.

Like your own eye
Lord keep us safe
Who union seek.

Cleanse and bless us,
Infuse us ever
With loving care.

Gracious source
Of holy power!
Do guide your folk.

Sublime and holy One,
Do turn to us,
Of holy chant.

Receive our prayer,
Do hear our cry,
Who secrets knows.

Through time and space
Your glory shines
Our blessed One

Barukh Shem Kevod Malkhutoh
l'Olam Va'ed

Q: Do you do intercession with the person in the same room?

Reb Zalman: Sometimes I would ask the permission of the person. For instance in a hospital I would ask the person, "Do you mind if I take your hand and we pray together?" Because for some people who are not used to praying for themselves it feels like I have to be very special, I have to do something extraordinary before I dare to pray. So when I take that person's hand with their permission and I say can we pray here, they sort of look at me, yes, please do it. They don't usually feel that they can do it themselves, but then when I begin in a very simple way and say, "*Ribbono shel Olam*, (Master of Eternity/ Universe) please help this person in whichever need they have." Whether it is in the hospital for a healing or anything that is taking place, or in a consultation space where I'm talking with that person, depending on the situation, sometimes I pray in Hebrew. And when they ask what did I say, I tell them, I wasn't talking to you I was talking to God. God understands the Hebrew. That is sometimes necessary. At other times I would say what I prayed for or I would even pray in English. Or if that person needs me to pray in Yiddish, depending on whom they are and what their background is, I find that whenever I do it in Yiddish, for the people who understand Yiddish, the tears come up so fast. Something gets loosened in their heart and they feel a lot better and sometimes it's necessary also psychologically for a person to have the notion, someone cares and I deserve to get better and I deserve to have that help. And that makes a difference.

So I encourage the person to pray with me out loud. Then I say, "How about you saying something, so I can say 'Amen' and follow along with you." Very often there is at first a resistance and a kind of shame, because those people very often don't have any experience in that and they feel so awkward about it. But with a gentle way and if I show beforehand, using simple and direct language, that helps them too.

Q: How Often Do You Do an Intercession?

Reb Zalman: Sometimes you pray for a whole bunch of people that are on your list. Yesterday was *erev Rosh Chodesh* (eve of the monthly New Moon Festival) and I went to my box in which I have all my students' pictures and I looked at those pictures and I was praying for each one of them. When I came across someone's picture sometimes I felt that there was something special that needed more prayer, or perhaps a sense that I need to get in touch with that person because we haven't talked for a long time.

So sometimes you do this wholesale. There was a time that Reb Avrohom Yehoshua Heschel, the Apter Rebbe, had people come to him from all places and before Rosh Hashanah (New Year) they had given him a whole series of *kvitlekh* (petitions for intercessory help written on little bits of paper). Usually he would pray for each *kvittel* separately but there was a whole big pile so he had his *shammes* (assistant) bring the pile of *kvitlekh* and put it on the table where you read the Torah, the *shulkhan ha-kriyah* and he put his hand on that pile and said, *Ribbono shel Olam* for all these people I pray that whatever they need *v'tashlim mish'alot libam l'tova* (fulfill their heartfelt inquiries for the good). In this way I did a wholesale thing and sometimes that's necessary.

Q: Did you get any messages about *gemilut chassadim* (deeds of lovingkindness), *tzedakah* (financial donations to charitable causes) and other practices, which you were guided to do in compensation for expending spiritual capital by your advocacy in the intercession?

Reb Zalman: My late Rebbe, Reb Menachem Mendel of Lubavitch, once suggested to me that with each intercession I should put some money into a *pushke* (*tzedakah*, charity box) and that was a very important thing for me. It had the sense of put up or shut up. It's not a question of how much. I have my little *shtiebele* (wallet) and I put change into it and when it comes to intercession and when I come to the verse *v'ata m'ha'ye'h et kulam* (You [God] revive all; [Nehemiah 9:5] that is found in the morning prayers, I take out 36 cents and put them in the *pushke*. There are many stories how prayer gets potentiated with *tzedakah*.

When I pray with people who come to visit the sick or who ask me to pray on behalf of someone then I ask them also to give some charity and I hope, *im yirtzeh Hashem*, (God willing) that the woman who wants to receive a get today (this session was dedicated in prayer for a woman that was hoping to receive a get that day) when she gets freed, that she should also give some *tzedakah* for other *agunot* who need help that way. *Im yirtzeh Hashem* I'm going to put some money in the *pushke* on her behalf today and *yehi ratzon*, (may it be God's desire) I can say this – "*Ribbono shel Olam*, the hardened heart of that husband who is really needed to give his full consent, that the get be able to happen, *yehi ratzon* that his heart should soften, that he should remember the love that he had for that person, that he doesn't want to injure at all. He should let go of his vindictiveness, and that his *neshama* (soul) is willing to listen to what the *Bet Din* (religious court) has to say to him, to bring about peace for his soon to be ex-wife and even for himself; that this should happen with great ease today; that people should go away today with a sense of forgiving each other and be able to say the *hareini mokhel* (I am ready to forgive). Amen."

Q: Can one link with others to increase the power of prayer?

Reb Zalman: Of course it often happened in the *yeshiva* and the synagogue that we would be told to pray for somebody and we would then gather around and the favorite was to recite Psalm 119 that I mentioned above. At times I ask people in a teaching session to assign merit to a person who is the target of prayer, like we prayed before for the *aguna* to be freed. In this case I hope that all of you, when I was saying the *tefilah*, (prayer) joined me in your heart to free this woman from having been anchored. (The word *aguna* means like a ship that's anchored and can't move) so that that person should be free. So I take a breath and I want to say that whenever we are in *shul* together and we begin with "*ana El na refa na la*—Please God, please heal her." [Numbers 12:13] We do this together. Yes, it builds strength, like a stronger battery.

Q: If we get a clear indication that the person we're praying for is on his or her deathbed, and that the family needs to go immediately and say their goodbyes, how do we appropriately convey this information, or any other critical information, for that matter, directly to the family?

Reb Zalman: There's always a risk and it's a risk that is very well worth taking. The worst thing that can be is that the people will not appreciate what you're saying and they'll be angry with you, but I do have a sense that if they are fully informed and hear the urgency that they won't be angry with you. Sometimes it's really necessary to wake people up because sometimes a chronic situation has been *shlepping* for years and they don't have the sense of the urgency, but you who come there at that point have a feeling that time is short. Then you have to speak about it.

In my early days as a rabbi I came to New Bedford in Massachusetts and there was a man who was dying of leukemia. The family was sitting around him and they were telling me that, yes, he likes to go fishing and I should make plans, when he gets better, to go fishing with him. I was young and green and my heart was telling me that this was inappropriate and that this person was dying, which I could see on his face, but I played along with them. I'm still ashamed to this day that I didn't say to the members of the family, "you let me talk with that person alone." Then to say to the person, "tell me what's in your heart, what do you really feel is happening?" Then I could have said *vidui* (final confession) with him and I could have talked about after-life, and could have prayed with him about the concerns he still had for members of the family. Nothing of this was I able to do because I let myself be snowed by the conspiracy of silence. I give you all a *brukheh* (blessing) that when you are in such a situation, you should have the *chutzpah* (temerity) to speak up.

Q: Could you think of something happening in the last year that you could share with us that might bring up a different modality of prayer on behalf of someone?

Reb Zalman: Let me begin by saying it's comparatively very easy to pray with people who are of our *hevra*, our colleagues and friends. So for instance, a woman has ALS here in Boulder and I came to her house and prayed with her. Somehow for all the heartache that I also had to see that this is a progressive disease etc., yet I prayed with her and it was OK.

What is sometimes different is when you come to people who are not your *hevra* (friends, congregants or colleagues). I've been asked sometimes to come to the hospital. One case there was a physician who was under special care and who had asked for a visit from a rabbi. I had never met him before. Nevertheless, an important thing is to just be silent and sit for a while with the person. If you sit there fully present to them, there is a tendency on the part of people to break the silence and start saying what's on their heart. That opens a conversation, which is good.

Sometimes you visit people who are not *b'nei brit*, people who belong to another covenant, another faith. I was once called to visit a Moslem woman and I asked her if she minded if I held her hand. At first she was a little bit embarrassed because that doesn't quite fit the situation, but being sick, she allowed me. Then I started to chant *ya-shafi, ya-mafi, ya-kafi*. These are Arabic words that are *wazifas*. By saying those words that were familiar to her that mean, "oh healer, oh healing, oh medicine" in Arabic, and repeating that with her, feeling how familiar that was to her; that was wonderful.

The same kind of situation exists when you come to be with a Christian and you can then say, "Address your prayer to Jesus and I will say amen to that too." I might remind the person about the healings that are written in the New Testament, like about the woman who had a menstrual flow and it didn't stop, and then she touched the hem of his (Jesus') garment and she was healed.

Of course there are also all wonderful stories that are addressing Mary. The other day I had a conversation with someone about that and I was saying *bozhe matka*, using the Polish word for Mother of God and their eyes lit up hearing that I could identify that source that would listen to their prayer. There's a joke about a woman who was standing in front of a statue of Mary in prayer, and the priest didn't like it. So he hid behind the crucifix and he said, "You should talk to me." And she said, "Shut up, Junior, I'm talking to your mother!"

Q: What daily practices do you recommend for building our soul strength for intercessory prayer?

Reb Zalman: Let me tell you how I incorporate intercession into my daily *Amidah* prayers. First of all *davven* (pray) every day. If you have at least time for prayer at dawn and dusk that makes some sense. So in my prayer space at home I have a list of people for whom I pray. When I come to *refa'einu* (the blessing in the *Amidah* that is addressing healing) on my list are members of my family, other people who need healing, people who are in need of *refuat hanefesh*, mental healing, and of social healing. In the family; where children and parents don't get along and communicate, I pray for them too. And there are some people that are not on your immediate emergency list, but people with chronic situations that have been there for a while. My *minhag* (custom) for quite a while, since I have some people who are not Jewish, instead of sealing this blessing in the *Amidah* with *rofei cholei amo yisrael* (Blessed is the One who Heals his people Israel), I say *rofei kol bassar u-mafli la'asot* (Blessed is the One Who heals all flesh and make miracles). This makes an inclusive statement rather than one that limits the response to only Jewish people.

In *barekh aleinu* (The blessing in the *amidah* that deals with the bounty of the earth and asking for livelihood) I have a list of people who have *tzuris* (trouble) with *parnassah* (finances for living) and I read that list and pray for them that they should have *parnassah* according to their capacity to serve. I know of one person for whom I care a great deal and who could do a lot better than be a cab driver but *nebikh* (as it goes) has to do that as his *parnassah* so he is daily in my prayer: "*Ribbono shel Olam* find him the right *parnassah* in which his talents would be able to come out."

Now in *t'ka b'shofar gadol l'cheirutenu v'kabtzeinu yakhad me'arba kanfot ha'aretz*, (blessing in the *amidah* that calls for us being gathered together from the four corners of the earth) I pray for people who want to find *shidukhim* (life partners) that they should be able to meet their *bashert* (soul mate) in a good way.

Then there are some people who have cases pending in court or are under scrutiny by legal authorities so I pray "*hashiva shofteinu k'varishona...melekh ohev tzedakah u'mishpat* — turn to us justly, O King who loves charity and justice." (From the blessing for justice in the *Amidah*) Sometimes I even include them in a prayer when I come to *la-malshinim* (The *Amidah* blessing that deals with false accusers), that the people who accuse them for nothing should be silenced for that.

When I come to *al ha-tzaddikim v'al ha-hasidim*, (blessing for the righteous ones and for the pious ones) I certainly pray for my *talmidim* (students) and for the people and the institutions that are supporting the work we do in renewing Judaism.

Regarding *li-yrushalayim ikrha b'rakhmim tashuv* (Blessing for God's return to Jerusalem) just before the elections, I had some strong prayers not only that there should be a good coalition to be able to govern Israel but also that the new cabinet of Hamas should get softer in their relationship.

When you keep these concerns as part of your reality, it makes a lot of sense to incorporate them in your regular prayer.

Q: In one of your articles you suggest that we should put on the mantle of the tzaddik, so to speak, for the time of intercession. Could you elaborate more about how to do this?

Reb Zalman: Humility is a wonderful virtue to cultivate. However, there are times when an intercessor can't afford to be too humble. Let me tell you another wonderful *meisseh* (vignette). It happened before Reb Shneur Zalman of Liadi had become the Rebbe and he had decided to be with his older colleague, Reb Mendele Vitebsker. (Rabbi Mendel of

Vitebsk) At one time Reb Mendele was out of town and Reb Shneur Zalman was hanging out with the *hasidim* talking and singing when somebody bursts into the *beit midrash* (study hall) with a big *geschrei* (cry) and calls, "Please I need to talk to the Rebbe - I need his intercession." All the *hasidim* in the beit *midrash* said, "Who are we? We are not *rebbe*s, we can't pray." So Reb Shneur Zalman gave them the following *mashal* (parable): Once upon a time there was a king and the king had children and they were always quarreling one with the other. They would burst into the throne room when the king was busy with all kinds of things and bring their quarrels there and the king said, "I can't handle that." So he appointed a major domo, somebody to be in charge of the kids and he said, "If they need something you come to me and I will take care of it, but I don't want them to come and make a tumult." One day the major domo was away and one of the kids got injured and they said, "Let's go and talk to Papa." The other kids said, "No, no, no, he said we should never interrupt him." One of the children said, "Only when we quarrel do we need to have one person to speak for us. But if we're all agreed that our brother needs help then we can all go in and Papa will be all right."

So Reb Shneur Zalman said, "Even if the Rebbe is away we can pray at this point" and he took on the role that is necessary at that point. If you take upon the role of an intercessor, you need to have that kind of *chutzpah*. This is holy *chutzpah*, one that is on a level of "*nitzkhuni bonai nitzkhuni banai* - My children have defeated me (says God)" [Bava Matziah 59b]. There's *nakhas* (satisfaction) that *Ribbono shel Olam* (God) has when a person says I'm not praying for myself. So to pray for another you can, sometimes you even have to become a *tzaddik* (holy one) for that moment, provided you don't continue feeling inflated when your job is completed.

Q: How can we pray for specific person or situation when we humans don't always see the big picture?

Reb Zalman: There are some people who have made empirical tests and report extensively about this subject. Larry Dossey, for example, has pointed out that one is not to insist on a particular form of healing or particular outcome. On the other hand, in the case of some cancers people have focused on a particular target in their prayer and yielded amazing results. I find it easier and closer in my heart to ask the soul of the afflicted person to join me in a general prayer. The *neshamah* (soul) knows what it needs. The people who have been doing this kind of work for a while say that if this is for the highest good of the person in this incarnation, let such and such be the outcome, but always qualifying if that is for the highest good.

Q: When you have interceded for someone and it appears that help is not forthcoming – the person gets sicker or if the person finds their beloved but in the end it doesn't work out, etc., how do you feel and what do you tell yourself? Is it easy to be philosophical, i.e., a higher wisdom beyond our understanding is determining the course of events, or do you look for faults in your own practice? Do you return to the person and try again to intercede?

Reb Zalman: The Talmud says that even if you have a sharp sword against your neck don't give up hope [Talmud Berachot 10 a]. *Kol zman sheh ha-neshamah b'kirbi*, (as long as the soul is in me), one continues to pray. It's true that sometimes prayer doesn't seem to help. Eve (Reb Zalman's wife) and I were in Rio at one time and we were called over to a child who was presumed to be brain dead already and we prayed and brought a *shofar* (ram's horn) and had hoped to be able to do our thing and *nebukh* (as fate would have it, unfortunately) a few days later they had to disconnect her from the support system and it didn't work. So what can you do? Not every *g'zeira* (Heavenly decree) are we able to turn.

On the other hand there are some situations where you have to have *hutzpa klapei shamaya mehania*, (religious audacity). You have to be really tough and come back again and again and again before God and the heavenly court to undo this *g'zeira* (decree).

Sometimes even a Rebbe gets caught in a difficult situation. There was a time when Reb Mendele Kotzker was in a dilemma. There was a woman who was having a tough time giving birth and there was a man who was having a tough time dying. The question was for whom should he pray? If it was for the woman giving birth it would mean that this man would have to die and his *neshamah* (soul) would have to go into the baby. Or, if he prayed for the man then the woman would have trouble with her birth, and maybe have a stillbirth. So he was walking up and down in his room being upset not knowing what to do. Again Reb Tomashover comes into the room and asks, "Rebbe, what's going on?" and he tells him. And he says, "Rebbe, there are other neshamas (souls) whom you can assign to the newborn, you are not the only one. Who asked you to stay in the dilemma?"

I remember myself once feeling caught in a dilemma like that and I prayed *Ribbono shel Olam*, You are *kol yakhol* (fully empowered), You can do it differently. Sometimes we have to insist and not give up. On the other hand if the person we are praying for is saying, "I'm tired already of the struggle. I don't want to have to struggle anymore. I'm tired." So then we can join that person and pray for her to be relieved. Say, "*Ribbono shel Olam* please help that person to have an easy transition."

Once you decide you're going to be an intercessor you can't worry about the dangers of the practice. You want to be a rabbi? It's plenty dangerous! You're taking risks! If you're going to start asking all these *shailas* (questions) to begin with, it's going to paralyze you in your prayers. Yes, you have to protect yourself spiritually but you can't pray with fear in your heart about your own safety. If you are still scared then maybe don't venture into the more sophisticated ways of interceding and just do it simply. The Baal Shem Tov once said "I am *peti ya'amin l'khol davar, l'hol* — I am a simple small person." And then you can say, "*Ribbono shel Olam*, this person needs help. I don't know, I don't have any *z'khus* (merit), I don't understand big *chokhmas* (wisdom) I don't want this and I can't do this, but I'm the mouthpiece for that part in your heart that wants healing to happen."

Q: Could you please share us your *shitah* (method) of intercession using the Tree of Life?

Reb Zalman: This is what I would do when I have more time and am in a place of *mokhin de'gadlut* (expanded consciousness). From my Rebbe Reb Yosef Yitzchak I heard, that you can go up to that place where, in *Adam Kadmon* (Kabbalistic term for the highest level of existence, where everything is possible) every person is there in the fullness of their capacity. If I can bring down something from that *Adam Kadmon*, blessing for that person, that's what's indicated. Mostly this goes well until you take it through *Chokhmah*, through *Binah*, through *Chessed*. And then you come to Gevurah. And that's when the thing becomes a little bit difficult because there you start figuring that this person hasn't really learned their lesson; they're still not dealing with their problems the right way and judgment comes against them at that point. That's where we get hung up. We have to really deal with that with what's called *ha-m'takat ha-dinim*, the sweetening of the decrees. To be able to say *af al pi chen* (even though he/she may not deserve it still we ask). That's where tiferet *rakhamim* (heart-space compassion) comes in, to be able to say, yes. If a person needs to have the *z'chut*, the right kind of merit on their side then there is no problem. But if there isn't the right kind of merit there, we still say "Have *rakhamim* (compassion) *Ribbono shel olam* (Master of the world)!" When do we need mercy and compassion? *Davka* (even more so) at that point when it's necessary to overcome a harsh judgment. One has to watch out for judgment in *gevurah*.

Coming down past Tiferet you get to *Netzakh*. Sometimes at that point it pays to be silent for a little while and to be open in the mind to see if there is somebody that needs to be counseled and if there is somebody who is instrumental for dealing effectively with the situation at hand.

There is a story that happened when I was in the *yeshiva*. We had a wonderful woman who was the cook, and she loved the *yeshiva bokhurim* (young male students) and was very, very caring for us. The Rebbetzin Dinah, wife of Reb Yosef Yitzchak would come down from time to time to the kitchen to taste the food that was prepared for the *talmidim* (students). She looked at this woman who was the cook and she said, "What's the matter, you look to me wan. Something is wrong." So she answered, "I haven't been feeling well lately." The Rebbetzin said, "From the whole world people come to my husband to ask for his prayer and for his blessing, so why didn't you talk to me about that?" Right away the

Rebbetzin said, "Come!" and with the apron still on she *shlepped* the cook through a couple of blocks to the Rebbe's house and went right up the Rebbe's place. The Rebbe talked to her a little bit, went inside himself to check in and then took out notepaper. He wrote a note and put it in an envelope and sealed it and said, "I'd like you to go to Dr. Bondy in Washington Heights." Dr. Bondy was one of those Viennese doctors who was supposed to be a great doctor. So she went to the doctor and he looked her over and found nothing wrong. Then she pulled out the letter of the Rebbe and showed it to him. He looked at the Rebbe's letter and then examined her again. Then he took her very quickly to the hospital, she had surgery and she recovered. So it's so amazing to me. How did the Rebbe know to give an indication to the doctor about what to do? But that's what comes from being in touch with the *netzakh* part of the prayer.

Hod is the place to pray for quick recovery, for elegant settlements in cases of dispute, for win-win outcomes. *Yesod* is connected with the life-force, called *ki* or *chi* in Eastern systems. Pray that the energy should be replenished, that it flows freely along amud *ha-emtza-i* (center column of the *Sefirot*).

In *Malkhut* we pray for the good outcome in reality. Sometimes we hear in medicine the phrase "the surgery was successful but the patient died." In *Malkhut* we pray that all the work of alignment and intercession that we have affected in all the upper nine *Sefirot* will produce a positive, long lasting outcome in the reality in this world.

In this way you answer the call to be present to each one of the *Sefirot* and bringing it down all the way to *Malkhut*.

In conclusion, I bless you in your decision to take on the important and powerful practice of *melitz yosher* and I urge you to maintain your spiritual practices so that you can do so in healthy ways. I also wish to give you a prayer, in Hebrew and English that I found in an old *siddur* (prayerbook) that will serve you well.

A Prayer for All Occasions *(I found it in an old Siddur)*

Our God, our parents' God
You hear the prayers of our pleading
of all of us who turn to You.
May it please You
to hear also my own prayer.
I approach You and plead with You
Knowing well
that I come without merit and worth
and without worthwhile deeds
I am embarrassed to raise my face to You
To pray for myself and for other people—-yet,
it is Your boundless compassion and kindness

that encourages me to trust
that You will not scorn me
but that You will support me
and come to my aid.

May my poor song be pleasing to You
in hearing our prayers with compassion.
I come with a sore heart to plead with You
Please, in Your great compassion
take pity on the remnant of Your people Israel
help us all and extricate us from our confinements
save us from our oppression
help us to leave poverty and humiliation behind
and keep us from a scarcity mentality
help us from all kinds of ruinous happenings
erupting upon the world.

Those who are healthy among us
Your people Israel,
guard them that no illness befall them,
no suffering enter them *Khalilah*!
Those, among Your people,
the house of Israel,
who are ill hasten
and send them a complete recovery.
Release all hostages to freedom
and a save our people, the house of Israel
from all pain and damage, assaults and accidents.
Compassionate One save us from such.

Childless couples,
bless them with vigorous children,
proper, good and kosher offspring,
that are well thought of by You
and all the children of Your people,
may their parents,
their fathers and their mothers merit
to raise them to the study Torah
and to serve You God
so that they might walk in a straight path

and be attuned to awe of You.
Let no childhood disease take hold of them.
May they be protected from demonic influences
and from ill winds in the world,
from plagues and accidents,
so that they might be healthy and wholesome
involved in serving You
and studying Torah all their lives.
Those mothers to be who are carrying new life
make them carry to term in peace and without pain.
When the time for their birthing comes
protect them from all hurt and damage
help them through labor with ease
and without any complications.

Above all, may Your great mercy protect
the Exiled people Israel,
and the remnant of Your holy Torah.
May all who oppress them
become aware of Your retribution
and not shed innocent blood.
And those of Your people Israel
who have gone astray
-may they find ways to approach You again.
Receive them in complete *T'shuvah*.
Your right hand of grace is stretched forth
to welcome those who repent.
Send us Your life and Your truth,
to guide us to live up to Your intention
in great compassion help us to come home
and redeem us with a lasting redemption.
Amen *Selah*!

יְהִי רָצוֹן מִלְפָנֶיךָ ד' אֱלֹקֵינוּ וֵאלֹקֵי אֲבוֹתֵינוּ

שׁוֹמֵעַ קוֹל שַׁוְעַת עֲתִירָה

שֶׁתִּשְׁמַע לְקוֹל תְּפִלַּת עַמְּךָ בֵּית יִשְׂרָאֵל וּבְתוֹכָם תִּשְׁמַע גַּם תְּפִלָּתִי אֲשֶׁר אֲנִי מִתְנַפֵּל וּמִתְחַנֵּן לְפָנֶיךָ,

וְאִם אָמְנָם יָדַעְתִּי מְעוּט עֶרְכִּי וְדַלּוּת מַעֲשַׂי וְאֹשֶׁר בּוֹשְׁתִּי וְנִכְלַמְתִּי לְהָרִים פָּנַי אֵלֶיךָ וּלְהִתְפַּלֵּל לְפָנֶיךָ עַל עַצְמִי וְכָל שֶׁכֵּן עַל אֲחֵרִים

אוּלָם עַל רַחֲמֶיךָ הָרַבִּים וַחֲסָדֶיךָ הַגְּדוֹלִים בָּטַחְתִּי אֲשֶׁר בַּל תִּבְשֵׁנִי מִשְׂבְּרִי וְתִסְעָדֵנִי וְאִוָּשֵׁעָה

וְשִׁירַת רָשׁ יִהְיֶה יָקָר בְּעֵינֶיךָ וְתִשְׁמַע לְקוֹל תְּפִלַּת עַמְּךָ יִשְׂרָאֵל בְּרַחֲמִים, וּבְלֵב נִשְׁבָּר וְנִדְכֶּה הִנְנִי לְהִתְחַנֵּן לְפָנֶיךָ

אָנָּא מָלֵא רַחֲמִים רַחֵם נָא עַל פְּלֵיטַת עַמְּךָ יִשְׂרָאֵל וְתוֹשִׁיעֵם וְתוֹצִיאֵם מִכָּל צָרוֹתֵיהֶם וְלַחֲצֵיהֶם וְדַחֲקֵיהֶם

וְתַצִּילֵם מִדַּלּוּת וּמִשְׁפְלוּת וַעֲנִיּוֹת וְאֶבְיוֹנוּת וּמִדִּקְדּוּקֵי עֲנִיּוֹת וּמִכָּל מִינֵי פֻּרְעָנִיּוֹת הַמִּתְרַגְשׁוֹת וּבָאוֹת לְעוֹלָם, וְהַבְּרִיאִים אֲשֶׁר בְּתוֹךְ עַמְּךָ יִשְׂרָאֵל תִּשְׁמְרֵם שֶׁלֹּא יִשְׁלוֹט בָּהֶם שׁוּם חֹלִי וְשׁוּם מַדְוֶה חָלִילָה, וּלְכָל חוֹלֵי עַמָּךְ בֵּית יִשְׂרָאֵל תִּשְׁלַח רְפוּאָה שְׁלֵמָה בִּמְהֵרָה, וְתִקְרָא לִשְׁבוּיִים דְּרוֹר וְלַאֲסִירִים פְּקַח קוֹחַ וְתַצִּיל אֶת עַמְּךָ בֵּית יִשְׂרָאֵל מִכָּל צַעַר וָנֶזֶק וְשׁוֹד וָשֶׁבֶר רַחֲמָנָא לִצְלָן, וְתִפְקוֹד לְכָל חֲשׂוּכֵי בָּנִים בְּזֶרַע שֶׁל קַיָּמָא זֶרַע טוֹב וְכָשֵׁר וְהָגוּן וְרָצוּי לְפָנֶיךָ

וְכָל יַלְדֵי עַמְּךָ יִזְכּוּ אֲבִיהֶם וְאִמָּם לְגַדְּלָם לְתוֹרָה וַעֲבוֹדַת ה

וְשֶׁיֵּלְכוּ בְּדֶרֶךְ הַיָּשָׁר וְיִהְיוּ מְדֻבָּקִים בְּיִרְאַת

וְאַל יִמְשׁוֹל בָּהֶם אַסְכָּרָה וְשֵׁדִין וְרוּחוֹת רָעוֹת בָּעוֹלָם וְכָל פְּגָעִין רָעִין וּמַרְעִין בִּישִׁין כִּי אִם יִהְיוּ בְּרִיאִים וּשְׁלֵמִים לַעֲבוֹדָתֶךָ וְתוֹרָתְךָ כָּל הַיָּמִים

וְהַמְעֻבָּרוֹת שֶׁל עַמְּךָ בֵּית יִשְׂרָאֵל תִּשְׁמְרֵם שֶׁלֹּא תַּפֵּלְנָה וְלַדְוֹתֵיהֶן חָלִילָה, וְיִגָּמְרוּ יְמֵי הֵרָיוֹן בְּשָׁלוֹם וּבְלִי צַעַר חָלִילָה

וּכְשֶׁיַּגִּיעַ זְמַן לֵדָתָן תֵּשְׁמ רֵם בְּעֵת לֵדָתָן מִכָּל צַעַר וָנֶזֶק

וְהֵתֵר חֶבְלֵיהֶן בְּנַקֵּל, וּבְלִי שׁוּם מִכְשׁוֹל חָלִילָה וְעַל כֻּלָּם יֶהֱמוּ נָא רַחֲמֶיךָ עַל שְׁאֵרִית תוֹרָתֶךָ הַקְּדוֹשָׁה וְעַל נִדְחֵי עַמְּךָ יִשְׂרָאֵל וְתִנְקוֹם נִקְמָתְךָ וְנִקְמַת דַּם עֲבָדֶיךָ הַשָּׁפוּךְ, וְכָל פּוֹשְׁעֵי עַמְּךָ יִשְׂרָאֵל תַּחְתּוֹר חֲתִירָה מִתַּחַת כִּסֵּא כְבוֹדֶךָ לְקַבְּלָם בִּתְשׁוּבָה שְׁלֵמָה לְפָנֶיךָ כִּי יְמִינְךָ פְּשׁוּטָה לְקַבֵּל שָׁבִים וְסוֹשְׁלַח לָנוּ אוֹרְךָ וַאֲמִתְּךָ וּתְנַחֲמֵנוּ בִּמְהֵרָה עַל דְּבַר קָדְשֶׁךָ וְתָשִׁיב שְׁבוּתֵינוּ בִּמְהֵרָה בְּרַחֲמִים רַבִּים וְגָאֲלֵנוּ גְּאֻלַּת עוֹלָם

אָמֵן סֶלָה

Recommended Reading

Goldie Milgram, *Meaning and Mitzvah: Daily Practices for Reclaiming Judaism through Prayer, God, Torah, Hebrew, Mitzvot and Peoplehood*, Jewish Lights, 2005. Includes several examples of contemporary Jewish intercession.

Zalman Meshullam Schachter-Shalomi, *Spiritual Intimacy: A Study of Counseling in Hasidism*, Jason Aronson, 1996

Part IV

Understanding and Cultivation of *Middot*
(Ethical Qualities)

Transparencies of the Divine: Formation, Contemplation and Spiritual Guidance in the Teachings of Rabbi Shalom Noach Brazovsky

by Howard Avruhm Addison

Rabbi Howard Avruhm Addison, PhD, is an Assistant Professor of Humanities at Temple University and serves as spiritual leader of Congregation Melrose B'nai Israel Emanu-El in Cheltenham, PA. A founding teacher of Lev Shomea, the first institute for training spiritual directors in the Jewish tradition, he is the Scholem Professor of Jewish Spirituality at the Graduate Theological Foundation. The author of several texts on kabbalah, the Enneagram and interfaith traditions of spiritual guidance, he is co-editor with Barbara Breitman of *Jewish Spiritual Direction: An Innovative Guide from Traditional and Contemporary Sources* (Jewish Lights).

The Question: Who Are You, My Child?

This was the question posed to our Father Jacob when he came before his own father in search of blessing [Genesis 27]. Wrapped in a mantle of deceit, Jacob presented himself as Esau, his darker, more vigorous twin, that aspect of himself that had been externalized in the womb,[51] whose shadow traits Jacob had demonized 'til that very day. Although his ruse momentarily succeeded, it would take Jacob twenty years of journey and exile, of those closest to him mirroring back his own mendacity, of wrestling with external discord and inner evasion until he could finally discern God's voice calling him home. Alone, amidst a dark night of struggle, a fearful but wiser patriarch was again asked his identity. "Jacob," he replied. "No more," answered his angelic interlocutor, "Your name shall be Israel, God's Champion, he who successfully wrestles with the human and the divine."

Each day God asks us the same question: "Who are You, My Child?" The clarity with which we as spiritual directors discern and respond to this call is vital both to our own spiritual growth and to our ability to serve those seeking sacred guidance.

The Slonimer

As we search for responses to the question of our essential identity, insightful counsel can be found in the writings of the late Slonimer Rebbe, Shalom Noach Brazovsky (1911-2000). Born in Belarus, Brazovsky established the Bais Avraham Yeshiva (Talmudic

---

51   On Jacob and Esau as identical twins see the Pentateuch commentary of Samson Raphael Hirsch, Judaica Press, 1973, on Genesis 25:24.

academy) in Jerusalem in 1941, which combines classical rabbinic studies with the teachings of Hasidism as conveyed by the dynasty of Slonim, founded by Rabbi Avraham Weinberg (1804-1883). Following the near devastation of the Slonimer dynasty during the Holocaust, Brazovsky's *yeshiva* became a primary kernel of rebirth for that Hasidic sect. In 1981 Rabbi Shalom Noach succeeded his father-in-law as the Grand Rabbi of Slonim, a position he held for almost two decades. Brazovsky's wisdom embodies a rare synthesis of contemplative, Hasidic kabbalah with the analytic and behavioristic elements found in the Lithuanian *yeshiva* and *mussar* (ethicist) movements. Brazovsky was actually introduced to the possibility of blending these varied spiritual teachings by the diverse orthodox faculty of Yeshivat Torat Chessed where he trained as a student in Belarus. Conceived in the late twentieth century, Brazovsky's thought also reflects many insights of contemporary psychology. One non-Hasidic sage went so far as to deem Brazovsky's seven volume magnum opus, *Netivot Shalom* (Pathways of Peace), the key modern text in Jewish spiritual formation, comparing it favorably with an earlier *mussar* classic, *Messilat Yesharim* (The Path of the Upright), written by the eighteenth century mystic and moralist, Moshe Chaim Luzzatto.[52]

Given Brazovsky's unique blending and transposition of traditional streams of Jewish spirituality into a contemporary key, his insights can prove invaluable to us in our quest to discover and become who we are called to be.

Awareness and its Obstacles

For the Slonimer Rebbe the quest to understand who we truly are begins with enlightened awareness. This quality, known in Hebrew as *Daat*, goes beyond a mere consciousness of one's surroundings to denote an intimate, heightened attention to the divine that underlies and pervades all things.

> The foundation of service and the pillar of the hasidic way is the quality of enlightened awareness (*Daat*)...When one is enlightened with genuine awareness one's eyes are opened; this is referred to in the verse, You have attained enlightened awareness that YHVH is God; there is nothing else (Deuteronomy 4:35) One perceives YHVH's presence infusing all worlds, inherent in all worlds, enveloping all worlds—there is nothing else. [Introduction: Pathways of Awareness 1:1 - 2:1][53]

---

52   On the life and career of Rabbi Shalom Noach Brazovsky see Shlomo Katz [ed], Hamaayan / The Torah Spring, Vol. XIV, No.48, September, 2000 at www.torah.org/learning/hamaayan/5760/

53   The translations from *Netivot Shalom* found in this essay combine elements of my own translations together with those of Rabbi Jonathan Glass. Glass' translation can be found at www.geocities.com/ ravjglass/netivot*shalom*.

The radical implications of this statement can hardly be exagerated. Echoing the near acosmic spiritual monism of Hasidism's second teacher, Rabbi Dov Ber, the Maggid (Preacher) of Mezeritch (d. 1772),[54] the Slonimer Rebbe here asserts that God is the sole reality of the world.

Therefore we human beings are, in essence, local manifestations of the divine. As such our task in life is to make ourselves nothing less than transparencies of God.

The Hebrew term for such transparency is *ayin*, literally "No-Thingness." As indicated in the passages below, *ayin* does carry connotations of humility and emptiness that can seem to border on self abnegation. However, in Kabbalah *ayin* is used as a synonym for the first *Sefirah* (Manifestation of the Divine Personality), *Keter* (literally "Crown"), which is the point of transition between *ayn sof*, the mysterious, unlimited God, and the revealed God of Kabbalah's *etz chayyim* (Tree of Life). Hence becoming *ayin* is not a matter of mere personal abasement. One who attains the emptiness of *ayin* literally becomes a point of transition between Divine potentiality and actualization.

> The essence of Jewish sacred service is to enter into the state of No-Thingness (*ayin*), to become a complete transparency of the divine (one's sense of being a separate, material self is extenguished in God)...A person in such a state of no-thingness takes up no space and has neither needs nor requests. Therefore s/he has neither jealousy nor hatred—for no-one stands in one's way. S/he suffers neither provocation nor self inflation nor craves the fulfillment of appetite and pleasure. The trait of love is embedded in one's soul, which seeks to acquire nothing for the self but is free to love the Blessed Creator... [Pathways to Purifying the *Middot* 3:3]
>
> Only in the state of *ayin* does one adhere to the Unknowable, Boundless divine, the blessed *ayn sof* [Introduction: Pathways of Awareness 4:3].

If we are indeed local manifestations of God and summoned to be transparencies of the divine, what deceptive mantle shrouds our awareness of who we truly are? The Slonimer Rebbe would answer with two words: Material egocentricity, known respectively in Hebrew as *yeshut* and *anokhiyut*.

---

54   For a detailed analysis of the theology of the Maggid of Mezeritch see Rivka Schatz Uffenheimer, *Hasidism as Mysticism*, Princeton University Press and The Magnes Press, 1993.

What is the cancerous root (root of wormwood and gall) [Deuteronomy 29:17] that produces a person's negative traits...human egocentricity. When one sees only personal benefit and only worries about the self, the holy Baal Shem Tov illumined this dynamic through the verse [Deuteronomy 5], I stood between YHVH and you—egocentricity stands as a partition separating YHVH from us...

Egocentricity is always accompanied by the perception of having an independent, material existence... This expression of separate and independent existence is likened to idolatry for the essence of idolatry is the assertion that there is some separate existence that is not nullified before the Blessed Creator. There is nothing else (besides YHVH). You (YHVH) enliven all. To the extent that something asserts independence and separation from the Blessed Creator, it is a kind of idolatry. [Pathways to Purifying the *Middot* 3:3]

While Jacob was trying to deceive his father Isaac with a goatskin coverup, our misidentification of who we are with the cloaks of our physical existence can transmute life enhancing human impulses into a web of excessive, negative character traits (*middot ra-ot*) that alienate us from God, others and ourselves.

...every character trait of a person is good at its root level; the reason for its negative expression is the fact that the trait has been clothed in physicality. [Pathways to Purifying the *Middot* 2:5]

The sages teach [Avot 4]: "Envy, desire, and pride remove a person from the world." These three traits are the roots of one's negative behavior... In his commentary "Derech Chaim" the Maharal (Rabbi Judah Loew of Prague d. 1609) explains that each of these traits are, in fact, necessary for the healthy functioning of a person in society; it is only when a person invests them with an inordinate amount of energy that "they remove one from the world." Without desire a person would neither eat nor drink nor beget children; the trait of jealousy encourages one to be involved in positive, creative activity as the rabbis have said [Baba Batra 21a], "the jealousy of scholars increases wisdom." A measure of pride is also essential for without it a person would walk around naked and perform abhorrent acts with no shame. These three traits are actually positive and essential for human survival...It is only when a person is excessive in these traits that they become destructive. [Pathways to Purifying the *Middot* 3:1]

Purifying One's Traits

The Hebrew title that many contemporary Jewish spiritual directors have adopted is one that is popular in the hasidic world, *mashpia*. The etymology of this word actually evokes the imagery of an irrigation system, with the Source of Life as the Wellhead emanating a flow of divine guidance and grace, *shefa*, to a thirsty world. The *mashpia* is therefore a conduit who reverently and intentionally places him or herself into this flow of grace to help channel its guidance and blessing to those whom they serve. The spiritual direction encounter establishes a reciprocal loop that flows back and forth between the director and the seeker, spiritually edifying both and ultimately returning that flow to further strengthen its divine source.

Like any channel, the purity and strength of that which flows through it is directly proportional to its freedom from blockages. Therefore we who would serve others as *mashpi'im* must continually endeavor to clear our psyches of any negative character traits (*middot ra-ot*) that might obstruct or distort our ability to discern the divine embedded in the unfolding narratives of life. As the Slonimer states, "Guidance (Torah) is only bestowed upon those who purify their traits (*middot*)." [Pathways to Purifying the *Middot*, Introduction]

The first step we must address in identifying the *middot ra-ot* is through self observation and the recording of one's own habitually negative responses to life situations. Echoing the insights of the twentieth century psychologist Carl Jung, the Slonimer also indicates that we find our own shadows mirrored back to us by others. [Pathways to Purifying the *Middot*, 4:3 & 7:3] If we respond spontaneously, intensely and irrationally to certain characteristics of others it is fairly sure that we ourselves also manifest those negative traits.

Practices Leading to Spiritual Purification

Having identified those traits we must engage, the Slonimer offers six different approaches to self purification. The first two are behavioral while the last four are contemplative. The following is a synopsis of his prescriptions with my own formulations of spiritual practice to engage and transform our spiritual character.[55]

---

55   Techniques for identifying, recording and engaging ones negative traits can be found in *Mussar* classics like Rabbi Menahem Mendel of Satanov's *Cheshbon Hanefesh* (The Inventory of the Soul) trans. Dovid Landsman, Feldheim, 1993, as well *Everyday Holiness* by Alan Morinis, Trumpeter Publ., 2007. I have found the Enneagram system of personality typing a particularly effective tool for identifying one's passions [see H A Addison, *The Enneagram and Kabbalah*, Second Edition, Jewish Lights, 2006].

I. Engaging One's Aversions

Maimonides writes: "How are they (*middot ra-ot*) healed? One who is prone to anger should accustom oneself to remain completely unperturbed even when cursed...and continue in this way until this tendency to anger is uprooted. Those who are arrogant should humble themselves... until arrogance becomes uprooted." The author of *Noam Elimelech* (R. Elimelech of Lizhensk, d. 1786) writes of this that s/he should spend forty consecutive days in conduct opposed to one's nature...

II. Embracing their Corresponding Virtues

An additional approach is through the statement of the *tzaddik*im (righteous) on the verse [Psalm 34], turn from evil and do good...One should strive to perform many commandments in the very area that pertains to one's negative trait. One who discerns that s/he is highly egotistical should increase acts of kindness to others. This will prove transformative for, "deed overpowers thought" [Kiddushin 59b].

The above two methods are complimentary. Together they can help a person to reach a state of character purification. A word of caution: Given what we now know about addiction I don't think we should apply these principles of the Slonimer to counseling addicts to engage their addictions (ie. alcoholics visiting bars to test their sobriety) as a means to advance abstinence.

III. Elevating a Harmful *Middah* to its Divine Source

It is said in the name of the Baal Shem Tov that "no evil comes from Above." ... Accordingly, every character trait of a person is good at its root level...the root level of desire is the capacity for love that the Holy One gives a person for the purpose of divine love. When a person does not refine this capacity it becomes corrupted and expresses itself as base desire... Every negative desire is, in fact, a gift from Heaven with the intent that a person elevates the desire to its root. Through this one becomes elevated and is saved from negativity.

Compose a list of all of your negative *middot* and a second list of their corresponding virtues (e.g., selfishness/generosity). Enter into a contemplative state and imagine yourself breathing out each of the negative traits one by one, with the breath beginning at the soles of your feet ascending upward through the body, past the crown of your head and onward towards their divine source. Pause after completing your list and then begin breathing in the virtues one by one, imagining the breath entering through the crown of your head and filling your whole body down to your soles. As part of my personal practice I breathe out an acrostic list of negative *middot* in Hebrew from through *tav* and then breathe in a reverse acrostic of godly *middot*, with the flow of each breath to the cadence of the High Holy Day confessional, *Ashamnu*.

IV. Recognition of Powerlessness and Surrender to God

Another superior path is when a Jew utilizes the Higher Power which is accessible to the soul. This is what is necessary on occasions when our natural powers are of no effect. When a person is confronted with a test such as "the harmful inclination (*yetzer ha-ra*) overwhelmed one to the point of utter possession" [see Nedarim 9b], our only recourse is soul surrender...when we are confronted by overwhelming desires, a time when the light of Torah and service are unable to assist us, the Blessed Holy One has provided the remedy of the Higher Power which we can access through complete surrender of our essence and of all our natural powers to God.[56][57]

Consider those negative aspects of your life which, no matter how hard you struggle, you are powerless to change: family history, brain chemistry, certain hurtful impulses or addictive behaviors. Prayerfully confess each one (I am powerless over ___) and following each confession breathe in the entreaty from the liturgy of our Sukkot *lulav* and *etrog* procession, Hoshannah, God please redeem me. After the last confession recite the concluding words of that Sukkot prayer, *Ani VaHo Hoshiannah*, I through God, shall be redeemed.

V. Inviting Divine Light to Penetrate the Darkness

There is another general approach through which light will dwell within a person... This approach is indicated by the process of creation. The earth was unformed and void; darkness was on the face of the deep. God said, "Let there be light" and there was light. Each person is a miniature world: each person contains a Godly soul and potent spiritual energies as well as forces of darkness and confusion.... In the absence of spiritual light a person becomes increasingly self-centered...; s/he simply cannot move beyond the self... When, however, s/he instills one's being with spiritual light—You shine forth the sun, they disappear [Psalm 104]—all the dark places of the soul become illuminated.

---

56   The selections from the Slonimer are exerpted from *Netivot Shalom*: Pathways to Purifying the *Middot* 2:4-6. The concept behind Practice IV was suggested to me by a friend who is acquainted with the principles and practices of 12 Step fellowships. Practice V was taught to me by my spiritual director of many years, Sr Barbara Whittemore, while the question posed in Practice VI was brought to my attention by a fellow participant in one of Helen Palmer's Enneagram trainings in the late 1990's.

57   To compare this teaching with Steps 1-3 of the 12 Step Programs see *Alcoholics Anonymous*, 4th Edition (Alcoholics Anonymous World Services, Inc, 2001) Ch 5

After entering into a contemplative state, imagine the *middah ra-ah* or spiritual challenge you are facing as a dark cloud or knotted mass before you. Invite the light of God into the darkness or the tangle and then wait hopefully as you discern what guidance might unfold to help you better understand and respond to this troubling trait or occurrence.

VI. Seeing through the Perspective of Heaven

You have seen that I spoke to you from the heavens. [Exodus 12]…The meaning of the verse is that I speak to you "communicating a state of elevated consciousness." When one looks at the world with this (heavenly) consciousness one sees the insignificance of so much that people put their efforts into…negative traits fall way. Mountains melt like wax before YHVH, the Lord of the earth [Psalm 97].

When caught in the thrall of some unworthy response spawned by a negative trait, meditate on the question, "What is this to Eternity?" Clear guidance can come by pondering the importance of this issue in relation to the timeless God's vast sweep of creation or by imagining the response to this moment by which we'd like to be remembered at the end of time.

A Never Ending Journey

Just as those who offer spiritual direction must continue to be in direction themselves so to must we, as *mashpi'im*, continue the process of purifying the conduits that are our souls by refining our character traits. As the Slonimer states: The *middot* (godly traits) are the vehicle (*merkavah*, lit. "chariot") by which guidance (Torah) is conveyed. [Pathways to Purifying the *Middot*, Introduction]

Because we are composed of not only the physical and the spiritual, but of the emotional and intellectual as well, it is important to combine the behavioral and contemplative practices listed above with ongoing prayer, empathetic reaching out to others and the study of Torah and works of *mussar* and ethical refinement. [See recommended reading.] It is only by integrating all four aspects of our humanity, reflecting the *arba olamot*, kabbalah's Four Worlds or dimensions of reality, that we might dedicate the entire self to becoming the ever clearer transparency of God that we as directors must strive to be.

Do we ever reach our destination? Is *ayin*, transparent no-thingness, a state of being or merely a station at which we but occasionally arrive? According to the Slonimer, for the vast majority of us the process is an ongoing journey:

It is a constant, even exhausting struggle... one needs to cultivate deep awareness of the degradation of negative traits and the goodness of positive ones.... Character traits require one's constant awareness and attention; if one becomes inattentive the negative traits will just arise again.

 —Pathways to Purifying the *Middot* 2:4

However, it is the faith that God is with us in that struggle that allows us to dance even when we only perceive thin threads of spiritual light. [PPM 4:4 &7:3] And it is that same faith that can impel us to sustain the struggle and thus be worthy of the name of that patriarch, which we bear – Israel, those willing to wrestle with the all too human within us for the sake of those we serve and the divine.

Acrostic of the *Middot* by Howard Avruhm Addison
Negative (*Middot ha-Raot*)

1.	*Anokhiyut*	Egocentricity
2.	*Batlanut*	Sloth
3.	*Ga'avah*	Arrogance
4.	*Dibat Ra-ah*	Slander
5.	*Hitrom'mut*	Self Inflation
6.	*V'Kashyut Lev*	Hard Heartedness\Indifference
7.	*Z'donut*	Maliciousness
8.	*Chayma*	Rage\Anger
9.	*T'faylut*	Trivial Diversions
10.	*Yeshut*	Materialism
11.	*Kavod*	Status Seeking
12.	*Laytzanut*	Ridicule
13.	*Merirut*	Melancholy\Bitter Resentment
14.	*Nivul Peh*	Vulgarity
15.	*Sikhlut*	Foolishness
16.	*Ervah*	Misdirected Sexuality
17.	*Pakhad*	Fear
18.	*Tzarut Ayin*	Narrowed Perspective
19.	*Kinah*	Envy
20.	*Resha*	Wickedness
21.	*Sheker*	Deceit
22.	*Ta-avah*	Craving\Lust

Acrostics of the *Middot* by Howard Avruhm Addison
Positive/Godly (*Middot Tovot*)

22. *Timimut*	Simplicity
21. *Shelemut*	Wholeness
20. *Rakhamim*	Compassion
19. *Kedushah*	Holiness
18. *Tzedakah*	Righteousness\Charity
17. *Pi-ilut*	Effective Action
16. *Anavah*	Humility
15. *Savlanut*	Patience
14. *Ne-emanut*	Faithfulness
13. *Mekhilah*	Forgiveness
12. *Lev Tov*	Good Heartedness
11. *K'vod Ha-briyah*	Respecting God's Creation
10. *Yosher*	Integrity
9. *Taharah*	Purity
8. *Chessed*	Loving Kindness
7. *Zerizut*	Enthusiasm
6. *V'Hokhmah*	Wisdom
5. *Hoda-ah*	Gratitude
4. *Daat*	Enlightened Awareness
3. *Gedulah*	Greatness\Maturity
2. *Bekhirah*	Freedom from Compulsion
1. *Elohut*	Godliness

Recommended Reading

Howard A Addison, *The Enneagram and Kabbalah, Second Edition*, Jewish Lights Publishing, 2006

Nilton Bonder, *The Kabbalah of Envy: Transforming Hatred, Anger, and Other Negative Emotions*, Shambhala, 1997

> *The Kabbalah of Food: Conscious Eating for Physical, Emotional, and Spiritual Health*, Shambhala, 1995

> *The Kabbalah of Money: Jewish Insights on Giving, Owning, and Receiving*, Shambhala, 2001

Sylvia Boorstein, *Pay Attention, For Goodness Sake*, Ballantine Books, 2002

Rabbi Menachem Mendel of Satanov's Cheshbon Hanefesh (The Inventory of the Soul) trans. Dovid Landsman, Feldheim, 1993

Alan Morinis, *Everyday Holiness*, Trumpeter Publishing, 2007

Rivka Schatz Uffenheimer, *Hasidism as Mysticism*, Princeton University Press and The Magnes Press, 1993

Ira F Stone, *A Responsible Life*, Aviv Press, 2007

Joseph Telushkin's A Code of Jewish Ethics, Volume I: You Shall Be Holy, Oxford University Press, 2006

Leaping and Waiting: Reflections on a Slonimer Text
A *Shpatzir*[58] in Four Movements
by Elliot K. Ginsburg

Rabbi Elliot K. Ginsburg is Associate Professor of Jewish Thought and Mysticism at the University of Michigan, rabbi of the Pardes Hannah *minyan*, and a member of the academic *va'ad* of the Aleph Ordination Programs. He is the author of *The Sabbath in the Classical Kabbalah* and translator (with a critical commentary) of *Sod ha-Shabbat: The Mystery of the Sabbath* by Rabbi Meir ibn Gabbai. Editor of an innovative website on mystical *piyyut* (poetry), he is currently at work on a multi-tiered study of Judaism as spiritual practice.

Haqqafah Alef: Spiral One, by way of an Introduction: To Wait or To Leap, that is the question.

"What is the meaning of *HoKhMaH* (Wisdom)? *HaKeh MaH.*
Since you can never grasp it (quickly), *chakkeh*, 'wait,' for *mah*, 'what' will come and what will be: wisdom emerging out of No-Thing (*ayin*)."
—Moshe de Leon, Sheqel ha-Qodesh, 26.[59]

First thought, best thought.
—governing principle of one Allen Ginsberg

"The correct answer to any question concerning (spiritual) practice always is: do what you need to stay balanced."
—Sylvia Boorstein, oral communication.

To lead the spiritual life, it has been said, one must learn to do two things: to fast and to wait.[60] In the language of Song of Songs [2:7, 3:5], *im ta'iru ve-im te'oreru et ha-ahavah ad she-tekhpotz*, don't awaken love until it is ripe, or as soul-singers The Supremes had it,

---

58   Lexical note: ***shpa-TZEER***, Yiddish for a promenade or amble (which would make this note the preamble)

59   I am slightly emending Daniel Matt's translation in Essential Kabbalah, p. 70.

60   ff. Siddhartha's realization in Hermann Hesse's classic that he can do the spiritual work: "I can fast, I can wait." I was reminded of this text by Shefa Gold.

"You can't hurry love." Indeed, much of Jewish spiritual practice ranging from "the path of blessing"[61] to the deep pause of *Shabbat* (Sabbath),[62] entails the practice of slow-cooking, of attentive listening to *pirpurei ha-nefesh*, the subtle movements of soul.[63] From the Slonimer Rebbe's lingering with the Beloved at a festival's end (*atzeret*)[64] to the Izhbitzer Rebbe's cultivation of *yishuv ha-da'at* (settled mind) when surrounded by a sea of rage;[65] from Nachman of Breslov's Sighing Practice,[66] in which one sends a Deep Breath of Patience[67] to our places of brokenness and discontent to the *Netivot Shalom*'s practice of *bikkurim*, where one doesn't rush to consume the "first fruits" but offers them up as gift[68] —all these teachings suggest a subtle balance of doing and restraint, surrender and openness, interiority and the holiness of "the between"—in short, a willingness to patiently surf the *ratzo va-shov*.[69] One can learn this movement not only from the *halakhically*-based ethical literature, but also from those profound "latecomers," Buber and Rosenzweig, who in 1920 counseled a kind of "readiness," an alert and confident waiting to see what unfolds, en route to their dream of a Jewish Renaissance. To practice "readiness," they taught, is to resist the urge to too quickly fill in the blank with ready-made plans or words. Instead, one should carve out wider channels of awareness, and so deepen

---

61   To recite a *brakha* (blessing) is to stop time for a blink or two in order to engage in holy triangulation, in which the bless-er links the proximate cause (be it a sandwich, a sunset, or a glass of water); one's awareness; and *der eybeshter* (the Ultimate cause). As Heschel put it, the goal of religious living is "to experience commonplace deeds as spiritual adventures." [God in Search of Man, 49]

62   *Shabbat* may be seen as a Fire-Break in the week, a day of "holy disengagement from the world that we so need to change." (Heschel) Or as Nachman the Breslover put it, *Shabbat* is the day of the Deep Breath, *arikhut ha-neshimah*, when we can breathe light into those parts of our embodied being that have become asphyxiated in the rush of doing. See *Liqqutei MoHaRaN 1:8, Liqqutei Halakhot, OH hilkhot shabbat sect. 1*, and below.

63   I borrow this phrase from the Piasetzner, Kalonymus Kalman Shapira, *B'nei Makhshavah Tovah*, sec. 11.

64   *Netivot Shalom, Mo'adim, d'rush* for Shavuot. For biographical information on the *Slonimer* Rebbe, Shalom Noach Berezovsky (1911-2000), see Avruhm Addison's essay in this volume and A. Nadler's article, cited in the bibliography to this article.

65   Mordechai Yosef Leiner, *Mei ha-Shiloach* to parashat Noach

66   Yid., krekhtzn.

67   In Nachman's words, *erekh appayim, arikhut ha-neshimah*.

68   *Netivot Shalom, D'varim, Ki Tavo*

69   The ebb and flow of the life-force, ff. Ezek. 1:14 as reread by the kabbalists: *veha-hayyut ratzo va-shov*.

Jewish learning and living.[70] As Rabbi Zalman Schachter-Shalomi is wont to say of the unfolding path, "*va-anahnu lo neida mah na'avod et YHVH ad bo'einu shamah* — We won't know with what we shall serve God until we get there." [Exodus 10:26]

The orienting term for me is *mishma'at*, Hebrew for a spiritual discipline that is simultaneously a hearing. Ears and heart open, poised (or attuned) to respond to what is aborning. In the spiritual math of the *B'nei Yissaskhar*, *LaG ba-omer* follows *LeV ba-omer*, for when the heart (*Lev*) is open, one sees differently.[71] Thus, *GaL einekha*—open your eyes anew (now that your heart has opened)—*va-abita nifla'ot mi-toratekha*, and see the wonders as they unfold [Ps.119:18].

Unfold. I write this word as a mnemonic for myself, *ke-mazkeret*, for I must confess that this skillful waiting is not the most obvious part of my temperamental *yerushah*, or inheritance.[72] I have always been drawn to the exuberant *geshrei*, the whoop of joy, and to the blink, the *khap*, the quicksilver flare of insight. The playful pun and the verbal improv that rises from the adaptive unconscious[73] like preternatural late-night jazz. The deeper calm that I can now more steadily access is a gift of *Shabbes* (the Sabbath), daily practice,

---

70   See esp. N. Glatzer, ed. *Franz Rosenzweig: His Life and Thought*, 222-25, On Being a Jewish Person:

Have confidence for once. Renounce all plans. Wait. People will appear who prove by the very fact of their coming...that the Jewish human being is alive in them...To begin with, don't offer them anything. Listen. And words will come to the listener, and they will join together and form desires...Desires that join and people that join together.

The unlimited cannot be attained by organization. That which is distant can be reached only through that which is nearest at the moment. Any "plan" is wrong to begin with—simply because it is a plan. The highest things cannot be planned; for them, readiness is everything.

Confidence is the word for a state of readiness that does not ask for recipes, and does not mouth perpetually, 'What shall I do then?' and 'How can I do that?' Confidence is not afraid of the day after tomorrow. It lives in the present....

Or as poet William Whyte put it, "The life you can plan/ is too small for you/ to live."

71   LaG and its numerically identical form *GaL* גל in gematria are each 33, following *LeV* (32). Reading mystically, *GaL*, new eyes, follows the 32 days of cultivating one's *LeV*, or heart. In the Dynover's view, the first 32 days of the Omer create readiness, so that or *ha-ganuz*, Deep or Primordial Consciousness, may break through and carry one to Sinai. The seam between Days 32 and 33 is the tipping point, the crowning or break-through. See there for details.

72   It was the exceedingly wise Barry Barkan who once said to me: "You don't have to accept every gift you've been given."

73   On this term, see Malcolm Gladwell, *Blink: The Power of Thinking Without Thinking* (2005).

and I'm convinced, middle age. Now my father was an exceptional man who had survived the *shoah* (the Holocaust) living by his wits, leaping and breaking free at the "right" time. Much later, in peacetime, it seemed to me that he was ever *zitzn af shpilkes*, sitting (if that is the right term!) on pins and needles, ready to spring into action. I sensed that the world was not a safe place, that safety necessitated being (preemptively, proleptically) in motion. *De-hayynu* (meaning), I drank in a certain restlessness with my father's milk. Perhaps it was from my mother, who lost her own mother as a two-year old in the flu epidemic of 1918-19, that I learned more about the long twisting path, the possibility that ultimately, *akhar ha-d'varim ha-elleh*, things would be ok.

So one may wait for many good reasons: to tamp down or sublimate the flames of anger or sexual desire;[74] to simmer or slow-cook what must not be raised to a boil; or to build up spiritual energy like a battery recharging to full-strength, or a preacher falling back and building to a crescendo. We may pause to wait for a friend, to say thank you to another, to acknowledge moments of fleeting beauty and grief, to watch a shy leaf skitter along a curb. So too, we may pause to grow into parts of ourselves, to break reflexive (often unskillful) patterns that seize us like fever, or to turn habitual judgments into something more playful: curiosity. To untangle mind and give it some "air." Many is the time I have watched my wife Linda sit with perplexities and confusion, till a deeper knowing emerges. There are some things which must bubble up from the unconscious depths, or emerge sidewise, crystallize, or take their own bittersweet time.

To fast and to wait. To practice patience with oneself and others.[75] But comes a time, when the spiritual path also demands a gravity defying vault: a leap into the breach. At such moments of decision, there can be no more slow-cooking of our *neshamah*, no more special pleas to grow a touch more "refined." For, there are situations when you will never be ready enough. As Nachman of Breslov avers, there is a moment on the spiritual path (on the ladder of Return to the One), where one is suspended in liminal space, caught between the rungs. Even if one stretches to one's full stature, the gap is sufficiently large that one cannot simultaneously have one's feet on the rung below and one's hands on the rung above. One can only jump into thin air, and hang for a moment between, where there is no Ground or sure hand-hold. Such is the practice of *emunah*, daring to push

---

74   On anger, see the Izhbitzer to Noah, noted above; on sexual waiting, see Gen. 37:11: ואביו שמר את הדבר and the commentators ad loc., as well as Gen. 39:8 on Joseph and Potiphar's wife. And for a Jewish Tantra, if you'll *fargin* (indulge) me that turn of phrase, see my *The Sabbath in the Classical Kabbalah*, Appendix 2, and more amazingly, Moses Cordovero, *Or Yakar* to Zohar, 3:26a.

75   Thus Nachman (attributed): צריך אדם להיות סבלן גדול גם עם עצמו (A person must be very patient, even with himself.)

forward, by even a few centimeters, the leading edge where one's Elemental Trust meets one's elemental Lack of Trust.[76]

I think about my own life: Do I think things will be ok? For me, my loved ones, Israel and Palestine, the planet? Are we held in the Everlasting Arms? On a macro-scale, I experience successive, and shifting layers of Fundamental Trust and Doubt. (It is easier in these early days of President Obama.) Most days (but not always) I feel: a calm at the bottom of the Sea. For this I feel blessed. But I know, deep in my *kishkes* (guts) that not all of us have been dealt a fair hand in this life, that some of us have experienced childhoods where our parent(s) couldn't protect us, or where society's safety-net has proven to be hopelessly threadbare. (We must speak of this, we who haven't fallen through.) The gifts of love and resilience are not equally distributed in this world, and our task is to find ways, large (systemic) and small (face to face), to better re-balance the flow of love and resources.

Y'hi shalom be-heilekh, shalvah be-arm'notayikh —May peace come to our ramparts [Ps. 122:7] to our borderlands and outer edges, to the places where we brush up against the world; and may tranquility come to our innermost sanctuaries, even reaching our palaces of power.

But let us return to the rampart at hand, the boundary situation of *Beshallakh*. Behind us the aversive forces draw ever nearer,[77] while ahead awaits the Sea of Reeds, uncharted, unknown, a tangle of unlikely hope. In an astonishing inter-splicing of the mythic imagination *Mekhilta de-Rabbi Ishmael* sees the Binding of Isaac happening again:

> At the moment when the Children were poised to enter the sea, Mount Moriah began to move from its place, and the altar for Isaac set, the whole scene as it had been arranged...Isaac as if he were bound and placed upon the altar, Abraham as if he were stretching forth his hand, taking the knife to slay his son...

A trauma that was half-repressed is revisited on the worn bodies of Isaac's descendants. To use the image of Auschwitz survivor Charlotte Delbo, "the skin of memory," of deep sequestered memory, suddenly ruptures, flooding consciousness. To be and not to be: that is the question.[78] As Abraham's knife comes down, Moses stands at the shore locked in

---

76   Cf. Nathan of Nemirov, *Liqqutei Halakhot*, on the Days of Awe, the leap of *teshuvah* and the parallel dance of the divine lovers. They separate from their back-to-back cleaving, risking the nesirah (and enduring separation) that they might come together face-to-face.

77   Ah, but perhaps in some iteration of the story we are those aversive forces....

78   I.e., the urge to life and the affect-storm of trauma (that sinking, visceral knowing that "I am cooked") are excruciatingly, simultaneously present. I borrow the emended Shakespearean phrase from Elie Wiesel and from my colleague, Henry Greenspan, author of *On Listening to Holocaust Survivors*.

prayer, unable to go forward. But Moses rallies, raises his staff to go forward and so pulls out Abraham's knife.... from our heart.[79] The People cross over.

Amid this backdrop, the spiritual question becomes not only whether to leap but when? And how, with eyes shut or open? Carrying what memories and whose bones? Is one's staff stretched forth confidently in a bid for power or frozen in the familiar somatic patterns? That staff in your hand, is it a conductor's baton for the symphony on the Other Side or a bowed walking stick to keep you from slipping on the sea-slick rocks? In terms of the Jewish spiritual year, the question of leaping is the question of Passover, all the more so on its seventh day. Another impasse? So soon? What adventures are we really open to, knowing that with change we must also change our lives? (Only now do we understand the comforts we left behind.)

What becomes decisive is not the "simple" (awesome) act of leaving Egypt (the work of the first day), but the next checkpoint and the next, the breach of *Mitzrayim*'s territorial waters, the birth into another stage of being.[80] *Shevi'i shel Pesakh* (the seventh day of Passover), Rabbinic tradition has it, is the day of Leaping, of Crossing Over with new eyes. It is a moment of surpassing joy, of risk and breakthrough, radical God-visioning,[81] of slave-legs learning to free-dance. Come the next day, however, the hung-over celebrants are left to ask: How do we live in light of that momentary glimpse? How do we nurture and integrate that liberating vision? What of those of us (and those parts of us) that remain on the Other Side? Important clues are provided in the practice of *sefirat ha-Omer*, the seven weeks of spiritual "walking"— the *shpatzir* between the liberation of *Pesakh* and the revelation of Shavuot. In the kabbalistic tradition, this is a time for catching one's breath: for refining one's *middot* or spiritual-ethical qualities—the intricacies of love and discernment, compassion, perseverance and gratitude, the *eros* of connectedness, of integrated being, as well as impeccable speech. Each week is dedicated to refining another *middah*, as a way of slow-cooking our hearts. As Rabbi Jeff Roth has it, this practice doesn't necessarily lead to perfection, but to heightened sensitivity to the ebb and flow of being, the *ratzo va-shov*. As he puts it, practice makes practice.

---

79   *Mekhilta, Shirta*, s.v. Yose ha-Galili, spliced together with the famous poem "Yerushah" (Inheritance) by Haim Gouri, in which Isaac is spared but the knife enters his descendants' hearts. I intend to discuss these texts at length elsewhere. Thanks to Oran Hesterman for kinesthetic (keen-aesthetic!) insight into the lifted knife.

80   Jewish mystical tradition likens Egypt to a womb that sustained the People at an earlier point, but soon grew perilously small. To remain there any longer was to court death...On Exodus as a birthing, see also Ilana Pardes' *The Biography of Ancient Israel* (2000).

81   See the famous *Mekhilta* on the maidservant: זה אלי ענו ואמרו below. But also see Yitzchak of Radwil, conventionally, "this is my God they answered and exulted," but here read homonymically "This is my God, anu [אנו], us," as though to say, in the expanded awareness at the Sea, Israel came to realize that they too are part of the Godfield. At this level of consciousness, altz iz Gott!

What we are invoking here is the rhythmic art of finding points of balance, of practicing Trust in accord with the rhythms of the Sacred Year. (This cycle gives us a framework and a language we can draw on in the unpredictable and often messy course of our own lives. And best of all, it gives us company on the way. As Reb Zalman once taught, sometimes if we can give ourselves over to a miraculous Order, healing can take place.) So, leaping and waiting. This *koan* flows from Sacred Time into the sequence of daily life: Should we leap, or should we wait to ripen?[82] How do we discern which of the two broad options to embrace? When is Waiting a leap, a motionless dance? I am speaking of the *asana* of faith, the balancing of opposing virtues. As Niels Bohr put it: "The opposite of a truth is a falsehood. But the opposite of a profound truth is another profound truth." Breslov tradition calls this the dialectic between the straw fire and the well-cooked heart. In Nachman's words, "Even more than God wants the straw fire, God wants the well-cooked heart"— the discipline of slow, steady deepening. Now it may be true that the subtle movements of spirit hold the key to the deepest transformations, but in the pages that follow I come to speak in favor of the leap, the blaze, the breakthrough, the melt, the whoop and morph, without which we cannot be easily freed from spiritual grid lock, or from narrowing vision. Without leaping, no hope.

> "Prayer takes place in the space between Life and Death"
> —Rabbi Shefa Gold
> (a certain Roadrunner-Rabbi <meep meep> from New Mexico)

The ensuing text has been a kind of *shiviti* text for me—a text that opens a window to the divine presence—since I first came across it some years ago. Given over by the Slonimer Rebbe, Shalom Noach Berezovsky (d. 5760/2000), it focuses on the moment of crossing the Sea. The *d'rush* (exploratory teaching) insinuates: You think that the exodus from Egypt was the end of liberation? Think again...for six days later the Children of Israel were at the Sea, the Enemy forces closing in from the one side and the Sea from the other. This is the moment of leaping, a covenant forged (a la Nachman) "between the rungs."[83]

---

82   Rabbinic tradition cites *B'nei Efra'im* as the classic example of those who couldn't/didn't wait till the right moment, and disastrously jumped the gun. See 1 Chr. 7:22, TB Sanhedrin 92b, Ex. Rabbah 20:11, ibn Ezra to Song of Songs 2:13, et al.

83   While the Leap spoken of here is momentous, a matter of life-and-death, I sometimes think of a continuum of leaps: from gaping life-and-death situations, to questions of changing professions, jobs, names, to entering into or leaving relationships/homes, or letting go of loved ones. But I also think of leaps in less dramatic, more mundane fashion: e.g., when do I decide to get up and eat lunch, or leave the endlessly fascinating faculty lecture, or agree to sponsor a student? Or, to get really minute, when I am meditating and my knees begin to ache: do I simply watch my reactions and thought patterns, or send myself some love, or do I actually "leap," i.e., re-arrange my body? And how closely can I track my decision-making process? Is the moment of decision a thinking or adrabbah, a non-thinking?!

For the Slonimer it is the gift of *emunah* —Elemental Trust—which enables one to make the leap. (Or perhaps Trust itself is the leap!) One can never be wholly ready for such moments of daring. As Nachman (and in his wake, my teacher teacher Arthur Green) expound on the verse, "*ve-lo yakhlu le-hitmahmeyah ve-gam tzeidah lo asu la-hem* — and the children of Israel could not tarry; they made no provisions for the way" [Ex. 12:39], there is no way to adequately prepare for certain journeys. One will never be ready enough. Leaving *Mitzrayim*, the narrow straits, was one such moment. Had the children of Israel waited until they were primed, why, they would still be in Egypt until this very day! Thus far, Reb Nachman.[84] The Slonimer begins his text by limning three levels of Trust: Trusting Mind, Trusting Heart, and Trusting Limbs/Embodied Trust. If the Exodus from Egypt required Trusting Mind and Trusting Heart, the leap into the sea required Trusting Limbs, which the Slonimer sees as the highest/hardest stratum of faith, a trust that is baked into one's embodied being. Elemental Trust, *emunah sh'lemah*, requires the integration of all three levels. In the next *haqqafah*/go-round, I offer my translation of the Slonimer's *vort* (short teaching), taken from his major work *Nevitot Shalom*, "The Paths of Peace." The core-text can be found on *Shabbat Shirah*, the *Shabbat* of Song,[85] with an alternate *girsa* in his homilies on the Seventh Day of Passover. Afterwards, I will append some brief comments to the text and suggest a way to turn the Teaching into a spiritual practice.

Haqqafah Beit. Text in translation.

"Confidence isn't something we have…it's something we practice."
        —Sylvia Boorstein

The Slonimer Rebbe on Crossing the Sea.
(*Netivot Shalom, Parashat Beshallakh*)

A.

It is taught in the *Mekhilta* [Beshallah, chap. 6], how great was Israel's faith in the One who spoke the world into Being. As reward for Israel's trust/*emunah* in YHVH, the holy

---

84   Or more precisely his *talmid-chaver*-channel Nathan of Nemirov, *Liqqutei Halakhot*, YD *hilkhot gilluakh*, section 3. And see Arthur Green's marginal glosses to Michael Strassfeld's The Jewish Holidays, p. 38. Paraphrasing Nachman he writes: "When you are about to leave Egypt—any Egypt—do not stop to think, 'But how will I learn a living out there?…' One who stops to 'make provisions for the way' will never get out of Egypt." A comment (Green adds) "to be repeated annually for college seniors, midlife-crisis confronters, and all the rest of us 'wage-slaves' as Marx would have it."

85   Shemot, parashat Beshallakh, 113-115

spirit rested on (*shartah*: but by way of punning, sang in) them and they broke into song (*amru shirah*), as it is said: "And they trusted the One and Moses, God's servant. Then Moses and the Children of Israel sang." [Ex. 14:31-15:1]

B.

    This requires some explanation, for already as Israel left *Mitzrayim*, they attained the rung of Trust. Even though it said "The People had faith" [Ex. 4:31] [when they were still enslaved], in leaving they didn't offer up song. This they only did at the Parting of the Seas...(He later explains why this was so, initially the song remained inward: *raq bi-fnimiyut ha-lev*.) There are three rungs of *emunah: emunat ha-moakh*: Trusting Mind; *emunat ha-lev*: Trusting Heart; but there is a rung still higher, *emunat ha-evarim*: Trusting with your limbs or embodiment, where *emunah* penetrates every fiber of your being, where horror can't seize you for your whole body feels the protective divine presence. Complete *emunah* occurs when it unfolds in all three dimensions. As King David said [Ps. 84:3] "*Libi uv'sari yerannenu el el chai* — My heart and my flesh (my body) sing to the Living God." Not just the heart, but also the flesh, our skin and our muscles, our bones and limbs also sing to the Living God, for *emunah* suffuses our entire being. This is "all my bones say, O Yah, who is like you — *mi khamokha*!" [Ps. 35:10] For bones are the densest part of our physical body...They are suffused by the Presence until they too cry out, "O God who is like you!" And so, the entire person comes to embody Trust—from the balls of one's feet to the crown of one's head.

C.

    Israel attained this rung as they crossed the Sea....jumping into the Sea in pure devotion (*mesirat nefesh*: surrender, handing over the soul-body)....in *emunat ha-evarim*. As our Sages said [*Mekhilta, Shirta* chap. 3], "the [simplest] handmaiden at the Sea saw what was beyond the vision of Ezekiel the Prophet. All Israel saw *Zeh*/This: "This is my God, and I will exalt This!" [Ex. 15:2]...They attained the highest rung of Faith.

D.

    And since they trusted in the One, the Holy Spirit rested/sang in them, and they broke into Song. (Whereas when they left Egypt, they sang only inwardly, in their innermost heart,) at the Sea — *partzah ha-hutzah gam ba-evarim*—it broke forth into their limbs.

E.

    In the *Noam Elimelekh* (of hasidic master Elimelekh of Lizhensk) in his *Liqqutei Shoshanah*, it is explained that "Israel walked on dry land —in the midst of the Sea—*u-v'nei yisrael halkhu ba-yabbashah be-tokh ha-yam*." [Ex. 14:29]. This means that even on dry land they felt the presence of the miracle, the wonder that visited them at the Sea (when swimming inside the divine)...There are some who feel the divine presence only during the most extraordinary events (*nisim*), but not in the mundane. At the Parting of the Sea, Israel attained the rung of walking as though they were in the Sea, as Ramban [Nachmanides on the Torah, parashat Bo, end] teaches: from the largest miracles, one comes to acknowledge/recognize/be grateful for (*modeh*) the small and hidden ones....

F.

The Splitting of the Sea was pure Love: but the *yir'ah* the People experienced [see Ex. 14:31] was the overflow of Love (its deepening into radical awe)...When their hearts and their embodied beings sang to the living God at the Sea, they attained the highest rung of love of God, the sense of awe that emerges (not from thou shalt not) but from the sense of permission (*heter*) or spaciousness.

G.

It is told of the *Sabba Kaddisha* (the Holy Grandfather), the Rebbe of Slonim:[86] Once on the seventh night of *Pesakh* he was sitting at his holy *tish* (the table around which his followers gathered) and he was moved to ask: Who would want the plunder, the riches of the Sea? One of his *hasidim* (adherents) answered: We only want the *emunah* of that moment, seeing God like the maidservant did....seeing the This-ness of the One, "This is my God, I will exalt This!"

Haqqafah Gimmel. Comments to the Text:

paragraph B:

"as Israel left Mitzrayim": This was only one stage in the process of liberation, not its full extent. After the liberation from the Narrow Straits, the people may think it is home free: but no, six days later, the people find themselves at an even greater impasse, hemmed in between angry armies and the angry Sea. Even after the crossing, not three days later, as the people grow hungry, they kvetch from their bellies in bitterness at *Marah*, longing for the comfort food of the *di alte heim* (the old home). Enlightenment, like liberation, is not once and for all. Rather, the practice is ongoing...two steps forward, one and a half back. (On a good day!) Practice makes....for an interesting dance.

---

86   The first Slonimer rebbe, Avraham Weinberg (1804-84), author of *Yesod ha-Avodah, Hesed le-Avraham*, novellae on the *Mekhilta*, et al.

"there is a rung higher still.": Perhaps the Slonimer is speaking too globally here. Some of us may come to embodied Trust more easily than to its affective or cognitive dimensions. Still, I tend to sympathize with his characterization. Trusting in one's *kishkes*, in one's bones, muscles and sinews may, for many of us, come last. To what extent has this been especially true of Jewish bodies? Is there some sort of ancestral "memory" encoded in how we learn to carry ourselves before power? So too, consider someone who has undergone deep trauma, which is literally encoded in the body in ways that defy ordinary languaging and ordinary memory. (This, of course, has correlates in the brain.) Sometimes, bodily trust comes alive only after the work has been done on the other levels of being. In my reading of the astonishing *Mekhilta* passage, wherein the *Akedah* starts to unspool, I suggest that precisely because that ancient trauma was uncovered—and the knife/staff lifted—some modicum of healing could take place. First the awakened memory, then a softening, and a gradual letting go. One indicator of healing: to be able to recall the trauma, without viscerally reliving it. See Barbara Breitman's comments in Arthur Waskow's *Godwrestling Round Two* (217-18) on Remembering and Forgetting Amalek; and Avishai Margalit's *The Ethics of Memory*, esp. chap. 4.

"*mi khamokha*! Who is like You?!": This phrase is found both in Psalm 35:11 and in Exodus 15:11 at the Song of the Sea. The Slonimer brings the two textual citations—a *gezerah shavah* (verbal analogy)—into alignment, rubbing the one verse against the other as though they were flint stones, sparks flying.

"Complete *emunah*": encompassing *Moakh, Lev, EHvarim* (mind-heart-body). Turn it into an acronym and it becomes: *MaLEH*: the fullness, or pleroma. Put in the lexicon of neo-*CHaBaD* or Renewal Kabbalah (feminist hasidism?!), this is an integrated trust, encompassing cognitive knowing (the world of *Beriyah*), relational trust including the world of emotions (*Yetzirah*), and trust that stretches beyond the language centers of the brain, encoded in the very limbs (*Assiyah*). The whole integrated gestalt suggests a fourth level of trust, parallel with the highest world of kabbalah, *Atzilut*, the realm of Being.

"horror cannot seize you": I see this as a larger confidence that can envelop and absorb smaller discomforts, doubts, even certain systemic shocks, like a tall building in San Francisco built to withstand not only buffeting winds, but the shifting of tectonic plates. Or perhaps better, it is not that one no longer has fears, but that one no longer becomes that fear. (I owe this distinction to Parker Palmer, *The Courage to Teach*, 57.) I am also drawn to Sylvia Boorstein's wise qualification: "Confidence isn't something we have....it's something we practice."

Paragraph C:

"as they crossed into the Sea": The Slonimer is ambiguous on this point here. He seems to suggest that one first has the embodied Trust and thereafter makes the leap, but one can also read the Hebrew to suggest that one attains embodied Trust only as one begins to walk. Some initial Elemental Trust makes possible the first steps, but confidence solidifies only in the walking. The parallel Slonimer text in *Shevi'i shel Pesakh* supports this second reading.[87]

"*mesirat nefesh*": a leap into Groundlessness, which is to say into the No-Thing/*Ayin*, that is really the Ground of Being. The obverse paradox (the conundrum of divine embodiment) is captured in Deuteronomy 33:27, *u-mitakhat zero'ot olam*: and underneath are the Arms of the World/the Everlasting, as though to say (in Reb Zalman's inspired reading): "you can't fall out of the arms of God."[86]

Zeh: "This-ness" as a name for God. The One who deeply Is, who is known only in the this-ness of the moment. Linguistically, the word zeh is a deictic particle. It has denotative meaning only when one can point the finger to it, in the present tense, right here. God at the Sea is that radical presence, a *zeh*, a panting recognition that is barely a word at all…."This" was my son Noah's first word in Hebrew, coming when he was 12 months old. Isolating a digit on his left hand, he pointed and cried out: "*et zeh*." (I want This! Zeh was vanilla ice-cream.) I call the profound awareness of This-ness *ZeHn* Judaism, by way of triple pun: as a "Zen" breakthrough, a sword that cuts away all illusion and discursive narration, all superfluity; and closely related, *Zeh* זה (in Hebrew): a being with what-is, barely worded, radically present, right here; and finally, Zehn in Yiddish, זען, a deep seeing or envisioning. The deictic becomes eidetic.[88] In the Rabbinic tradition this revelation at the sea is one of pure Love.[89] The Slonimer will later add (par. F): a love that deepens into *yir'ah*, radical awe: *va-yir'u ha-am et YHVH* (Ex. 14:31). The Song of the Limbs emerges from this amazement. In recent years I have been working with this name of God, Zch or

---

87   *Netivot Shalom* al ha-Mo'adim, 282: "They (Israel) attained this rung [of *emunat ha-evarim*] in the act of jumping into the sea [*ule-madregah zo higi'u al yedei she-qaftzu p'nimah el tokh ha-yam*], an act facilitated by the luminous Trust they had in God…Thus they attained the brightest (most transparent form of) Trust for this Trust penetrated even their embodied limbs."

88   God as World: this is Spinoza, made up-close and personal.

89   Dare I try a fourth? (Fat Chan-ce) זאל זיין : *zol zen*, from the Yiddish root to be. As in "That was me sitting *zol zen*. All Shabbes long: *zol zen sha* — (Well you got that one, Velvel, faster than a Gladwellian blink…)

in the feminine *Zot* (a kabbalistic name for *Shekhinah*)[90] as a kind of continuity practice. *Et zeh, et zot*! When, I ask, is this (This!) a *shem*, a naming, a recognition of Presence? A final addendum: this pointed *zeh* also recalls the Rabbinic teaching [Bavli Ta'anit 31b and B'nei Yissaskhar to Tu B'av] which envisions Messianic consciousness as a circle dance in which the righteous are dancing with the Holy One, the dancer par excellence — *rosh choleh*. Here no person is higher than another, there is no one-upsmanship (*taharut*), no beginning or end. In this circle everyone is pointing out, "*Zeh*: this is God!" Recasting the passage, I ask: "Is everyone present in the circle also another face of God? *Zeh eli*! This is my God.....*Ve-anvehu*: I will celebrate this one! And this one...and this one..."[91]

A meditation on the quality of This-ness. Nachman of Breslov relates a dream within a dream. He wakes up from the dream within the dream, and—still within the dream—is puzzled by it. He asks a wise man who is standing near him: "What is the meaning of my dream?" The sage replies: "This is my beard and this (tugging at the beard) is the meaning of the dream." Nachman is befuddled: "I don't understand." The sage responds: "Ok, in that case go to the next room and you will find the meaning of the dream." Nachman goes there. It is an endless room with endless shelves on which sit endless books, each one filled with different commentaries on the meaning of the dream. Nachman adds: "And every page I opened, there was another interpretation on the meaning of my dream." [*Chayyei MoHaRaN* 3:3 ff. *Liqqutei MoHaRaN* 1:20]

Words cannot exhaust the meaning of this dream. Indeed, the continual interplay of words seems to generate meaning. But, perhaps the words also deflect us from Meaning (with an upper case M), endlessly defer it, or (a la H.N. Bialik) even conceal its absence. The other side of the spectrum is the beard-tug, this is the meaning of the dream. "This-ness"— signifying that which is self-evident, non-languaged, or barely so. Simple unadorned Is-ness. The question of meaning is hereby solved, which is to say, dissolved. That is the zeh of the revelation of the Sea...And the revelation of Torah at Sinai, with its Written Torah and Oral Torah? Perhaps it points to the endless library filled with infinite commentaries and ever-more layers of meaning. Following Nachman, we might say that *eillu ve-eillu*, both revelations, or interpretive models, are "true."[92]

---

90   See Arthur Green, "The Children of Israel in Egypt and the Theophany at the Sea," *Judaism* 24 (1975): 446-456, and Daniel Boyarin, "Carnal Israel".

91   See, e.g., Moshe Cordovero's *Pardes Rimmonim*, Gate 23; and the work of Betty Roitman, including "Sacred Language, Open Text" in S. Budick and G. Hartmann, eds, *Midrash* and *Literature*.

92   On human "faces of God," see Nachman's tale "The Portrait" and the introduction to Arthur Green's *Seek My Face, Speak My Name*.

Paragraph D:

"Song....into their limbs": What is the singing of the limbs, if not also dance! *Shirat ha-Yam*, the Song at the Sea, becomes the dance of the People Israel, the dance of Miriam. As Rabbi Andrea Cohn-Kiener once quipped, "if you are singing, and more than two of your limbs are moving, you might as well give in and dance." Cavorting tenors! *Salsafied altos*!

Paragraph E:

Noam Elimelekh's teaching: Many of the commentators have tried to unknot this text, e.g., reading it sequentially: first they stood in the water, and then the Sea parted, so that they were able to walk dry-shod on land. But it is possible to read this as referring to the simultaneous occurrence of the miraculous and the mundane. Only the stages of realization are sequential. Following this interpretation (advanced by the Noam Elimelekh and the Slonimer), the Crossing of the Sea is something that can happen at each moment. Here the Sea of Reeds is a cipher for the Sea of the divine, expanded consciousness. According to one midrash, the waters stood up in columns, as transparent as glass,[93] and the children of Israel walked through the hollowed out space (*charut*: freedom, the space of possibility), fully seeing.[94] Read kabbalistically, from the vantage point of this transparent consciousness, they could see that all is God. God is the water that surrounds (and implicitly, suffuses) all being. And yet, the more lasting revelation is not of the Sea-Consciousness in and of itself—call it *mohin d'gadlut*, the realm of expanded awareness—but perhaps this: that on the "dry land" i.e., the sand—*Heb.*, *hol*—which also means the ordinary, it was as though they were still "in the midst of the Sea." (Somatic memory: once when I was 20, I spent a whole *Shabbat* body surfing and swimming near Netanya. Long after I returned home that Sunday, I still felt the waves...)

As Israel attained the expanded *mohin* of the Sea, wave-consciousness, they came to realize that the divine presence, the *zeh* or This-ness, is always here, even in the smallest thing, the most ordinary ground or moment. Wave: particle—*di zelbe zakh, hayynu hakh* (the same thing). Or as Blake would have it, the world in a grain of sand. *Mammish*! (For real)

---

93   See his seminal essay, *Gillui ve-kissui be-lashon* (English: "Revealment and Concealment in Language")

94   *Mekhilta Beshallakh*, chap. 4: הקפיא להם את הים לשני חלקים ונעשה כמן כלים של זכוכית — the sea congealed on both sides and became a sort of glass crystal.

Paragraph F:

awe...from the sense of permission (*heter*) or spaciousness: This is the difference between *yir'ah chitzonit*, the fear that stems from proscription, and *yir'ah p'nimit*, the awe/trembling that arises freely, from the welling up of a great love. The Slonimer is pointing to that sense of radical amazement, where one looks upon a beloved and thinks: Please God, I just don't want to do anything that harms or brings suffering to this one.

Paragraph G:

plunder of the Sea, *bizat ha-yam* (taken from the Egyptians). What they wanted was not "God-loot," so much as *gadlut*, expanded consciousness, and its correlate — embodied and integrated Trust.

Haqqafah Dalet.
Crossing the Sea: Torah into Spiritual Practice.

One of the spiritual tasks I have embraced in recent years is turning Torah (Rooted Teaching) into Spiritual Practices that weave together mind, heart, and body. I do so by way of experiment, to dislodge the habitual and offer up elements of learning and devotion that often remain hidden to discursive mind. I do this as a provisional offering: as serious play and as a prayer for *tikkun*/healing in the self, between communities, and in the world. So for example, after studying this text with a group, both using critical tools and exploring its potential resonance in our lives, I invite the participants to practice a Leaping or Crossing. Much depends on there being some basic trust between the participants who are learning together. I would not do this if we could not build a safe space or a mishkan (tabernacle) that honored the work of the heart. It is especially powerful to do this practice on the seventh day of *Pesakh* itself, where mythic and personal calendars coincide. (An all too rare opportunity in our postmodern world, *tsu loyfn mit der tzeit*.)[95] As we move into practice, I extend the textual by way of sound and movement. To allow us to imaginatively hear the Sea (and the Sea within us), I play "Improvisations on *Ay visto lo mappamundi*" an Italian Renaissance song, as performed by the aptly named Waverly

---

95   To use Reb Shneur Zalman of Lyadi's sly locution for "keeping up with the times": *dos heyst Breshis, Noyekh, Lekh Lekho!* This surrender to sacred calendar is a challenge to many Renewal (or liberal) communities, which generally lack the social density or unwavering commitment to communal practice prevalent in the more traditional or Orthodox worlds. It was Peter Berger who pointed out the haunted sense of constructedness that sometimes visits those doing the work alone. So it's a special delight to *davven* be-havruta, and even better to do so *be-tzibbur p'nimi*, among a quorum of spiritual friends, family, seekers, and what the hey, a few *stam yidn* :-)

Consort. This is a deeply transporting melody, at once deep and calm that evokes the sea's ebb and flow, the lapping of waves, the journey to the unknown. One hears the play of a *tenor viol*, *vihuela*, and recorder amid the coruscating tide... In silence, we line up into two facing rows,[96] and enter into an extended breathing meditation on the divine Name, YHVH—Is-Was-Will Be. With a forward rocking motion, the first side breathes out Yaaaah, rocking back to receive the antiphonal breath from the other side, a soft crescendo of Haaaaah. Side one breathes out Vaaaaah, side two breathing it in deeply and responding Haaaah. And so on back and forth, call and response, inspiration and expiration, *ratzo va-shov*, all held together in our circular breathing. *Yah hah Vah hah*:[97] we aspire the Name into Wholeness, in the process becoming wavelike ourselves, rocking and being rocked, breathing and being breathed, awash in the Sea of God. Then, our kabbalistic breathing stills and our rhythmic rocking turns to a gentle, reed-like sway. Wave consciousness recedes to the back-burner[98] and I find myself holding that profound (and profoundly "ordinary") opposing truth: that we are individuals, with particular (maybe even conflicting) dreams, sufferings, bodies and biographies. We realign to face each other intently, ready to receive our first wayfarer. As we behold the person passing through the hollowed-out space, we each bear witness to the unique mystery (and the sheer facticity) of that person who is in front of us, vulnerable, gifted, crossing over.

Here's how it works. The person who is at the front of one of the lines walks over and sits in a chair that has been placed at the head of the two columns, set in the empty space between them. (The chair is thus symbolically still in *Mitzrayim*, at the edge of the Sea.) She sits down, facing the Sea (two slowly undulating columns of Waves/Witnesses). The first Crosser (*Ivri-YaH*) is invited to wrap herself in a garment or *tallit*, and when she is ready to cross—having some *kavvanah* in mind—she must leap: i.e., reposition her body to stand up, and in the manner that suits her best, walk dance crawl leap or swim through the open channel, even as the others present (both waves of the divine and distinct personalities/particles) bear witness to her Presence.[99] As she joins the end of the line, the person now at its head moves to the chair, and so forth, until everyone has crossed, seen and been seen. Holding the silence, we then form a circle and dance, in solemnity and joy—on the Other Side—as the Waverly Consort music continues to loop around, its

---

96   Again, I think of the connections to *B'rit bein ha-Betarim*.

97   I wish I could calligraph the letters here in wave-like form. I learned this breathing practice nearly twelve years ago from David and Shoshana Cooper.

98   Or if you prefer your metaphors musical: it becomes a sustained drone, the tambura of consciousness.

99   The alchemy of Hebrew words reaches a high point here. *Gal* (noun): a wave. *Gal* (verb): to open the eyes (to see). *Ed*: a witness. *Gal-ed*: a monument, or here, the invitation to become a living witness to what has trans/spired.

strains growing ever fainter. Finally, we lift our hands, break the circle, and bless each other silently, with our eyes, for the journey ahead—Sinai and the steady work of slow-cooking the heart.

It is uncomfortable for me to mandate that everyone make this "leap," especially since I know that for some folks, *ad she-tekhpotz*, the time is not yet ripe, so I suggest another possible *kavvanah* (intention) for entering into the practice. I note that this spiritual exercise is, in all likelihood, not the moment of actual existential leaping, but rather a real "practice at it." Even with this disclaimer, I know that some of us are not ready to even practice-leap: some participants must still slow-cook, and practice waiting. For those in that place, I suggest they walk through with simple *Zeh*-consciousness, being with what is, in the most ordinary fashion: walking, trusting (or at least exploring) the movement of the limbs. That too, is a high rung—maybe even higher—for as *Sefer ha-Bahir* teaches (sec. 150), the secrets of Torah can only be plumbed by one who is willing to stumble. To walk in this world is hard. Simply walking can be an act of elemental *emunah*, of deep trust. For what is walking if not a falling and a catching, a falling and a catching...

Recommended Reading

Sylvia Boorstein, *Don't Just Do Something, Sit There*, Harper Collins, 1996

Malcolm Gladwell, *Blink: the Power of Thinking without Thinking*, Back Bay Books, 2007

Arthur Green, "The Children of Israel in Egypt and the Theophany at the Sea," *Judaism* 24 (1975): 446-456

Henry Greenspan, *On Listening to Holocaust Survivors*, Praeger, 1998

Melvin Konner, *The Jewish Body*, Schocken, 2009

Avishai Margalit, *The Ethics of Memory*, Harvard, 2004

Parker Palmer, *The Courage to Teach*, Jossey-Bass, 1998 and *Let Your Life Speak*, Jossey-Bass, 2000

Ilana Pardes, *The Biography of Ancient Israel: National Narratives in the Bible*, California, 2002

Polly Young-Eisendrath, *The Resilient Spirit*, Addison Wesley, 1996

In Hebrew:

S. Arazi, M. Fechler, B. Kahana, eds. Ha-Hayyim ke-Midrash, "Life as Midrash", *Yediot Achronot*, 2004

Alan Nadler, "The Value of Torah Study in Slonimer Hasidism" in *Yeshivot U-vatei Midrashot*", ed. Immanuel Etkes; Merkaz Shazar, Jerusalem, 2006

Music:

The Waverly Consort, 1492: Music from the Age of Discovery, EMI, 1992. Digital download: "Improvisations to Ayo visto lo mappamundi"

This is the Path: Twelve Step in a Jewish Context
by Rami Shapiro

Rabbi Rami Shapiro, an award winning author of over two dozen books on religion and spirituality, co–directs One River Wisdom School, writes a regular column for *Spirituality and Health* magazine called "Roadside Assistance for the Spiritual Traveler," and hosts the weekly Internet radio show, *How to be a Holy Rascal* on Unity On-line Radio. www.rabbirami.com

When *adam* (humanity) eats from the Tree of Knowledge of Good and Evil, God says we became *ekhad mimenu* [Genesis 3:22], not "like one of us," as many English Bibles translate it, but "unique from us," that is cut off and alienated from God. The hallmark of becoming *akhad* is fear [Genesis 3:10], which is, perhaps, the hallmark of all addictions. *Akhad* is our core addiction, the cause of all our suffering. As long as we insist on the delusion of separateness, the delusion that we are apart from rather than a part of the Whole that is God, we play god with a brutality that wrecks havoc throughout the world. The Twelve Steps of Alcoholics Anonymous, when adapted to the disease of *akhad*, can help us overcome our addiction to playing God and awaken to the fact that God is playing us. Exploring just how this is so is the goal of this essay.

Step One

We admitted we were powerless over our sense of isolation–that our lives had become unmanageable.

Unlike other creation stories where God defeats the dragon of chaos and establishes an orderly world out of its carcass, creation in Genesis gives us no such security. The world is *tohu va'vohu*, wild and untamed [Genesis 1:2], and God never tames it. Creation, Genesis tells us, is a linguistic veneer over a deeper madness. God calls the world into existence, and must do so continually if the façade of order is to be maintained. As Rav Kook wrote in his commentary to Psalm 100: "God's relationship with the universe did not end after its initial creation... We would not exist if God did not constantly sustain our existence."

If not for God, nonexistence would trump existence. If not for God chaos would defeat order. But even with God nonexistence and chaos are ever present. And this is never clearer than when we place our trust in our own efforts, and seek to create an ordered life for ourselves. It is then that order devolves into chaos, and our lives become dances of the macabre.

Life is unmanageable; we are powerless. That's what makes living interesting. The disease of *akhad* promotes the ridiculous notion that life can and should be controlled by us; that we can and should get everything we want. Indeed, it is our desire for power and control, the symptoms of being *akhad*, isolated from God, that lead us to secondary addictions to alcohol, food, sex, etc. Substance abuse dulls the pain of our helplessness. It keeps us from hitting rock bottom, and realizing that *tohu va'vohu* is the warp and woof of reality. We don't hit rock bottom when we drink. We hit the real rock bottom when we stop drinking!

As long as we can numb ourselves with alcohol, food, sex, drugs, etc., we can wallow in self-pity, imagining that we could have been in control if only we were different, better, other than we are. Religion, too, can be a numbing drug, and one no less permeated with magical thinking that the others. If I do "x" God will do "y". The Torah tells us this over and over again: If we keep God's *mitzvot*, God will grant us rain in its season, good harvests, long-life, and children [Deuteronomy 11:13-15].

Thought of this way, the *mitzvot* aren't commandments from God but commands to God; magical rituals that coerce God into giving us what we want. All addicts are failed magicians. All addicts are alchemists wrongly believing they can make gold out of a life lost to alcohol, food, or even religion. And as long as we are trapped in magical thinking we never hit rock bottom.

Rock bottom comes when we stop numbing ourselves. It is then that we realize that there is no lifeline, and without the illusion of a lifeline we fall into the absolute abyss of true powerlessness. It is then that we take the First Step, not as an intellectual conceit or an act of rational will, but as an act of desperation. We take our first step only when we exhaust all other options; only when we hit rock bottom and we know we are about to die; only when Reality slams us into the wall of our own insanity so hard that we cannot shield ourselves any longer. It feels like hell, yet it is an act of pure grace.

Step Two

**Came to believe that a power greater than
ourselves could restore us to sanity.**

How do we come to believe? Not by reason, nor by revelation, but by sheer grace. All of a sudden, and out of the depths of our suffering, we suddenly know there is something greater than ourselves. What that something is, or who that something may be, we have no idea, for if we did have an idea that something would simply be our own ego masquerading as "other." It would just be more madness.

Sanity is living without the delusion of knowing, and illusion of security and surety that such knowing allows. Sanity is realizing that there is no security or surety in this world; that life is *havel havalim* [Ecclesiastes 1:2], impermanent and transitory. Sanity is surrendering to insecurity and learning how to live it with humility, grace, humor, justice, and compassion.

Twelve Step programs don't nurture the illusion of order; they tear it down. They don't substitute one delusion—"I am in control"—for another: "God is in control." They strip away all notion of control, and leave us, Job-like: broken by life, caught up in the terrifying whirlwind that is God, and bereft of balance and grounding.

"Who is this that darkens counsel by ignorant speech?" [Job 38:1]. Who is this that substitutes talk for wisdom, theology for experience, ideology for reality? It's us; it's what we do. We talk a good game, the way God spoke the world into existence. But unlike God we mistake talk for truth, the ism for the is. Unlike God we pretend chaos is dead and order reigns, but the only way we can stay convinced of this is to stay drunk. And when the drink or the drug no longer protects us, we bite our tongue and play the supplicant:

"I lay my hand upon my mouth, I have spoken once, and I will not answer; twice, but will proceed no further," [Job 40:4-5]. We pretend to surrender in hopes that God will leave us alone. But there is no "alone" with Reality, there is no hiding from God. So the whirlwind continues, and the last clinging to salvation ends, and at last Job renounces his words, his pretense of knowing, and surrenders to not–knowing, realizing that he is nothing but dust and ash [Job 40:6].

It is only when we are surrendered to Reality, it is only when we give ourselves completely to the wildness of the moment and discover we are but dust and ash that we can begin to navigate the chaos. Navigate it, not defeat it or escape it. Sanity isn't the capacity to order life, but rather the ability to live constructively in the seeming disorder that is life.

Step Three

Made a decision to turn our will and our lives over to the care of God as we understood God.

How do you understand God? However you answer, you are wrong, for your understanding of God is merely a reflection of your knowing, and your own knowing is but a figment of your imagination. There is no knowing God, there is only knowing our understanding of God, which isn't God at all.

Step Three contains a subtle trap: if you mistake your egoic understanding of God for God you are never going to "relent and surrender," and the chaos will never be navigated. And yet what else can we do? Even as the initial silence of Job gave way to more words and theologies, isms and ideologies, so we again mistake the map for the territory, and our isolation from Reality continues. Here we must take guidance from the Prophet Micah: "walk humbly with your God" [Micah 6:8]. Why "your God" rather than simply "God"? Because God is beyond words, beyond knowing, beyond our imagination, and any idea we have of God is not God. We cannot avoid words about God, theories about Reality, but we should walk with them humbly, never mistaking the menu for the meal. For me, God as I understand God is Reality, and Reality is change. God is *ehyeh asher ehyeh* [Exodus 3:14], not the static, durative, sense of I am that I am, but the fluid, future tense we encounter in these words that also mean "I will be whatever I will be." God is perpetual surprise, and thus meeting God is, as Abraham Joshua Heschel tells us, the ecstasy of "radical amazement.

Deciding to turn our lives over to God is deciding to turn our lives over to the unknowable, and to live with wonder, surprise, and not–knowing. "Just as you do not know how the breath comes to the bones in the mother's womb, so you do not know the work of God, who makes everything." [Ecclesiastes 11:5]

This is the deep faith of the Twelve Steps, not surrendering to one god or another, but surrendering to the One God beyond knowing. Surrender to not–knowing, and act out of the deep and humbling realization that "you do not know what will prosper." [Ecclesiastes 11:6]

This doesn't make living easier; it makes it more interesting. Curiosity replaces control, and we live the wildness creatively and without expectation. In this way we "banish anxiety and put away pain" [Ecclesiastes 11:9], and with it the need for our numbing drug of choice.

Step Four

Made a searching and fearless moral inventory of ourselves.

Torah tells us to examine our ways and test them [Lamentations 3:40], and when we do so we find two forces at work: *yetzer ha-rah*, the frightened, hiding, defended, and self-isolating force seeking to control the chaos; and *yetzer ha-tov*, the fearless, compassionate, and self-integrating force seeking to navigate it. The former brings pain to oneself and others. The latter, though not immune to suffering, brings compassion.

Yetzer ha-rah cuts against the grain and swims against the current. Its way is harsh, jagged, and exhausting. *Yetzer ha-tov* cuts with the grain and swims with the current. Its way is yielding, soft, creative, and fresh. We contain both ways and must constantly choose between them.

What our inventory shows is that more often than not, we choose *yetzer ha-rah* and the control it promises. At the heart of our foibles is the hunger for control. Because control is impossible, actions we take in hopes of achieving control can only cause us and those we meet more suffering.

Step Five

Admitted to God, to ourselves, and to another human being the exact nature of our wrongs.

We admit the insanity of our lives to God only when we can no longer hide from it. We admit the insanity of our lives to ourselves only when we are ready to think differently. We admit the insanity of our lives to another only when we are ready to live differently.

"When I kept silent, my bones wasted away through my groaning all day long. For day and night Your hand was heavy upon me; my strength was sapped as in the heat of summer...Then I acknowledged my sin to You and did not cover up my iniquity. I said: 'I will confess my transgressions to *HaShem*,' and You forgave the guilt of my sin," [Psalms 32:3-5].

To keep silent is to deny the mess we make of life when we live the way of isolation and coercion. To deny the mess is to live under its crushing weight until at last we must admit our own powerlessness or die. God's heavy hand is not punishment, but grace. It leads, if we let it, not to damnation but liberation.

When we admit our insanity the hiding ends; there is no more need to lie or pretend. We are not free from our failings, but we are free from the need to hide them from ourselves and others. We can no longer be blackmailed by our own guilt for "You forgave the guilt of my sin."

The guilt but not the sin is forgiven. We cannot undo what has been done. We cannot erase the pain we have caused. Just because we admit to hurtful behavior does not release us from responsibility for that behavior. We are relieved of the guilt of what we have done, but not of the obligation to set it right. We are free to turn from evil and do good [Psalm 37:27], but we cannot pretend the evil is not real.

Step Six

Were entirely ready to have God remove all these defects of character.

Being "entirely ready" means that we have no choice. Being "entirely ready" means that we can no longer hide from our disease; we can no longer excuse our insanity; we can no longer pretend to power and control. We see Reality for what it is and our lives for what we have made them, and we have no choice but to change. Step Six is choiceless: We either live differently or we die. "Behold I place before you life and death, blessing and curse. Choose life." [Deuteronomy 30:19]

Choosing life means choosing the unknown and unknowable. It means choosing the authentic wildness over the drug–induced delusion of order and control. Choosing life means shattering the idol of ego and being surrendered to the whirlwind of God. Few of us do this willingly or happily. Most of us do this desperately, or perhaps we don't do it at all. Our defects define us, and we love them even as they kill us. They are not taken from us lightly. They are torn from our grasp, and our fingers bleed in the process. As my friend and teacher Rabbi Shefa Gold says, "God is like a knife that cuts away all that is not essential for life."

This is the gift that God offers: a stripping away of all you think you are and imagine yourself to be. This is the fierce love that is God. This is what Job discovers in the whirlwind; the wind sheers every notion from his mind until there is nothing left of him but dust and ash. Are you entirely read for the torment of sobriety? Few of us really are.

Step Seven

Humbly asked God to remove our shortcomings.

To ask humbly is not to ask meekly but desperately; not to speak as a servant to the master, but to gasp for salvation as a drowning man gasps for air. Anything less is a ploy, a stratagem, a con, a lie. There is desperation and fierceness to the Twelve Steps and that is what makes it work. This is not a gentle path with a grandmotherly god. This is a brutal path with a fierce God whose infinite love is granted only when we have nothing else to hold on to. "I am a jealous God" [Deuteronomy 5:9]. If we love anything else, we are doomed. Only when all our gods are shown to be idols, and we are falling into the abyss of our own insanity, only then is God known and we discover we are no longer falling not into hell but rather into the infinite embrace of the Divine.

This is the ecstasy of Step Seven. For a moment there is a deep release, ani ("I") becomes *ain* (the Divine No-Thing) [ed. Note: also transliterated as *ayin* and *a'yin* in this volume]. I am no longer playing God, and realize that God is playing me the way a tree "plays" the branch or an ocean "plays" the waves. My defects are gone, my madness erased, I am free from the insanity of living in a world of my own imagination, and free to live in the world as it is: wild, untamed, and chaotic. I desire only to live lightly, humbly, simply, and without having to deal with the past. But the past is never past, and so the Steps continue.

Step Eight

Made a list of all persons we had harmed, and became willing to make amends to them all.

No, no, no, no, no! Aren't I done with this? Am I not forgiven and healed and freed? Aren't my sins, "once red as scarlet now white as snow?"[Isaiah 1:18]

Yes, but this does not mean we forget the past; this means that we are now at last ready to deal with it.

Our list is a portrait of our insanity, a narrative of our descent into hell—not in some imagined afterlife, but in this life. Every name recalls a story, and every story deepens our humility and we see things not from the defensive perspective of an isolated ego, but from the radically vulnerable perspective of one who is connected to all, a perspective that allows us to feel the suffering of those we used and harmed in our desperate quest for power and control. It is a list drenched in tears, and the tears wash away the ego's defenses, and we are, at last, ready for *teshuvah*, ready "to turn from evil and do good," [Psalm 34:14].

Step Nine

Made direct amends to such people wherever possible, except when to do so would injure them or others.

This is the practice of *tikkun*, making whole, re-pairing. The key word here is "direct." The persons we have harmed must be met. We must see them so that the last vestiges of hiding are burned away in the searing encounter of two broken hearts. There is no defense in this brokenness. There is no excuse or story or hiding behind the madness of addiction. There is no "because," only "what is." "Why" doesn't matter, all that matters is that you meet the ones you have harmed with the love and compassion with which you have been gifted by the fierce grace of God.

Sometimes this is an uneven asking of forgiveness, while the other, the injured party, is left with a burning passion for revenge. But at its best it is the meeting of two shattered souls who, each having lived life's wild ecstatic dance of suffering and delight, see in each other the One Who is All. In this meeting is the realization that being broken is the key to becoming whole. If there is healing in the Twelve Steps it begins here. We have realized our brokenness, and now we live from it. Not as a person seeking a false wholeness through drugs and alcohol, food or sex, but as a person who knows that being broken is part of the human condition. We meet not as Jacob, still clinging to another's heel, but as *Yisrael*, the wounded Godwrestler who limps from his encounter with divinity [Genesis 32:25] and realizes this wound is the ultimate gift, allowing us to walk at the pace of the nursing calves and babies [Genesis 33:13].

When we face our own brokenness and the lives we have shattered we discover that even in this there was God. The illusion of a whole in opposition to brokenness is the fuel that drives our vicious quest for power and control. The realization that wholeness includes brokenness is the key to true liberation.

Step Ten

Continued to take personal inventory and when we were wrong, promptly admitted it.

There is no end to this path. We are never free from *yetzer ha-rah* and the disease of *akhad*. We don't break bad habits, but allow ourselves to be broken to the point where the habits cannot take hold. The shattered life that is the life lived with wonder and abandon.

It is not that we willfully refrain from "this" and "that", we simply no longer find them compelling. But one habit drops only to have another beckon. There is always the allure of power, the fantasy of control. There is always the hope that life isn't chaos, that God isn't change, and that we can be in control. There is always the wish that salvation isn't through the shattering but an alternative to it. And so we are ever susceptible to wrong choices based on anxious lies propping up fearful ignorance.

Yet once we have seen the truth, once we have been broken on the altar of Reality, once we have been awakened to the fact that we are but dust and ash, the lies are bitter on our tongues and we cannot swallow them, but spit them out. We gag where once we gulped the bitter waters of our infidelity to Reality [Numbers 5: 11-31]. And as we catch ourselves in the midst of our madness we find it is easier to admit the truth, clean up our mess, and move on.

Step Eleven

Sought through prayer and meditation to improve our conscious contact with God as we understood God, praying only for knowledge of God's will for us and the power to carry that out.

Prayer and meditation, at their best acts of self-emptying, become, when forced into fixed form and technique, egoic acts of magic seeking to tame God and conjure that which will fulfill our desire for power and control. True prayer is a wordless sigh, a surrender of the breath back to the One who breathes it into us [Genesis 2:7]. Authentic meditation is seeing what is without the illusion that it should be other than it is.

We cannot set out to see, for this only narrows our vision. We cannot set out to surrender, for this only masks the deeper quest for control. We can only be surrendered to what is because there is no alternative to what is, and in this gift of grace we become still and know [Psalm 46:10]; we taste and see [Psalm 34:9]; and we seek peace and pursue it [Psalm 34:14]. In this alone is there conscious contact with God, *ehyeh asher ehyeh*, Reality ever unknown and unfolding. In this alone is God's will revealed to us.

What is God's will for us? The same as God's will for God: To be and become; to birth and to die; to unfold and even unravel in infinite possibility. We are part of God's unfolding, we are the way God is God in our particular situation. We are the way God knows Reality from our unique perspective. We are a way God comes to know the wild majesty of the formless and the formed, the darkness and the light, the depths and the shallows, and to say, "Wow!"

God breathes consciousness into *adam* (humanity) [Genesis 2:7] that we might name the world of God's unfolding [Genesis 2:19]. This naming comes from knowing, from sharing a common source and substance with all that is. Our naming is not an imposition but an invocation. We know and then name, rather than name and then know. Naming is an act of ecstatic wonder and intimacy. God's will for our lives is for us to learn the art of awe and wonder, to cultivate the capacity to know and name and say "Wow!" This is the gift of God's fierce grace forever pulling the rug of control out from under our feet that we might time and again be surrendered to the divine free fall that is living the wildness of God.

Step Twelve

Having had a spiritual awakening as the result of these steps, we tried to carry this message to others, and to practice these principles in all our affairs.

We are like a sleeping woman who awakes at midnight to find a deadly serpent coiled on her bed. Terrified, she stiffens in horror and prays for rescue. At dawn she discovers that the snake is only a belt she failed to put away the night before. Suddenly her fear is gone, and she laughs with joy and a sense of life's absurdity.

Unlike this woman, who gets up and goes about her day, however, we fall back to sleep only to awake the next night terrorized yet again. We are never free of our terrors. We are never without the disease of *akhad* and the machinations of *yetzer ha-rah*. We are never surrendered once and for all, only now and again.

The only question is whether we engage the world from fear or from love; from the mind of *akhad* (separation) or from the heart of *ekhad* (integration); from a desperate need to play God or the simple realization that God is playing us.

Recommended Reading

Kerry M. Olitsky and Stuart A. Copans, *Twelve Jewish Steps to Recovery: A Personal Guide to Turning from Alcoholism and Other Addictions*, Jewish Lights Publishing, 1991

Abraham J. Twerski, *Addictive Thinking, Second Edition: Understanding Self-Deception*, Hazelden, 1997

Additional Website(s):

Jewish Alcoholics and Chemically Dependent Persons and Significant Others offer retreats, resources and support. http://www.jacsweb.org

The Outstretched Arm is the newsletter of The National Center for Jewish Healing, "Addiction, Recovery and Jewish Healing" is the theme of Summer 2008 issue. http://www.jewishhealing.org/outstretched.html

Fear, Loss, and the Power of Yielding
by Burt Jacobson

Rabbi Burt Jacobson completed his training as a spiritual director at the Mercy Center in Burlingame, CA in 1995. He serves as a *mashpia* for the Aleph Ordination Programs and as a founding faculty member of The Aleph Ordination Program in Jewish Spiritual Direction. He has been a student of the teachings of the Baal Shem Tov for thirty-five years, and is currently engaged in writing a book that will offer a vision of the Baal Shem Tov's spiritual philosophy through the lens of Neo-Hasidic teachings.

A Divorce, a Death and a Fire

In the late 1980s my seven-year marriage began to come apart, but I was oblivious to the signs. When my wife informed me that she was going to file for divorce, I was stunned by her decision, and this opened out into fear and dread as my world began to come apart. And then, only a few months later, my mother died. I'd had a difficult relation with her as a child, but in my adult life Mom and I had become close friends, sharing a mutual interest in spirituality, the visual arts, culture and politics. I was shaken by her loss, all the more so because it came on the heels of my marital breakup. I felt as if my life had fallen into a black hole, and I wasn't sure whether or not I would survive. Somehow I needed to accept what was happening, but I didn't know if this would be possible.

Years before, my spiritual director, Rev. Ted Pecot, had told me that I was too unyielding, and that I needed to learn to abandon myself to God. "I'm willing to abandon myself to God's goodness," I had told him, "but not to God's evil. How can I surrender to the God who allowed the Holocaust to happen?" "No," he replied, "When you give yourself to God, you abandon all of yourself to all of God." I didn't really grasp what he was saying and his proposition seemed impossible to me. If I gave my self to God, what then would be left?

A few years later, Judith Binetter, a good friend of mine from Israel and a woman possessed of great insight into the human soul, told me that she experienced me as being overly controlling. "Let go!" she would shout at me in her German accent. "Why do you hold on to this image of yourself? Each moment is different. Each moment is unique. Let go of the past and be in the present." But again I didn't really understand what she meant.

The day my wife informed me about the divorce I called Ted, who offered me his deepest consolation. Then I called Judith in Tel Aviv. She shouted at me over the phone, "Let it go! Let it go, Burt. Don't hold on!" I put the phone down. "How could she be so callous?" I thought, angered by her response. Much later I came to see that Ted had responded as one kind of spiritual director and Judith had reacted as another kind of director—or perhaps a Zen master—trying to shock me into accepting the present situation in its fullness, rather than wallowing in self pity. It took a great deal of time, but slowly the truth of what Judith and Ted had observed and shared with me over the years began to sink in.

I came to recognize that if I was to survive these two losses, I would have to learn to surrender, to abandon my wounded ego to God. I was not thinking of the Baal Shem Tov at the time. I did not know that he had spoken about these sorts of issues. I turned instead to the biblical book of Job.

Job was a righteous man, and his goodness was rewarded by God with all the blessings of family, wealth and privilege. But Satan tempted God, wagering that given the chance, he would be able to make Job break faith with God. And so Job loses everything he had, and in his anger he challenges God's lack of justice. Finally, God appears out of a whirlwind and reveals to Job his majesty, mystery and power. And then God interrogates Job: "Just who do you think you are to challenge Me, the Creator of both order and chaos?" Job realizes that there is a larger cosmic will that dwarfs his own notions of morality and righteousness. In utter humility he surrenders to God.

Reflecting on the tale of Job put my struggles into a larger perspective. I realized that Ted and Judith had both been right: I had attempted to stake my life on a rigid idea of how my life needed to be. But I could no longer do this. Like Job, I had to learn to surrender, to yield to God. I had not engaged in regular spiritual practice for twenty years, ever since I had left the bounds of traditional Judaism, but now I undertook a form of daily meditation in which I simply gave my self over to God.

In the summer of 1991 I went to San Antonio for the unveiling of my mother's gravestone. When I returned to Berkeley, the final divorce papers were waiting for me. Two weeks later a firestorm swept through the Oakland and Berkeley hills. Hundreds of homes were destroyed, including the house I lived in, and virtually all of my belongings went up in smoke. (One of the few things I took with me as I escaped from the house that day was my research on the Baal Shem Tov!) But this immense destruction did not affect me emotionally. The loss of the two women closest to me loomed so much larger than the loss of mere possessions. More important, I had already begun to surrender my life and destiny to the Divine. I came to see the fire as a kind of testing: How far had I come in learning to yield? The months after the fire were difficult, but I was not shattered. After all, I was alive and no one that I knew had been killed. I had lost only possessions.

Of course, the ego doesn't give up easily. Over and over again I have had to re-learn the necessity of surrender. Every day I experience resistance as I engage in my meditative practice. Yet, I persist.

The Orphan

Israel Baal Shem Tov was the founder of the revivalist movement called Hasidism in Poland during the 18th century. I have been a student of his teachings for over thirty-five years. When I first encountered his insights regarding fear, loss and yielding, they spoke to my heart with a deep sense of truthfulness, and have since provided me with a spiritual framework for experiences of this kind. They have also helped me immensely in my work with my spiritual directees. In his teachings the Baal Shem discusses why human fear exists, and how one can use fear as a catalyst to bond with the Divine.

Legend tells us that the Baal Shem's parents were extremely old at the time of his birth. His father, Eliezer, spent a good deal of time with the boy, but he died when Israel was about three years of age. It is not clear what role his mother, Sarah, played in his life. The tale recounting the *Besht's* (acronym for Baal Shem Tov) childhood states that it was the villagers of Okupy who attempted to care for the boy following his father's death. His mother goes unmentioned.

Before he died, Eliezer tried to prepare his child for his life alone, saying to him, "I see that you will light a *yahrzeit* (memorial) candle for me every year on the anniversary of my death, and that I will not have the pleasure of rearing you..." And then, perhaps because he saw fright in the boy's eyes, he added, "My beloved child, remember this all of your life: God is with you. Do not fear anything." After his father's death, Israel acted out his fear, pain and anger at school. He wouldn't behave, and he would run into the woods to be alone. Israel's experience of loss was repeated during his adolescence: He was married at about age sixteen, but his wife died only a year later.

Through his study of ancient and medieval Jewish religious thought, Israel came to understand the place of fear in the spiritual life. His own ruminations about fear have to do with the relation of personal loss to the terror of annihilation and the fear of God. The key to transforming this fear into love comes through the act of yielding the ego to the greater reality of cosmic consciousness.

Our External Fears

I live in California's East Bay, an area that is periodically subject to earthquakes. This morning's newspaper carried the following caption on the front page: "BIG ONE: IT'S ZERO HOUR". Below these words is the following headline: "Scientists call next massive quake imminent; when it strikes, hundreds of thousands of people could be left homeless."

Fear fills our lives. We fear losing our jobs or losing our partners or losing our homes. We fear the ravages of cancer and AIDS. We fear environmental degradation. We fear weapons of mass destruction. We fear for the kind of world we are handing down to our children. We fear death.

Our ancestors feared plagues, pogroms, poverty, loss of respect and death. The Baal Shem believed that all of these fears have to do with loss, which we perceive as a diminishment of the self. He taught:

> Your anxieties have to do with fear of loss,
>   the loss of anything you value:
>   honor or wealth, or life itself.
>
> But once you have actually suffered the loss,
>   your uncertainties will disappear.
>
> Lose all of your money,
>   and you no longer fear the loss of wealth.
>
> And, of course, when you die,
>   you will no longer fear death.
>
> —Tzofenat Pa'ane'akh 49c

Many times people believe that such outer fears are punishments for wrongdoing, but to the Baal Shem, this was not the case.

> All of these are merely external fears.
>
> They are the same as the fears
>   suffered by all living creatures:
>
> The mouse fears the cat; the cat fears the dog;
>   the dog fears the wolf...
>
> —Tzof'nat Pa'ane'akh 49c

God's Presence in Our Fears

But there is something at the core of our fears that goes beyond the fears themselves. The Baal Shem Tov taught:

"There is no place devoid of the Divine."

—Tikkunei Zohar

"God's reign embraces everything."

Yes, the Divine is present,
   even where potent evil exists,
   even where the demonic seems to rule,
   as it is written, "You enliven all things."

But what appears to be evil is merely a shell.
Crack the shell open, and you find the kernel within.
If you grasp this truth, you will no longer fear evil,
for you will know that the Light of goodness
dwells at its core.

It is this Light that you are to hold in awe and fear.

—Yativ Panim, I: 119

In the Baal Shem's spiritual philosophy, Divinity is everywhere, even in the worries, anxieties and terrors we experience as we face the difficulties of this world. But why would God create fear? What is its purpose?

The Divine intent is that these external fears
   serve as stepping stones to the higher fear,
   bringing you to the realization that there is no
   fear other than the fear of God.

—Me'or Einayim, Yitro

But just what is the fear of God, and why is it superior to our ordinary human fears? Unlike our external fears, which are brought on by extrinsic concerns, the fear of God is inward in nature. It comes about through radical amazement and awe at the vastness, incomprehensibility and majesty of the Creator, the ineffable Mystery that underlies and fills all existence. We know that at every moment the Creator is infusing being and life into creation, into us. But God's gift of life comes with a proviso: there can be no life without death. When I realize fully that my life must end, I experience the fear of my own annihilation. The Baal Shem once exclaimed:

O my body!
I am amazed that you do not shatter
out of fear of your Creator!

—Rishpei Eish, 111

And he taught:

Look deeply into the nature of existence,
 and you will stand in awe of the Divine,
 the Master and Ruler, Ground and Root
 of all worlds.

You will realize that if the Holy One were to withdraw
 the Lifeforce that energizes all worlds
 for even an instant—God forbid!—
 all these worlds would cease to exist.

Such astonishment will sear your awareness,
 and you will be filled with fear and trembling
 until all of your limbs become faint
 because of God's cosmic power!

—M'or Einayim, Yitro

This teaching reminds me of Job's terror-filled epiphany, and his final yielding to the Divine. It also calls to mind Robert Oppenheimer's reaction to the explosion of the first atomic bomb at Alamogordo on July 16, 1945. He uttered the words of the Hindu god Brahman from the *Bhagavad Gita*, "I am death, the shatterer of worlds."

The great terror—the fear of God—then is, at essence, the realization that that our lives can be snuffed out at any moment, that we have no real control over our destiny. I could walk out of my office, begin to cross the street, and be run down by a passing automobile. Tomorrow I could be given a diagnosis by an oncologist that I have only three months to live. And even if my life runs its course, and I live to age eighty or ninety, I know that I will one day die. Such thoughts astound me. I recognize my total dependency on both the Lifeforce that is upholding and sustaining me, and on the Divine origin of this Lifeforce.

The Baal Shem believed that such fear is one of the cornerstones of true spirituality. "The beginning of wisdom is fear of YHWH," we read in the book of *Proverbs* (1:7).

> Everything has as its goal the fear of God.
> Without such fear, our sages teach,
> all of our wisdom is without value or worth.
> The true purpose of wisdom is to lead us to such fear.
>
> —Keter Shem Tov 391

It is foolish to forget the existential character of our lives. Fear reminds us of our finitude in relation to the Infinite, our transience in relation to Eternity. It thereby enables us to cultivate true humility. We know that we have only a certain amount of time on this plane, and that each of us must use this time to accomplish the particular mission with which we have been entrusted.

For the mystic, the experience of the fear of God bears a special significance. The shock of this recognition—said the Besht—empties us of our selfhood and our desires. Neither the thought of death, nor the fear of Hell stirs the heart; there is only the yearning to yield one's self fully to the Source of life. At this point the "I" becomes "nothing" (*AhNY* becomes *AYiN*). In such a state all the harshness of the external world is eradicated, because there is no self to experience it (Tzof'nat Pa'ane'akh, B'Shalakh 5). Because we are nothing—no thing—there can be nothing at all to fear.

> Like our external fears,
>   the inner fear of God involves a loss:
>
> For when you bind your self to the Life within all life,
>   you know that you are one with the One,
>   and you lose your independent existence.
>
> —Tzofenat Pa'ane'ackh 49c

From Fear to Love

According to the Baal Shem, such fear may be the beginning of wisdom, but it is not wisdom's end. Such fear leads the heart to love, for when the ego surrenders and becomes nothing, it can then become purified and, when it reappears once again, it will have been transformed. Entering into our selfhood, we are struck by the wonder of it all. For we have not been annihilated after all! We exist, we are here! I experienced this when I was driving over the Bay Bridge to San Francisco to escape the flames of the firestorm. Full of concern and worry over the destruction taking place, I suddenly felt a giddy sense of relief, a lightness of being. Yes, virtually everything I owned was most probably gone. But I was here, alive.

We are constantly being supported by the Lifeforce that upholds us, providing us with the gifts of life and consciousness and the mitzvot—the Divine directives—that guide our lives. And because we recognize the precious character of the tiny bit of life we have been graced with, we can finally love the Source of our life and consciousness with all of our hearts, all of our souls, and all of our passion. For the Baal Shem Tov then, the love of the Divine comes about out of gratitude for what we have, and the simultaneous recognition that what we seem to possess is not ours forever. The master taught:

> When you experience Divine love and kindness
>   showering upon you,
>   through God's enormous mercy,
>   you will then realize that the purpose
>   of all your external fears
>   was only to waken you to the inner fear of God.

> It is just then that your fear of God becomes transformed
>   into the love of God, and you are able to
>   accept all of your outer fears in love.
>   At this point, you will recognize that
>   there is nothing at all in the world
>   that can make you afraid!

> —Tzof'nat Pa'ane'akh, B'Shalakh, p. 5

When we experience God's great love, we can only respond by loving God in return. Then we come to understand that the purpose of the external fears we suffered was only to arouse us to go inward and to cultivate inner fear, which now opens out into love. With this recognition, we can accept all of our external fears, all adversity in love. The Baal *Shem* puts it this way:

> The essence of your spiritual striving is
>   the cultivation of the fear of God.

> Then the love of God will be given to you
>   as a great gift from Heaven.

> —Devarim Hekhmadim Avot, Chapter 1

A man once asked the Baal Shem Tov:

"How is one to live in this world with all the suffering
   we are forced to bear?"

The master answered:
   "Accept everything that happens to you in this
   world in the spirit of love,
   and then both this world and the next
   will be yours."

—B'er Hakhasidut 142

Thus we see that human fear and love are merely two different but interrelated responses to the exact same phenomenon: the contingent nature of existence. Fear comes about when we reflect on the possibility that our lives may end at any time. Love comes out of the recognition of the miraculous existence of existence itself, and gratitude for the divine gift of life and consciousness. But in reality there is no dichotomy between fear and love. Fear turns out to be merely another face of love.

Fear and Spiritual Practice

The Baal Shem Tov offers a cognitive spiritual practice that we can engage in when we experience any kind of external fear. This practice is a kind of self-interrogation that allows us to make use of our reason in the service of recalling the awesome character of existence, and our innate divine nature. This, in turn, can help us place the fearful emotions that appear to be overwhelming us into a larger perspective, and we are no longer held captive by the external fear that had been plaguing us.

The moment you experience either love or fear,
   ask yourself:

"Where is this feeling coming from?...

Why it must be coming from God,
   for doesn't every feeling derive from Divinity?

Even ferocious animals experience love and fear.

Aren't these emotions part and parcel
    of what it means to be alive?

Everything was broken when
    the cosmic vessels holding the Divine Light
    were shattered at the beginning of creation.

But the Light did not disappear—it can be found
    in each and every fragment of physical existence.

Why, then, should I be afraid of this single spark of Divinity
    that comes to me in the guise of fear?

Wouldn't it be better for me to bind this fear
    to the great fear of God alone?

When a feeling of love rises within you,
    or any feeling whatsoever,
    find the Divine spark lying within it,
    and lift it up to its Source.

This is why we have been gifted with divine souls:
    to uncover the divine sparks hiding in every aspect
    of our physical existence, and return them
    to their Source

      —Tziv'aat HaRivash 127

Fear and *Hashpa'ah*

How might a *mashpia* make use of the Baal Shem's notions of fear, loss and the power of yielding when working with a *mushpa*?

Jan has been in spiritual direction with me for about two years. She has spoken about her fears in many of our sessions. Jan lives by herself and experiences a great deal of loneliness. She is cut off from her family of origin. She is middle aged and has begun to think about her death, and she is fearful that no one will remember her. Although she has a PhD. in psychology, Jan has been inhibited in pursuing her life goals because she has allowed her fears to rule her. Six weeks ago, I decided to share the Baal Shem's perspective on fear with her.

"Jan, is your fear altogether bad — or could it contain a spiritual message for you?" "What do you mean?" she asked. I rephrased my question: "The Kabbalah teaches that 'There is no place devoid of the Divine.' From that point of view, where might God be present in your fear?" She said that she would have to think about this. I then explained the Baal Shem's view about fear to her. Then I asked her to close her eyes and take a few deep breaths. "Now let yourself enter the fear that you have been talking about... Can you describe it?... What does it feel like?... Can you let yourself fully yield to the fear?... What does this feel like?... The Baal Shem Tov teaches that every fear can lead us to God. Can you allow your fear to open out into God?... What does this feel like to you?..."

I gave Jan a few minutes for each of these questions, and she slowly spoke about her experiences.

When she opened her eyes, I asked her how the exercise had been for her. "Something has shifted for me," she answered. "The fears are still there, but I don't feel like I'm a victim now." I suggested that every time she experiences some anxiety or fear, she should ask herself the question, "Where is this fear ultimately coming from?... How can I bind this feeling of fear to God?..." I also suggested that when she wakes up in the morning and before she goes to sleep at night she might say the final verse of the *Adon Olam*: "In Your hand I entrust my spirit, before I sleep and when I wake. And with my spirit, my body, too. You are with me—I will not fear.

When I met with Jan this past week she told me that she has been practicing the Baal Shem's approach to elevating fear, and that this practice has been working for her. "I say to myself, 'God is with me. I know I'll be okay.' I'm finding that I experience greater calm and relief and equanimity. I know that God is always with me, and that I can bear whatever happens to me."

Recommended Reading

Niles Elliot Goldstein, *God at the Edge: Searching for the Divine in Uncomfortable Places*, Bell Tower, 2001

> *Forests of the Night: The Fear of God in Early Hasidic Thought*, Jason Aronson, Inc., 1996

Miriam Greenspan, *Healing Through the Dark Emotions: The Wisdom of Grief, Fear, and Despair*, Shambhala, 2003

Entitlement, Blessings, and Miracles
by Mitchell Chefitz

Mitch Chefitz is the author of *The Curse of Blessings*, a story collection, translated into German, Korean, and Mandarin. His novel, *The Seventh Telling*, is a Los Angeles Times bestseller. He is Scholar-in-Residence at Temple Israel of Greater Miami where he teaches on subjects related to Jewish spirituality. www.mitchellchefitz.com

In my experience there is no greater impediment to the happiness or growth of a *mushpa*, a spiritual directee, than a sense of entitlement, and no greater opening to the flow of *shefa*, Cosmic love and abundance, then the acknowledgment of blessing.

First, an exploration of the nature of entitlement, and then a look at how this might be addressed through spiritual assignments. Entitlement is the sense that one is worthy of, or deserves:

1. Things.
2. Relationships.
3. Processes.
4. Attributes.

Entitlement to Things

You might believe you have an entitlement to your home, your car, your college tuition, or financial aid for your child's college tuition. You might believe you have an entitlement to two homes, two cars, graduate school tuition, financial aid for your grandchild's tuition. You might believe you have an entitlement to everything you possess, or everything you need that you don't yet possess, or everything you want that you don't yet possess. You might believe you have an entitlement to the Interstate free of accidents, free of traffic. Before this becomes absurd, jot down, not in permanent ink, those things to which you might just possibly be entitled. Be generous. You can erase them later, if need be.

Entitlement to Relationships

You might believe you are entitled to a loving relationship with parents, with a spouse, with children, with grandchildren. A caring relationship with friends, with partners, with students, with clients. A kind relationship with waiters, attendants, clerks, service people.

After all, aren't you loving, caring, and kind? Aren't you entitled to love, care, and kindness in return?

Again, in the same medium, pencil, pixels, or erasable ink, jot down those relationships to which you think you might be entitled.

Entitlement to Processes

Externally, you might believe you are entitled to the cycle of seasons, to gravity, to the laws of nature. Internally, you might believe you are entitled to health of body and a sense of wellbeing, that you deserve happiness, fulfillment, and a livelihood.

That sounds so good.

Go ahead and jot away. Really, do it.

Thinking about it isn't the same as making even an impermanent list. It may require you to put this book down for a moment, to go to the computer, or pick up a pad.

Entitlement to Attributes

What might you list under attributes?

You might believe you are entitled to your appearance, your ability to empathize, your creativity, your sense of self.

Please, write. Come back when you're done.

Had you written in ink, the exposure might have been too great to bear.
Better that you wrote in pencil.

Reviewing Things

To what things are you entitled?

Consider what you own. Perhaps your resources are such that you have acquired a home, two cars, and a plethora of miscellaneous objects. You may have worked hard to attain them. Aren't you entitled to them? Aren't they the fruits of your hard labor?
Now consider what owns you: Your home, two cars, and a plethora of miscellaneous objects. They command your time, your energy, your resources. Aren't they entitled to your care and maintenance?

If the goal towards which you work is no more than the material, and, once you have acquired that material should you experience it as an entitlement, you will find no joy in it, for it is merely what you deserve. So, any joy in acquisition will be fleeting. You will learn in short order that what you own, owns you. You will become resentful of the obligation. Moreover, should you lose what you have gained through a downturn of fortune, resentment will fill the emptiness.

Resentment is burning anger reduced to coals that smolder forever. Sometimes, quite literally, resentment can eat your guts out, consuming you, leaving as residue the ashes of entitlement.

So, review your list of things to which you are entitled. The longer your list, the greater your exposure.

Reviewing Relationships

To what relationships are you entitled?

Perhaps you have listed parents or a partner. Children. Relatives. Friends.

There are models of how such relationships should be: honor due to parents, love received from children, faithfulness from a partner, trust and honesty from friends. You, of course, are at one end of those relationships, with your responsibilities, and they are at the other end, with theirs.

If you feel entitled to such a relationship, and the returned honor, love, faithfulness, trust, not be according to your sense of what you deserve, the result will be – resentment.

Should you lose such a relationship, either through the alienation or death of the other, resentment will fill the emptiness.

Resentment is burning anger reduced to coals that smolder forever. Sometimes, quite literally, resentment can eat your guts out, consuming you, leaving as residue the ashes of entitlement.

Lest you pale at the repetition and balk at reading further, recall the title of this article: "Entitlement and Blessings." We'll get to the blessings. We have only two sections of entitlement left to endure.

Reviewing Processes

To what processes are you entitled?

The sun rises, the sun sets. You rely on the steady passage of time. A minute is a minute. An hour is an hour. A year is a year.

But have you noticed that every year goes by faster than the last? That "The Golden Years" of retirement are often not so golden?

If you have notions concerning the passage of time, and consider yourself entitled, when experience gnaws away at that entitlement, the result is – resentment.

Hot is hot. Cold is cold. Is that a process to which you are entitled? From time to time you've likely made the error of touching what you thought to be cold and found it to be hot, so hot that a finger is burned and a mouth curses, expressing anger at the fool (likely you) who put the obstacle in your way.

But these external expressions of entitlement are trivial compared to the internal.

Internally, health is all that matters. "So long as you have your health..." That's the wisdom we hear from elders. What's on your list as an entitlement?

> The ability to see? To hear? To walk? To talk?
> To use your hands? To lift your arms?
> To remember? To think?
> To sleep? To wake up? To go to the bathroom?
> To function sexually?

Reviewing Attributes

To what attributes are you entitled?

This is more difficult conceptually. What have you written?

Appearance? There are large industries devoted to those who take appearance as an entitlement. Plastic surgery, cosmetics, diet systems. If you've written "appearance," it's likely to cost you an arm and a leg to fill in wrinkles and remove excess fat. If the cost doesn't produce the desired result, just imagine the resentment!

Ability to empathize? There are some people who have a knack for it. To them, empathy comes naturally. It's another form of being attractive, appealing to others. But for even such people, that ability occasionally goes behind a cloud. There can be periods of depression. If the ability to empathize is accepted as an entitlement, in its absence depressions are likely to be deeper.

Creativity? Do you have talents you listed as entitlements? Sometimes a person mentions a talent in response to the question "What do you do for a living?" If that talent is impaired, the resulting resentment might make life seem not worth living.

Your sense of self? Surely, you might think you are entitled to your self. If so, I'm sorry, not for you, but for me, because if I write well enough and bring you through this spiritual journey, you may be deprived of that entitlement, too, and be resentful – of me!

"Blessings" – a Temporary Description

Blessing springs from the sense that one is unworthy or undeserving of:

1. Things.
2. Relationships.
3. Processes.
4. Attributes.

I'm about to ask you to list your blessings under these four headings, each listing something you do not intrinsically deserve, but have nonetheless. They come as gifts, as an act of grace from an agency outside your self. Please be generous. Don't be superstitious.

Do you really believe if you count your blessings they will disappear? This listing isn't for the purpose of counting. This is a listing for the purpose of appreciating.

Please come back with your list when you're done.

If any of these is on your list of entitlements, you are guaranteed a life of misery. Why? Because, as you age, your ability in almost all of the above will diminish and in some cases disappear.

As you lose each ability, since it is no more than something you deserve, something to which you are entitled, each loss will be greeted with – resentment.

I can't bear to repeat the definition again.

Perhaps just one word – bitterness. That's often used to describe elders who lose faculties one by one. They become – bitter.

I hope your lists are long. As you read further, you might come back and add to them.

Before continuing, we need the definition of another term.

Miracles

First, what miracles are not:

Miracles are not the splitting of seas, the sun standing still, the dead coming back to life, or the apparent extraordinary lapses within the laws of nature or the extraordinary happenings within the progression of our lives.

Rather miracles are the laws of nature and the ordinary happenings within the natural progression of our lives. If miracles were only the extraordinary events, whether actual or mythical, we would experience only a few, if any, in a lifetime.

We have collective memory of past extraordinary events. Such memories frame our thinking and view of the world. Whether or not the events happened is not significant. The collective memory as it has evolved through the years is real and significant. But that's memory, not miracle.

We experience miracles daily, but have a tendency to take them for granted, because... we experience them daily.

That my fingers open and close is miraculous! Such a wonder! If I consider how many physical, biological, chemical, mathematical ratios and laws must be in continual balance just for me to open and close my fingers, then I know it is miraculous. That I see. That I have children. That I have clothes to wear. That I stand up straight. That I ...

All of these are miracles.

If you would, please, go back to your lists of "Blessings" and replace the heading "Blessings" with "Miracles."

What you've written is really a list of miracles, not blessings, but if I had asked you at the outset to write a list of miracles, you might have been confused, and your list would have been shorter.

So, if your "blessings" are now miracles, what are blessings?

A blessing is the acknowledgment of the miraculous, an expression of thanks for something one receives through the agency of another, as a gift or as an act of grace.

For me a blessing is a "thank you" for something to which I am not entitled.

I suggest now an exercise that goes beyond writing.

Consider each item or relationship or process or attribute you have listed, one at a time, and find the miraculous within it. When you do, speak words of blessing.

What are words of blessing? The form is, "Thank You that I have the benefit of..."

You'll likely find better words, but that's the form.

For a thing, for the motorcycle sitting in my garage, for the masterpiece of technology I am privileged to ride, I say, "Thank You."

For a relationship, with my wife or with my children, each relationship curving the direction of my life in unexpected and wondrous paths, I say, "Thank You."

For a process, my recovery from illness and recapture of physical abilities nearly lost, I say, "Thank You."

For my creativity, the stories that appear so miraculously on the monitor before my eyes, I say, "Thank You."

The "You" is the source of the miracle you bless.

If we are successful in this work, our lists of miracles will grow longer and our expressions of blessings more eloquent.

Alas, a Lament

Most everything you have written on your page of blessings, now re-titled your page of miracles, will likely diminish or be lost as you age. Such change is inevitable.

However, whereas the loss of an entitlement leads to resentment, the loss of that which evokes a blessing leads to... sadness.

From resentment there is no recovery, only burning and bitterness that keeps one from continued growth in the world.

From sadness there is recovery. The process is called mourning. After a loss, trivial or profound, one learns how to stand in balance, albeit in a different world, and continue growing, finding new experiences of the miraculous, evoking still new blessings.

And, Lastly, a Wish

My wish is within your power to achieve.

I wish that all your entitlements be transformed into blessings so you might live a life sailing from miracle to miracle, leaving behind you a wake of blessings.

If you, as spiritual director, are able to accomplish that, then your wake of blessings becomes a path for your directees to follow.

Supervision: An Essential Support for the *Mashpia*
by Sandra Sarah Cohen

Dr. Sandra Sarah Cohen has received *smicha* (ordination), from Rabbi Zalman Schachter-Shalomi as a *mashpi'ah ruchanit* and *maggid*, and a certified teacher and mentor of his Age-ing to Sage-ing work. She is a graduate of The Shalem Institute for Spiritual Formation, an interfaith institute. A psychotherapist in private practice, Sarah also provides both individual and group spiritual direction supervision. She serves as a spiritual director and adjunct faculty member at the Reconstructionist Rabbinical College as well as serving as a faculty member and *mashpi'ah* for The Aleph Ordination Program in Jewish Spiritual Direction.

This chapter attests to the value of and insists upon the requirement of peer group or individual supervision for all who work as Jewish spiritual directors. It is a professional standard in the Aleph Ordination Program and this article details both why and how supervision works and matters.

Let's begin with an example of why supervision is essential to the healthy delivery of Jewish spiritual direction. I am a member of a peer supervision group that meets monthly. At the time of this experience, we had been meeting for several years. It was my turn to present. Our model of peer supervision is that a director shares herself in response to a particular session with a directee that has evoked a response significant enough to bring to supervision. What we share about the directee, while being absolutely mindful of the directee's total anonymity, is what it was in that particular session that was evoked in the spiritual director personally.

What Does Supervision Offer?

Once when it was my turn to present in supervision, my husband had just received a heart transplant and my beloved sister, to whom I was as close as the dearest of friends, had just died in her sleep. I chose to present about a person who decided that she did not want to continue to work with me. She felt I had somehow let her down. My impression of our work was that it was going well, that many very sensitive issues were brought to God together and we would surely continue our sessions the following year.

Upon sharing this story with my peer group, one of the members said, "Sarah, it sounds like you feel betrayed." Well, the word "betrayed" triggered such a deep response in me that I literally shouted, "Betrayed, yes! Betrayed, by God! 'Who do You think YOU are?! Taking with one hand, giving with the other, come and FACE me!" All the while I was crying and calling out my pain. My precious spiritual direction peer supervision group held me in silent prayer, as I railed and raged against God who I felt had betrayed me, not the directee.

This gift of being held in a sacred, safe, loving, judgment- free silence by my peer supervisors led to insight into how I might hold this directee with open-heartedness and blessings for her future work in spiritual direction. And, perhaps more importantly, where I was with God at that time in my life. In the way that wondrous things happen, the very next day I had a scheduled appointment with my own spiritual director to whom I brought my profound experience in the group supervision session. She and I then reflected on such questions as: Why didn't I know how angry I was at God? What kept me from knowing? How old was I in the God concept I was holding? Wasn't my God able to hold me and love me through my anger and pain and loss? It was then that my own inner healing and reconnecting with God were able to begin.

A *mashpi'ah* is called to use her self in a conscious way to be a helpful guide and teacher in the process of offering *hashpa'ah*. Supervision is required so that she serves the other with support in her service to God. Social work and other counseling modalities set as a core value that any counselor engages in the "conscious use of self" to screen out unconscious personal agendas and create directee safety.

Consider Issues of Difference

Spiritual Guidance, particularly in the *hashpa'ah* model, is a profession that is founded on the ability to cultivate positive relationships with people who may be very different from us. There may be differences in age, personality, gender, socioeconomic status, health, sexual orientation, rank, power, and privilege, as well as beliefs regarding theology and politics. The experience of these differences can cause a *mashpia* to feel emotionally, cognitively, and/or spiritually disturbed. The ability to become aware of, and consciously attend to these internal disturbances, will affect the quality of relationship we are able to establish in providing this sacred service to those we serve. Supervision is the place to bring such disturbances for deep reflection and prayerful consideration.

In spiritual direction, the guide is asked to prepare by emptying herself of the small ego, so that God's guidance can be available to the *mashpia* and *mushpa* for the benefit of the *mushpa*. Self-awareness is among the first prerequisites for accomplishing this goal. In order to get oneself out of the way, one must be willing to listen with an open heart, to be open to the other's view of the world and his or her theology, prayer life and differences in general from one's own views.

Self-awareness in relational theory suggests that self-awareness is a process that occurs alongside the flow of the client's *hashpa'ah* process with you. Within this theory self-awareness refers to the ability to recognize our own thoughts, beliefs, emotions, personality traits, personal values, habits, biases, strengths, weaknesses, and the psychological needs, and theology that drive our behaviors. It includes the ability to recognize how we react to cues from the other and how our emotions and personal history may affect our way of relating to others.

Mindful self-reflection in our professional growth as spiritual guides requires a plan for every spiritual director to engage in daily examination and refinement of self-awareness. For example, journaling about the impact upon you of a particular session with a person you are guiding, bringing questions awakened in you by the directee to your own spiritual director and/or into supervision, bringing your questions into your private prayer time, and being willing to accept that at times the person being guided is being sent as a messenger/angel for what you need to recognize at this time in your life.

What is important here is that this self-reflection and discernment take place outside of the session with your *mushpa*. The ability to put those self-awarenesses on hold unless they help you change your interaction on the person being guided's behalf in that very session is essential. The cardinal rule is that we stay clear about the nature of our agreement as contracted with the *mushpa*. We are in this process together for the sole purpose of the *mushpa*'s growth toward God in all aspects of their lives. We sometimes gain a secondary benefit toward our own growth toward God.

Additional Examples of Supervision

Whether serving as a spiritual guide or while mentoring others in becoming *mashpi'im* (pl), peer group or individual spiritual direction and supervision is vital, or we will inevitably miss blind spots about what is evoked in us when with a directee.

A clergyman comes to me for supervision. Let's call him Harold. Harold brings a verbatim about a woman for whom he serves as spiritual director who has wanted to separate from her husband of many years. What arose in Harold's awareness as she shared was the question: How could he be there for a woman who wanted to leave her husband when he, Harold, was in such despair in his life about a similar circumstance?

Harold is a man who is in his early fifties, a clergy person who is going through a very painful divorce. His wife is angry with him and wants to take their children to Brazil with her to live with her family. He is distraught about this.

Harold asked: "Where is God in this? Why is God doing this to me at this time?" These were excellent questions for us to begin our work together that day. As he began to explore his inner reactions, anger, projections, and counter transferences, he was able to grow in compassion for his client and her circumstances as well as in compassion for himself. He was brought closer in his relationship with God's love for him. Harold was then able to bring this Godly love back to his work with his directee. He helped her discern what God was asking of her and what she might ask of God during this painful time in her life. The director came away feeling ready to pray for his own client's guidance and to walk with her as she experienced her pain. Vital to his effectiveness was the clarity he attained in our supervision session for himself, and that he had his own spiritual director and his supervisor for the support he needed.

Now let's move to a different issue in supervision, a sexual issue. Esther, my supervisee, has several years of experience in spiritual direction; she is a married woman with three teenage children. Her directee, whom she has been seeing for almost a year, is in her early thirties. The client has shared with her that she is entering the process of sex-change and is planning gender reassignment surgery. The process will take a long time, she has seen the doctors, etc. and she wants and really needs her spiritual guide to stand by her and help her on this journey. My supervisee reports being "freaked out." What does she know about any of this? Will she be filled with counter-transference? Could God really want this? Is she the right spiritual director for the task?

We met together in supervision for almost a year regarding these and other questions that arose in her. She came to feel that God was asking her to grow in relation to these life issues in another so different from herself. She discerned that it was her opportunity to journey with her directee, with God. And she would serve as a *mashpia* is meant to do, as a spiritual friend, aide-to-awareness, and nurture growth in herself.

Two Models of Supervision: Individual and Group

Individual supervision is offered in several ways. First, the supervisor asks for a verbatim to be forwarded by the spiritual director prior to the meeting. In preparation for writing the verbatim the spiritual director reflects on how God was moving in her during a recent session with one of her own directees. She then writes in the verbatim what she recalls as having transpired during the session: who said what, silences, prayerfulness and questions for discussion during the supervisory meeting. This model is very useful when a spiritual director feels stuck in her work and really wants direction from her supervisor in order to understand and progress with a particular situation, as in the above example.

Peer group supervision focuses primarily on the spiritual director and less on the directee. The model we use in our peer group is the model some of us learned at the Shalem Institute for Spiritual Formation. There are three steps in this process. First, a convener, a member of the peer group who has volunteered to facilitate the presenter's work, opens with a prayer, bringing the group's attention to being present with God on the presenter's behalf. About five minutes of prayerful silence follow. Next, the convener invites the presenter to share. The presenter shares herself in relation to a particular session with a directee that evoked something in the spiritual director. When the presenter is finished sharing, the convener asks for several moments of silence in which any questions of information clarification may arise from group members. After the silence, the convener asks for question of clarification only. Then silence again for about five minutes, so that the members can take into prayerful silence what they have heard. The convener then asks for questions for reflection by the presenter. The presenter responds to the questions or relates what arises in her at that time. As in my own peer group experience above, one rarely knows what can arise. The convener then asks for prayerful silence so that the presenter can hold what she has taken in. The final step of this model is for the peer supervision group to process the time with the presenter. Did the presenter feel that spiritual direction had happened for her? Was God present in the experience? What were other members experiencing during the work with the presenter, for themselves, and for the presenter? The convener then closes with a prayer, a *niggun* (wordless traditional melody), or whatever seems appropriate at the time.

The power of supervision to create personal and professional growth for the evolving spiritual director, enhancing safety and insight that might be important for the *mushpa*, cannot be overemphasized. For those seeking a supervisor, many of the very experienced spiritual directors do take on supervisees. You could surely seek to commission such support from any author in this volume if he or she has schedule space available.

Recommended Reading

Maureen Conroy, *Looking into the Well, Supervision of Spiritual Directors*, Moorehouse Press, 2005

Mary Rose Bumpus and Rebecca Bradburn Langer, *Supervision of Spiritual Directors, Engaging in Holy Mystery*, Church Publishing Inc., 2005

Part V

Hashpa'ah in Communal
and Interfaith Settings

Farginnin: A Mussar-Inspired and Kabbalah-Based Process for Synagogue Leadership and Membership Empowerment

by David Zaslow

Rabbi David Zaslow is the spiritual leader of Havurah Shir Hadash, a Jewish Renewal synagogue in Ashland, Oregon. He is the author of the *siddur Ivdu et Hashem B'simcha*, and *Jesus: First-Century Rabbi* published by Paraclete Press. He and his wife Devorah travel around the country leading *shabbaton* weekends and interfaith workshops. His website is www.rabbidavidzaslow.com

As a tribe we make jokes about two Jews having four opinions, or the single Jew who built two synagogues on a desert island – one that he goes to, and one that he'd never set foot in. *Oy*! It's good that we can laugh at ourselves, but maybe it's time to address the problem that underlies our self-effacing humor. Even in synagogues that are relatively free of *lashon ha-rah* (destructive gossip), there is often plenty of *r'khilut*–general griping,[100] chattering, and complaining about what is not right. Too often we hear indiscreet judgments among board leaders, committee chairs, and other volunteers about how so-and-so is doing something wrong. We often find well-meaning leaders and committee chairs offering advice or feedback to a volunteer in a manner that actually disempowers the individual rather than empowering him or her. We see the same ineffective, albeit well-intentioned, behavior between individuals who serve so tirelessly on the Board of Directors.

Most synagogue leaders, committee chairs, and volunteers have nothing but the best of intentions for their beloved *shul* (affectionate Yiddish term for a synagogue community). Yet the technology seems to be lacking effective forms of communal empowerment among the leaders themselves and among the members of particular committees. We end up with a higher kvetch (Yiddish for complaint) and gossip quantum than is useful, burnout increases as gratitude decreases, and many of our synagogues end up wondering why there is a lack of volunteers.

When members kvetch about leadership, leadership *kvetches* about membership, and committee members kvetch about the way other volunteers are carrying out their tasks,

---

100   The Chafetz Chaim defines *lashon ha-rah* as derogatory or damaging (financially, physically emotionally, or socially) communication whereas *r'hilut* is any communication that generates animosity between people. *R'hilut*, one of the most common forms of gossip, is sharing facts about another person (true or untrue) that increase the listener's negative feelings about that person. As you will see, unchecked *r'hilut* within a synagogue community is one of the most potent forces to destroy leadership and volunteer efficiency. *R'hilut* works against the positive, healing, and elevating energy of *farginnin*.

this communal neurosis is called *t'lunot*. This is usually translated as "murmuring," and is recorded in many of our Torah stories. The root of this Hebrew word is pronounced loon and simply means "to lodge." In the Torah the idea of "lodging" is metaphorically extended to the notion of an individual's obstinacy. An obstinate "unwillingness to move" or an emotional or intellectual position by one group in relation to another has weakened the Jewish people throughout our history, and continues to plague some of our synagogues today.

The techniques described in this discourse may be very effective in dealing with these problems. Learning to *fargin* one another can increase efficiency and the sense of joy when carrying out the day-to-day business of the *shul*. Obviously, *farginnin* can be applied to family communication, within businesses, and in any kind of organizational setting, but because it is a uniquely Jewish concept, the techniques derived from *farginnin* are especially suited to synagogues. The process of *farginnin* is what we call a *kiddush HaShem*, a sanctification of God's Name in our world. If synagogue leaders and volunteers elect to follow a *farginnin* model for mutual empowerment, this can create an inspiring model for others to follow and be spiritually uplifted in their work and personal lives.

Nu, So What is Farginnin?

Yiddish dictionaries define "*farginnin*" in the positive – by saying that the verb "to *fargin*" is "to grant" or to "to afford" something personal from you to someone else. It is related to another Yiddish word *fargenigen* which simply means "enjoyment". Reb Zalman extends the idea by saying that "to *fargin*" is "to send positive energy to someone." But to really grasp the idea of *farginnin* we have to understand what it is not – what it means "not to *fargin*." When you "*fargin*" someone you bless them with your hope for continued positive outcomes. Not to *fargin* someone is called *nisht farginnin* in Yiddish. Reb Zalman teaches us that *nisht farginnin* is "to begrudge."

In Israel when the modern Hebrew verb *l'fargen*[101] is used it implies an action that is opposite to giving someone what our ancestors called *ayin hara*, the evil eye. If we look askance or skeptically at someone's good fortune, for example, we are confiscating energy from that person. When we give a person the good eye–when we *fargin* them, i.e., when we are happy for them, we actually transmit energy to the person.

There are two kinds of *nisht farginnin* that often occur within volunteer relationships in synagogues. The first is when one leader or volunteer believes he/she can do a volunteer job better than another person who has agreed to take on that task. The second happens when envy or resentment arises between members who have taken on volunteer tasks. The deliberate practice of *farginnen* can transform these negative situations.

---

101   *l'fargen* is used in modern Hebrew and etymologically comes from the Yiddish *farginnin*

Remember that *farginnin* is not simply a person's ability to feel enjoyment. Rather, *farginnin* is the ability to enjoy the enjoyment of others even when you lack that enjoyment yourself (e.g., your neighbor wins the lottery and you don't). So the ability to *fargin* has the potential to energetically release the person who believes s/he can do a job better than someone else from the prison of his/her opinion. Even if that opinion is correct he/she has to accept that someone else has already taken on the task in question, and realize that disdain for another volunteer only creates animosity and separation. S/he should offer polite and respectful advice, but must release the temptation to control the other person to do the job "the right way." Thus *farginnin* becomes an act of faith and trust that the job will ultimately be completed. This not only benefits the congregation, but also fosters the self-worth of the volunteer.

It's important to understand that *farginnin* is not sentimental approval of everything anyone does in the *shul*. It does not mean that the person who fargins abandons his/her opinions at the door. What it does mean is that these opinions are stated with humility and honor. I may have a constructive critique about how someone else is doing a job, but I must bear in mind that I am not the one who volunteered to carry out the task. I might do a particular job differently (maybe even more effectively), but I do not have license to resent the way in which my fellow volunteer is executing the task, or to talk to others about how I could do it better.

When envy and jealousy are involved, the process of *farginnin* becomes more difficult. If my neighbor wins the lottery, can I fully *fargin* him/her without feeling envious? If a person is in a higher level of leadership than I am within a synagogue, and if I am a bit envious of that status, can I be emotionally free enough to *fargin* him/her to do his job? Can I do it without subverting his/her efforts in small ways: gossipy *r'khilut* – chattering behind his back; offering unnecessarily long winded opinions in meetings; not completing the tasks that I have taken on, or making subtle, negative facial gestures as he/she is speaking?

The second application of *farginnin*, then, has to do with *farginnin* another when you are actually envious of the other person. This level takes both discipline and practice. Let's say you're single and have been searching for your *basherte* (your soul mate) for years. Suddenly someone you know finds his/her *basherte*. Sure, you are happy for the person, but deep inside you feel a twinge of envy too. When you *fargin* your friend, you will actually utilize the energy of the envy. Rather than suppressing it, feeling guilty about it, or ignoring it, you can utilize and transform the very same energy that allows you to feel the envy into a blessing.

Imagine this possible scenario: there's a rabbi in a small *shul*. The more affluent Conservative *shul* in his town receives a major financial gift from a local philanthropist who has supported both synagogues for many years. The rabbi of the smaller *shul* experiences intense envy, and it literally takes him years to be able to *fargin* the rabbi of the neighboring *shul*. In his practice of *farginnin*, he says to *HaShem* (God), "I realize that this financial gift will do much good, but I still feel envy." On the spiritual plane, it is the rabbi who eventually is able to *fargin* his neighbor who receives the greatest gift – the ability to transform his envy.

Now, apply that lesson at the more everyday kinds of volunteerism and leadership tasks within your synagogue or *havurah*. *Farginnin* someone you are envious of – deliberately invoking the practice of sending them vibes of your goodwill even while acknowledging that you still have some envy inside – can have an extraordinary impact on your own emotional and spiritual health. And, thus, it will ultimately improve the emotional and spiritual health of your Jewish community."

An Anecdote

When Rabbi Zalman Schachter-Shalomi read the first draft of this article he called me to tell me about a plaque that he has. In Dutch it reads "*Volledige Vergunning*," variously translated as "full license," "full authorization," or "total permission." This is a common phrase in that hangs on signs in establishments that sell liquor, and are used for other kinds of public permits. Consider the *kavannah*, the intent of this phrase and imagine yourself as having the generosity of spirit to offer your synagogue peers, leaders, and fellow committee members "full license" on energetic, emotional, and intellectual levels as they fulfill their sacred tasks within the synagogue. Becoming aware, through communal and individual spiritual direction that rather than taking energy from them you can actually transmit energy to them is a vital perspective and related skills set that a *mashpia* can elicit or convey.

Reb Zalman also teaches that we don't know of any way to eliminate the envy we often feel at another's good fortune. Rather the process of *farginnin* is a spiritual practice that allows us opportunities to utilize the energy of the envy (rather than suppressing or ignoring it) as we give blessings and permission to one another. In other words, when we *fargin* we may still feel the envy but we don't let the envy stop us from giving one another emotional and spiritual allowance.

Imagine your peers offering you this same *volledige vergunning*, full license, when you take on a community task. What a wonderful spiritual practice for synagogue leadership and general membership to learn and to master! Wouldn't you prefer to have *volledige vergunning* from your peers, rabbi, and synagogue leaders when you volunteer for a particular project? Who wouldn't? So, first apply it to others and see how it feels.

Farginnin Exercise #1: Next time you hear that someone is volunteering for a particular leadership position in the community sit with your response. Be a friend to any discomfort you feel. Do you have some creative language to describe this? Similarly observe your response if you feel joy. Stay with the sense of all that. Ask what is between you and your being able to support this person's appointment or efforts? Notice what emerges in your inner knowing, not in your mind, rather in the place of the still small Voice. Perhaps it will help to consider what you need in terms of jobs, roles, and opportunities for your own future, or where you feel unacknowledged and so disinclined to support another. Now that you are in touch with your own domain of needs and possibilities, set your healthy boundary by releasing that person from your energetic negative hold. Imagine yourself "sending them some energy." You can picture this in a physical sense, as if you could see the positive energy going from you to them in the hope they will have a joyous and successful experience. Should it feel safe and worthy, you might consider offering him/her assistance, now free of the desire to criticize or judge him or her unworthy of the task.

Farginnin Spiritual Practice #2: Imagine yourself about to disparage a person who has taken on a volunteer task on behalf of your synagogue. A voice inside you whispers, "I could do it better" or "He's not doing it correctly." Imagine yourself being aware of the thought as it is happening. Imagine yourself turning to the person and *farginnin* him by saying, "I acknowledge the fullness of your intention. Deep inside I am grateful you are taking on this task, and I bless you for the fulfillment of it. Let me know if I can help."

Farginnin Spiritual Practice #3: Imagine hearing some terrific news about your synagogue community (e.g., money has been raised for a project, the mortgage has been paid off, a rabbi has been hired, etc.). Suppress any immediate sense of envy or resentment, and see yourself as sharing in the happiness of the community. Check in with your immediate feelings. Acknowledge any sense of envy or resentment. Just notice it. Then recall a scenario where you have felt happy, generous and loving toward someone rejoicing (maybe *kvelling* {Yiddish, rejoicing} over a child or grandchild's success). Let that feeling come into your heart and body until you feel it strongly. Then consciously transfer that feeling to the situation or person(s) you have felt resentment for. Keep trying to sustain that feeling and radiate it to them.

How to *Fargin* the Communal Leadership in your Synagogue

The following practices are, I believe, the core skill-set necessary to be able to *fargin* one another. These practices can be used in several different but overlapping ways within any spiritual community:

- Individual synagogue leaders might apply this practice to one another as sensitive, emotionally charged, controversial, or other important decisions are being made. It is suggested that synagogue leaders *fargin* one another as much as possible for both organizational efficiency and spiritual efficacy.

- Committee members might consider applying these principles and practices within committees themselves. It is good to see the application of the *farginnin* practices as an authentic Jewish spiritual practice.[102]

- Members might consider applying these principles when hearing communal news, when attending a community meeting, when considering what committee to join, or when working with other members on any group volunteer project.

- All of us might consider applying these same principles to our family decision making processes, and to ourselves. *Farginnin* is an excellent psychological template that will have great benefits to all who practice it as an emotional and spiritual discipline.

Synagogue leadership members often work tirelessly on behalf of the community, and burnout occurs when community gratitude, trust, and honor are lacking. When envy, begrudging and nitpicking are prevalent within a committee or the general community it is hard to draw down the spiritual effluence that is available from the Holy One to accomplish our holy tasks. Once the synagogue leadership masters the above practices of *farginnin* they can be taught to the members of each of the committees, and eventually to the general community. Ultimately, the aim is for these ethical and empowerment principles to infuse the synagogue, radiating from leadership to individual synagogue members to committees and back again.

Middot - **Ethical Qualities:** The first step in community-wide behavior is to cultivate the following general attitudes toward one another.

- Giving the benefit of the doubt: Be deliberately mindful that most people mean well most of the time. Don't begrudge the job a volunteer is doing. Pitch in and help. *Fargin* one another by giving one another the benefit of the doubt. Do you have a constructive suggestion? Make it in a way that is not begrudging.

---

102   *Farginnin* has many parallels to the Buddhist Vipassyna practice known as the Meta Practice

- Trusting one another: It is crucial for synagogue leadership members, committee members, and general membership to engage in trust at a very deep level. This doesn't mean simply trusting each other's honesty and integrity (that should be a given), but consciously trusting and projecting that your fellow community-worker will find the most efficient and economical way to accomplish his or her sacred task even if you would do it differently.

- A sense of our holy task: We must all cultivate the sense that our work is inspired by a higher source, and that our tasks are like the flow of oxygen within the body of our planet. In other words, our little actions make a difference and are important components of something greater than ourselves. We are agents of God, acting by the guidance of Torah, within the body of Israel.

- *Farginnin* is not democracy: To *fargin* someone is to empower the person by observing and then overriding our own urge to meddle, criticize, kvetch, or offer opinions that weren't asked for. The core of the practice is to deliberately trust that your community leader or committee member is doing the best he/she can. This does not mean you suppress your desire to offer help and/or constructive feedback, but it does mean that you don't get a vote on the execution of every task. This is where trust and *farginnin* intersect.

- *Farginnin* is releasing control: To *fargin* is to foster the sense that though you may know how to do a job better than someone else, your faith in *Hashem* (God) and trust in your neighbor trumps your impulse to control over the world around you. As beneficial as *farginnin* is for the one who is *farginned*, it is even better for the *farginner*.

- The perfection of imperfection: Synagogues are comprised of many more volunteers than professionals. The paid staff needs help, and the volunteer helpers have busy lives. Reality check: we must remember that volunteer tasks can't always be carried out to the level of perfection that comes from professionals. When this is the case, the practitioner of *farginnin* not only releases control, but releases his/her expectation of perfection. For many synagogue tasks "good enough" is plenty.

In 1937 the psychologist Dr. Wilhelm Reich described this process of *farginnin* and mutual empowerment with the term "work democracy" in a pamphlet titled: *Die Natürliche Organisation der Arbeit in der Arbeitsdemokratie* (The natural organization of work in a working democracy), which essentially teaches that those who volunteer on a project get to decide how to best carry out the steps in that process. It may not be perfect, and the project may not done exactly as you would have done it, but your role is to *fargin* your neighbor the way you would want him/her to *fargin* you. If you have good advice, offer it kindly, without attachment. If you want control, then take on the task yourself next time.

On an energetic level, your *farginnin* will actually aid your fellow volunteer to discover for him/herself the most effective and efficient way to implement a project. It seems that the best *rebbe*s are masters of *farginnin*. Rather than trying to control their students and *hasidim*, these *rebbe*s empower others with the trust that underlines the ability to *fargin*. When someone is not fully capable of carrying out a particular task efficiently, the rebbe's *farginnin* of the disciple has the power to elevate his self-worth and draw down a Divine effluence that raises the disciple's actions to a higher level of functionality.

Wisdom Teaching: Rabbi Samuel Weintraub says, "Open up, give space, understand that our hearts and minds are capable of infinitely greater love and patience than we normally assume. Every argument need not be zero-sum."

Spiritual Practices: Imagine that your synagogue leadership makes a decision with which you disagree:

1. Ask yourself: "Am I ready to be part of the volunteer leadership team to help make the changes I would like to see?"

2. Ask yourself "Why am I thinking in zero-sum terms? Why do I think that if my synagogue goes in one direction (e.g., hiring a full-time rabbi) that this direction precludes other decisions (e.g., expanding or purchasing a building) in the future?"

3. Third, ask yourself: "Can I open up and give space to the idea that our synagogue community can be prosperous, bountiful, and diverse in meeting the many dreams of our diverse membership?

4. Finally, again ask yourself, "Am I willing to join a synagogue committee now to help make my dreams for my synagogue come true?

The Inner Work Necessary for *Farginnin*: Making a Personality Inventory

I suggest that that *farginnin* is actually a *mussar*[103] practice, and that it requires the kind of learning and discipline that the *mussar* praxis can offer. Alan Morinis teaches,

> "*Mussar* is a path of contemplative practices and exercises that have evolved over the past thousand years to help an individual soul to pinpoint and then to break through the barriers that surround and obstruct the flow of inner light in our lives...The goal of *Mussar* practice is to release the light of holiness that lives within the soul. The roots of all of our thoughts and actions can be traced to the depths of the soul, beyond the reach of the light of consciousness, and so the methods *Mussar*...are all intended to penetrate down to the darkness of the subconscious, to bring about change right at the root of our nature."[104]

Jewish Virtues or Personal Character Traits – *Middot*

The refinement of any of our personality traits is beneficial both to our physical and spiritual health. The discipline involved in the self-control of natural physical instincts permits a higher degree of "control" by our souls within our lives. Our choices are elevated to a new and emotionally exciting new level. When we move the ego aside as we are about to choose what to say to another person we create a kind of vacuum whereby the ever present flow of God is allowed a bit of room to express Itself within our lives.

These *middot*, or character traits, are refined through the performance of mitzvot – the spiritual commandments outlined in the Torah. Parallel to fulfilling mitzvot we can each work on refining and elevating our God-given personality traits even as we interact with our fellow synagogue leaders and volunteers. In Morinis's book *Everyday Holiness*, an inventory or map of personality traits, is offered for which *mussar* refinement practices might be effective:[105]

---

103   The Hebrew word *mussar* literally means "discipline" and "instruction".

104   http://www.*mussar*institute.org/wisdom-way.htm

105   I have modified or added to the interpretations that Morinis uses for some of the *middot*.

- **Humility/Modesty – *anavah*:** Be humble when you think you know how to accomplish a particular job better than the person who has taken that task on. Do you have good advice and constructive criticism? Then offer it with sensitivity and humility, being sure not to shame or embarrass the person you are trying to help.

- **Patience - *savlanute*:** *Fargin* each other to move at a pace that is only humanly possible in our busy community and personal lives. In Hebrew *savlanut* implies that patience requires a bit of suffering. Don't rush each other even as you help each other complete sacred tasks.

- **Gratitude - *hakarat ha-tov*:** Literally "Consciousness of goodness." Only from a place of gratitude toward other volunteers in your synagogue will you be able to *fargin* them in their work. Thank people out loud and in public for the good that they are doing.

- **Compassion – *rakhamim*:** Related to the Hebrew word *rehem* meaning "womb." I also like the Yiddish variant *Rakhmunis*. When you show *Rakhmunis* toward one another you are expressing a high level of empathy (womb-like compassion) for one another. *Rakhmunis* is like saying "*Oy*, it could have been me having to do that task. I feel for you. I want to send you energy and my compassionate blessings."

- **Order/Arrangement – *seder*:** If you work in an orderly manner you not only carry out your own tasks more effectively, but you will have more spare energy to *fargin* others around you as well. Also, by arranging your thoughts before you speak you are taking the first step in the *farginnin* process.

- **Equanimity - *menukhat ha-nefesh*:** Literally "a resting soul." Practice being level-headed and level hearted in your emotional reactions to each other's ideas and behaviors. As you cultivate a restful soul you will able to *fargin* others to achieve their goals.

- **Honor/Respect - *kavod*:** Honor your friends in private and public. Related to the Hebrew word "heavy." It is not a light thing to honor someone. When people *fargin* each other they are actually displaying a heavy-duty level of *kavod*, honor. When you *fargin* another person you are energetically sending them the *kavod* they deserve for the tasks they have taken on.

- **Sufficiency/Simplicity - *histapkut***: Believe that what you already have is enough. Bless yourself and others to believe that what we already have is actually sufficient even though it may less than what we desire. It is from this simple sense of sufficiency that an energetic opening is created for the Divine flow to flow to help us move towards greater abundance.

- **Alertness and agility - *zerizut***: Be creative, agile, and alert when involved in a problem-solving process. Don't feel attached to old ways of accomplishing a task – be open to the call of *Shekhinah* (God's indwelling presence) to solve a problem in some innovative, new way. Once you are intellectually agile it will be easier for you to *fargin* others.

- **Silence - *sh'tikah***: Be as silent as possible in meetings. As Jews we joke about the fact that we often have a little something to say about both sides of every issue (one Jew, two opinions). This can be good, but it can be inefficient in committee meetings. Restrain yourself and say as little as possible - only that which is crucial to the discussion.

- **Generosity of Heart - *nedivat lev***: Be generous on many levels. Start with your own financial contributions to the community, and go all the way to the way you are generous with your praise for one another. This is a key character trait in being able to *fargin*.

- **Truth - *emet***: Keep truth as your highest virtue. *Farginnin* is only effective if it comes from a place of authenticity and truth.

- **Moderation/The Golden Mean - *shevil ha-zahav***: Be moderate in your words, judgments, and criticism. Practice seeing reality from the center –neither left nor right, neither passive nor aggressive. Cultivate the ability to "be" with fellow committee members without having to withdraw or intervene. Talk less, do more. Analyze less, trust your intuition more.

- **Loving-Kindness - *chessed***: Do you realize what an honor it is to be in synagogue leadership with your spiritual brothers and sisters? *Farginnin* comes from being loving and kind to one another.

- **Responsibility - *akhrayut***: When you take on a task be responsible and complete your tasks as you agreed to. In colloquial Hebrew *ahrayut* implies "leave it to me; it's taken care of!" Your taking responsibility for a project implies your need for *farginnin* by others.

- **Trust - *bitakhon***: Practice having the highest level of trust for each other. These *mussar* practices are not in a hierarchical order since they are all threads in a single fabric, but *bitahon* is the stitching that holds the fabric together. Practicing trust in each other is foundational to cultivating a *farginnin* attitude.

- **Faith - *emunah***: In Hebrew *emunah* means faith connected to trust and confidence. It is an affirmative word like when we exclaim "*amayn*" (Amen) at the end of someone else's prayer. There are two interconnected levels of faith in Judaism – faith in *HaShem* and faith in each other.

  1. Faith in each other: believe in each other even when it seems unreasonable. Based on your faith in the Holy One – draw down that faith and extend it to your synagogue brothers and sisters who have taken on the sacred tasks of the community.

  2. Faith in *HaShem*: know that there is a God above and within who loves you for what you are doing and for who you are. Have the *emunah* faith to know that even when you make mistakes (which you will) there is a process called *teshuvah* (returning to God) which gives you a way back home.

- **Awe of God - *yirat HaShem***: Be in awe of God, this process, your ancestors, and your tradition, and the Torah.

More Virtues or Personal Character Traits - *Middot*

In addition to the classical *mussar* (moral attributes) inventory items just presented there are additional *middot* (qualities) to consider. We are blessed by the Creator to each possess so many unique personality traits within us, and are doubly blessed to be able to artfully refine ourselves like a sculptor working on his/her beautiful creation. I am sure you will add other character traits to the list as well.

- **Enthusiasm - *hitlahavut***: From the Hebrew word for "flame." Practice being positively inflamed and enthusiastic about what other leaders and volunteers are taking on and accomplishing in your synagogue.

- **Integrity - *yosher***: From the Hebrew word "to straighten." Know that everyone who volunteers in your synagogue probably means well and has the highest level of straightness and integrity.

- **Clarity - *b'heerut***: From the Hebrew word for "brightness." Be clear, bright, and lucid in the planning and execution of sacred synagogue tasks.

- **Simplicity - *pashtut***: Take the path of least resistance in accomplishing the work needed by your community. Don't make things more complicated than they need to be. Needless complexity takes away the energy needed for *farginnin*.

- **A Cool Spirit/Calm - *kore ruakh***: The Hebrew words for "cool" and "close" share the same root. When you actually experience that your emotional spirit is already close to God, all that will remains is a "cool" and joyous sense of calm. It is from this place that you can *fargin*.

- **Hope - *tikvah***: Related to the Hebrew word for "pool." Maybe hope is an emotional and spiritual *mikveh* (spiritual bath) pool. Hope in the positive outcomes of your work within the Jewish community.

- **Commitment – *m'khuyavute***: Only from commitment and a sense of joyous obligation to God, Torah, and Israel will volunteer tasks get accomplished efficiently.

- **Care/Concern - *d'ahgah***: Express the highest level of care and concern for one another. We know that our synagogue *hevre* (community) are all leading busy lives (probably too busy). Your care for another person is often the key to unlock the gates of *farginnin*.

- **Intentionality - *kavannah***: Originally an archery term meaning "aim." It has the extended meanings of "concentration, devotion, and conviction." So, focus clearly and aim well. See each other as having only the best of intentions for the community even when you disagree with other people about how they are carrying out their volunteer task – especially when you disagree with them.

- **Practice - *tirgul***: Etymologically similar to the English word "legwork." Know that that volunteer tasks have a learning curve. They take practice and hard legwork to get things done in an efficient, fulfilling, and sacred manner.

Farginnin is not so much a goal as it is an ongoing practice that requires intention and intention so that what happens among volunteers in a community is elevated to the level of holiness.

Recommended Reading

Menachem Mendel of Satanov, *Cheshbon ha-Nefesh* (*Accounting of the Soul*) translated by Dovid Landesman, Feldheim Publishing, 1996.

Goldie Milgram, "Preparing the Surface of Your Life" in *Reclaiming Judaism as a Spiritual Practice: Holy Days and Shabbat*, Jewish Lights Publishing, 2005, pp. 25-30

Alan Morinis, *Everyday Holiness: The Jewish Spiritual Path of Mussar*, Trumpeter Press, 2007

Rami M. Shapiro, *The Sacred Art of Lovingkindness: Preparing to Practice*, Skylight Paths Publishing, 2006

Ira F. Stone, *A Responsible Life: The Spiritual Path of Mussar*, Wipf & Stock Publishing, 2013

Exploring the God-Field: A Systems Approach to Spiritual Direction/*Hashpa'ah* in Communal and Organizational Life

by Shawn Israel Zevit

Rabbi Shawn Zevit, the rabbi of Mishkan Shalom in Philadelphia, PA, offers spiritual direction for individuals, groups, communities and organizations. He serves as *mashpia* and Associate Director for The Aleph Program in Spiritual Direction, and was a spiritual director at the Reconstructionist Rabbinical College from 1999-2007. An organizational consultant, congregational rabbi, teacher, author, recording artist and performer, he is the author of several works including, *Offerings of the Heart: Money and Values in Faith Communities* (Alban Institute) and co-editor of *Brother Keepers: New Perspectives in Jewish Masculinity* (Men's Studies Press).

The Jewish mystical tradition views each human being as a creative spark awaiting more kindling on his or her soul journey. This *nitzutz* (divine spark) is often the nurturing focus of *hashpa'ah* (spiritual direction). Yet if we expand our Godly lenses to a broader, "satellite" view of God's Presence in this Universe, then exploring this Presence in the context of faith community, family systems, organizations and societies in which we live and work, live and die, is equally important. In a holographic, non-dualistic world-view, there is no place outside of Godly existence.

Bringing "God" or "Spiritual/Ethical Values" to congregational planning, ritual and policy decision-making, conflict, and values clarification can be a gateway to engaging and releasing untapped Godly potential. These approaches are keys to unlocking the very spiritual, emotional, and intellectual energy that may be dormant or blocked in a congregational, organizational or larger communal system.

Take for example this text, taught in the Warsaw Ghetto, where discerning the sacred mission, and "God's will" for a community was just as important in times of life-threatening crisis:

> "Our association is not organized for the purpose of attaining power or intervening in the affairs of community or state, whether directly or indirectly. Quite the opposite: Our goal is to gradually rise above the noise and tumult of the world by steady, incremental steps. It is not consistent with our goals to hand out awards as to who is advanced and who lags behind. The whole premise of our group is the vast human potential for both baseness and elevation. Our bodies and souls are currently quite un-evolved, but our potential for holiness is very great.

Holiness is our key and our primary value; honors and comparisons serve no useful purpose.[106]

Even in the midst of times of questionable survival, Rabbi Shapira and his community in Warsaw were taking a stand for a clear God-centered mission and saw the importance for a shared, openly articulated purpose for being together as a faith community. We may do individual work in *hashpa'ah* to clarify our own purpose and spiritual path, but are we asking ourselves within the collective context of a living system?

Spiritual Direction: A Systems Perspective

Beginning in the 1960s and 1970s, "systems theory" emerged in the fields of family therapy, anthropology, and communications, as well as in the business world. A systems approach looks at the totality of a social organization and the interaction within it. This approach recognizes that the parts interact with complexity, with the whole being greater than the sum of its parts.

As applied to group life, a systems approach sees the totality of a communal or organizational system and the interaction of the component parts, rather than looking only at individual roles and functions. Mordecai Kaplan wrote:

> The human being is not a self-contained atom, but is the product of the biological, historical and social forces that operate in the group to which he belongs…. What has been said of words in relation to their context is true of human beings in relation to their communities; they are not "pebbles in juxtaposition"; they have only a communal existence; the meaning of each interpenetrates the others.[107]

Congregations, communities and organizations also go through lifecycles, just as an individual who may come to us for spiritual direction does over time. The process of communal *hashpa'ah* requires assessing what the roles are of current leadership in this community at this moment in its development. For example, working with a board of a newly formed congregation or a congregation-in-transition in a group spiritual direction process may reveal that, while solving complex and long-reaching presenting issues may be the goal of certain individuals in leadership positions, divisiveness may prevail if secondary

---

106   Rabbi Kalonymus Kalman Shapira, *Conscious Community*, translated by Andrea Cohen-Kiener, Jason Aronson Inc., Northvale, N.J.: 1999. p. 3

107   Rabbi Mordecai Kaplan, *The Future of the American Jew*, Macmillan, NY, New York: 1948, p.148.

stages of stability and consolidation are not reached beforehand. A group *mashpia* can help the leadership tune into where God, or Truth, or Mission and Vision are clear and accessible, a coming together of spirit that can form a healthy grounding for the work at hand of group or communal spiritual formation.

Note: Each group will have a comfort level and language of its own to describe God-experience; the *mashpia* must be careful not to assume anything, nor to impose one's own.

Walking the "God-field": Creativity and Choice-Making in Community

A 300-household Jewish congregation wished to reconnect with its founding principles and mission, with its pre-building, pre-rabbi, pre-staff stage of communal life, which began two decades ago. They described themselves as having lost their spiritual center, despite have achieved programmatic diversity and increased membership. People had joined the community for the warmth, inclusivity and creativity of services and programming. Even so, leadership and members could not articulate the mission of the community or consciously understand why the community in fact felt the way it did to them. The approach to group *hashpa'ah* selected for this community was "creative" both in the sense that they employed narrative, imagery, role playing, and imagination, as well as in the sense that they were generative of something new, unexpected, and alive.

We began the first session together gently with some moments of quiet reflection, with a familiar ritual, a *niggun*—a wordless melody that brings focus to the group's energy and acts as a reminder of the sacred intent of our gathering and the commitment to the relationships formed in the name of community. I put a chair in the center of the group and invited them to think of God/Holy of Holies/Core Values (whatever language worked for people) as in the center or seated in this chair bearing witness to what they were about to share- and as a locus of holy inquiry to turn to for clarity and vision as needed.

Next, we projected a photograph that was taken at the original meeting two decades ago where the idea of starting the congregation was hatched. Both seasoned and new members were invited to use the body language and expressions of the people pictured to suggest what they were thinking. Wonderful stories came to the fore from the founders, and creative interpretations were offered by newer members, especially children and youth. More photographs were then projected from the congregation's twenty-year history, with an invitation for sharing of more real or imagined thoughts or dialogue for those pictured. When we arrived at a current photo of the synagogue itself, participants were asked to find a partner and share what it was they believed this building would want prospective members to know about its people and its history, and what God as Eternal Witness would remind them was important even before a *mikdash* (sanctuary), holy space, had been built around this Sacred Heart.

The final image was a supersized version of the congregation's mission statement, which the president was invited to read aloud. Then everyone was invited to "become" the adjectives included in the mission statement, e.g.:

> *You are 'warm and welcoming'—Why are you in the mission statement and what are you here to remind us of?*

> "I am here to remind everyone that we are to always be an open tent like the one our ancestors Abraham and Sarah had, like the ancient festival celebrations in Jerusalem that welcomed in the Israelite and the stranger," one participant responded.

> "That we are to be open to people who may have been alienated from religious life and are seeking a non-judgmental home to return to," offered another.

We went through all the descriptive words in the mission statement in this way: "You are 'egalitarian'...you are 'inclusive'... you are 'valuing tradition'... you are 'innovative.'" More and more voices joined the exploration, each contribution punctuated by a return to the *niggun* with which we had begun, and a moment of contemplation. Following each third or fourth offering, I asked what they felt "God was for them" or "where they experience their soul's Truth" in response.

I offered appreciation for the mission statement and thanked its initial crafters for the wisdom they imparted through it. Participants were next asked to explore what they had learned from the document that expressed the reason for their community's existence. An hour later, with the conversation still buzzing, the evening was brought to a close by my offering a series of questions for everyone to consider in preparation for the next day's session: "Imagine that you are back at that founding meeting 20 years ago. Would you change this mission statement in any way and why? What values would like to see reflected in it? What does your soul (God/Truth) tell you is most important to remember, reclaim, change, from this foundational time, when you were wanderers coming together to find a place of promise? Imagine that it is five years from now and you are looking at a photo of this weekend: What was said at this time that supported the congregation in growing and thriving in the years that followed?"

That evening the past was present and the future was glimpsed. Individual and congregational stories were brought to the table, later to become inspiring references for the work ahead. On subsequent days of the retreat, we began each session with a group spiritual direction session, and contemplatively studied texts on living in community from the Torah, the Talmud, and the hasidic masters, pausing whenever someone felt moved to share an insight or response to a text that connected them to sense of purpose, touched their own spiritual life or evoked a call to realize an aspect of their own community.

We looked at other congregational mission statements and a previous five-year plan to examine the elements needed to help build a conscious, supportive, and spiritually and intellectually vibrant community. We broke into subgroups to revise the mission statement, to clarify the value of a variety of religious practices and the synagogue's worship style, and to explore educational issues that needed to be addressed in the year ahead. During prayer, we paused when one of the values or themes being explored in our work together surfaced in the liturgy, and we added additional prayers for those values (e.g., creativity, love, deep listening, unity, etc.) to be present in the work of the board and committees, the clergy, and teachers in the year ahead. There were no activities—study, group dialogue, worship, brainstorming, or late-night conversation—that were seen as being outside the process and goals of the weekend or the subsequent year in the life of the community.

This is just one example of the power of *hashpa'ah* or spiritual direction using systemic modalities in work with communities or organizations. Process and outcome, form and content become mutually enhancing and interdependent ways of realizing the divine potential of individuals, communities, and larger organizational systems, especially when conflict, stagnation, and habit are exerting stress on the congregational or organizational system.

Giving Voice to the Unexpressed

There are many ways to interact with our sacred texts and to weave in how we experience the Divine working through us now. For example, a number of the psalms include dialogue with God. Similarly, one way to work with both young people and adults in the area of congregational decision-making, visioning, and planning is to ask them to write a "Dear God/Source of Life," "Dear Self," or "Dear Congregation" letter, allowing for a variety of comfort levels with personal theological language. This exercise provides an avenue to voice what is not in scripture but is informed by it; or to voice something that is in an individual's heart but is not conventionally expressed. Sometimes I ask participants in this exercise to also write their own answering letters addressing their particular queries or areas of conflict or concern. What often emerges from this exercise is a soul response that is more expansive, flexible, and capable of holding polarities (even when resolution is not always accessible) than is produced by opinion sharing or conceptual discussion. The suspension of judgment and deep listening to the words beneath the words are very important in any of these exercises, just as they are in group spiritual direction or consensus-building exercises.

If we believe that the classroom, the sanctuary, the community center, the workplace, the home, are all places in which we engage in life-long learning, then to live a God-centered life is to actively and consciously express and participate in the life-narrative we are co-creating with each other.

> The intersection of theology and creativity invites us into a relationship with the Divine that is a dynamic process, not a static conceptualization: not for the noun God do we look. What we had experienced was not static ENTITY. So VERB and PROCESS are words that fit better.[108]

Bibliodrama and God-Centered Theatre as Group *Hashpa'ah*

On the twentieth-first century stage God becomes not necessarily less holy or powerful, only infinitely more approachable. This dramatic exploration of human-Divine encounter, or trying to give voice to new *midrash* about God, whether bibliodramatically from sacred texts, or improvised and scripted new plays, requires sensitivity. Peter Pitzele, a therapist and psycho-dramatist, structured the process which emerged in some Jewish and Christian circles in the 1970s and 1980s into a form of interpretive play he termed "bibliodrama." He spells out some of the parameters in his book "Scripture Windows":

> "There are times when a bibliodramatic scene cries out for the presence of God. Directors should be guided by their own theological scruples as to whether they will or will not bring God onto the stage. Some may rightly fear the reduction of the mysterium tremendum to the scale of play; others may feel that the personification of the divine offends their own sense of religious decorum or may offend members of the group. Others may feel that God needs to be brought into the drama so that people can find ways of being in dialogue with the divine."[109]

There is a sense here that the sacred text, and the narrative of our lives, is not merely acted upon, but rather part of God working through us, the working tools of the Holy One, in ongoing creation.

Another exercise involves asking group members to create a human "sculpture" around a particular value as it relates to an issue requiring a decision that will impact the community at large. In the case of an explicit contract to examine the God-center

---

108   Rabbi Zalman Schachter-Shalomi, *Paradigm Shift*, Jason Aronson, NJ, 1993, p. 141.

109   Peter Pitzele, *Scripture Windows: Towards a Practice of Bibliodrama*, Torah Aura Productions, Los Angeles, CA, 1997-98, p. 221.

or spiritual core of a community, group or organization's life; this exercise can be titled "Aspects of Divinity in Our Community" or "Points of Purpose in Our Mission."

For example, if *tikkun olam* (social justice and community activism) is the chosen issue about which members are trying to develop priorities, resolve conflict or self-educate, participants can be asked to create a sculpture representing the various values, causes or organizations under discussion. The exercise begins with one person striking a pose expressive of the cause or value they represent (e.g., "anti-hunger," "environment," "international relief," etc.). One by one, others take positions in relation to the first person and offer a one-word description of the aspect of *tikkun olam* they represent. During the exercise, the facilitator can interview various people as to why their cause is a priority. The different members of the sculpture can be invited to dialogue among themselves. Those remaining seated can be invited to offer what they observe and how the dialogue impacts their view of which causes to invest congregational human and financial resource in, and in what priority.

The art of inviting participants—whether in study, during worship services, in youth or adult educational settings, at meetings or retreats—to give voice to the unspoken thoughts and feelings of characters or situations in scripture can also be a powerful way to assist members of a community to unlock insights in the Bible ("bibliodrama" or "*drashodrama*" or "contemporary midrash") and discover their relevance to contemporary issues.

When exploring the dynamics of leadership with congregational or organizational boards, committees, clergy, and staff, I often use the story of Moses receiving and acting on his father-in-law's advice about delegating and avoiding leadership burnout as a text to explore the dynamics of leadership [Exodus, Chapter 18, or Deuteronomy 1:9-15]. Exploring the scripture bibliodramatically might involve reading a few verses of text, then inviting people to offer suggestions as to why Jethro felt compelled to give Moses his advice, or asking participants to consider what Moses really thought when he heard Jethro's advice and why he decided to listen to him. What is gleaned from this enactment and the text itself that relates to leadership and communication issues in the community can then be explored in discussion.

It is important to recognize that there are different comfort levels each of us may have with setting up these scenarios or taking on the task of giving voice to God. Only do what you and your participants are comfortable with. At the same time, I have done these exercises with groups ranging from interfaith, multi-faith, orthodox and self-professed atheists, corporate executives and line-workers, clergy and lay leaders, with moving and long-term transformative results. Both children and adults are able to express and reflect on the beliefs they hold about a Higher Source in the universe, how that does or does not align with their actions in the world, and what it tells them about who they long to be Jewishly, and as a human being in general.

Re-telling the Story

Telling a community's story through a scriptural lens, or creating vignettes of the history of one's congregation, school, or organization and the values it stands for can help a group realize how it can live in and create sacred community. To translate an older theological view of "And God said to Moshe, tell the Israelites..." we could offer a key question of *hashpa'ah* in a larger system such as, "To where do we understand as a community or organization that God/Higher Vision/Fulfilling our Mission is calling us?" This creative and maximalist approach is central to a productive values-based decision-making process that can be employed for crucial issues in the life of a faith-based community. A paradigmatic model based on that suggested by Dr. David Teutsch, Director of the Center for Ethics at the Reconstructionist Rabbinical College, consists of:

—study of the sources, religious and cultural traditions and practices

—study of current information from the natural and social sciences (including organizational dynamics, systems theory, etc.)

—reflection on personal and communal values analysis of the impact of each possible decision on each affected party

—democratic and inclusive processes that maximize the number of participants along the way to a final decision.[110]

To this approach, I have added the creative techniques for reflecting on personal and communal values, or what we might express as the search to understand "God's direction" described earlier in this article, as well as role playing to help in analyzing the impact of possible decisions. An in-depth process such as this may take a year or more in the life of a community, so this is not a model I would recommend for making minor decisions. However, in the areas of religious services, board governance, operating practices, financial resources, education, and involvement in social justice causes in the larger world, combining creative techniques with this serious approach to discernment can powerfully impact the level of participation, the outcome and ownership of decisions.

---

110   Richard Hirsch, "Decision Making in the Congregational System," *The Reconstructionist*, Volume 65, No. 2, Spring 2001, pp. 13-21 and David A. Teutsch, "Values Based Decision Making" *The Reconstructionist*:, Volume 65, Volume 2, Spring 2001.

Cultivating Active Participation

Many faith communities and organizations employ such participatory processes to engage the entire congregation in renewing and reinvigorating worship services, coming to deeper ownership of congregational *Shabbat* practices and guidelines, and other areas of ritual. The role of clergy as teacher and guide as well as active participant—is crucial to the success of such endeavors. By trusting that when we openly look at and name the dynamics of power, authority, and responsibility that we, as clergy or lay leaders, have in a congregational or organizational system, we can facilitate ownership by other members of the community for their part in the decision-making process—to everyone's benefit.

An example of this occurred recently in my own life, when I became the visiting rabbi at a historically lay-led congregation in Pittsburgh, a faith community experimenting with a hybrid of leadership models. In this congregation, we arranged for the signing of the rabbinic contract to be a ritual event. After the president of the congregation convened the evening, the leadership of the *havurah*, a subgroup within the community that, with the support of the larger congregation, had accepted responsibility for bringing a visiting rabbi to the congregation each month, shared what it meant for them to arrive at this moment. The *havurah* liaison and I both shared that we experienced the contract negotiations as a truly holy conversation. We then discussed the themes of power, authority, and accountability as they occur in any group or organizational system, studied biblical and contemporary texts on leadership, and explored our hopes for our rabbi-congregational relationship.

Next, using a ritual format often used at Jewish weddings, the president handed me the contract, asking if I agreed to the covenant of our terms. He then did the same with the *havurah* liaison. After we had signed the document, other *havurah* members were invited to sign as witnesses if they so chose. Afterward, we chanted the traditional *Shehekheyanu* prayer, thanking God for being the sustaining Source and for bringing us to this day. This was followed by a shared meal, where we traded stories about our personal journeys. Finally, we embarked on a three-hour planning session that laid out the year's activities for the *havurah* and how it would interface with the congregation as a whole. People remarked upon how our study together and the sacredness of the signing ritual had directly contributed to the energy, creative thinking, and enthusiasm for the decision-making and planning that followed. At evening's end, I invited the leadership to share what they were taking away from our first collective working session. A number of participants commented that their fear of losing their voices with a rabbi present had given way to new energy, empowerment, and a sense of being supported to take on greater roles in their spiritual and communal lives. One person shared: "God is in this place and we, we CAN know it!"

Weaving together ritual, individual and congregational stories, study, prayer, a shared meal, administrative objectives, and program planning can mutually enhance each of these components, helping to build relationships and a sense of sacred community at the same time.

I have discovered that capital campaigns and efforts to decide what type of membership dues or fee structure a community will adopt can also be enhanced by these types of creative values-based decision-making approaches. Creative and participatory approaches to the spiritual life of any community are enhanced the more people see themselves as active participants in their individual and congregational religious life. This can help narrow the divide between practices and expressed values both within a faith community and outside its walls. In addition, seeing adults become more invested in the major issues that determine the current and future actions of their community can also inspire young people to become involved.

Of course, we can misuse any creative or participatory process—to block needed action and consign decision-making to an endless process of processing, for instance. As with an individual *mushpa* or directee, we want to pay attention to a person's movement away from or towards more holy and holistic consciousness. We can hide behind anti-authoritarian approaches, undermining clergy and leaders by insisting that everyone needs to approve every decision or that consensus is required at every turn. To avoid these pitfalls, it's important to be aware of the shadow side of any creative process when we approach core issues in sacred community creatively and with maximal member involvement. Ultimately, when we enter into discussion about an important issue in our community, we are entering sacred ground. Godliness can manifest through the approach and content of our decision-making. We are, in short, striving for a process that contains Godly values and yields an outcome that fulfills the mission of our community and the spiritual growth of the participants.

Whatever approach we take, it's crucial that we do our homework beforehand, trust in the development of our own styles of leadership and the social and spiritual bonds in the community we are committed to. We also must recognize that we might have a strong bias in favor of a particular outcome. This is part of the creative tension when we move decision-making from an elite activity into greater communal participation. Moses faced this tension with a burgeoning community at Sinai. Managing polarities is part of the decision-making process. In the moment of a creative encounter—as in any artistically alive and spiritual moment—our task is to be present to what the relationships and dynamics in the room are calling out for, in balance with the mission and values of that community. The insights, healing, enjoyment, and challenges people will experience depend on this practice of presence, and the creativity, compassion and conscious choice-making that can be its result.

There are some key questions to hold in your heart as you encourage or guide others into this holy inquiry: What moments have you most strongly felt your faith or a Divine presence, present in a major decision or activity in the life of your faith community or organization? What was the role of spontaneity and creativity in this experience? What was the role of study, weighing values and open discussion of different viewpoints?

We have seen how the process of communal *hashpa'ah* also invites the individual to see him or herself in relationship to the smaller and larger systems in which they live and move along their own soul's interactive journey. In the hasidic mystical foundations text, *Likutei Amarim*, known as *The Tanya*, we read of how a face to face or relational field is necessary even for independent Divine Energies to function without collapsing in on themselves:

> "*Tohu* (disorder) refers to the state of the original *Sefirot* (Divine Emanations), as unformed and unordered points. *Tikun* (restitution; reformation) refers to the state of the *Sefirot* rearranged, mended and reformed...Thus among the *Sefirot of Tohu* there is no inter-relationship... no mutual inclusion- each on its own, without relating to its opposite. The *Sefirot of Tikun*, on the other hand, compound one another...permitting the mitigating influence of Wisdom, and are, therefore, able to inter-relate."
>
> —Reb Schneur Zalman of Liadi

We are not inherently broken and in need of repair. We are inherently whole, but not always in relationship with this sense of *Ekhad* (Unity), our Godly potential, with each other and with the world. Perspectives or systems may be broken; their repair happens when we reaffirm our covenant with the Source of Life Itself and take our values and beliefs from the prayer book and the study halls, the mission statement and the budget lines into every aspect of our lives.

A Closing Prayer

Holy One of Blessing
Your invitation is to locate our acts
Of building sacred community
In honesty, in justice, in love for ourselves,
Loving each other and the world.

Without You we may start to believe
We alone are the source and judge
Of what is a right course of action
Without taking our prayers
Out of the sanctuary into the streets
We risk seeking comfort and escape
From the cries around us.
All of the natural world
Has its own song to the universe
When we lovingly open our hearts
When we strive for Godly connection within
And outside the walls of our communities
Then our *tefilot* and mitzvot can become
A grounding source for our God-conceptions
And a grounding force for Godly actions.

Recommended Reading

Richard Hirsch, "Decision Making in the Congregational System," *The Reconstructionist*, Volume 65, No. 2, Spring 2001, pp. 13-21

Editor, *Rabbi-Congregational Relationship: A Vision for the 21st Century*, Reconstructionist Press, 2001

Rabbi Kalonymus Kalman Shapira, *Conscious Community, translated by Andrea Cohen-Kiener*, Jason Aronson, Inc., 1996

Peter Pitzele, *Scripture Windows: Towards a Practice of Bibliodrama,* Torah Aura Productions, 1997-98

Rabbi Shawn Zevit, *Sacred Trust: Values-Based Leadership and Governance*, Reconstructionist Press, 2001

and Rabbi Shira Stutman, *Money and Jewish Values: A Twelve-Week Curriculum*, Reconstructionist Press, 2004

and Rabbi Shira Stutman, *Jewish Communal Leadership and Congregational Governance: A Resource Manual for Training and Developing Effective Boards and Committees,* Reconstructionist Press, 2005

Additional Website(s):

Institute for Contemporary Midrash. http://www.icmidrash.org

Integrating Reb Zalman's Deep Ecumenism into the Practice of Spiritual Direction
by Raachel Nathan Jurovics

Rabbi Raachel Jurovics, Ph.D., serves as the spiritual leader of Yavneh: A Jewish Renewal Community in Raleigh, NC, and conducts a private practice in spiritual direction. Rabbi Jurovics was ordained by the Aleph Rabbinic Ordination Program and received a second *smicha* (ordination) in spiritual direction from Rabbi Zalman Schachter-Shalomi. Her commitment to social justice has involved her in fair housing, human rights, reproductive rights, and interfaith activism.

The practice of spiritual direction creates a safe vessel in which to explore our relationship with God, so as to enhance and deepen that relationship, a practice sustained by the shared conviction of seeker and guide that such interconnection with divinity unfolds over a lifetime. *Mashpi'im*, guides, serve as spiritual mentors; as open channels of insight and *shefa* (divine abundance), spirit and compassion; as midwives to transformation; as holy listeners. Some participants refer to the process as one of triangulation, as having an alchemical or catalytic effect by means of disinterested companionship and teaching, of calling attention to signposts, of witnessing the integrity of individual spiritual experience, of modeling the ever-present Presence.

Above all, the holy listener is open to anything the seeker might bring,[111] which means that authentic spiritual direction, whole-hearted spiritual companionship, requires a deeply felt, deeply experienced ecumenism, a loosening of denominational boundaries, precisely because it is predominantly about faith and faithfulness, not about religion, much more about experiencing God than about the particularities of how we get there. Authentic spiritual direction demands our recognition of the providential component of what we inherit or learn from other traditions at the highest common denominator, the *madregah* (rung) at which all spiritual seekers transparently manifest their varied ways of interacting with Divinity, our varied way of honoring the theotropic nature of being.

Even when engaged in *hashpa'ah* (spiritual direction) with Jews, we cannot anticipate what theological reality will present itself to/through the seeker (or through the *mashpia's* receptivity to the Presence). In the delicate processes of God-seeking, there is no way to overestimate the centrality of the experiential; it is our holy obligation to open our minds, hearts, and souls to the Reality of God and to the reality that God loves diversity, nearness, and surprise. As Rabbi Zalman Schachter-Shalomi has often suggested, we may be constrained and hobbled by traditional images without even realizing it; for example:

---

111   Margaret Guenther, *Holy Listening,* Cambridge: Cowley Publications, 1992, p. 145

What if the *Shekhinah* is not in the *galut* (exile) we imagine, but fully present to all who welcome Her, all who recognize that exile is an artifact of our fractured spirits, struggling against the mysterious illusion of duality? Of course, to recognize, we have to pay attention; as Tamar [Genesis 38:25] says, "*ha-kerna*"–take a look, and see not what you expect or think you want, but what's truly there.

Mashpi'im don't get to select "appropriate" divine imagery for seekers; seekers uncover their unique experiences of presence, absence, intimacy, distance, fear, love, awe, and joy. One who thinks he doesn't know what to ask trips over God at the base of Mt. Sinai one *Shabbat* morning, and falls in love with the *parashiot* (Torah portions) — with God as Torah. One who as a child experienced murderous betrayal finds no basis for trust in the universe, yet perseveres for decades in her service to *tzur olamim*, the Rock of the Worlds. One who buried God in intellectual anger, who rejected divinity along with the narrow, stringent and cold-hearted religiosity of his youth, uncovers an as-yet-uncharacterizable Presence in the company of other souls–finds it enough that people choose to gather in community to welcome a great Something. A woman accustomed to a persistent Divine whispering loses touch with the Guidance on which she depends, and looks to the migratory faithfulness of Canada geese for a sign of Present Love. An observant Jewish woman, sitting in a guided meditation on compassion, finds her interior vision filled–and her heart broken–by the image of Christ crucified.

For guides and seekers both, the practice of spiritual direction invites us to revel in the universal Sacred Heart. In an evolving cosmic reality defined by distributed functioning (as in our bodies, emotion, intellect, and spirit manifest throughout, not within narrow bounds), spiritual direction invites us to experience the widely distributed compassion and abundance of the Universal Organism of which we are a microcosm, no less, of course, than are all other forms of being. As our teacher Moshe Cordovero monistically insists, "God forbid you should tell me that rock is not God![112] "*V'rahamav al kol ma'asav* — and God's infinite mercy, compassion, and yearning pour into all being" [Psalm. 145:9], bringing wholeness and healing. Indeed, as with all forms of spiritual practice, spiritual direction supports the Divine will to heal, whether experienced as the *Shekhinah* hovering over the sickbed; as the Sacred Heart of Jesus–perhaps located in *Tiferet b'yetzirah* (a location on the mystical Tree of Life), feeling the suffering of all sentient being–or, as the shattering of Avelokiteshvara,[113] yearning to effect a complete *tikkun* (healing, repair).

How many times a day do we say, "*yitgadal*" ("may it be magnified," relative to The Great Name)? And how shall we mean it? Deep ecumenism requires us to accept the

---

112   Shi'ur Qomah, Modena Ms., 206 b, cited in Daniel C. Matt, *The Essential Kabbalah*, SF: Harper San Francisco, 1995, p.24.

113   A manifestation of the Bodhisattva of Compassion, who, momentarily disconcerted by the extent of the suffering of sentient beings, shattered into countless fragments.

consequences of radical monotheism/monism/Oneness: One is One and One is All, and we are obligated to bring the reality we pray into being in our lives and, B"H (with God's help), into the lives of those whom we serve as teachers and guides. Reb Zalman has counseled his rabbinic students to understand themselves as *shomrim* (guardians) of God's communication to us. As *shomrim*, we keep, observe, protect, and transmit. As authentic *shomrim*, we are obligated to transmit what we receive, even when it breaks through into something we don't yet recognize, just as Moshe Rabbenu (Moses our teacher) sought to transmit the ineffable *Ehyeh* [Exodus 3:14], the great "I AM," to our skeptical and impatient ancestors.

As spiritual directors, our service is to *binyan ha-malkhut* (the building of the Kingdom, the domain of the *Shekhinah*), expanding the God-field to which we connect through our yearning and our will for ever more abundant life, a yearning and a will that we share with the One Who Will Be. The process of spiritual evolution is interactive, unbounded by denomination, and unpredictable, and if we choose to participate in it, we must accept that it implicates us in the service of universal well being; when we open our hearts to the movement of Divinity, the Presence manifests as it will and dwells in the form of its own deepest need. "*V'asu li mikdash, v'shakhanti b'tokham* — if they make me a tabernacle, I will dwell among them." [Exodus 25:8]

Authentic spiritual direction cultivates a sympathetic ear for other traditions; failing this, we cannot reach the people we're called to serve. Having this ear, however, does not require us to disregard our own spiritual understandings or compromise our personal religious practices. If deep ecumenism has a boundary, it is in the realm of practice, at the point where we sense something damaging to the spiritual immune system, which I understand as something that calls into question for us the integrity and beauty of Jewish teaching. Within the protected heart-space of spiritual direction, we support the seeker's experience, listening for hope, watching for signposts, feeding devotion. Within our own practice, we sink our roots gratefully into the spiritual soil that most nourishes us, and seek our flourishing in that familiar garden.

The neighbor's garden, though, has its own divine delights. As Huston Smith likes to remind us: "Everything that we find flowering in the historical religions, monotheism, for example, is prefigured in the primal ones in faint but discernable patterns."[114] Recently, something in the Joseph narrative invited me to think about Australian aborigines. As Smith describes aboriginal religion, he notes that their understanding of life reflects an integral connection between their ordinary life and what anthropologists used to call their mythic world, but which they now refer to by the aborigines' own term, "the Dreaming."[115] Just as we understand that our dreams represent a part of our larger life experience,

---

114   Houston Smith, *The World's Religions* , SF: HarperSanFrancisco, 1991, p. 366

115   Ibid., 367.

although at what we tend to consider a less "real" level of experience, for aborigines, ordinary life and the Dreaming represent alternative ways of experiencing a single world.

The world of ordinary aboriginal experience is measured out by time – the rolling of season into season, generation into generation. The Dreaming provides a stable backdrop for this unending procession of life events, an "everywhen" untouched by time. In a waking state, aborigines seek to conform their actions to the model of the archetypal heroes who people the Dreaming, and in such conforming, feel themselves truly alive. Houston Smith notes: "The occasions on which they slip from such molds are quite meaningless, for time immediately devours those occasions and reduces them to nothingness." So, "aboriginal religion turns not on worship but on identification, a 'participation in,' and acting out of, archetypal paradigms. "The entire life of the aborigine, insofar as it rises above triviality and becomes authentic, is ritual."

What it might mean to live in the Dreaming, in a cosmic moment seamlessly connected to ordinary life, in which every routine act of life holds the potential to express spiritual reality? What links us now to this early spiritual teaching, what evolution in our own historical faith has been seeded in aboriginal Dreaming? Nothing less than our constant cosmic moment: the linking of Dreaming and ordinary time, of the realm of divine grounding and generational change, expresses itself for Jews in an elegant system of mitzvot, in the covenanted relationship between Israel and the God we serve. When we live the mitzvot, when we strive to fulfill our part of the Covenant, we link ourselves to the divine will that creates and sustains all that we are, all that is, and we, too, live fully and authentically in our everywhen.

In another corner of the garden, Maggid Yitzchak Buxbaum calls our attention to an insight into the meaning of eating as a sacrifice, brought down by Rabbi Tzadok ha-Cohen of Lublin: "A clear spiritual perception of the meaning of eating comes from the power of a person's better side, the soul, which is a part of God. When that side dominates during eating, then the enjoyment of your soul during the meal is nothing less than the pleasure above from a sacrifice–because the part is equivalent to the whole." Maggid Yitzhak continues: "So when you eat with a full awareness of the spiritual meaning of eating, that God in [divine] love and humility is 'serving' you and feeding you, giving you life and pleasure, you can go from being the receiver to being the giver. You can serve [God] with everything you do during the meal. When you do this, and eat in holiness, it is as if you were 'feeding' God."[116] If you are a monist, it is as if you were exchanging your substance with God, just as God has served you out of the divine substance.

A complementary tale about the table of the *Besht*, (the Baal Shem Tov, founder of Hasidism) from Rabbi Yitzchak of Drohobitch: "Immediately after the *kiddush*, our master and rabbi... placed before himself a small silver plate on which the name YHVH

---

116   Yitchak Buxbaum, *Jewish Spiritual Practices*, Jason Aronson Inc., 1990, p. 270.

was engraved, and he rested it against his thumb. For it was his holy practice to have this little plate before him when he ate; and whenever he took food into his mouth he looked at the Name and so would he do through the whole course of the meal."[117] It is no wonder to me that when I am present at communion, every sacramental gesture resonates with my experience of Jewish practices of holy eating, of experiencing myself as fed by and of the substance of divinity; *"v'akhalta, v'savata, u'verakhta et Adonai Elohekha* — and you will eat, and you will be satisfied, and you will bless the Lord your God."

We return to our beginning: above all, a holy listener must be open to anything a seeker might bring, which means that authentic spiritual direction requires a deeply felt, deeply experienced ecumenism, a loosening of denominational boundaries, precisely because it is predominantly about faith and faithfulness, about *emunah*, not about particularistic practice, *avodah*. Authentic spiritual direction invites us to rise to the *madregah* (rung) at which all spiritual seekers transparently manifest our varied ways of honoring the theotropic nature of being.

After we recite the *Aleinu* prayer ("It is incumbent upon us to praise the Lord of All"), our assertion and acceptance of our entanglement with divinity, of our obligation to praise *adon ha-kol* (the Lord of All), we confirm Zechariah's [14:9] expansive vision: *bayom ha-hu yi'yeh Adonai ekhad u'sh'mo ekhad* ("On that day, God shall be One and God's name shall be One")." In that moment, we understand ourselves as *ha-m'yakhadim et sh'mo*, unifiers of the Name. Yet, as we re-experience with each reading of *parashat Sh'mot*, when the Holy One announces the most hidden name, *Ehyeh*, we receive a name that, to quote Rabbi Arthur Green, "fills all names,... all words, all things, all times and places, [such that] *any* name you Give Me, will indeed be mine." [Exodus 1:1-6:1] In all our acts of faith and of practice, then, especially in our service as *mashpi'im ruhani'im* to our companions in seeking the One of Infinite Being, may we be blessed to encounter the great *Ehyeh*, that our hearts may remain open to every new possibility of divine entanglement. By whatever Name, my dear friends, *"Adonai Eloheikhem Emet* - the Lord your God is True."

---

117   Ibid., p. 242.

Reducing Professional Isolation: The Rabbi and the Priest, *Hashpa'ah* with a Christian Colleague

by Wayne Dosick

Rabbi Wayne Dosick, Ph.D., D.D., is the spiritual guide of The Elijah Minyan in San Diego, and the host of the Internet radio program *SpiritTalk Live!* He is the author of nine books, including *Living Judaism, Soul Judaism, 20 Minute Kabbalah,* and *When Life Hurts.* His most recent book is *The Real Name of God: Embracing the Full Essence of the Divine.* www.RabbiWayneDosick.com

You've probably heard all the old priest-rabbi jokes. In my favorite, my priest friend — we'll call him Tom — asks me, "When are you finally going to eat a ham sandwich?" I reply, "At your wedding reception."

I met Father Tom decades ago, when we were both teaching at the local Catholic university. He is a kind, gentle, deeply spiritual man. He is revered and adored by everyone, for he is the sage, mentor, and compassionate friend to whom so many turn for guidance and direction. One of his colleagues once described him as "a priest who creates holy ground wherever he walks." And — making him even more beloved — he has a warm Irish sense of humor and a great love for the game of golf.

Tom did not know any Jews when he was growing up, and, as a youngster, he was taught to pray for the "perfidious Jews," because they had killed Christ and didn't accept Jesus as their messiah. And I am the one who was beaten up by the Catholic kids in the old neighborhood for "killing their Lord." Yet, we have grown beyond our childhood upbringings to know and appreciate each other's faiths and communities.

Tom and I often had lunch together. We talked of the things that friends discuss — our work, our families, our backgrounds, our training, our jobs, university politics, theology, sports. We tell each other all those old priest and rabbi jokes. We wonder if the next Pope will be any more liberal, and if the next Israeli government will bring peace. I tell him that if the next pope is chosen the way popes should be chosen — by the Holy Spirit — then, he is sure to be the next pope — Pope Tom the First. And, through his amused embarrassment, he tells me that if that ever happens, he'll bring me to the Vatican as his closest advisor — and give me one of those red yarmulkes that the cardinals wear.

On campus, we were known as the "Stodgy Radicals," for we both cherish the traditions of our faiths, while, at the same time, we are known as innovative thinkers who advocate fundamental and sweeping reform and change in the theology, practices, and institutions of our religions.

One of the very best moments for both of us was when a student came up to us and said, "You know, when I came to this university, I did not know any Jews. There weren't any where I grew up. And, to tell you the truth, I held some prejudice against Jews from all the stories I had heard. But, if the two of you can be friends, then I guess that I can meet some Jews and become friendly with them. You two are a living sermon."

Fr. Tom and I became such close friends that I read the Hebrew Scripture at his mother's memorial mass, and he read Psalms at my father's funeral. So, I was more than surprised when, one day, Fr. Tom asked me to act his "spiritual advisor." I know that, within the Church especially, this is a highly respected role, for being entrusted with the guidance of a precious soul of God is an extremely deep and serious responsibility. I felt neither deserving nor worthy. I was more than uncomfortable, because I did not want to violate the boundaries of our friendship. So, before agreeing, I asked Fr. Tom to explain the situation at hand, and to tell me why he was choosing me for this task.

I already knew that, at the time, he was about seventy years old, and that he had been in the active priesthood for more than fifty years. He is a Jesuit, whose training — especially in the "old days" — was strict and rigid. He has a deep, personal, intimate relationship with God; he gets up at 5:00 o'clock every morning, and spends at least one hour in prayer, meditation, and conversation with God. But he has little use for the Church, its hierarchical rules, and canon law. He thinks that it is ridiculous that, as he puts it, "a bunch of old celibate men makes rules for human sexuality — birth control, and abortion, and marriage and divorce, and priestly celibacy, women's rights and roles in the Church."

Now, he told me: His Provincial — the Jesuit equivalent of a Bishop — (who is 30 years his junior) is telling him that he must return to his home Province for a new assignment. At one level, he feels he must go, because he took on a vow of obedience that he has followed for fifty years. At another level, he, who has little use for the rules of the Church, feels that at his age, and with his record of experience and service, he should be able to decide his own work and location. He feels infantilized by the demand, and wants to refuse the new assignment. Yet, he is in serious conflict between his lifetime of obedience and service, and his human desire for freedom of choice and personal soul satisfaction.

He never has any desire for things of the material world: he owns two "priest suits," two sweaters, one pair of shoes, and a set of golf clubs. No one can give him a Christmas present, because he gives it away (to "someone who needs it more") within an hour. The only gift that I ever gave him that he had to keep was golf balls embossed with his name. Yet, he is not dependent on the Jesuits for his care and well-being in his old age, for, if he ever needs or wants it, there is family money available to him. So the ultimate "sword" of a place to live, food to eat, and health care that the Provincial can usually hang over the heads of his priests does not effect Fr. Tom.

He cannot discuss this dilemma with any of his priest-colleagues, for he knows what their response will be, and he is reluctant to go to a secular therapist, because he does not want to go outside the Church with this conflict. So, he came to me, his rabbi-friend, whom he surmises will understand the issues, and help him come to a solution from a spiritual, God-centered place.

In our few "sessions" together over this issue, we did not have to begin where many, if not most, *hashpa'ah* sessions begin: we did not have to go seeking God, nor "work" to invite God in. When, as a rabbi, I guide worship services, my task is to create "holy space," a safe and sacred place where people can connect and communicate with God. In spiritual direction, the need is the same. So, I often invite people into chant, prayer, meditation, and visualization to open the channel to God. I did not have to do this with Fr. Tom.

Catholic priests trade much of the responsibility and pleasure of this world - by taking vows of poverty, chastity, and obedience - for power. Unlike "mere mortals," they have a direct "pipeline" to God; their word turns a cracker and a glass of wine into the body and the blood of their Lord; their word grants forgiveness to a penitent's most grievous sin. Those priests who are not fully conscious of having made this "trade" sometimes very sadly abuse the power politically, financially, or sexually. Those who are aware use their power for the highest good. Fr. Tom - being fully aware of his persona, place, and priesthood - could use his "pipeline" not only for the good of the Church and its people, but, in this case, for his own benefit. And since I knew of his deep relationship with God, that is where we could begin.

So, I asked Fr. Tom to "tune into" God. Instead of focusing on what the Church and Provincial wanted from him, I asked him to focus on what God wants for him. I asked him - and I have always considered this is as a core principle of *hashpah'ah* - to focus on intention. What is God's intent for him, for his service? And what is his intention? Is it pure or is it selfish? Is it a choice - in words he would use - that is ephemeral or for eternity?

It is important for the *mashpia* not to impose language or idiom, but to use, as much as possible, the language and idiom that are most familiar and comfortable to the spiritual seeker. So, in his language - in this case the language of the Church - I asked Fr. Tom questions - one leading to another based on the responses he gave.

Does God want him to remain a loyal servant of the Church and its rules, as he has known and lived them? Does God want him to follow rules that hold a higher good than he is seeing in this moment? Does God say that there is a worthy freedom within loyal obedience? Does God give the Provincial special wisdom to know Fr. Tom's heart better than he does? Is he just feeling old and tired, "burnt out" and cynical? Do the old Church rules — articulated in the Name of God — hold enduring wisdom that supersede time and space, and "over"-rule personal desire? Is God testing him?

Or, does God want him — as he expressed it — to give blind obedience? Does God want him to give rote service? Does God want him to feel like a child, forced to obey a demanding and unreasonable parent? Does God want him to feel stunted and diminished? Does God want his humanity squashed and his spirit broken? Or does God want something else? Does God want joyous and freely given service? Does God want to celebrate personal freedom and choice? Does God want to elevate the human spirit? Does God want this long-time loyal servant to continue to serve in the best way his own wisdom and experience guide him?

The challenge of these sessions was to get "ego" out of the way, and listen to God. This was not particularly difficult, because Fr. Tom is one of the least ego-centered people I know. Yet, his whole life is at stake. For, at his age, he was probably making the penultimate, if not the ultimate, career and locale decision of his life. His personal proclivities, and desires, and choices, were sure to keep seeping into the process.

My biggest role, as the spiritual guide, then, was not to bring God into the process — for God was surely there — but to keep the focus on listening to God. Again and again I reminded Fr. Tom, in the words of the Scripture he knows so well, to "render unto Caesar what is Caesar's, and unto God what is God's." His problem, of course, is that given the structure of the Church, he continues to perceive that Caesar (in this case, the Church/ Provincial) is God's duly appointed spokesman. Since throughout his entire life, the Church has spoken to him in the Name of God, he has great difficulty in seeing the separation between the two.

Here he was being asked (perhaps for the first time in his life) to separate the two: to understand that the Church is made of men who make up rules for men and women, but clothe them in the "word of God." And, to understand that the perfect God — the God to whom he speaks in intimacy each morning, and serves each day — is pure Spirit, pure Love.

So, the task and goal of the *hashpa'ah* sessions was to make a clear delineation between the Church and God, and to listen, listen, listen, to God's word and will. My own biggest challenge was to keep myself out of the way, to keep from expressing, or even indicating my feelings, my hopes, about how my friend Fr. Tom would choose.

I was never concerned that Fr. Tom would decide that "my will is God's will," seeking to impose his desires on God, or acting as if what he thinks that he might want is what God wants for him. He would listen, listen, listen to God, to discern what God really wants for him, always affirming, "Thy will be done."

In the end, Fr. Tom's listening gave him a clear channel to and from God. His listening to God led him to joyfully take responsibility for his own life. He decided that God wanted him to serve in the fullness of his being, not to be dictated to, or, ever, bound by, another human being —no matter what his position in the Church. For, he finally understood and celebrated the difference between God and the Church. He decided —in his words—to "grow up," and begin acting like an adult instead of a child. He warmly embraced his newly found freedom to choose. He informed his Provincial that he would, indeed, return to the home Province, but he would not take the assignment that the

Provincial gave. He consulted with fellow priests and administrators at the local Catholic university, and he carved out a set of tasks that bring him much soul-satisfaction — and that he can do at his own time and pace. He made his own living arrangements, so that he would not be forced to live in a place or situation that would not be both spiritually and physically comfortable for him. He negotiated a salary for his services—not that he keeps much of the money, but he is not on the monthly priestly "dole" of the Province, which gives him a sense of self-reliance and independence.

Now, a number of years later, Fr. Tom reports that he has never been happier or more soul-satisfied in his entire life. He loves his job. He loves the community in which he chose to live. Although the weather — and the golfing opportunities — are not nearly as fine as what he left behind, he is glad to be "back home," where he has renewed acquaintances with friends of four and five decades.

He feels a real sense of balance in his life. He still has his deep personal, intimate relationship with God, and he has put the Church into the perspective he thinks it deserves. Father Tom has even forgiven the Church for how he perceives that it stifled his humanity and "emotionally abused" him over the years.

Needless to say, the personal drawback for the two of us — now separated by thousands of miles—is that we do not get to "hang out" very much anymore. But, for both of us, that is a small price to pay for the great personal growth and newly found joy in my friend Fr. Tom's life.

And it was all brought about through *hashpa'ah*, where Fr. Tom put God at the center, and listened, listened, listened, as God spoke to him. Sinai is ever-present. God always comes to the cleft of the Rock.

Acknowledgments

We are grateful to the contributing authors for your generous donation of carefully thought through professional articles to this volume.

We are also grateful to the co-editors and proofreaders who have donated so much loving care and worked through the challenges of the multi-lingual aspects of each addition.

And also to Lawrence M. Monat
for the remarkable cover photo.

And to the Holy One of Blessing
for the gift of life, creativity
and our capacity for learning and healing.

Index

20854960R00220

Made in the USA
Middletown, DE
10 June 2015